Successful Business English

Lois J. Bachman
Community College of Philadelphia

Norman B. Sigband
University of Southern California

Theodore W. Hipple
University of Tennessee

Second Edition

Scott, Foresman and Company
Glenview, Illinois
London, England

To Joanie, Marge, and William

ISBN 0-673-18472-2

2 3 4 5 6 MKN 91 90 89 88 87

Preface

"The ability to communicate effectively is probably the single most important factor influencing an individual's advancement and progress in today's organization." Variations on this statement, based on research and personal experience, have appeared in the Wall Street Journal, Harvard Business Review, *and many other publications time and again in recent years.*

Few people will argue the point. Nor will they deny that wordy, illogical, poorly phrased, or incorrect communications hurt careers. Managers, accountants, businesspersons, stockbrokers, bankers, office supervisors, and administrative assistants are perceived as less competent in their areas of expertise when they make errors in writing or speaking.

Successful Business English has been designed to help you sharpen your communication skills. Regardless of your present position or your career goals, you will find this book valuable. If you are now a good communicator, this text will make you even better. If you are only a fair communicator, this text will improve your performance appreciably.

The format of Successful Business English *is innovative. It is designed so you will learn and enjoy yourself while you do so. And that enjoyment will grow as you see the progress you're making.*

OBJECTIVES

In this book we have stressed the fundamentals of effective communication. Not only will you speak and write more correctly when you complete your course of study, but you will be able to use English with greater facility. Both the discussions and the exercises will help you achieve this end.

More precisely, the emphasis in this book is on effective communication in business situations. *While not all of you will go into business, you will all find communication skills of value. Your work with sample letters and memos, as well as exercises, will help acquaint you with the daily operations of many organizations.*

SPECIAL FEATURES OF THE SECOND EDITION

Following the suggestions of our reviewers and adopters, we have kept our First Edition's strongest features and revised and expanded all others to offer the type of learning tool needed to master business English. Here are some noteworthy changes:

- *We have included two additional chapters, one devoted entirely to* Verbs *and the other expanding coverage of the common marks of* Punctuation. *There are 19 chapters in all, with expanded explanations and exercises and new end-of-chapter* summary charts.

- *The* Parts of Speech *and* Parts of Sentence *chapters (Chapters 5–12) have more explanatory sections and many more examples to enable you to grasp and retain the principles and their applications.*

- *There are new, cumulative* Chapter Review Exercises *throughout the book that retest your retention of the materials previously presented.*

- *The* Self-Check Exercises, *revised and expanded, continue to allow you to evaluate yourself and determine if you need additional review on a topic. These exercises are easy to complete and simple to score—you need only refer to the key at the end of the text.*

- *The end-of-chapter* Application Exercises *have been expanded to include more opportunities to write effective sentences applying the principles presented in the text. These exercises review each chapter's contents and give you a chance to check your progress with the help of your instructor. In addition, the new and stimulating* Challenge Exercises *are provided to test your overall knowledge of each chapter's contents.*

- *Also included are revised and additional* Dynamic Business Vocabulary Lists—*one after each chapter—with many up-to-date word-processing and data-processing words and terms. These lists will increase your skill in using important business words and terms as the words are listed, defined, and used in sentences. When the lists are used with the accompanying* ABC's of Business Vocabulary, *you will be able to test your knowledge of today's business vocabulary.*

- *The sample* Letters and Memos, *revised and updated, help familiarize you with actual business situations. Again, you have the opportunity to check your knowledge of language fundamentals, as well as to develop your business skills.*

- You Are The Editor *letters and memos, modified to include the errors existing in some unsuccessful business communications, allow you to edit others' communications and correct their mechanical imprecision.*

In short, in the Second Edition we have made every effort to accomplish the basic objective of developing your ability to communicate effectively and correctly in business situations.

ACKNOWLEDGMENTS

In the various phases of writing and revising Successful Business English, *we benefited from the advice of many colleagues. We would particularly like to thank the following for their counsel and support:*

Cecile Beckerman, Chemeketa Community College,
Barbara M. Blickensderfer, Community College of Philadelphia,
Fred H. Bremer, Saddleback Community College,
Janice A. David, Illinois Central College,
Judy Dresser, College of the Redwoods,
Alice F. Grottola, Diablo Valley College,
Phillip A. Holcomb, Angelo State University,
Betty Jacquier, American River College,
Mildred I. Johnson, Colorado State University,
Billie Miller Long, Cosumnes River College,

Ann Maloy, Oscar Rose Junior College,
Jane Mangrum, Miami-Dade Community College,
Charlotte Mathews, New Mexico State University,
Connie Roberts, Central Washington University,
Carolyn A. Simonson, Tacoma Community College,
Dan H. Swenson, Western Michigan University,
Jean W. Vining, Houston Community College,
Judy F. West, The University of Tennessee at Chattanooga, and
Mary Witwer, University of Akron.

CONCLUSION
The new edition of Successful Business English *is carefully designed to help you communicate clearly, correctly, and concisely. When the goal is accomplished, you will be a successful communicator. Only then will we feel that we continue to be successful authors.*

Lois J. Bachman
Norman B. Sigband
Theodore W. Hipple

Contents

1 Introduction to Business English

Picture, if you will, two office buildings. One structure may be 35 stories high and located in New York City, the other 5 stories high and in Belleview, Kansas. Regardless of location, the activities that take place in both buildings are fairly similar. Business is being transacted.

Business transactions involve a multitude of activities, but one factor that is common to all the transactions is *communication.* In one office a meeting of 14 managers is being held to disseminate information. Next door three people are on a conference call to their counterparts in California, Hawaii, and Japan. Nearby, a secretary is typing a report for Executive Vice President Baxter. In the same office, letters, memos, proposals, manuals, reports, and bulletins are being processed in the word-processing center.

In other offices, letters are being dictated, memos scratched out, recruiting interviews held, computer terminals monitored, phone calls placed, telex messages sent, articles written, speeches presented, briefings finalized, . . . and a hundred and one other communication activities are going on. You are now part of that communication "blizzard" or you soon will be. How well prepared are you? How competent are you? How *confident* are you?

Today industry has a tremendous need for effective communicators. One study after another tells us that executives rate effective communication as the most important skill an individual in business can possess. Regardless of how competent you may be in a technical area, you must still communicate your ideas to others. Your purpose may be to motivate, to inform, to persuade, or to compare; whatever it is, communication must be employed to achieve your goal.

Of course, communication may take many forms: It may be a brief letter or a memo; it may be a formal written report or a carefully prepared speech; it may be a meticulously structured conference or an interview; or it may be an informal briefing or a short presentation in an office. As you can see, some of these forms are written communications and others are oral. Is one form more important than the other? No! Both written and oral communications are important, and both should be mastered by anyone striving to succeed and advance in a business career.

In this book we are offering you the opportunity to enhance your knowledge of business English and to strengthen your writing skills. Learning the basic principles presented will help you become more expert in this very important area.

BUSINESS WRITING AND IMAGE PROJECTION

On March 5 the firm of Chicago Engineering Associates mailed a letter to a prospective client in St. Louis, Missouri. It was the first letter the St. Louis firm had received from Chicago Engineering. Does the letter in Figure 1-1 provide a positive or negative image of Chicago Engineering to Mr. Williams, the prospective client?

Certainly this letter says a great deal to Mr. Williams about the efficiency, competency, care, and attitude of Mr. Murray Y. Soong and the Chicago Engineering Company. Would you want a firm that sent out such a careless letter to have the responsibility of redesigning *your* plant?

Probably not!

Now Mr. Soong could protest and say that the letter was typed in a hurry; a deadline had to be met; the secretary was new and untested; Soong was out of town and could not review the

Figure 1-1. Chicago Engineering's letter.

 **CHICAGO ENGINEERING ASSOCIATES**
240 North Michigan Boulevard
Chicago, Illinois 60604
(312) 894-3913

March 5, 198_

Mr. Warren Williams, President
Williams Electronic Company
1515 East 53 Street
St. Louis, MO 63121

Dear Mr. Williams,

It was pleasure to recieve your letter of February 21 in which you
inquired about our interest in possibly submitting a bid to redesign
your plant #1 building which is over 80 yrs old but fundamentally and
strukerally sound.

From our initial on-cite survey we feel it is easily possible to give
you the 8000 sq. feet you are seeking; it would be quite easy to
remove the too central columns, enclose the present outdoor shipping
dock, and construct several more small offices in what is now the
upper (but unused) area.

At the same time, new electrical lines could be run to give you
the power resorses you need. Of course something like this doesn't
come cheap but if your looking for a first-class job, Chicago
Ingineering Associates can do the job. We have enclosed a blue-print
plus plus a tentative cost estimate form for your review,
analsis and possible exceptance.

Sincerely yours

Murray Y. Soong
Executive Vice-President

Enclosure

letter so his assistant had signed it for him; and on and on. But the damage had been done; the image has been formed. Chicago Engineering lost the opportunity to be selected for the $500,000 construction project.

Just as images are formed on the basis of communications—written and oral—that pass from one organization to another, so images are formed *within* an organization.

Suppose Mr. Fred Slight, sales manager of ZRM Electronics, requests a brief memo from Betty Kuperowski on the number of current, new, and dropped accounts this month as compared to the same month last year. Mr. Slight also asks for information on full- and part-time sales personnel for the same period. These seem like simple and logical requests on Mr. Slight's part. But Figure 1-2 shows the memo he received.

Does this memo present an image of Betty Kuperowski? Is the image positive or negative? That question is easily answered. The memo clearly says something about Betty's competence, her ability to organize ideas, her efficiency in presenting information, the tact she possesses, and perhaps her future with ZRM Electronics. Certainly all these will be scored in the minus column.

Don't let a negative evaluation be made of *your* attributes on the basis of a communication you submit. Don't let misspelling and errors in grammar, punctuation, and capitalization affect the dynamics of your writing. Be knowledgeable about the mechanics of English so that you can present your thoughts in writing without mechanical flaws.

If Betty had been knowledgeable in this area, the memo that she submitted would have been similar to Figure 1-3.

Figure 1-2. Betty's memo on ZRM accounts.

TO: Freddy S.

FROM: Betty K.

DATE: 2/3/87

SUBJECT: Sales

Fred-You asked for info on accts that are new, dropped, and current for this year month this year and this month last year plus numbers of sales personal and here are the infos you wanted which by the way may also be found in our quartely report.

For May of this yr we have 23,550 currant accts as compared to 21,500 last May. We dropped 518 this year (for May) and added 610. Thats not so good considering we added 870 last year (May) and dropped 310. As for sales personal we had 84 full time last year and 88 this year and 55 part time last yr May and 61 this year for May.

Although you did not ask for dollar sales, I'm adding it in case you want them: $2,650,000 this year and $2,300,000 for last May.

By the way, Jerry Korb has called you three times this week concerning a past-due remitence on your car.

Figure 1-3. Betty's improved memo.

TO: Fred Slight, Sales Manager

FROM: Betty Kuperowski

DATE: May 1987

SUBJECT: Sales Accounts and Sales Personnel Data:
           May 1986/May 1987

	May 1987	May 1986	Percentage Change
Accounts			
Current	$23,550	$21,500	+10%
New	610	870	-30%
Dropped	510	310	+65%
Sales Personnel			
Full-time	88	84	+ 5%
Part-time	61	55	+11%
Sales Volume	$2,650,000	$2,300,000	

WHAT CONTRIBUTES TO A POSITIVE IMAGE?

All your communications—written and oral—in the years ahead should not only be effective in content, but should also present a positive image of you. That image should "say" that you organize logically and you communicate clearly, correctly, completely, concisely, and courteously (the five Cs of good communication).

Can you detect the errors in the following examples?

1. *Write Clearly.*

   That meeting we discussed about selecting a new computer can be next Monday morning if you are available, or if you are not, you can select another time. [NOT an example of *clear* writing.]

   Revised and Improved
   The meeting to select a computer, discussed in our May 18 telephone conversation, can be held in my office Monday, June 3, at 10 A.M. if your schedule permits.

2. *Write Correctly.*

   Our winter conference will be held at the Holiday Inn in Saddle Brook, New Jersey, on June 23 next year. [NOT an example of *correct* writing.]

   Revised and Improved
   Our winter conference will be held at the Holiday Inn in Saddle Brook, New Jersey on January 23, 1988. [Winter conferences aren't held in June.]

3. *Write Completely.*

Here is the time, date, and plane information for your trip to Philadelphia: You will fly Eastern Air Lines on Monday, May 6. [NOT an example of *complete* writing.]

Revised and Improved
Your reservations are for Monday, May 6, on Eastern Airlines Flight #235, leaving Newark at 8:23 A.M., arriving in Philadelphia at 8:58 A.M.

4. *Write Concisely.*

One of the most important activities carried through today is the training of manager-trainees in the insurance industry so that the manager-trainee can be prepared to step into middle-management positions when they open up in various insurance companies. [NOT an example of *concise* writing.]

Revised and Improved
One of the most important activities in the insurance industry is the training of future managers. This practice ensures that trained personnel will always be ready when middle-management positions are available.

5. *Write Courteously.*

How do you expect us to send you the forms you requested if you carelessly omitted the identifying numbers? [NOT an example of *courteous* writing.]

Revised and Improved
If you will send us the form numbers, we will be glad to send you all the papers you requested.

These examples demonstrate five points:

Every sentence should be crystal clear.
Every word should be spelled correctly and chosen for appropriateness.
Every letter, report, or memo should be complete.
Every message should be stated in the fewest words possible.
Every statement should be tactful and courteous.

Certainly it is not difficult to be sure that your communications follow the principles of the five *C*s. All that is required is care, attention to detail, and a standard on your part that accepts nothing less than excellence.

MECHANICAL PRECISION

To develop skill, confidence, clarity, and effectiveness in your writing, you should strive for perfection in applying the basic rules of written language. In addition to the very important factors of good organization and context flow, commendable writing style and proper tone, and attention to the human relations aspect of effective writing, you must pay careful attention to *mechanical precision.*

Precision in grammar, spelling, punctuation, capitalization, and in number writing is essential for the effective communicator. A manager who relies on a secretary's skill and the correction capabilities of word-processing software to prevent mechanical flaws is in a very precarious position. Good communicators should master the principles and correct application of mechanical precision. Their support staff and electronic equipment, if available, can then double-check the material to eliminate mistakes.

Successful Business English provides the guidelines to be studied, examples to clarify the guidelines, and numerous exercises to help you apply what you have learned. Mastery of this text and frequent reference to its contents will increase your knowledge of basic business English.

BUSINESS VOCABULARY

To help you improve and expand your business vocabulary and learn to use the proper words and phrases in business situations, at the end of each chapter we have included a special section called "A Dynamic Business Vocabulary." Since word processors and computers are essential in today's offices, we have included some of the more popular commonly used terms that apply to the utilization of electronic equipment.

If you study the spelling, definition, and use of each word, you will become acquainted with the "in" language of successful people in business careers. If you have a question about the pronunciation of any of these words, you should refer to your dictionary.

By increasing your vocabulary and sharpening your English skills, you will be one step closer to becoming the effective communicator that government and industry need and want.

APPLICATION EXERCISES

A. Please edit the following letter. Circle errors in punctuation, grammar, and spelling. Write the correction above the encircled errors.

August 10, 198_

Mr. Robert Schwartz, Treasurer

Kemple and Kemple, Inc.

5555 South Market Street

San Francisco, CA 94101

Dear Mr. Schwartz,

We received your past due invoice #2828 in which you indicated our account was deliquent to the tune of $448.00.

This appears to be an error on your part, we sent you our check $4414 dated May 10, 198_, which shood have cleared the account. That check was for $448.00.

We are surprised that your firm made a mistake of this magnidude. It certainly doesn't help our credit reputation when firms make credit errors on there customers accounts.

If you did not recieve the check, we will have to put a stop on the original and issue a new one. Let us here from you as soon as possable so we can clear up this problem.

Sincerely yours

Cathlean Camber

Accounts Payible Clerk

B. Please edit the following memo. Circle errors in punctuation, grammar, and spelling. When you have finished, write your corrections above the encircled errors and rewrite the memo on a separate sheet of paper.

TO: Will Williams, Production Mgr.

FROM: Bob Writtendorf, Foreman #12

DATE: Nov. 4, 198_

SUBJECT: Reqst for materials

This is to request your aproval for the following items which are needed immetiately by this dept so that proper inventory can be maintained and continued. We need five number #201 brushes and 6 number #251 tools and three bilevel pumps of each two quart capacity, and 12 handsaws (model #300), and three screw driver sets (standard).

These items are requizitioned under Bulletin 404 and will be charged to our department budjet. Please expedite and hurry-up this request.

C. Please edit the following letter. Circle errors in punctuation, grammar, and spelling. When you have finished, write your corrections above the encircled errors and rewrite the letter on a separate sheet of paper.

HOWARD INDUSTRIES, INC.

82 FRONTAGE ROAD   FAIRFIELD, CONNECTICUT 06437   (203) 480-6995

2/12/8_

Mrs. Maria Song

1445 South Denton St.

Miami, FL 33143

Dear Ms. Song,

We were very pleased to receive your resent letter of 2-3-8_ in which you made inquiry conserning the possible purchase of a new Howard vacuum cleaner from a locale dealer in you're area and for which you wished to have charged to your VISA Credit card.

The local dealer in your area for Howard products is located at 1400 South Lyons Avenue in the Lyons Shopping Center in Miami, Florida. You will find that he carries a full line of Howard's cleaners in all

---

modles and prices. We know you will be pleased with your purchase and please right us if you have any questions.

By the way, all our appliances are fully guaranteed and carry a 2 year waranty.

Sincerly Yours,

Arnold Becker

Sales Manager

Challenge Exercise

Refer to Figure 1-1 on page 2. You will remember that the letter in this example, written by Murray Y. Soong, had many flaws. On a blank sheet of paper, write or type an error-free revision—one that would impress the recipient, Mr. Warren Williams, president of Williams Electronic Company. Double-check your spelling, grammar, capitalization, and punctuation, and proofread your finished copy for writing or typing errors.

Name _____

You Are the Editor

Review and edit this business letter. Correct spelling and punctuation and anything else you feel should be changed. Write your corrections between the lines.

APEX
MOTORS

240 Burr Street
Bamesville, Iowa 50011
(515) 998-6328

March 12, 198_

Mr. Carl Contini
1524 South Clifford Drive
Bamesville, IA 50011

Dear Mr. Coutini,

Thank you very much for your recent purchase of a new Ford from our facilities, we know you will be pleased with your purchase for many years to come.

We want to remind you that Apex Motor's Service Department is one of the largest and most effishunt on the east Coast. We service cars from 7:00 to 7:00 6 days each week. In addition, we offer a fine rental car service if such a need on your part or friends of yours should arrise.

11

We our pleased, Mr. Countini, that you chose Apex for your car purchase. We want to work with you every way possible to fill your needs, we do hope you will tell your friends and business associates about us so that our relationships may expand.

Sincerely yours,

Gerald Lotz, Owner

A DYNAMIC BUSINESS VOCABULARY

To improve your vocabulary, study the spelling of these words, their definitions, and their use in sentences. In addition, check their pronunciation by referring to your dictionary. An exercise to test your mastery of this list follows.

Absenteeism

Continued absence from work or other duties either deliberately or habitually.

Absenteeism of plant personnel at the Acme Corporation contributed to the 10 percent drop in productivity.

Accountability

The assignment of responsibility for actions, decisions, goals, and performance.

The company has assigned accountability to each department head for any losses sustained.

Acronym

A word that is formed from the first letter of words or parts of words in a term, title, or name. Examples are NASA and FORTRAN.

The ZIP in ZIP code is an acronym for zone improvement plan.

Actuary

An individual qualified to analyze rates and systems to determine future situations, usually involving financial matters and time.

The firm's actuary computed the long-term benefits for all life insurance policies.

Adjudicate

To carry through a judicial procedure for the primary purposes of settling claims.

The judge was requested to adjudicate the claims and counterclaims made by the parties involved.

Affidavit

A statement written and sworn to in the presence of a notary public.

Because Mr. Marquez could not be present for the court case itself, he submitted an affidavit setting forth his understanding of Acme's responsibilities.

Affiliate

In business, to associate one business with another, as in a subsidiary of a business.

The University of Southern California School of Accounting is affiliated with the university's Graduate School of Business Administration.

Agenda

A list, outline, or plan of things to be considered or done at a meeting.

Dee typed an agenda for Thursday's department meeting.

THE ABC'S OF BUSINESS VOCABULARY

Throughout this book there are lists of important business words to learn and use in your business writing. The first list, on the preceding page, includes several words beginning with the letter *A.* Check your knowledge of these words by completing the following exercise.

1. The meaning of the verb *affiliate* is _____

   _____

2. The definition of the noun *absenteeism* is _____

   _____

3. Define the noun *acronym.* _____

   _____

4. Compose three short sentences using one of the following words in each sentence:
   (a) accountability, (b) actuary, (c) adjudicate.

   _____

   _____

   _____

   _____

   _____

   _____

5. A statement written and sworn to in the presence of a notary public is a/an (a) bank statement, (b) monthly statement, (c) persuasive communication, (d) affidavit.

6. A program listing of activities to be addressed and carried out at a future meeting is the (a) appendix, (b) assessment, (c) agenda, (d) minutes of a meeting.

Part One
Which Word, and How Is It Spelled?

Study these sentences:

1. *The personal in the outer office were most courteous. ["Personal" should be* personnel.*]*

2. *That is the first occurance of that error. ["Occurance" should be spelled* occurrence.*]*

3. *What are the principals that guide your behavior? ["Principals" should be* principles.*]*

4. *The affect of the reorganization was most positive. ["Affect" should be* effect.*]*

5. *Juanita's most recent memo supercedes her previous one. ["Supercedes" should be spelled* supersedes.*]*

6. *At least two thiefs were involved in the robbery. [The correct plural of "thief is* thieves.*]*

7. *Ms. Clark, will you please prepare a reciept for Ms. Jensen? ["Reciept" should be spelled* receipt.*]*

8. *The secretaries brought there notebooks. ["There" should be* their.*]*

9. *That is alright with me. ["Alright" should be spelled* all right.*]*

10. Incidentally *contains four syllables. ["Incidentally" has* five *syllables.]*

All these sentences contain errors (corrected in brackets) that involve only one word. That is, the authors misused single words, using them incorrectly or misspelling them or choosing the wrong form. (In later sections you will encounter errors of other kinds involving whole groups of words.)

These are errors you can avoid, provided you work at it. The next three chapters will help you. The first chapter teaches you about using the dictionary. You'll learn that it is truly an effective tool, one you should keep close at hand when you write.

Chapter 3 covers spelling, surely one of the most difficult areas for many writers and, ironically, one of the easiest for many others. We cannot help you become a great speller if you are not one already, but our suggestions will assist you in becoming a better speller than you are now.

The final chapter in this section of the book deals with confusing words. Should you use affect *or* effect? personal *or* personnel? to, too, *or* two? *Having studied this chapter, you will be better able to answer these kinds of troubling questions.*

Mistakes made in single words often reveal not only an uninformed writer, but also an uncaring one who will not take the trouble to learn or look up the correct form. These chapters will help you avoid presenting this image.

2 The Dictionary

Suppose that, in response to the newspaper advertisement in Figure 2-1, you decided to apply for the administrative assistant position at Ortega Imports. While writing your letter of application, you might have the following questions:

1. Which is the correct spelling—*superviser, supervisor, supervizer,* or *supervizor?*

2. When you type your letter of application, you discover that only part of the word *employer* can go at the end of the line, with the rest of the word in the next line. You know that you should break words between syllables. What is the correct syllabification (word division) of *employer?*

3. The newspaper advertisement says "salary negotiable." What is the meaning of *negotiable?*

4. Suppose in an interview you have to discuss the word *negotiable*. How do you pronounce it?

5. In your letter you have used the word *responsibility* several times, and instead of using it again, you would prefer to substitute a synonym. What is a good synonym for *responsible* or *responsibility?* (A synonym is a word that means almost the same as another word.)

In what one book can you find the answers to all these questions? The answer is, of course, the dictionary. It is one of a writer's best friends, whether that writer is a world-famous novelist, a copywriter for department store catalogs, a writer of collection letters for a loan company, or a student taking a course in business English.

In almost any standard dictionary you can find the spelling, syllabification, pronunciation of a word, the part or parts of speech a word may be, its meaning or meanings, and its synonyms. Additionally, in many dictionaries you can learn something about the history of a word, special abbreviations, rules of grammar, examples of sentences containing certain words, illustrations, locations of colleges and universities, biographical information, and foreign terms and their meanings.

Figure 2-1. Help wanted.

ADMINISTRATIVE ASSISTANT Excellent opportunity with local
importing company. Able to assume low-level management
responsibilities. Minimum 2 years college. Salary
negotiable. Send resume to ORTEGA IMPORTS, Box 3166,
Princeton, NJ 08540.

ABRIDGED AND UNABRIDGED DICTIONARIES

In all likelihood the dictionary you use will be *abridged*. That means it is a shortened, or abridged, version of a longer, *unabridged* dictionary. Unabridged dictionaries are found in libraries, often on special stands or tables. Usually they are about ten to twelve inches thick.

Even unabridged dictionaries do not contain all the words currently in use in the English language. Unlike a language no longer in popular use—Latin, for example—English is constantly changing, especially by the addition of new words. An unabridged dictionary of 1950 did not have the words *hippie, chip* (as in *computer chip*), *supply-side economics, user-friendly* (applies to electronic equipment), as well as many others we could mention.

For almost all your purposes, a good desk-size abridged dictionary will work fine. On the other hand, the paperback pocket-size dictionary you may carry to class is not detailed enough for the average business writer. It lists fewer words than the desk-size abridged dictionary and generally provides less explanatory information about the vocabulary that is listed.

ANALYZING A DICTIONARY PAGE

Note page 687 from *Webster's Ninth New Collegiate Dictionary* (an abridged desk-size dictionary) in Figure 2-2. Using just that page, you can find answers to these questions:

1. What is the meaning of *levity*? (Note that it has several meanings. Many words in English do.)

2. What is the plural of the noun *lexicon*? (Both *lexica* and *lexicons* are given. Although both spellings are acceptable, the spelling given first is preferred.)

3. What are the parts of speech of *levy*? (It is both a noun and a verb. Many words in English can be more than one part of speech.)

4. What are the five syllables in *lexicographer*? (Note the small dots that separate the syllables: *lex·i·cog·ra·pher.*)

5. What are some synonyms for the adjective *liable*? (Read their descriptions carefully and you will see that there are slight distinctions in the meanings.)

Also on this dictionary page, note the two guide words at the top: *leverage* and *libel*. These guide words help you find words in a hurry, as all the words on this page fall alphabetically between *leverage* (the first entry on the page) and *libel* (the last entry on the page).

Note, also, the capitalized word *Levi*. Many dictionaries provide definitions or explanations for names of famous people, places, or things.

PRONUNCIATION

Reading aloud someone else's writing, a lovely poem or a brief portion of a book can be a frustrating experience if you do not know the correct pronunciation of a word appearing in the written passage. Fortunately, the correct pronunciation of the word in question can be found in most desk-size and unabridged dictionaries. Most dictionaries provide the phonetic pronunciation of entry words between two slanted lines (virgules).

apricot   \ˈap-rə-kät, ˈā-prə-kät\

To determine the correct pronunciation of all vowels and some consonants and dipthongs (*th, ch*), you should refer to the phonetic chart or explanation usually appearing at the bottom of

Figure 2-2. Dictionary page.*

leverage • libel 687

[1]**le·ver·age** \'lev-(ə-)rij, 'lēv-\ *n* (1724) **1 :** the action of a lever or the mechanical advantage gained by it **2 :** POWER, EFFECTIVENESS ⟨organizing . . . to gain greater professional, economic, and political ~ — *Change*⟩ **3 :** the use of credit to enhance one's speculative capacity ⟨buying stocks on margin is a form of ~⟩

[2]**leverage** *vt* **-aged; -ag·ing** (1937) **:** to provide with leverage

lev·er·et \'lev-(ə-)rət\ *n* [ME, fr. (assumed) MF *levret*, fr. MF *levre* hare, fr. L *lepor-, lepus*] (15c) **:** a hare in its first year

Le·vi \'lē-ˌvī\ *n* [LL, from Heb *Lēwī*] **:** a son of Jacob and the traditional eponymous ancestor of the priestly tribe of Levi

levi·able \'lev-ē-ə-bəl\ *adj* (15c) **:** capable of being levied or levied upon

le·vi·a·than \li-'vī-ə-thən\ *n* [ME, fr. LL, fr. Heb *liwyāthān*] (14c) **1 a** *often cap* **:** a sea monster represented as an adversary defeated by Yahweh in various scriptural accounts **b (1) :** a large sea animal **(2) :** a large oceangoing ship **2** *cap* **:** the political state; *esp* **:** a totalitarian state having a vast bureaucracy **3 :** something large or formidable — **leviathan** *adj*

levi·er \'lev-ē-ər\ *n* (15c) **:** one that levies

lev·i·gate \'lev-ə-ˌgāt\ *vt* **-gat·ed; -gat·ing** [L *levigatus*, pp. of *levigare*, fr. *levis* smooth + *-igare* (akin to *agere* to drive) — more at LIME, AGENT] (1612) **1 :** POLISH, SMOOTH **2 a :** to grind to a fine smooth powder while in moist condition **b :** to separate (fine powder) from coarser material by suspending in a liquid — **lev·i·ga·tion** \ˌlev-ə-'gā-shən\ *n*

lev·in \'lev-ən\ *n* [ME *levene*] *archaic* (13c) **:** LIGHTNING

le·vi·rate \'lev-ə-rət, 'lē-və-, -ˌrāt\ *n* [L *levir* husband's brother; akin to OE *tācor* husband's brother, Gk *daēr*] (1725) **:** the sometimes compulsory marriage of a widow by a brother of her deceased husband — **le·vi·rat·ic** \ˌlev-ə-'rat-ik, ˌlē-və-\ *adj*

Le·vi's \'lē-ˌvīz\ *trademark* — used esp. for blue denim jeans

lev·i·tate \'lev-ə-ˌtāt\ *vb* **-tat·ed; -tat·ing** [*levity*] *vi* (1673) **:** to rise or float in the air esp. in seeming defiance of gravitation ~ *vt* **:** to cause to levitate

lev·i·ta·tion \ˌlev-ə-'tā-shən\ *n* (1668) **:** the act or process of levitating; *esp* **:** the rising or lifting of a person or thing by means held to be supernatural — **lev·i·ta·tion·al** \-shnəl, -shən-ᵊl\ *adj*

Le·vite \'lē-ˌvīt\ *n* (14c) **:** a member of the priestly Hebrew tribe of Levi; *specif* **:** a Levite of non-Aaronic descent assigned to lesser ceremonial offices under the Levitical priests of the family of Aaron

Le·vit·i·cal \li-'vit-i-kəl\ *adj* [LL *Leviticus*] (1535) **:** of or relating to the Levites or to Leviticus

Le·vit·i·cus \-kəs\ *n* [LL, lit., of the Levites] **:** the third book of canonical Jewish and Christian Scripture consisting mainly of priestly legislation — see BIBLE table

lev·i·ty \'lev-ət-ē\ *n* [L *levitat-, levitas*, fr. *levis* light in weight — more at LIGHT] (1564) **1 a :** excessive or unseemly frivolity **b :** lack of steadiness **:** CHANGEABLENESS **2 :** the quality or state of being light in weight **:** BUOYANCY

le·vo \'lē-(ˌ)vō\ *adj* (1938) **:** LEVOROTATORY

levo- — see LEV-

levo·do·pa \'lev-ə-ˌdō-pə\ *n* (1969) **:** L-DOPA

le·vo·ro·ta·tion \ˌlē-və-rō-'tā-shən\ *n* (1882) **:** left-handed or counterclockwise rotation — used of the plane of polarization of light

le·vo·ro·ta·to·ry \-'rōt-ə-ˌtōr-ē, -ˌtȯr-\ *or* **le·vo·ro·ta·ry** \-'rōt-ə-rē\ *adj* (1873) **:** turning toward the left or counterclockwise; *esp* **:** rotating the plane of polarization of light to the left — compare DEXTROROTATORY

lev·u·lose \'lev-yə-ˌlōs, -ˌlōz\ *n* [ISV, irreg. fr. *lev-* + *-ose*] (1871) **:** FRUCTOSE 2

[1]**levy** \'lev-ē\ *n, pl* **lev·ies** [ME, fr. OF *levee*, act of raising — more at LEVEE] (13c) **1 a :** the imposition or collection of an assessment **b :** an amount levied **2 a :** the enlistment or conscription of men for military service **b :** troops raised by levy

[2]**levy** *vb* **lev·ied; levy·ing** *vt* (14c) **1 a :** to impose or collect by legal authority ⟨~ a tax⟩ **b :** to require by authority **2 :** to enlist or conscript for military service **3 :** to carry on (war) **:** WAGE ~ *vi* **:** to seize property

lewd \'lüd\ *adj* [ME *lewed* vulgar, fr. OE *lǣwede* laical, ignorant] (14c) **1** *obs* **:** EVIL, WICKED **2 a :** sexually unchaste or licentious **b :** OBSCENE, SALACIOUS — **lewd·ly** *adv* — **lewd·ness** *n*

lew·is \'lü-əs\ *n* [prob. fr. the name *Lewis*] (1743) **:** an iron dovetailed tenon that is made in sections, can be fitted into a dovetail mortise, and is used in hoisting large stones

lew·is·ite \'lü-ə-ˌsīt\ *n* [Winford L. *Lewis* †1943 Am. chemist] (1919) **:** a colorless or brown vesicant liquid $C_2H_2AsCl_3$ developed as a poison gas for war use

lew·is·son \'lü-ə-sən\ *n* (ca. 1842) **:** LEWIS

lex \'leks\ *n, pl* **le·ges** \'lā-(ˌ)gās\ [L *leg-, lex*] (15c) **:** LAW

lex·eme \'lek-ˌsēm\ *n* [Gk *lex*is word, speech + E *-eme*] (1940) **:** a meaningful linguistic unit that is an item in the vocabulary of a language — **lex·emic** \lek-'sē-mik\ *adj*

lex·i·cal \'lek-si-kəl\ *adj* (1836) **1 :** of or relating to words or the vocabulary of a language as distinguished from its grammar and construction **2 :** of or relating to a lexicon or to lexicography — **lex·i·cal·i·ty** \ˌlek-sə-'kal-ət-ē\ *n* — **lex·i·cal·ly** \'lek-si-k(ə-)lē\ *adv*

lexical meaning *n* (1933) **:** the meaning of the base (as the word *play*) in a paradigm (as *plays, played, playing*) — compare GRAMMATICAL MEANING

lex·i·cog·ra·pher \ˌlek-sə-'käg-rə-fər\ *n* [LGk *lexikographos*, fr. *lexikon* + Gk *-graphos* -grapher] (1658) **:** an author or editor of a dictionary

lex·i·co·graph·i·cal \ˌlek-sə-kō-'graf-i-kəl\ *or* **lex·i·co·graph·ic** \-ik\ *adj* (1791) **:** of or relating to lexicography — **lex·i·co·graph·i·cal·ly** \-i-k(ə-)lē\ *adv*

lex·i·cog·ra·phy \ˌlek-sə-'käg-rə-fē\ *n* (1680) **1 :** the editing or making of a dictionary **2 :** the principles and practices of dictionary making

lex·i·col·o·gy \ˌlek-sə-'käl-ə-jē\ *n* [F *lexicologie*, fr. *lexico-* (fr. LGk *lexiko-*, fr. *lexikon*) + *-logie* -logy] (ca. 1828) **:** a branch of linguistics concerned with the signification and application of words — **lex·i·col·o·gist** \-jəst\ *n*

lex·i·con \'lek-sə-ˌkän, -si-kən\ *n, pl* **lex·i·ca** \-si-kə\ *or* **lexicons** [LGk *lexikon*, fr. neut. of *lexikos* of words, fr. Gk *lexis* word, speech, fr. *legein* to say — more at LEGEND] (1603) **1 :** a book containing an alphabetical arrangement of the words in a language and their definitions **:** DICTIONARY **2 a :** the vocabulary of a language, an individual speaker or group of speakers, or a subject **b :** the total stock of morphemes in a language **3 :** REPERTOIRE, INVENTORY

lex·is \'lek-səs\ *n, pl* **lex·es** \-ˌsēz\ [Gk, speech, word] (1960) **:** LEXICON 2a

ley *var of* LEA

Ley·den jar \ˌlīd-ᵊn-\ *n* [*Leiden, Leyden*, Netherlands] (1825) **:** an electrical condenser consisting of a glass jar coated inside and outside with metal foil and having the inner coating connected to a conducting rod passed through the insulating stopper

L–form \'el-ˌfȯrm\ *n* [*L*ister Institute, London, where it was first isolated] (1948) **:** a filterable form of some bacteria that may be a specialized reproductive body appearing chiefly when the environment is unfavorable and resembling typical pleuropneumonia organisms

Lha·sa ap·so \ˌläs-ə-'äp-(ˌ)sō, ˌlas-ə-'ap-\ *n, pl* **Lhasa apsos** [*Lhasa*, Tibet + Tibetan *apso*] *often cap A* (1935) **:** any of a Tibetan breed of small dogs that have a dense coat of long hard straight hair, a heavy fall over the eyes, heavy whiskers and beard, and a well-feathered tail curled over the back — called also *Lhasa* \'läs-ə, 'las-\

Lhasa apso

li \'lē\ *n, pl* **li** *also* **lis** \'lēz\ [Chin (Pek) *li*³] (1588) **:** any of various Chinese units of distance; *esp* **:** one equal to about $^1/_3$ mile (0.5 kilometer)

li·a·bil·i·ty \ˌlī-ə-'bil-ət-ē\ *n, pl* **-ties** (1794) **1 a :** the quality or state of being liable **b :** PROBABILITY **2 :** something for which one is liable; *esp, pl* **:** pecuniary obligations **:** DEBTS **3 :** one that works as a disadvantage **:** DRAWBACK

li·a·ble \'lī-ə-bəl, *esp in sense 2 often* 'lī-bəl\ *adj* [(assumed) AF, fr. OF *lier* to bind, fr. L *ligare* — more at LIGATURE] (15c) **1 a :** obligated according to law or equity **:** RESPONSIBLE **b :** subject to appropriation or attachment **2 a :** being in a position to incur — used with *to* ⟨~ to diseases⟩ **b :** exposed or subject to some usu. adverse contingency or action ⟨watch out or you're ~ to fall⟩

syn LIABLE, OPEN, EXPOSED, SUBJECT, PRONE, SUSCEPTIBLE, SENSITIVE mean being by nature or through circumstances likely to experience something adverse. LIABLE implies a possibility or probability of incurring something because of position, nature, or particular situation; OPEN stresses a lack of barriers preventing incurrence; EXPOSED suggests lack of protection or powers of resistance against something actually present or threatening; SUBJECT implies an openness for any reason to something that must be suffered or undergone; PRONE stresses natural tendency or propensity to incur something; SUSCEPTIBLE implies conditions existing in one's nature or individual constitution that make incurrence probable; SENSITIVE implies a readiness to respond to or be influenced by forces or stimuli. ***syn*** see in addition RESPONSIBLE

usage Both *liable* and *apt* when followed by an infinitive are used nearly interchangeably with *likely*. Although conflicting advice has been given over the years, most current commentators accept *apt* when so used. They generally recommend limiting *liable* to situations having an undesirable outcome, and our evidence shows that in edited writing it is more often so used than not.

li·aise \lē-'āz\ *vi* **li·aised; li·ais·ing** [back-formation fr. *liaison*] (1928) **1 :** to establish liaison **2 :** to act as a liaison officer

li·ai·son \'lē-ə-ˌzän, lē-'ā-, ÷'lā-ə-\ *n* [F, fr. MF, fr. *lier*, fr. OF] (1809) **1 a :** a close bond or connection **:** INTERRELATIONSHIP **b :** an illicit sexual relationship **:** AFFAIR 3a **2 :** the pronunciation of an otherwise absent consonant sound at the end of the first of two consecutive words the second of which begins with a vowel sound and follows without pause **3 a :** communication for establishing and maintaining mutual understanding (as between parts of an armed force) **b :** one that establishes and maintains liaison

li·a·na \lē-'än-ə, -'an-ə\ *or* **li·ane** \-'än, -'an\ *n* [F *liane*] (1796) **:** a climbing herbaceous or woody vine esp. of tropical rain forests that roots in the ground — **li·a·noid** \-'än-ˌȯid, -'an-\ *adj*

li·ang \lē-'äŋ\ *n, pl* **liang** *also* **liangs** [Chin (Pek) *liang*³] (1827) **:** an old Chinese unit of weight equal to $^1/_{16}$ catty

li·ar \'lī(-ə)r\ *n* [ME, fr. OE *lēogere*, fr. *lēogan* to lie — more at LIE] (bef. 12c) **:** one that tells lies

Li·as \'lī-əs\ *adj* [*Lias*, division of the European Jurassic, fr. F, fr. E (a limestone rock)] (1813) **:** LIASSIC

Li·as·sic \lī-'as-ik\ *adj* [modif. (influenced by *Jurassic*) of F *liasique*, fr. *Lias*] (1833) **:** of, relating to, or being a subdivision of the European Jurassic

lib \'lib\ *n* (1970) **:** LIBERATION 2

li·ba·tion \lī-'bā-shən\ *n* [L *libation-, libatio*, fr. *libatus*, pp. of *libare* to pour as an offering; akin to Gk *leibein* to pour] (14c) **1 a :** an act of pouring a liquid as a sacrifice (as to a deity) **b :** a liquid (as wine) used in a libation **2 a :** an act or instance of drinking often ceremoniously **b :** BEVERAGE; *esp* **:** a drink containing alcohol — **li·ba·tion·ary** \-shə-ˌner-ē\ *adj*

li·bec·cio \li-'bech-(ē-ˌ)ō\ *or* **li·bec·chio** \-'bek-ē-ˌō\ *n* [It] (1667) **:** a southwest wind

[1]**li·bel** \'lī-bəl\ *n* [ME, written declaration, fr. MF, fr. L *libellus*, dim. of *liber* book — more at LEAF] (14c) **1 a** *archaic* **:** a handbill esp. attacking or defaming someone **b :** a written statement in which a plaintiff in certain courts sets forth his cause of action or the relief he seeks **2 a :** a written or oral defamatory statement or representation that conveys an unjustly unfavorable impression **b (1) :** a statement or representation published without just cause and tending to expose another to public contempt **(2) :** defamation of a person by written or representational means **(3) :** the publication of blasphemous, treasonable, seditious, or obscene writings or pictures **(4) :** the act, tort, or crime of publishing such a libel

\ə\ **abut** \ᵊ\ **kitten**, F **table** \ər\ **further** \a\ **ash** \ā\ **ace** \ä\ **cot, cart**
\au̇\ **out** \ch\ **chin** \e\ **bet** \ē\ **easy** \g\ **go** \i\ **hit** \ī\ **ice** \j\ **job**
\ŋ\ **sing** \ō\ **go** \ȯ\ **law** \ȯi\ **boy** \th\ **thin** \th̲\ **the** \ü\ **loot** \u̇\ **foot**
\y\ **yet** \zh\ **vision** \ȧ, k̲, ⁿ, œ, œ̄, ue, ue̅, ʸ\ *see* Guide to Pronunciation

By permission. From *Webster's Ninth New Collegiate Dictionary* © 1986 by Merriam-Webster Inc., publisher of the Merriam-Webster ® Dictionaries.

the dictionary pages. The chart consists of phonetic letters with accompanying short familiar words to indicate the correct pronunciation.

    ə (as in) **abut**   ä (as in) **cot**
    ā (as in) **ace**   a (as in) **ash**

Note that the word *apricot* has two pronunciations—one beginning with a short *a* sound and one beginning with a long *a* sound. The second pronunciation is considered as acceptable as the first by most educated speakers. It is safe to conclude when you see pronunciation variants (more than one way to pronounce a word) in your dictionary that all examples given after the entry word are satisfactory. ☑

HELPFUL SUGGESTIONS FOR FINDING A WORD IN THE DICTIONARY

Searching for a word in a dictionary is particularly troublesome when the first and second letters of the word are not known. To solve this problem, the following information can be helpful:

1. If a word begins with the sound of *f,* you should check *ph* as well as *f.*
    COMPARE   *f*oam WITH *ph*one
                    *f*roze WITH *ph*rase
                    *f*arm WITH *ph*armacy

2. If a word begins with the sound of *s,* you should check *c* as well as *s.*
    COMPARE   *s*eize WITH *c*ease
                    *s*ealing WITH *c*eiling
                    *s*eller WITH *c*ellar

3. If a word begins with the sound of *k,* you should check *c* as well as *k.*
    COMPARE   *k*ite WITH *c*oat
                    *k*issed WITH *c*ost
                    *k*eep WITH *c*ape

Self-Check Exercise 1

Refer once again to the reproduced dictionary page. Locate specific words and respond to questions about their pronunciation, syllabification, definition, and parts of speech. You can check your answers in the key at the end of the chapter.

1. Are there different pronunciations for *liaison*? If so, explain the difference.

2. How many syllables does *levitation* have? What are they?

3. Define *¹levy* and *²levy.*

4. What part of speech is *liability*?

4. If a word begins with the sound of *en,* check *in* as well as *en.*

      COMPARE   *en*close WITH *in*sight

                       *en*circle WITH *in*cline

                       *en*act WITH *in*active

THE MEANING MAKES THE DIFFERENCE

Of course you want to be extra careful about eliminating all errors in spelling from your communications. You therefore refer to your dictionary each time you are unsure of the correct spelling of a word that you select. When you locate the particular word, however, you must check not only the spelling, but the definition of the word as well. The following situation indicates why this two-step process (checking spelling and checking definition) is important.

Suppose you are in the process of composing a business letter and decide to include the following sentence: "We must follow the (principals?) (principles?) set down by the organization's guidelines." You stop and ask yourself which one of the two words in parentheses is correct. When you refer to your dictionary, you find both *principal* and *principle,* but you may not know which spelling to use in your business writing. You can make the correct choice, however, if you carefully study the definition of each word.

Always refer to the meaning of a word before deciding that you have located the correct spelling. (In the above sentence, the correct spelling choice is *principles* because of its meaning. It is defined as "a comprehensive fundamental law or doctrine.") What word would you choose in the following sentences? ☑

The straw hat (compliments, complements) the woman's Easter outfit. [The answer is *complements,* which means "something that fills up, completes, or makes perfect."]

Of the two nieces, the younger inherited the (lessor, lesser) amount of money. [The answer is *lesser,* which means "smaller or inferior."]

He is the (sole, soul) owner of the record shop. [The answer is *sole,* which means "having no sharer and being the only one."]

Self-Check Exercise 2

Test your ability to locate in the dictionary words that begin with the sound of *f, s, k,* or *en.* In the following sentences you are asked to select the correct spelling. Do so by referring to your dictionary. After underlining your answers, you can compare them with the key.

1. A stamp collector is a (filatelist, philatelist).

2. The policewoman received a (citation, sitation) for her bravery.

3. The Muslims' holy book is called the (Coran, Koran).

4. He sells modern (enamel, inamel) jewelry in his store.

5. She was (interrogated, enterrogated) by the detective.

6. A flying insect with transparent wings is a (sicada, cicada).

THE PREFERRED SPELLING

Occasionally you will have a choice of spelling when there are two acceptable ways to spell a word. Some dictionaries permit choices, such as judgment or judgement, acknowledgment or acknowledgement, and traveled or travelled. Generally, the spelling given first is the preferred spelling. Thus, in the examples just given, *judgment, acknowledgment,* and *traveled* would be the preferred spellings as they appear first in most dictionaries. Make a selection in the following sentences:

> The manager-trainees (benefitted, benefited) from their in-service seminar. [The spelling usually given first is *benefited.*]
>
> The generosity of the senior citizens (equalled, equaled) that of the Boy Scout troop. [The spelling usually given first is *equaled.*]
>
> Our attorney and our accountant serve as (advisors, advisers) to our association. [The spelling usually given first is *advisers.*]

HOW MANY WORDS?

Have you ever wondered whether a vocabulary item was one or two words? For example, *post office* is two single words, while *postmark* is one word. Also, if you refer to a dictionary, you will learn that *already* and *all ready* are both correct, depending on the writer's meaning. Lastly, *all right* is the spelling considered correct by most informed writers. Some dictionaries list *alright,* but this spelling is rarely accepted. ☑

> COMPARE *lower class* (two words) WITH *lowerclassman* (one word)
> *tidal wave* (two words) WITH *tidewater* (one word)
> *tea bag* (two words) WITH *teacup* (one word)

Self-Check Exercise 3

Refer to your dictionary and select the correct words in the sentences below. This exercise requires that you understand the meaning of a word, select the preferred spelling, and determine whether a term is written as one or two words. After choosing your answers, check them in the key.

1. The district attorney will (persecute, prosecute) the criminal.

2. The innocent and childlike employee was said to have an (ingenuous, ingenious) manner.

3. Here are the (principal, principle) items in the procedure manual.

4. They received their (cancelled, canceled) checks.

5. The instructor (refered, referred) to yesterday's *Wall Street Journal.*

6. An assertive person sometimes has an (over bearing, overbearing) manner.

7. The area that is being considered for the warehouse is described as (underdeveloped, under developed).

SUMMARY

Samuel Johnson is quoted as saying, "To make dictionaries is dull work." That may be true, but the finished product—the completed dictionary—is an important, vital reference book.

Who would debate the value of the dictionary to all writers and users of standard English? Referring to a dictionary helps the writer select the correct words in each situation, pronounce the selected words, divide these words on the written or typewritten page, and find synonyms so that the writer's choice of words is not repetitious.

In addition, as indicated at the beginning of this chapter, a dictionary can help in writing employment communications and in communicating orally with confidence. Yes, all three—the pocket-size dictionary you bring to class, the desk-size dictionary you use at home, and the large unabridged dictionary you use in the library—are invaluable writing tools.

APPLICATION EXERCISES

A. Use your dictionary to find the definition for each italicized word, and place the letter for the best answer in the blank at the left.

_____ 1. A *vendor* is a person who (a) buys, (b) sells, (c) removes garbage, (d) works in a courtroom.

_____ 2. *Wholesale* is the opposite of (a) neutral, (b) beautiful, (c) retail, (d) illegal.

_____ 3. A *mortgage* is (a) a claim on property used as security, (b) a down payment on a house, (c) the final payment on a loan, (d) interest on an investment.

_____ 4. To *compile* means (a) to stack dirt, (b) to collect and arrange, (c) to determine guilt, (d) to become older.

_____ 5. A *cerulean* tile is (a) purple, (b) red, (c) blue, (d) white and green.

_____ 6. *Quid pro quo* is a Latin term meaning (a) useless, (b) this for that, (c) in the first place, (d) all for one and one for all.

_____ 7. A *component* is (a) a part, (b) a competitor, (c) a doctor, (d) a price.

_____ 8. A *statute* is (a) a large stone figure, (b) a law, (c) a plan to end something, (d) a new beginning.

_____ 9. Another name for a *mortician* is (a) lawyer, (b) undertaker, (c) teacher, (d) writer.

_____ 10. *Pecuniary* has to do with (a) food, (b) water, (c) money, (d) medicine.

_____ 11. A *brochure* is (a) a partner in a business venture, (b) a large building, (c) a pamphlet or booklet, (d) a decision made by a judge.

_____ 12. *Toxic substances* are (a) useful in preparing food, (b) poisonous, (c) found only in Central America, (d) usually sold in their natural form to restaurants.

_____ 13. A word beginning with *deca* possibly has to do with the number (a) 1, (b) 5, (c) 10, (d) 100.

_____ 14. A *ketch* is (a) a small shop, (b) a windowless room, (c) a major stockholder in a company, (d) a boat.

_____ 15. A *fortnight* lasts (a) about three or four hours during the early evening, (b) two days, (c) four days and nights, (d) two weeks.

_____ 16. A *stentorian* voice is (a) soft, (b) loud, (c) very high, like a soprano, (d) whiny.

_____ 17. A *misogamist* is unlikely to (a) get married, (b) succeed in business, (c) live beyond 40, (d) do his or her own bookkeeping.

_____ 18. *Tempera* or *tempora* is a process of (a) constructing condominiums, (b) fixing food, (c) painting, (d) worrying.

_____ 19. *Ophthalmologists* are doctors who work on (a) eyes, (b) ears, (c) hearts, (d) feet.

_____ 20. A *goober* is a (a) small bolt, (b) ring, (c) musical instrument, (d) peanut.

_____ 21. A *necropolis* is (a) a city of the dead, (b) a kind of fruit, (c) a disease of the central nervous system, (d) a huge wart.

_____ 22. *Grog* is (a) a Hollywood monster, (b) a kind of liquor, (c) sleepiness, (d) a tree with large leaves.

_____ 23. If you have *halitosis,* you need (a) a cane, (b) glasses, (c) a mouthwash, (d) a hearing aid.

_____ 24. A *rhea* is (a) a lizard, (b) an elephant found only in Alaska, (c) a kind of sweet fruit eaten by Australians, (d) a South American bird.

_____ 25. *Hypertension* has to do with (a) blood pressure, (b) food poisoning, (c) extreme heat, (d) stormy weather.

B. Use your dictionary to find the correctly spelled word in each set of four below, and put the correct letter in the space at the left.

_____ 1. (a) government, (b) goverment, (c) governmant, (d) govarnment

_____ 2. (a) subordinate, (b) subbordinate, (c) subordenite, (d) subordineight

_____ 3. (a) receit, (b) reciet, (c) receipt, (d) reciept

_____ 4. (a) embarass, (b) embarras, (c) embarrass, (d) embaras

_____ 5. (a) minamize, (b) minimise, (c) minimize, (d) minamise

_____ 6. (a) acommodate, (b) accommodate, (c) accammadate, (d) accomodate

_____ 7. (a) occurence, (b) occurance, (c) occurrence, (d) occurrance

_____ 8. (a) manufackture, (b) manufacture, (c) manufakture, (d) mannufacture

_____ 9. (a) typewriter, (b) typriter, (c) tipwriter, (d) typewritre

_____ 10. (a) maskerade, (b) masquerade, (c) maskuraid, (d) masqueraide

_____ 11. (a) efficiensy, (b) eficiency, (c) effishancy, (d) efficiency

_____ 12. (a) inventorie, (b) innventory, (c) inventory, (d) invenntory

_____ 13. (a) acountent, (b) accountant, (c) accountent, (d) acountant

_____ 14. (a) custodian, (b) kustodian, (c) custodienne, (d) custodien

_____ 15. (a) restrant, (b) resturant, (c) restaurant, (d) restourant

_____ 16. (a) freight, (b) frate, (c) frieght, (d) freit

_____ 17. (a) warrentee, (b) waranty, (c) warranty, (d) warenty

_____ 18. (a) enjenir, (b) enginere, (c) enginer, (d) engineer

_____ 19. (a) aparently, (b) apparently, (c) aperently, (d) aperantly

_____ 20. (a) landromart, (b) laundermat, (c) laundromat, (d) laundrymat

_____ 21. (a) evaluation, (b) evalyation, (c) evaluashun, (d) evaleation

_____ 22. (a) mashinary, (b) macheenery, (c) machinery, (d) machenery

_____ 23. (a) apraizal, (b) appraisle, (c) appraisal, (d) appreisal

_____ 24. (a) cirriculum, (b) curriculum, (c) caricullum, (d) curricullum

_____ 25. (a) aluminum, (b) alluminum, (c) alluminumm, (d) alumenumm

C. Indicate in the blanks at the left what part or parts of speech each of the following words can be.

_____ 1. establishment   _____ 14. sincerely

_____ 2. contractual   _____ 15. cooperative

_____ 3. orderly   _____ 16. electronic

_____ 4. optic   _____ 17. transmit

_____ 5. guarantee   _____ 18. recommend

_____ 6. itemize   _____ 19. confidentially

_____ 7. analysis   _____ 20. negotiable

_____ 8. him   _____ 21. summarize

_____ 9. factory   _____ 22. agriculture

_____ 10. beside   _____ 23. secretarial

_____ 11. Spanish   _____ 24. business

_____ 12. incentive   _____ 25. and

_____ 13. interview

D. Divide each of the following words into syllables, writing them in the blank at the left. Put a slash (/) between syllables.

_____ 1. architect

_____ 2. incidentally

_____ 3. participation

_____ 4. sanitarium

_____ 5. insurmountable

_____ 6. voltameter

_____ 7. healthfully

_____ 8. parenthesis

_____ 9. contamination

_____ 10. school

_____ 11. opportunity

_____ 12. substantial

_____ 13. electricity

_____ 14. management

_____ 15. transcontinental

_____ 16. convocation

_____ 17. zoologist

_____ 18. photography

_____ 19. beautician

_____ 20. criminologist

_____ 21. equivalent

_____ 22. reimbursable

_____ 23. mechanically

_____ 24. impersonate

_____ 25. budgetary

E. Find two synonyms for each of the following words and put them in the blanks at the left.

_____   _____   1. secret

_____   _____   2. intention

_____   _____   3. responsibility

_____   _____   4. rich

_____   _____   5. beneficial

_____   _____   6. begin

_____   _____   7. costly

_____   _____   8. punish

_____   _____   9. temerity

_____   _____   10. insanity

_____   _____   11. insipid

_____   _____   12. solitude

_____   _____   13. border

_____   _____   14. mercy

_____   _____   15. splendid

_____   _____   16. flagrant

_____   _____   17. task

_____   _____   18. difficulty

_____   _____   19. mystery

_____   _____   20. concise

_____   _____   21. authentic

_____   _____   22. distribute

_____   _____   23. invent

_____   _____   24. proficient

_____   _____   25. thin

Challenge Exercise

Using a dictionary—and you may need an unabridged one, which you can find in libraries—answer as many of the questions below as you can. Some of these are difficult, but try them anyway.

1. Use the word *run* in at least five different ways.

   (a) _____

   (b) _____

   (c) _____

   (d) _____

   (e) _____

2. Which American city is larger, San Francisco or Dallas? _____

3. Who was William Makepeace Thackeray? _____

   _____

4. What does the abbreviation PGA stand for? _____

   _____

5. What is an *acronym*? _____

   _____

   Give an example of one. _____

6. Would you put an *ascot* (a) on your kitchen table, (b) around your neck,

   (c) next to the telephone, (d) in a swimming pool? _____

7. Where is Ohio State University located? _____

8. *Greengage* describes (a) dogs, (b) crayons, (c) plums, (d) weeds. _____

9. The British are likely to put an extra letter in *color*. What is it and where does it go?

   _____

10. Who is most likely to know something about *colophons*? (a) librarians, (b) gardeners, (c) dentists, (d) tennis players _____

11. In what state is Mount Shasta and how tall is it? _____
_____

12. Your letter to the President of the United States should begin: _____
_____

13. What is the plural of the word *datum*? _____

14. What is an *iguana*? _____

15. How many syllables are there in *antidisestablishmentarianism*? _____

16. One thousand meters is equal to _____ miles.

17. What does the word *Tebet* refer to? _____
_____

18. The term *gerrymander* is named after what American statesman? _____
_____

19. *Zed* is the British word for what letter? _____

20. What is the plural of *brother-in-law*? _____

21. What is *Vassar*? _____

22. According to your dictionary, the *i* in *mile* is pronounced like the *i* in what word? _____
_____

23. The island country of Sri Lanka was once called _____

24. When it is twelve noon (standard time) in New York City, what time is it in London? _____

25. What is the capital of California? _____
_____
_____

You Are the Editor

TO: Marilyn Kowalski, Accountant

FROM: Teresa Sanchez, <u>Supervizor</u>

DATE: August 12,198_

SUBJECT: <u>Takking</u> College Course Work on Company Time

I have discussed your <u>bequest</u> to take a course at <u>Sante</u> <u>fe</u> Community College on <u>thursday</u> afternoons with our <u>subordinate</u>, Mr. Riley, and he says that <u>its</u> <u>alright</u> with him. It will be <u>excepted</u>, however, that you will make up the time away from your work here by <u>retaining</u> after dinner in the evenings.

The company <u>polisy</u> <u>inquires</u> that you put in at <u>lest</u> <u>fourty</u> hours a week in order to maintain all the fringe <u>beneficiaries</u> to which you are <u>entitlement</u>. It will be possible for you to work, <u>to</u>, on <u>saturday</u> mornings from eight <u>oclock</u> until <u>Noon</u>. I think that, if we <u>mainstream</u> this new schedule, <u>they'res</u> not <u>likeable</u> to be many problems.

Thank you for your <u>patients</u>.

Key to Self-Check Exercises

Exercise 1

1. Yes. Pronounced like ′lē-ə-zän, ′lē-ā-zän, ′lē-ā-zän, or ′lā-ə-zän.
2. Four syllables (lev i ta tion).
3. ¹*Levy* means "the imposition or collection of an assessment, etc." ²*Levy* means "to impose or collect by legal authority, etc."
4. *Liability* is a noun.

Exercise 2

1. philatelist
2. citation
3. Koran
4. enamel
5. interrogated
6. cicada

Exercise 3

1. prosecute
2. ingenuous
3. principal
4. canceled
5. referred
6. overbearing
7. underdeveloped

A DYNAMIC BUSINESS VOCABULARY

Here are some more business terms for you to master.

Allocation

A designation or assignment of responsibilities, costs, etc., for a certain purpose or organization.

An allocation of $80,000 was made to the new Department of Research and Development for its first year of operation.

Amortize

To liquidate or extinguish an indebtedness, usually by periodic payments made to a sinking fund, a creditor, or an account.

It would probably be wise to amortize the loan over a ten-year period.

Analysis

The separation and comparison of results in a study, theory, idea, etc.

An analysis of the explosion showed that it was caused by a faulty shut-off valve.

Annuity

An income or allowance paid over a fixed period of time.

The annuity on John's insurance policy would take care of his wife for the rest of her life.

Aptitude

The ability to learn and retain information; a natural ability.

Carlos had an aptitude for geometry and physics.

Arbitration

The hearing and determination of a dispute by an impartial party.

Commissioner Franklin acted as an impartial third party in the Conwin-Keller arbitration meeting.

Bank draft

An order for the payment of money drawn by one bank on another.

The Corwin Company settled the claim with a draft of $30,000 drawn against its reserve fund.

Bankrupt

Reduced to a state of financial ruin. If unable to pay debts, an individual, corporation, etc., may make formal petition to a court to declare insolvency.

Barney's Emporium went bankrupt after the Golden Apple opened across the street.

Name _____

THE ABC'S OF BUSINESS VOCABULARY

Thus far you have studied two lists of business vocabulary. Are you familiar with the words and their definitions? See if you can accurately complete the following quiz.

1. The definition of the noun *arbitration* is _____

_____

2. The meaning of the verb *amortize* is _____

_____

3. Compose three short sentences using one of the following words in each sentence: (a) annuity, (b) aptitude, (c) bankrupt.

_____

_____

_____

_____

_____

_____

4. The separation and comparison of results in a study, theory, or idea is a/an (a) program, (b) list, (c) analysis, (d) column.

5. A designation or assignment of responsibilities, costs, etc., for a certain purpose or organization is a/an (a) allocation, (b) gift, (c) award, (d) liability.

3 Spelling

This chapter deals with the mysterious world of English spelling. It is mysterious partly because English words are often spelled in ways you would not expect when you hear them pronounced. Partly, too, the mystery of spelling lies in our not quite knowing why two people of apparently similar schooling and intelligence can exhibit marked differences in their ability to spell.

Writing "I made a personal decision" when you meant "personnel decision" creates a serious error in meaning, but many misspelled words do not foster this much confusion. If you wrote "concret blocks" or "forty kartons of cereal" or "two [or even "to"] secrateries," most readers would be able to follow your meaning, but they would certainly criticize your spelling.

Occasionally spelling is an important contextual clue—it can alter meanings. It is always an important social clue—it offers significant insight into your ability to communicate. Suppose you received the letter in Figure 3-1 from Mr. Don Hunt of Brighton Mutual Insurance. What would be your impression of Mr. Hunt? Would you like to do business with him? Do you see the necessity to spell as well as you are able?

Like it or not, your lapses in spelling will be noticed by your readers, and they may suspect your other communication skills to be equally weak. Is your communication the result of careful thinking and writing, or because of its spelling inadequacies, does it appear to have been carelessly thrown together? After all, your readers may wonder, if you will not take the time to ensure that your spelling is correct, what other shortcomings does your written communication have? Is it logical? Are your facts straight?

We cannot, in this chapter, promise to make you a *perfect speller,* though we do believe that the principles we present and the advice we give will help you become an improved speller.

A SPELLING PRETEST

Self-assessment is a good point at which to start improving your spelling. Take the following spelling test. You will note that it differs from more common spelling tests in which an instructor dictates words and you write them. In this one, a silent test, you must find the one incorrectly spelled word in each line. This kind of test provides a useful examination of your spelling potential because it presents a spelling of a word and asks you to determine its correctness, just as you have to do with words you write. You should not be too surprised if you sense you are making mistakes, as it is a difficult test.

SPELLING TEST

One word in each line is not spelled correctly. Put its letter in the blank at the left.

_____ 1. (a) central, (b) accomodate, (c) believe, (d) exaggerate, (e) definition

_____ 2. (a) simplify, (b) exhaust, (c) aversion, (d) its', (e) finally

_____ 3. (a) seperate, (b) organic, (c) tenderness, (d) sensitive, (e) cowardly

———— 4. (a) intelligent, (b) decision, (c) occurence, (d) cafeteria, (e) asterisk

———— 5. (a) misery, (b) solicit, (c) calendar, (d) strategy, (e) alright

———— 6. (a) technique, (b) physician, (c) relevent, (d) correspond, (e) wholly

———— 7. (a) bargain, (b) advertisement, (c) weird, (d) committment, (e) maneuver

———— 8. (a) peculiar, (b) confidence, (c) banana, (d) thier, (e) nuisance

———— 9. (a) mathematics, (b) disease, (c) license, (d) institute, (e) accidently

———— 10. (a) extention, (b) parallel, (c) symptom, (d) thief, (e) accomplice

———— 11. (a) architect, (b) bulletin, (c) allotted, (d) paragraph, (e) occassion

———— 12. (a) mediocre, (b) apparrently, (c) clothes, (d) receipt, (e) baggage

———— 13. (a) overwhelm, (b) perseverence, (c) faucet, (d) exceed, (e) February

———— 14. (a) conscious, (b) proffessor, (c) significance, (d) existence, (e) rhyme

———— 15. (a) passtime, (b) reservoir, (c) sphere, (d) eligible, (e) courtesy

———— 16. (a) duplicate, (b) feminine, (c) criticizm, (d) preferred, (e) loneliness

———— 17. (a) therefore, (b) permissible, (c) pursuit, (d) privelege, (e) publicly

———— 18. (a) aquaintance, (b) bruise, (c) athlete, (d) temperature, (e) marriage

———— 19. (a) medicine, (b) mispell, (c) experience, (d) warrant, (e) vengeance

———— 20. (a) intimate, (b) either, (c) variety, (d) miscelaneous, (e) attorney

———— 21. (a) vacuum, (b) leisure, (c) garage, (d) grievious, (e) subtle

———— 22. (a) budget, (b) liability, (c) rapport, (d) syllable, (e) reccommend

———— 23. (a) versatile, (b) imaginary, (c) balloon, (d) mayor, (e) disipline

———— 24. (a) contemptable, (b) parliament, (c) relieve, (d) difference, (e) division

———— 25. (a) government, (b) rehearsal, (c) doubt, (d) fasinate, (e) supplement

Refer to Application Exercise B, which shows the incorrect words. If you scored 20 or better, you are a superior speller. Scores between 15 and 20 put you in the average range. If you scored below 15, you need to identify the weaknesses in your spelling and take the following steps to help you overcome those weaknesses.

Figure 3-1. Letter from Don Hunt

 Brighton Mutual Insurance Company
140 Palisades Avenue
Englewood Cliffs, New Jersey 07632
(201) 492-3159

December 6, 198_

Dear studant:

We at Brighton Mutual Insurance are hopping to be able to servise all your insurance needs. While we are certenly not the largest insurer of colege studants, we beleive we are one of the most active companys. We offer to our subsribors a wide range of benafits and can accomodate our programs to your needs. Will you pleaze take a minate to complet the attatched card, and return it to us as soon as possable so that we might vissit you to explane our programe.

Thank you for your attenshun. We wush you continued good luck in school.

Sincerly yours,

Don Hunt

Insurance Agent

Attachment

STEPS TO IMPROVE SPELLING

Four steps can help you write communications that are free of misspelled words.

1. *Get a good dictionary.* Also purchase a spelling aid such as *Webster's Instant Word Guide.* Both books should always be close at hand when you write. To be sure, people often ask, "How can I look up a word if I can't spell it?" The fact is that most spelling difficulties occur in the middle or at the end of words. Seldom do the first few letters cause such a problem that you cannot find the word in one of these books.

2. *Become skeptical of your spelling ability.* If in doubt about the spelling of a word, look it up! The extra time required will be well spent if it saves you the embarrassment of misspelled words.

3. *Make a list of words that cause you difficulty.* One of the easier ways of keeping such a list is to put a few blank sheets of paper in the back of your dictionary. When you look up a word, write its correct spelling on a sheet and study the word's pronunciation and spelling. If possible, break the word into syllables to see which part of the word is difficult for you to remember. If you discover that you are frequently looking up the same words, devote additional time to memorizing their correct spelling.

4. *Use mnemonic devices to help you remember the spelling of troublesome words.* Mnemonic (pronounced /ni-'män-ik) devices are artificial reminders, like the piece of string you tie around your finger to remind you to do something. Some of these devices are simple and superficial, but that is not really a concern if you can remember them. Here are three examples:

   Separate has *a rat* in it. [Therefore, it is not sep*e*rate.]

   Congratulate also has *rat* in it. [Therefore, it is not congra*d*ulate.]

   All right is the opposite of *all wrong.* [Therefore, it is two words and not the frequently used but unacceptable *alright.*]

   A lot is the opposite of *a little.* [Therefore, it, too, is *two words,* not one.]

The best reminders, however, are those you make up yourself; you will discover that you remember them more easily than those provided for you in books or in rules.

SPELLING GUIDELINES

IE AND *EI* WORDS

Attend to spelling rules when you believe they will be helpful. To illustrate our point, let us first use one rule you may already know:

> *i* before *e*
> except after *c*
> or when sounded as *a*
> as in *neighbor* or *weigh.*

This is a useful rule, but like too many rules that describe English spelling, its exceptions are many. First there are those exceptions identified in the rule itself: except after *c* or when sounded as *a.*

rec*ei*ve (after *c*)   n*ei*ghbor (sounded like *a*)
rec*ei*pt (after *c*)   w*ei*gh (sounded like *a*)

Then there are other exceptions—special words such as *either, neither, weird, seize, height, counterfeit, foreign*—and these are not all the special exceptions. Thus, although this is a helpful rule to know, it is far from foolproof.

Some rules in English have fewer exceptions, and your knowing them can have enormous benefits for your spelling.

WORD BEGINNINGS

The addition of such prefixes as *de-, dis-, mis-, non-, re-, trans-,* and *un-* usually does not cause any alteration in the spelling of the root word to which the prefix is added. ☑

de + emphasis = deemphasis	dis + appear = disappear
mis + spell = misspell	non + conformity = nonconformity
re + commend = recommend	trans + form = transform
un + lawful = unlawful	

WORD ENDINGS

FINAL Y

Nouns that end in *y* (such as *baby*) require your special attention when you make them plural. If the final *y* is preceded by a consonant, change the *y* to *i* and add *es*.

Singular	Plural
baby	bab*ies* (*y* is preceded by the consonant *b*)
company	compan*ies* (*y* is preceded by the consonant *n*)
copy	cop*ies* (*y* is preceded by the consonant *p*)

Self-Check Exercise 1

Are you ready to apply the two guidelines that discuss *ie* and *ei* words and the joining of prefixes to root words? Complete the following exercise and check your answers with the key at the end of the chapter.

1. Can you (believe, beleive) that the drought is finally over in this area?

2. Never (decieve, deceive) your employer.

3. He subscribes to (*Foreign, Foriegn*) *Affairs* magazine.

4. The contractor has a (lien, lein) on her house.

5. She was (dissenchanted, disenchanted) when she heard the president of the company speak.

6. He is her legal (hier, heir) in her will.

7. What were (thier, their) (frieght, freight) bills last month?

If the *y* is preceded by a vowel, leave the *y* and merely add an *s.*

attorney   attorn*eys* (*y* is preceded by the vowel *e*)
monkey   monk*eys* (*y* is preceded by the vowel *e*)
delay   del*ays* (*y* is preceded by the vowel *a*)

DOUBLE OR NOT
In a two-syllable word, you sometimes have to double a final consonant before adding a suffix that begins with a vowel (i.e., *-ed, -ing*). Here are some easy guidelines to remember:

1. First pronounce the word to see if the accent is on the second syllable and if the second syllable has a short vowel (like the *e* in *bed*).

    e*quip*   pre*fer*   re*gret*   [NOT e*qual*   *can*cel   *tra*vel]

2. If the accent is on the second syllable and the second syllable has a short vowel, make the second syllable even heavier by doubling the consonant before adding the suffix.

    e*quipping*   pre*ferred*   re*gretted*   [compared to e*qualing*   *can*celed   *tra*veled]
    be*ginning*   con*curred*   con*troller*   [compared to cred*ited*   *pro*fited   *to*taling]

LONG AND SHORT VOWELS
In a one-syllable word, you may also have to double a final consonant before adding a suffix beginning with a vowel. Your decision "to double or not to double" will be based on the vowel in the root word. If the vowel sound is short (like the *e* in *bed*), double the consonant; if the vowel sound is long (like the *a* in *fade*), do not double the consonant. ☑

h*op*   h*opped*   BUT h*ope*   h*oped*   [h*ope* has the long vowel sound]
t*ap*   t*apped*   BUT t*ape*   t*aped*   [t*ape* has the long vowel sound]

Self-Check Exercise 2

Do you know when to drop the *-y* and add *-ies* or when to double the consonant to add a suffix beginning with a vowel? Answering the following questions will indicate how well you have mastered these spelling rules. You can check your answers with those in the key.

1. This table is the (sturdiest, sturdyest) I have seen.

2. Why haven't the (attornies, attorneys) contacted us by now?

3. The accused burglar was (acquitted, acquited).

4. His work shows that he is only a (beginer, beginner).

5. By now, Sears, Roebuck and Company should have (credited, creditted) my account.

FINAL E

If a word ends in a silent *e*, you usually drop the final *e* before a suffix beginning with a vowel, with the exception of *-able*.

serve	ser*ving*	[Drop *e* before *-ing.*]	brake	bra*king*
place	pla*cing*		apprise	ap*prising*

If a word ends in a silent *e*, you will usually *not* drop the *e* before a suffix beginning with a consonant.

endorse	endors*ement*	[Keep *e* before *-ment.*]	idle	idl*eness*	[Keep *e* before *-ness.*]
sincere	sincer*ely*	[Keep *e* before *-ly.*]	loose	loos*ely*	

Exceptions: Words frequently used in business that are exceptions to this rule include *truly, ninth, judgment,* and *acknowledgment.*

THE SO-CALLED SEED WORDS

Though none of the words actually end in *seed*, there are eleven, and only eleven, words in English that have more than one syllable and end with the *seed* sound. It may be easier simply to try to memorize them using some mnemonic device. Here are the eleven words:

-sede	**-ceed**	**-cede**
supersede	exceed	accede
	proceed	antecede
	succeed	concede
		intercede
		precede
		recede
		secede

Remember that there are four "seed" words that do not end with *-cede.* They are *supersede, exceed, proceed,* and *succeed.* Therefore, if you are using a "seed" word and it is not one of these four, its ending has to be *-cede.* It is that simple!

AN "IFY" ENDING

Does the word end in *-efy* or *-ify—liqu?fy, beaut?fy, class?fy, rar?fy, intens?fy.* Again, this rule is most easily remembered if you simply memorize the fact that only four of the words ending with this sound are spelled *-efy.* The four words are *liquefy, putrefy, rarefy,* and *stupefy.* All other words ending with this sound end in *-ify.* Examples include *beautify, clarify, classify,* and *intensify.* ☑

BEGINNINGS AND ENDINGS WORTH CHECKING

Be sure to keep your dictionary handy to look up words that do any of the following:

Begin with the sound of *per.*
Is it *per-* as in *per*ishable or *pur-* as in *pur*sue?

End with the sound of *ible.*
Is it *-able* as in pay*able* or *-ible* as in respons*ible*?

End with the sound of *ence.*
Is it *-ance* as in accept*ance* or *-ence* as in occurr*ence*?

Self-Check Exercise 3

Should you write *-ify* or *-efy; -sede, -cede,* or *-ceed*? Keep the silent *e* or take it out before adding a suffix? Those are good questions! Let us see if you can answer them correctly by completing the following exercise. Remember to check your answers with the key.

1. (Ninety, Ninty) teenagers attended the meeting.

2. The (arriveal, arrival) of the committee helped the situation.

3. She frequently used the complimentary close "Very (truley, truly) yours."

4. Do not (excede, exceed) the limit.

5. My students frequently confuse the words (procede, proceed) and (precede, preceed).

6. Her dynamic personality and enthusiasm will (electrefy, electrify) the atmosphere in the room.

7. The bank's profits are beginning to (recede, resede).

End with the sound of *ize*.
Is it *-ise* as in adver*tise*, *-ize* as in criti*cize*, or *-yze* as in anal*yze*?

End with the sound of *shun*.
Is it *-tion* as in inten*tion*, *-sion* as in exten*sion*, or *-cion* as in coer*cion*?

Now you can see why a dictionary is such an important reference book for any writer who wishes to avoid misspellings.

We have given just some of the more important spelling rules in this chapter. Learning them will produce dividends in improving your spelling. There are other rules, though some of them are rather complex or too filled with exceptions to make the time required to learn them worthwhile. ☑

ABBREVIATIONS

Shortened forms of words or groups of words are sometimes preferred in written communications. The overuse of abbreviations, however, is frowned upon by business writers because there is the danger of misinterpretation or confusion. The following guidelines should help you determine which abbreviations are generally acceptable for your business writing.

COURTESY TITLES AND FAMILY DESIGNATIONS

You should abbreviate most courtesy titles and family designations.

Mr. Earl Jones   Ms. Ellen Jones   Mrs. Eartha Jones
The award was accepted by James Seaton, Jr.
His father, James Seaton, Sr., was in the audience.

PROFESSIONAL TITLES

Abbreviated professional titles may or may not be acceptable.

Acceptable

Dr. William Seaton was proud of his nephew's accomplishment.
Seaton's cousin, George Smolinski, Esq., opened his law office in Center City.

Not Acceptable

Prof. State was on sabbatical leave. [Should be *Professor State.*]

The invocation was given by Rev. Boyle. [Should be *Reverend Boyle.*]

The speaker was the Hon. Gerald Juarez. [Should be the *Honorable Gerald Juarez.*]

ACADEMIC DEGREES

Academic degrees may be abbreviated.

The speaker is Marian Warner, Ph.D.

The consultant we hired is Louis Bateman, Ed.D.

He earned a B.S. in Education degree from Rider College.

I hope to earn my M.B.A. this June.

The lawyers were taught by Jonathan Lever, J.D.

Self-Check Exercise 4

Use your dictionary, if necessary, to choose the correct spelling in the following sentences.

1. She works in the (pursonnel, personnel) department.

2. Can you make your handwriting more (legible, legable)?

3. (Intelligance, Intelligence) is very important in an office-occupation career.

4. Please (emphasize, emphasise) my apology when you write to our customer.

5. What is the (occasion, occation, occacion)?

6. You may want to improve your (complesion, complexion, complextion).

7. The rude customer will not (apologise, apologize) to the saleswoman.

STATES

In the inside address of a letter, as on the envelope, abbreviate the state. Use the capitalized two-letter abbreviation to accompany the ZIP code. Here is the list of abbreviations accepted by the U.S. Postal Service:

Alabama	AL	Montana	MT
Alaska	AK	Nebraska	NE
Arizona	AZ	Nevada	NV
Arkansas	AR	New Hampshire	NH
California	CA	New Jersey	NJ
Canal Zone	CZ	New Mexico	NM
Colorado	CO	New York	NY
Connecticut	CT	North Carolina	NC
Delaware	DE	North Dakota	ND
District of Columbia	DC	Ohio	OH
Florida	FL	Oklahoma	OK
Georgia	GA	Oregon	OR
Guam	GU	Pennsylvania	PA
Hawaii	HI	Puerto Rico	PR
Idaho	ID	Rhode Island	RI
Illinois	IL	South Carolina	SC
Indiana	IN	South Dakota	SD
Iowa	IA	Tennessee	TN
Kansas	KS	Texas	TX
Kentucky	KY	Utah	UT
Louisiana	LA	Vermont	VT
Maine	ME	Virgin Islands	VI
Maryland	MD	Virginia	VA
Massachusetts	MA	Washington	WA
Michigan	MI	West Virginia	WV
Minnesota	MN	Wisconsin	WI
Missouri	MO	Wyoming	WY

Note: Do not abbreviate the names of cities!

COMPANIES, INSTITUTIONS, AND GOVERNMENT DEPARTMENTS

Abbreviate the names of well-known companies, institutions, and government departments. Since the following abbreviations are so familiar, periods are no longer placed between the letters. Use capital letters but omit the periods.

AT&T	American Telephone and Telegraph
IBM	International Business Machines
FBI	Federal Bureau of Investigation
USN	United States Navy
IRS	Internal Revenue Service
AFL-CIO	American Federation of Labor and the Congress of Industrial Organizations
UN	United Nations
PBS	Public Broadcasting Service

COMPANY, INCORPORATED, AND CORPORATION

Abbreviate *Company (Co.),* *Incorporated (Inc.),* and *Corporation (Corp.)* if a firm uses an abbreviation for these designations in its company name. Check for possible abbreviations on the company's letterhead.

Correct

> We buy our supplies from A. C. Smith, Inc.
>
> She previously worked for Bonomy Oil Corp.
>
> Have you written to Lord & Watword, Inc.?
>
> The reputable company I. Rothschild, Ltd., has been in business since 1921. [*Limited* is the British designation for Incorporated. The abbreviation is *Ltd.*]

Incorrect

> Which co. provides cleaning service? [Should be *company* as it is not part of a proper name.]
>
> A. T. Barnes is no longer a company but a major corp. [Should be *corporation.*]
>
> The two firms have merged and inc. [Should be *incorporated.*]

FAMILIAR TERMS

Abbreviate commonly used and easily understood terms.

GNP	Gross National Product
C.O.D.	cash on delivery
f.o.b.	free on board
a.m.	before noon *(ante meridiem)*
p.m.	after noon *(post meridiem)*

Abbreviations for the days of the week, months of the year, compass points, units of time, and weights and measurements are not used in sentences. They may be used, however, in tables, charts, or invoices. ☑

> We will meet on Monday, October 13, 1987. [NOT Mon., Oct.]
>
> Three weeks from now we will meet for about two hours. [NOT wks., hrs.]
>
> That board measured one yard three feet and four inches. [NOT yd., ft., in.]
>
> The college is about three miles northwest of the city. [NOT mi., NW.]

An *acronym* is a word formed from the first letters of a series of words.

COBOL	Comon Business-Oriented Language
EPCOT	Experimental Prototype Community of Tomorrow
NOW	National Organization for Women

AVOID MISSPELLING COMMON WORDS

You can probably get by with misspelling *antidisestablishmentarianism,* though even here some wary reader may catch you. However, many readers will notice if you use *its* when you need *it's* or confuse *to* and *too* or spell *occurrence* with just one *r.* To help you, we have included a list of 200 commonly misspelled words. Our best advice on these is to learn their pronunciation and their spelling, break the more difficult ones into syllables and analyze any trouble spots, and memorize them. Note that many of the words are relatively common, even simple, yet they are among the most frequently misspelled in the English language.

Self-Check Exercise 5

Check your ability to recognize the preferred use of abbreviations in business communications by completing the following exercise. Indicate errors that pertain to abbreviations. You may check your answers with the key at the end of the chapter.

1. What st. does she live on in Phila.?

2. The cost of gas is close to $4 a gal. in Italy.

3. Mail your finished report to Prof. Labio at Temple Univ.

4. We will see you in the p.m. on Wed., Sept. 3,

5. The F.B.I. has stringent hiring practices.

6. The city of NY is a favorite cultural center.

7. Ms. Maria Henderson will preside at the meeting.

8. The signature on the letter was that of Jeremiah Johnson, Junior.

9. He has an appointment with his dr.

10. They opened a branch office NE of Collins Avenue.

11. The name of her new co. is Handicrafts and Novelties.

12. Our economics prof. lectured on the GNP.

200 Commonly Misspelled Words

absence	affect	argument	changeable
accidentally	aggravate	assistant	clientele
accommodate	aggressive	athlete	committee
accompany	alignment	attendance	complexion
accumulate	all right	bankrupt	confident
achievement	already	believe	conscientious
acknowledge	analysis	beneficial	consensus
acquaintance	analyze	bureau	convenient
advertisement	apparatus	calendar	correspond
advertising	apparently	census	courteous

courtesy	guarantee	mileage	prevalent
criticism	guidance	minimum	privilege
criticize	height	miscellaneous	procedure
defense	hindrance	mischief	professor
definite	hypocrisy	misspell	pronounce
definition	illustrate	mortgage	pronunciation
desperate	imaginary	naturally	publicly
development	impatient	necessary	receipt
difference	importance	necessity	receive
disappear	incidentally	negotiable	recommend
discrepancy	incompetent	nineteen	relevant
doesn't	incredible	ninety	religious
doubt	indispensable	ninth	remember
economy	inevitable	noticeable	remembrance
efficiency	innocence	nuisance	repetition
eighth	intercede	occasion	respectably
eligible	interesting	occurred	respectfully
embarrass	irrelevant	occurrence	respectively
envelop (verb)	irresistible	omitted	rhythm
envelope (noun)	it's (it is)	opposite	ridiculous
exaggerate	language	optimism	schedule
exceed	legitimate	parallel	scissors
existence	leisure	pastime	secretary
extension	length	permissible	seize
familiar	liability	perseverance	separate
fascinate	liable	personnel	similar
February	library	phenomenon	sincerely
foreign	lieutenant	physician	sophomore
forty	loneliness	possession	strategy
fourth	loose	practically	strength
freight	losing	precede	succeed
government	maintenance	preference	sufficient
grammar	manufacture	preferred	superintendent
gratitude	mathematics	prejudice	supersede
grievous	mediocre	presence	syllable

symptom	tragedy	unanimous	Wednesday
tendency	transferred	undoubtedly	whether
therefore	treasurer	useful	wholly
their	truly	usually	withholding
thief	Tuesday	vacuum	writing

THE FINAL STEP

If you find that the correct spelling of the words on this list and all other words that confront you tend to elude you, this is the time to begin your personalized "Words to Spell Correctly" list. Tape the list to the back cover of your dictionary or this textbook and refer to the list *daily.* Once you master the spelling of a particular word on your list, cross it off. Before long you will be proficient in spelling the first few words on your list, enabling you to spend more time on the words you have recently added. You will find this is an ideal way to become an improved speller!

APPLICATION EXERCISES

A. As you know, the letter from Mr. Hunt in Figure 3-1 contained a number of spelling errors. It is reprinted below. Correct all the spelling errors you find by writing the correct spelling above the misspelled words.

Brighton Mutual Insurance Company

140 Palisades Avenue
Englewood Cliffs, New Jersey 07632
(201) 492-3159

December 6, 198_

Dear studant:

We at Brighton Mutual Insurance are hopping to be able to servise all your insurance needs. While we are certenly not the largest insurer of colege studants, we beleive we are one of the most active companys. We offer to our subsribors a wide range of benafits and can accomodate our programs to your needs. Will you pleaze take a minate to complet the attatched card, and return it to us as soon as possable so that we might vissit you to explane our programe.

Thank you for your attenshun. We wush you continued good luck in school.

Sincerly yours,

Don Hunt

Insurance Agent

Attachment

B. The words listed below are the misspelled words in the spelling test you took. In the space provided write the correct spelling.

_____ 1. accomodate   _____ 14. proffessor

_____ 2. its'   _____ 15. passtime

_____ 3. seperate   _____ 16. criticizm

_____ 4. occurence   _____ 17. privelege

_____ 5. alright   _____ 18. aquaintance

_____ 6. relevent   _____ 19. mispell

_____ 7. committment   _____ 20. miscelaneous

_____ 8. thier   _____ 21. grievious

_____ 9. accidently   _____ 22. reccommend

_____ 10. extention   _____ 23. disipline

_____ 11. occassion   _____ 24. contemptable

_____ 12. apparrently   _____ 25. fasinate

_____ 13. perseverence

C. In each set of four words, one word is spelled correctly. Mark its letter in the blank at the left.

_____ 1. (a) advertisement, (b) advertisment, (c) advertizement, (d) advertizment

_____ 2. (a) allready, (b) already, (c) alreddy, (d) allreddy

_____ 3. (a) aknowledgement, (b) acknowledgment, (c) acknowledgmant, (d) acknowlegement

_____ 4. (a) consensus, (b) consencus, (c) concencus, (d) consenses

_____ 5. (a) morgage, (b) mortgag, (c) mortgaje, (d) mortgage

_____ 6. (a) mischievious, (b) mischevious, (c) mischievous, (d) mischeivous

_____ 7. (a) exceed, (b) excede, (c) exsede, (d) exseed

_____ 8. (a) gramer, (b) grammer, (c) gramar, (d) grammar

_____ 9. (a) exagerate, (b) exaggerate, (c) exaggeraight, (d) ecksaggerate

_____ 10. (a) govermant, (b) goverment, (c) government, (d) governmant

_____ 11. (a) irelevant, (b) irrelevant, (c) irrelevent, (d) irelevent

_____ 12. (a) intresting, (b) intrasting, (c) interesting, (d) intaresting

_____ 13. (a) clarify, (b) clarefy, (c) clearify, (d) clearefy

_____ 14. (a) reccommend, (b) recommend, (c) recommind, (d) reccomend

_____ 15. (a) sincerly, (b) sincereley, (c) sincerlie, (d) sincerely

_____ 16. (a) stratdegy, (b) strategy, (c) stragety, (d) stratagy

_____ 17. (a) hindrance, (b) hinderance, (c) hinderence, (d) hindrence

_____ 18. (a) dissappear, (b) disapear, (c) disappear, (d) dissapear

_____ 19. (a) rember, (b) remember, (c) remimber, (d) remembre

_____ 20. (a) syllable, (b) sillable, (c) sillible, (d) syllible

_____ 21. (a) sucseed, (b) succede, (c) sucsede, (d) succeed

_____ 22. (a) guarrantee, (b) guarantee, (c) guarrantie, (d) guarantie

_____ 23. (a) embarras, (b) embarass, (c) embarras, (d) embarrass

_____ 24. (a) Februery, (b) February, (c) Febuary, (d) Febuery

_____ 25. (a) undoubtably, (b) undoutedly, (c) undoubtedly, (d) undoubtibly

D. In each of the following sentences some words are misspelled. Find them and write the correct spellings in the blank at the left. (All proper names are correctly spelled.)

_____ 1. Teresa did poorly in mathamatics, failing algebra her first year

_____ and geometry her third.

_____ 2. The Swenson Travel Agency regularly sends advertizements

_____ to it's most influential customers.

_____ 3. Sociologists report that newleywed couples have fewer argue-

_____ ments than those who have been married five to ten years.

_____ 4. Conservasheinists often try to persuad politicians to preserve

_____ the forests of America.

_____ 5. As a direct consequence of Jacob's diligence, he was made a

_____ lutenant at the earliest oportunity.

_____

_____

6. The factory was dilapidatted and provided too little safety for many of its personel.

_____

_____

7. The alinement of the charts must be acurate so that the architect can develop blueprints that are free of distortion.

_____

_____

8. Nielsen's Bakery is managed well, with relatively few occurences of either employee or customer disatisfaction.

_____

_____

9. Mary Anne tried hard to rember the material she had so studiously commited to memory just the evening before.

_____

_____

_____

10. When he made application for the position, Willie discovered that the fact that he had not been gradated from high school made him appear incompetant.

_____

_____

_____

11. *The Reader's Digest* attributes much of its popularity to its having a sereis of seperate articles instead of one or two lengthy pieces.

_____

_____

_____

12. Prospective employers are particularly conscious of good grooming during interviews and, therefor, it will pay dividends if you are as clean and neat as possable.

_____

_____

_____

13. Louis learned that the immediate vicinnity of his jewlry store was the best place for the posters announcing his February sale.

_____

_____

14. Maria accidently set the temperature too high, but the clothes were as riuned as if she had done it on purpose.

Challenge Exercise

In this letter are a number of misspelled words. Write the correct spellings above each misspelled word. Use your dictionary.

Oakville Community College

Office of Admissions and Records
Oakville, Alabama 35486
(205) 729-4217

June 10, 198_

Mr. Juan Garcia

123 Main Streit

Chicago, IL 60610

Dear Mr. Garcia:

Your request for admittence this coming autum to out

architectural program has been recieved in this office and

refered to Dean William Damico for his reply. Please

understand that, though Dean Damico trys to comunicate with

each applicent as soon as possible, it is sometimes

difficulte to accomodate all requests as early as we would

wish too. We hope, therefor, that you will be pateint.

Please be assured that all axpects of your application are alright and that you should be heering from Dean Damico about your request soon.

                                        Cordialy yours,

                                        Becky Goldman
                                        Secretary to Dean Damico

You Are the Editor

In the following memorandum are a number of misspelled words. Write the correct spelling above each misspelled word. Use your dictionary.

TO: Ms. Bernice Sikes, Office Staf

FROM: Ms. Susan Chin, Unit Maneger

DATE: March 12, 198_

SUBJECT: Complience with company polisy regarding lunch hours

Ms. Sikes, during the past several weeks it has come to my attention that you have frequantly returned to your desk up to a half hour late after you're lunch break. In this office we try hard to maintain our committment to the individuale worker. To do so, we offen overlook an occassional occurence of tardyness. We know that the lunch hour is sometimes, of necesity, the only time that office personal can get errands run, telephone calls made, appointments set up.

Yet their are those workers who continualy abuse these priveledges by remaining away from thier desks well beyond the alloted time. I do not wish to embarass you, Ms. Sikes, by bringing this matter to the attenshun of the devision managers. But I must ask that you exercize greater vigilance in retourning from lunch on time.

Key to Self-Check Exercises

Exercise 1

1. believe
2. deceive
3. *Foreign*
4. lien
5. disenchanted
6. heir
7. their, freight

Exercise 2

1. sturdiest
2. attorneys
3. acquitted
4. beginner
5. credited

Exercise 3

1. Ninety
2. arrival
3. truly
4. exceed
5. proceed, precede
6. electrify
7. recede

Exercise 4

1. personnel
2. legible
3. Intelligence
4. emphasize
5. occasion
6. complexion
7. apologize

Exercise 5

1. street, Philadelphia
2. gallon
3. Professor Labio, Temple University
4. We will see you in the afternoon on Wednesday, September 3.
5. FBI (no periods)
6. New York
7. Sentence has no errors.
8. Jeremiah Johnson, Jr.
9. doctor
10. northeast of Collins Avenue
11. company
12. professor

A DYNAMIC BUSINESS VOCABULARY

Here is another useful list of words that belong in your business vocabulary.

Basic

Acronym for *B*eginners *A*ll-Purpose *S*ymbolic *I*nstruction *C*ode, which uses English words and mathematical symbols to perform problem-solving operations on the computer.

In DP 111 the students are taught BASIC, one of the easiest computer languages to learn.

Beneficiary

A person who receives benefits, funds, etc., from a will, insurance, or some other form of settlement.

Melinda was made the beneficiary of her brother's will.

Bequeath

To pass on, give, or offer property to a certain recipient, as in a will.

Enrico will bequeath his home to his father, Alfredo, and his car to his sister, Maria.

Bona fide

Sincere, genuine offer "in good faith" (Latin).

The offer was bona fide and accepted as such by both parties.

Budget

A list of expenditures or income itemized for a certain period of time.

Every year the government must propose a working budget to Congress for approval.

Business cycle

Economic periods of alternating prosperity, depression, or stability.

The business cycle for the period 1965–85 made a major contribution to the stock market's fluctuations.

Bylaws

Rules and regulations governing an organization.

The board of directors of the company disagreed strongly when the new bylaws were presented for approval.

Capital account

An accounting of all funds and assets owners and stockholders of a business or firm have invested in the business.

The audit revealed that the firm's capital account was short almost $30,000.

THE ABC'S OF BUSINESS VOCABULARY

Check your knowledge of the business vocabulary words by answering the following questions.

1. A list of expenditures or income itemized for a certain period of time is (a) net assets, (b) annuity, (c) certificate, (d) budget.

2. The assignment to managers of responsibility for their actions, decisions, goals, and performance is (a) agenda, (b) accountability, (c) arbitration, (d) aptitude.

3. Economic periods of alternating prosperity, depression, or stability can be called a(n) (a) business cycle, (b) inflation, (c) deflation, (d) depression.

4. The definition of the noun *beneficiary* is _____

_____

5. The meaning of the adjective *bona fide* is _____

_____

6. The term *bylaws* can be defined as _____

_____

7. Compose three short sentences using one of the following words or terms in each sentence: (a) business cycle, (b) bankrupt, (c) BASIC.

_____

_____

_____

_____

_____

_____

4 Words Frequently Misused

THREE TALES OF WOE

Although we hesitate to begin this important chapter on a negative note, it is necessary that we do so. As we relate each sad story, you will see why these tales had to be told in this chapter.

STORY ONE

John Tagahashi, a sophomore at Crimson University, applied to a personnel agency for a summer job as a clerk-typist and transcriber. John was a B + student in the management curriculum and was proud of the 50 wpm typing skills he had acquired in high school. John was certain that he had passed the transcription test that he had taken in the personnel office because he had checked his spelling in a dictionary. He was also confident that his punctuation and grammar were flawless. John was, therefore, very surprised and quite disappointed when the interviewer told him that the memo he had transcribed did not meet employment standards, and consequently he was not being considered for employment as a transcriber.

Figure 4-1 shows John's memo. Can you detect the errors that John made?

John may have checked his spelling in a dictionary, but he certainly hadn't read our Dictionary chapter. The section "The Meaning Makes the Difference" would have helped him secure the summer employment he desired.

STORY TWO

Lucretia Burger, a secretary for six months at Systems Planning, was looking for her first merit raise. Her supervisor called her into his office yesterday for a performance review and complimented her on her punctuality, attendance, and generally cooperative attitude. He then dropped the bomb. He handed her copies of three letters she had typed the past week—all of them unsatisfactory and all of them with the same type of errors. It was obvious: Lucretia's raise was not to be. "How could that have happened to me?" asked Lucretia. "I always refer to my dictionary and check my spelling."

Look at one of Lucretia's letters (Figure 4-2). What else should have been checked besides the spelling?

STORY THREE

Allen Finio, a junior accountant for a prominent public accounting firm in Cleveland does not feel confident dictating his letters into a machine. He prefers to write out rough drafts for the typists. Since he arrived three months ago, he has been getting funny looks and snide remarks from many of the typists. Yesterday the supervisor of the typing pool approached him to complain about a number of his drafts. She said, "My typists claim that you are always confusing your words. Don't you ever check the definition of your words before including them in your letters?" The supervisor then showed Allen the rough draft he had submitted to be typed (Figure 4-3). She had circled his errors to emphasize her point.

Figure 4-1. John's transcription test.

TO: Laura Antilles

FROM: John Tagahashi

DATE: January 4, 198_

SUBJECT: Lock Device

The new lock device developed by foreman Carl Cope is extremely
ingenuous, and I recommend that we consider it's manufacture and
apply for a patent on it.

Carl has demonstrated great incite in it's design. His locking
device is smaller, more reliable, and less expensive then any on the
market. It also has a farther advantage and that is it's basic
simplicity. In addition, it is made of the finest medal.

I endorse it holy, and accept for one miner change (see attached
drawing), I recommend we go foreword on the project immediately.

mv

Enclosure

Figure 4-2. One of Lucretia's letters.

SYSTEMS PLANNING CORPORATION

11394 N.W. 23rd Street
Washington, D.C. 20071
(202) 564-8350

July 9, 198_

Mr. Edward Smith
623 North State Road
Cherry Hill, NJ 08012

Dear Mr. Smith:

Thank you for the employment inquiry you sent to our personal department.

Yesterday, we received a call from the imminent Reverend James Grahl, famous author and member of our Board, mentioning that he talked with you at the June Feat, and highly recommended you for the position we have open. Reverend Grahl said that you were illegible and seemed to have a flare for both sales and public relations work.

If you will fill out the job application form and return it to us in the enclosed envelop, we will contact you shortly to arrange for an interview.

Yours truly,

Lucretia Burger

Figure 4-3. Allen's rough draft.

Dear Mrs. Hooper :

(Hear) is the information that you requested.

In reference to the possibility of your adding to your cleaning equipment, the (duel) (dying) vats you inquired about will be (to) (expansive) for the present financial condition of your store. I am sure your financial backer, Jeremiah Henderson, will (disprove) of your making any more (disperse-ments) for cleaning and (dying) equipment.

Why don't we arrange to meet and discuss this at your store on Tuesday, March 22 at 9 a.m. Marilyn Horn will be (their) also.

Yours truly,
Allen Finio

Why did all three of these people make such flagrant errors in word choice if they used their dictionaries to check their spelling? That question is easy to answer. Allen, Lucretia, and John all made the very same common mistake—they checked the spelling but forgot to double-check the definitions of the words they selected. Had they carefully read the definitions, they would have realized that in many cases they had chosen the wrong words. All three were victims of the "frequently misused and confused word" syndrome.

SYNONYMS, ANTONYMS, AND HOMONYMS

Words that have *similar meanings* are called *synonyms*. Examples are happy–joyful; ask–request; give–donate; rapid–quick.

Words that have *opposite meanings* are referred to as *antonyms*. Examples are beautiful–ugly; slow–speedy; tall–short; fat–thin. Synonyms and antonyms are easy to learn and rarely cause serious problems in word selection.

Words that *sound exactly or nearly the same* but have different meanings are called *homonyms*. Examples are council–counsel; bizarre–bazaar; principle–principal; affect–effect. Homonyms cause many of us problems from time to time. And the problems can be serious, as you noticed in the "Three Tales of Woe."

If, for example, you mean *disinterested* and you use *uninterested,* your reader or listener may misinterpret what you mean. If you write *capital* instead of *capitol* or *minor* when you mean *miner,* you may very well confuse the individual with whom you are communicating.

But also of importance is what the error says about the person who made it and his or her ability to use the English language correctly.

There is a further point to consider involving the loss of words that results from their misuse. If enough of us in business, industry, and government, plus those who appear on radio and television, continue to misuse a word, that word will soon be lost. If, for example, the word *disinterested* is used for *uninterested* over and over, the former will eventually take the place of the latter, and we will have lost the present meaning of *disinterested,* which is to be *neutral about a subject.* English is a changing language, and it is made up of contributions from many cultures. However, we should not be responsible for *misusing* words. When we talk and write, we should make every effort to use words as carefully and as correctly as possible.

Some of the most common and troublesome homonyms are listed for you here so you may familiarize yourself with their spelling and definitions. Complete all the self-check exercises to test your ability to correctly use these vocabulary demons.

List

Accent: to stress or emphasize; a regional manner of speaking
Ascent: a rising or going up
Assent: to agree; agreement

Accept: to receive; to give an affirmative answer to
Except: to exclude; to leave out; to omit

Access: admittance or admission
Excess: surplus or more than necessary

Ad: abbreviation for advertisement
Add: to join; to unite; to sum

Adapt: to accustom oneself to a situation or to change something to fit a new use or situation
Adept: proficient or competent in performing a task
Adopt: to take by choice; to put into practice

Advice: counsel; a recommendation (noun)
Advise: to suggest; to recommend (verb)

Affect: to influence (verb)
Effect: result or consequence (noun)
Effect: to bring about (verb)

All ready: prepared
Already: previously

Allusion: a reference to something familiar
Illusion: an image of an object; a false impression
Delusion: a false belief

Altar: a place to worship or pray
Alter: to change

Altogether: completely or thoroughly
All together: in a group; in unison

Anyone: any person in general
Any one: a specific person or item

Bazaar: an establishment that sells merchandise
Bizarre: eccentric in style or mode

Biannually: two times a year
Biennially: every two years

Canvas: a coarse type of cloth
Canvass: to solicit; survey

Capital: a seat of government; money invested; a form of a letter
Capitol: a government building

Carat: unit of weight generally applied to gemstones
Caret: mark showing omission
Carrot: vegetable
Karat: unit for measuring the purity of gold

Cease: to halt or stop
Seize: to grasp or take possession

Censer: an incense pot
Censor: a critic
Sensor: an electronic device
Censure: to find fault with or to blame

Cereal: any grain
Serial: arranged in successive order ☑

List 2

Cite: to quote from a source
Sight: act of seeing; object or scene observed
Site: a place, such as a building site

Coarse: composed of large particles; unrefined
Course: a direction of progress or a series of studies

Collision: a clashing of objects
Collusion: a conspiracy or fraud

Command: to direct or order; an order
Commend: to praise or laud

Complacent: satisfied, smug
Complaisant: obliging

Complement: that which completes or supplements (noun); to complete or supplement (verb)
Compliment: flattery or praise (noun); to express flattery or praise (verb)

Confidant: one who may be confided in
Confident: positive or sure

Continual: taking place in close succession; frequently repeated
Continuous: no break or letup

Council: an assembly of persons
Counsel: to advise; advice; an attorney
Consul: a resident representative of a foreign state

Councillor: a member of a council
Counselor: a lawyer or adviser

Self-Check Exercise 1

You have studied and compared the homonyms in List 1 and can now check to see if you know them. Complete the following exercise, and then check your answers with the key at the end of the chapter.

1. (Accept, Except) for Yolanda, everyone has participated.

2. If you will (canvas, canvass) everyone on the committee, you will receive a favorable response to Proposition 13.

3. The (capitol, capital) invested was completely lost because of poor financial management.

4. I would not hesitate to (cease, seize) an opportunity like that.

5. The storage bin for the (serial, cereal) belonged to the breakfast food company.

6. The comptroller had (excess, access) to the books on the weekend.

7. The teachers decided to (adapt, adopt) this textbook for the fall semester.

Core: a center
Corps: a body of troops; a group of persons in association
Corpse: a dead body

Credible: believable or acceptable
Creditable: praiseworthy or meritorious
Credulous: gullible

Critic: one who evaluates
Critique: an analytical estimate or discussion

Currant: a type of fruit, a raisin
Current: timely; motion of air or water

Deceased: dead
Diseased: infected

Decent: correct; proper
Descent: going from high to low
Dissent: disagreement

Decree: a proclamation of law
Degree: difference in grade; an academic award

Defer: to delay or put off
Differ: to disagree

Deference: respect
Difference: unlikeness

Deprecate: to express disapproval of
Depreciate: to lessen in value because of use and/or time ☑

List 3

Desert: to abandon (verb)
Desert: a barren geographical area (noun)
Dessert: a course at the end of the meal (noun)

Disapprove: not to accept
Disprove: to prove wrong

Disburse: to make payments; to allot
Disperse: to scatter

Disinterested: neutral; not biased
Uninterested: not concerned with; lacking interest

Disorganized: disordered
Unorganized: not organized or planned

Dual: double or two
Duel: a contest between two antagonists

Dying: in the process of losing life or function
Dyeing: changing the color of

Elicit: to draw forth, usually a comment
Illicit: unlawful; illegal

Eligible: acceptable; approved
Illegible: impossible to read or decipher

Elusive: difficult to catch
Illusive: deceptive

Emerge: to come out
Immerge: to plunge into, immerse

Emigrate: to travel out of one country to live in another
Immigrate: to come into a country
Migrate: to travel from place to place periodically

Eminent: outstanding; prominent
Imminent: impending, very near, or threatening
Immanent: inherent

Envelope: container for a communication (noun)
Envelop: to surround; cover over or enfold (verb)

Expansive: capable of extension or expansion
Expensive: costly

Self-Check Exercise 2

How well did you learn the homonyms in List 2? Test your knowledge by completing this exercise. Your answers may be compared to those in the key.

1. Although she had been (deceased, diseased) for six years, a memorial service has not been held for her.

2. I would place more confidence in the statement if he could (site, cite, sight) the source.

3. For best results in using that coffeemaker, the beans should be (coursely, coarsely) ground.

4. There is no doubt that (collision, collusion) took place between the judge and the plaintiff.

5. I feel the best jam is the kind made of (currents, currants).

6. Making a contribution of that amount is a most (creditable, credible) act and deserves the publicity it got.

7. The German (consul, council, counsel) stationed in Los Angeles was born in Berlin.

Facet: a surface of a cut gem; aspect of an object or situation
Faucet: a spigot

Facilitate: to make easier
Felicitate: to greet or congratulate

Faint: to lose consciousness (verb); feeble, weak (adjective)
Feint: to pretend or simulate; a deceptive movement

Farther: refers to geographical or linear distance
Further: more; in addition to

Fate: destiny
Fete: to honor or celebrate (verb); a party or fair (noun)
Feat: an act of unusual skill ☑

List 4

Flair: natural ability
Flare: a signal rocket; a blazing up of a fire

Formally: according to convention
Formerly: previously

Genius: unusual and outstanding ability
Genus: a grouping or classification, usually on a biological basis

Self-Check Exercise 3

The third list has provided additional homonyms for you to learn. Test your ability to use some of the words that are listed. Complete the exercise, and check your answers with the key.

1. He has decided to (emigrate, immigrate) from England to settle in Hawaii.

2. The fog seemed to (envelope, envelop) the entire upper half of the mountains.

3. Her handwriting was absolutely (illegible, eligible).

4. It was most difficult to watch him (dying, dyeing) and know there was nothing that could be done to save his life.

5. The platoon seemed to be (unorganized, disorganized) 24 hours each day.

6. It was almost impossible to (illicit, elicit) a comment from Antoine.

7. She was more (elusive, illusive) than a rabbit; no one could ever catch her.

Hoard: to collect and keep; a hidden supply
Horde: a huge crowd

Holey: having perforations or holes
Holy: sacred, saintly
Wholly: entirely; completely

Human: pertaining to man or woman
Humane: kindly, considerate

Incite: to stir up
Insight: keen understanding; intuition

Incredible: extraordinary; unbelievable
Incredulous: skeptical; not believing

Ingenious: clever, resourceful
Ingenuous: frank, honest, free from guile

Its: a possessive singular pronoun
It's: a contraction for *it is*

Later: refers to time; the comparative form of *late*
Latter: refers to the second named of two

Load: a burden; a pack
Lode: a vein of ore

Loath: reluctant; unwilling
Loathe: to hate; to despise; to detest

Lose: to cease having
Loose: not fastened or attached; to set free

Magnate: a tycoon; important official
Magnet: a device that attracts metal

Marital: used in reference to marriage
Marshal: an official; to arrange
Martial: pertaining to military affairs

Maybe: perhaps (adverb)
May be: indicates possibility (verb)

Medal: a badge of honor
Metal: a mineral substance
Meddle: to interfere

Miner: an underground laborer or worker
Minor: one who has not attained legal age; of little importance

Moral: a principle, maxim, or lesson (noun); ethical (adjective)
Morale: a state of mind or psychological outlook (noun) ☑

List 5

Notable: distinguished
Notorious: unfavorably known

Observance: a customary practice, rite, or ceremony
Observation: act of seeing; casual remark

Self-Check Exercise 4

See how well you have learned the fourth list of homonyms by completing the following exercise. Can you easily select the correct answer in each sentence? The key gives you the correct choices.

1. Do not (loose, lose) your perspective when you are with him.

2. It was a (minor, miner) point, and I felt it should be overlooked.

3. In times of inflation, it seems silly to try to (horde, hoard) money.

4. I was (loath, loathe) to leave him unattended in his condition.

5. If the (load, lode) is too heavy for you, why not secure some assistance?

6. There (may be, maybe) a possibility that she will go with me.

7. Their (marshal, martial, marital) difficulties finally ended in a divorce.

Ordinance: a local law
Ordnance: military weapons; munitions

Peak: top of a hill or mountain; topmost point
Peek: a quick look through a small opening

Peal: sound of a bell
Peel: to strip off

Percent: should be used after a numeral (20 percent)
Percentage: for quantity or when numerals are not used (a larger percentage)

Persecute: to subject to harsh or unjust treatment
Prosecute: to bring legal action against

Personal: private; not public or general
Personnel: the staff of an organization

Perspective: a view of things or facts; the effect of distance or depth on the appearance of objects
Prospective: likely to come about; looking forward in time

Plaintiff: the complaining party in a lawsuit
Plaintive: sorrowful; mournful

Plane: to make smooth; a tool; a surface
Plain: area of level or treeless country; obvious; undecorated

Precedence: priority
Precedents: cases that have already occurred

Proceed: to begin; to move; to advance
Precede: to go before

Principal: of primary importance (adjective); head of a school; original sum; chief or official (noun); main thing or person
Principle: a fundamental truth; a rule; a law

Provided: on condition; supplied
Providing: supplying

Recent: newly created or developed; near past in time
Resent: to feel indignant ☑

List 6

Respectfully: with respect or deference
Respectively: in order named

Resume: to begin again (verb)
Resume or Résumé: a summary for employment application (noun)

Rise: to move upward; to ascend (rise, rose, risen)
Raise: to elevate; to pick up (raise, raised, raised)

Sometime: at one time or another
Sometimes: occasionally

Stationary: not moving; fixed
Stationery: writing paper or writing materials

Self-Check Exercise 5

List 5 had 15 pairs of words to challenge you. Can you use these words correctly in sentences? Complete the following exercise and compare your answers with those in the key.

1. The factory (personal, personnel) all received a substantial bonus.

2. It will be necessary to (prosecute, persecute) her in a court of law if justice is to be secured.

3. The (peal, peel) of the bells marked the end of the year.

4. Although it was a city (ordinance, ordnance), none of the citizens seemed to obey it.

5. His careful (observation, observance) of the laws won him the designation of "Citizen of the Year."

6. Although she was the (principal, principle) of the school, she could rarely be found in her office.

7. The (plaintive, plaintiff) howling of the wolves was certainly frightening.

Statue: a carved or molded three-dimensional reproduction
Stature: height of a person; reputation
Statute: a law

Straight: direct; uninterrupted; not crooked
Strait: narrow strip connecting two bodies of water; a distressing situation

Than: used in comparison (conjunction): "Joe is taller than Tom."
Then: relating to time (adverb): "First he ran; then he jumped."

Their: belonging to them (possessive of *they*)
There: in that place (adverb)
They're: a contraction of the two words *they are*

To: preposition, "to the store"
Too: adverb, "too cold" means *very* or *also*
Two: number, "two apples"

Vice: wickedness
Vise: a clamp

Waive: to give up; relinquish
Wave: swell of water; a gesture

Weather: a climate or atmosphere
Whether: an alternative

Who's: a contraction of the two words *who is*
Whose: possessive of *who*

Your: a pronoun
You're: a contraction of the two words *you are* ☑

Self-Check Exercise 6

You have just studied the final list of homonyms. Check to see if you can select the correct answers in the sentences in this exercise. The key is available at the end of the chapter.

1. It was really much (to, two, too) hot to sit in the sun any longer.

2. (Whether, Weather) you go or not makes little difference to me.

3. I believe (there, their, they're) going to Chicago without Maria.

4. Tom, John, and Mercurio were given five, ten, and fifteen free passes (respectively, respectfully) for the work accomplished.

5. The (vise, vice) was old and rusted and could not be used in the shop.

6. Although he was an attorney and was quite familiar with the law, he had never heard of that (statue, statute).

7. The administrative assistant was asked to order new (stationary, stationery) for the office.

OTHER WORDS FREQUENTLY MISUSED

Here are pairs of words that do not sound alike and are not spelled similarly, yet are still troublesome for many writers. You should compare the definitions of the words in the pairs so you do not misuse the words in *your* communications.

Aggravate: to increase; to intensify; to make more severe
Irritate: to exasperate or bother

Almost: nearly; only a little less than
Most: an informal use of almost; correctly, it means greatest in quantity or the majority of

Among: refers to three or more
Between: refers to two only

Amount: quantity without reference to individual units
Number: a total of counted units

Anxious: upset; concerned about a serious occurrence
Eager: very desirous; anticipating a favorable event

Balance: as an accounting term, an amount owed or a difference between debit and credit sums
Remainder: that which is left over; a surplus

Beside: by the side of, next to
Besides: in addition to

Can: refers to ability or capability
May: refers to permission

Healthful: giving or contributing to health (food, climate)
Healthy: having health (a living thing)

Imply: to hint at or to allude to in speaking or writing (the speaker *implies*)
Infer: to draw a conclusion from what has been said or written (the listener *infers*)

In: indicates location within
Into: indicates movement to a location within

Let: to permit
Leave: to go away from; to abandon

Likely: probable
Liable: legally responsible
Apt: quick to learn; inclined; relevant

Oral: spoken
Verbal: communication in words, does not involve action ☑

Self-Check Exercise 7

Can you correctly use these frequently misused words in sentences? Test your ability by completing this final Self-Check Exercise and then checking your responses with the key.

1. It was very difficult for me to make a choice (among, between) Yoshi, Margarite, and Tasha.

2. The (remainder, balance) of the canned food was to be divided between Mrs. Cole and Ms. Cable.

3. He was extremely (eager, anxious) to get the results of the football game.

4. If you wish to (imply, infer) by your statements that he is not honest, you have succeeded.

5. She found that California had a very (healthful, healthy) climate.

6. When I stepped (in, into) the bank's vault, I immediately knew that something was wrong.

7. He made a/an (oral, verbal) agreement when he spoke to Kelly yesterday.

8. Do not (aggravate, irritate) me when I am trying to meditate.

9. (Almost, Most) all of the people left before midnight.

10. What was the exact (amount, number) of box lunches you had left?

11. Who else went swimming (beside, besides) them?

12. (Can, May) I leave the dinner table now?

13. Do not (leave, let) her go by herself to the dinner meeting.

14. They are (likely, liable) to go to the office first.

Had John Tagahashi studied a chapter such as this, he would probably have been a successful transcriber and would have been considered favorably by the personnel agency. Instead of the memo in Figure 4-1, John would have submitted an error-free communication that resembled the one in Figure 4-4. Note the following corrections: *ingenious* instead of *ingenuous; its* instead of *it's; insight* instead of *incite; its* instead of *it's* (again); *than* instead of *then; further* instead of *farther; its* instead of *it's* (again!); *metal* instead of *medal; wholly* instead of *holy; except* instead of *accept; minor* instead of *miner; forward* instead of *foreword.* Twelve corrections!

Figure 4-4. John's improved memo.

TO: Laura Antilles

FROM: John Tagahashi

DATE: January 4, 198_

SUBJECT: Lock Device

The new lock device developed by foreman Carl Cope is extremely ingenious, and I recommend that we consider its manufacture and apply for a patent on it.

Carl has demonstrated great insight in its design. His locking device is smaller, more reliable, and less expensive than any on the market. It also has a further advantage, and that is its basic simplicity. In addition, it is made of the finest metal.

I endorse it wholly, and except for one minor change (see attached drawing), I recommend we go forward on the project immediately.

mv

Enclosure

Now that you have studied the troublesome homonyms and other frequently misused words, you can constructively criticize the errors in Lucretia Burger's letter in Figure 4-2. If you have not already done so, encircle each of her misused words. Now rewrite her letter so it is free of misspellings. You can check your revised copy with the key.

You will find the exercises that follow to be interesting and also helpful in strengthening your knowledge of frequently misused words.

APPLICATION EXERCISES

A. Write fifteen sentences in the spaces provided using the words listed.

1. Stationery _____

_____

2. Its _____

_____

3. Further _____

_____

4. Council _____

_____

5. Continuous _____

_____

6. Meddle _____

_____

7. Morale _____

_____

8. Principal _____

_____

9. Formerly _____

_____

10. Irritate _____

_____

11. Imply _____

_____

12. Healthful _____

_____

13. Beside _____

14. Capital _____

15. Site _____

B. Insert the correct words in the spaces provided.

_____ 1. When the girls were (altogether, all together), the train left the station.

_____ 2. His acceptance did not (alter, altar) the situation.

_____ 3. The Budapest (bizarre, bazaar) was an unforgettable collection of people, noises, and smells.

_____ 4. (Beside, Besides) Tom, Bobbie, and Ray, there were four other youngsters in the class.

_____ 5. If you will (canvass, canvas) the neighborhood, you will find that most of the homeowners are in agreement.

_____ 6. The (capital, capitol) building in Sacramento has been repainted recently.

_____ 7. His performance was excellent, and he deserved the (condemnation, commendation) he received.

_____ 8. Can you (adapt, adopt, adept) yourself to this very humid climate?

_____ 9. He registered for three (courses, coarses) this quarter.

_____ 10. Bob had (all ready, already) left the restaurant when we arrived.

_____ 11. I was able to divide the collection (between, among) Betty and Dorothy.

_____ 12. The ship's (compliment, complement) was 800 men.

_____ 13. He was extremely (eager, anxious) to attend the club's baseball game scheduled for next Sunday.

_____ 14. The (sight, site, cite) for the new building has not yet been selected.

_____ 15. There was some thought in my mind concerning (collision, collusion) between the two lawyers.

C. If a word has not been used correctly, strike it out and write the correction in the space provided. If all words are used correctly, write a C in the space provided.

_____ 1. The Brazilian council said his Miami office would be in the Smythe Building.

_____ 2. The Tenth Core attacked at dawn.

_____ 3. The water flowed over Niagara Falls continuously.

_____ 4. He complained continuously about high gasoline prices.

_____ 5. Saving the dog was a creditable act.

_____ 6. The troops disbursed when the artillery was directed at them.

_____ 7. She was disinterested in the conversation and strolled away.

_____ 8. The train had duel controls for the engineer and his assistant.

_____ 9. The fog should envelope the hill about midnight.

_____ 10. The railroad station was completely air conditioned and very comfortable for the tired passengers.

_____ 11. He decided to immigrate from England and come to the United States.

_____ 12. She was an imminent senator, and her opinions were respected.

_____ 13. He was arrested because of his elicit activities.

_____ 14. The collapse of the tower was imminent.

_____ 15. The choice of a judge for the trial was excellent; he was a completely disinterested individual.

D. Insert the correct words in the spaces provided.

_____ 1. I have always found her handwriting (illegible, ineligible).

_____ 2. Their (marital, martial) problems finally ended in a divorce.

_____ 3. Joe Banana was a (notorious, famous) gangster.

_____   4. The (peal, peel) of the bells filled her with happiness.

_____   5. The (moral, morale) of the employees was unusually high.

_____   6. It is quite (liable, likely, apt) that he will arrive in time for the wedding.

_____   7. The new silver (load, lode) was discovered by chance.

_____   8. If you will (let, leave) her attend, she will surely win a prize.

_____   9. It was an (ingenuous, ingenious) contrivance designed to open rusted locks easily.

_____   10. This is no time to (hoard, horde) money.

_____   11. If you (lose, loose) the money, we won't be able to buy food for a week.

_____   12. (Maybe, May be) the strike will end at noon.

_____   13. He walked about three miles (farther, further) than the other men.

_____   14. The (personnel, personal) in the factory were given a holiday.

_____   15. He will (persecute, prosecute) the criminal to the full extent of the law.

E. If a word has not been used correctly, strike it out and write the correction in the space provided. If all the words are used correctly, write a *C* in the space provided.

_____   1. The principal was based on well-known facts.

_____   2. The prophet was looked on as a holy man.

_____   3. The roll of the nurse in the play was not easy to portray.

_____   4. The statue was part of the Illinois criminal code.

_____   5. The vice could not be opened to release the metal bar.

_____   6. He will marry her providing she can secure a divorce by the end of this month.

_____   7. The principal objective is the improvement of working conditions.

_____   8. If you will waive the regulation, I will be able to secure a visa.

_____   9. The rope was so taught that it immediately broke under additional pressure.

_____ 10. The room was quiet, and I was therefore able to read in comfort.

_____ 11. His statute in the community was sufficiently high to assure his election.

_____ 12. If they will forfeit their rights to the land, we will begin construction today.

_____ 13. In a large office the cost of stationary is a big expense.

_____ 14. Do you know who's attending the football game?

_____ 15. Do you believe your the only one who has been in an accident?

Challenge Exercise

If you find a word incorrectly used in any of the sentences below, cross it out and insert the correction immediately above it.

1. Although he was aggravated by Betty's constant drumming of her fingers on the tabletop, he made no illusion to it as he continued to council her.

2. "Its really not very important weather you approve or disprove of the action we take," said Marty.

3. Although California is supposed to have a healthy climate, people must recognize that their health may suffer because of the smog.

4. Although Betty was anxious to attend the party, she knew it would be a breach of good taste to advice Joan of her feelings.

5. Its not likely that Ramon will except the invitation; if he does, it will be necessary for him to altar the plans he made with José.

6. The cite for the new capital building has not yet been selected by the legislative counsul of six representatives.

7. The Mojave Dessert is one of the most beautiful though desolate expanses of ground in the world.

8. The duel controls permitted both the driver and the passenger to control the vehicle.

9. His discrete inquiry concerning the eminent collapse of the bank was contained in the envelop that arrived in this morning's mail.

10. The marine's moral was high for he had reached the mountain's peek far ahead of the soldier and sailor.

11. The chances were good that I would receive a call from the plaintive in the case and not be able to attend the party.

12. Mr. King, Mr. Kelly, and Mr. Takahashi would receive a gold, a silver, and a bronze award, respectfully, at the dinner tonight.

13. The ship could enter the harbor providing it obeyed the legal statute of the nation's maritime law concerning passenger visas.

14. To be excepted by the city council and approved for display, the sign will have to be fixed in such a way as to make it completely stationery.

15. She had a natural flare for good fashion; of all our office personal, she was an outstanding model of good taste.

Name _____

You Are the Editor

In the exercise that follows, use your editor's pencil to strike out errors. Insert corrections directly above the word or words misused.

The Northern Company

806 Brunswick Road
Arlington, Illinois 60703
(312) 525-3020

January 23, 198_

Mrs. Rita Mendoza, Manager

Purchasing Department

Texas Metal Corp.

1472 South Jackson Boulevard

Alamo, TX 78516

Dear Mrs. Mendoza:

We thank you for your recent phone call telling us you were able

to adopt our No. 41 cutter for use on your Kellogg Grinders.

Although the cutter is not precisely manufactured for these grinders,

we were happy the small change you made on them permitted them to be

used.

Between the three cutters we had available (Nos. 40, 41, and 42), the

one you selected should give the longest service. We hope it will

not be necessary for you to altar the cutters we shipped.

I suggest that you purchase our knew Conrad Cutter line for use in your aluminum door frame manufacturing process. The Conrad is a duel cutter and can be used on aluminum or copper. I am confidant that you will find it satisfactory to use on bars, rods, or plane surfaces. A farther advantage that the Conrad Cutter possesses is it's complete reliability.

If you call us today, we can ship tomorrow; and, of course, we are always ready to offer consul on any medal-working problems you might encounter.

Sincerely yours,

Martin Anderson
Sales Manager

Key to Self-Check Exercises

Exercise 1

1. Except
2. canvass
3. capital
4. seize
5. cereal
6. access
7. adopt

Exercise 2

1. deceased
2. cite
3. coarsely
4. collusion
5. currants
6. creditable
7. consul

Exercise 3

1. emigrate
2. envelop
3. illegible
4. dying
5. disorganized
6. elicit
7. elusive

Exercise 4

1. lose
2. minor
3. hoard
4. loath
5. load
6. may be
7. marital

Exercise 5

1. personnel
2. prosecute
3. peal
4. ordinance
5. observance
6. principal
7. plaintive

Exercise 6

1. too
2. Whether
3. they're
4. respectively
5. vise
6. statute
7. stationery

Exercise 7

1. among
2. remainder
3. eager
4. imply
5. healthful
6. into
7. oral
8. irritate
9. Almost
10. number
11. besides
12. May
13. let
14. likely

Lucretia Burger's Letter (Figure 4-2)

Paragraph 1:
Use *personnel* instead of *personal.*
Paragraph 2:
Use *eminent* instead of *imminent.*
Use *Fete* instead of *Feat.*
Use *eligible* instead of *illegible.*
Use *flair* instead of *flare.*
Paragraph 3:
Use *envelope* instead of *envelop.*

A DYNAMIC BUSINESS VOCABULARY

To improve your vocabulary, study the spelling of these words, their definitions, and their use in sentences. In addition, check their pronunciation by referring to your dictionary.

Cartel

A group of independent business organizations set up to regulate pricing, production, and marketing of products.

Several oil companies banded together to form an independent oil cartel.

Cash flow

Money that is available for day-to-day operating expenses in a company, such as salaries and payment of bills.

Although the 28-unit apartment building was supposed to produce a cash flow to the owner of over $2,000 per month, the sum averaged 10 percent of that figure for the first year.

Cassette

A small plastic cartridge containing magnetic tape that is used in dictation equipment, word-processing machines, and other hardware.

The machine transcriptionist inserted the dictator's cassette in her new Lanier transcriber.

Centralization

A drawing together or concentration into one group.

The firm was reorganized to produce a centralization of authority in the New York office.

Centrex

An abbreviation for Central Exchange, a telephone system that permits direct dialing to a specific extension phone, bypassing a switchboard initially.

The Baltic Institute was pleased with the efficiency and overhead cost of the recently installed Centrex system.

Certification

A written statement authenticating a document, fact, or promise.

The certification received from the Securities and Exchange Commission permitted the firm to issue its stock on the open market.

Chip

A sliver of silicon on which thousands of complete electronic circuits are implanted. It contains all the circuitry needed to carry out computer operations.

The data-processing students found it difficult to believe that a minute microcomputer chip can contain the electronic circuits used to perform such intricate computer functions.

Class action

Legal action taken by one or more persons, usually against an organization, for themselves and others with an identical interest in the alleged wrong.

The suit brought against Health-More Pharmaceuticals by Lester Jameson in behalf of all individuals who had purchased Health-More Vitamins was a class action.

THE ABC'S OF BUSINESS VOCABULARY

You have had the opportunity to study four lists of business words. By now your business vocabulary should be expanding. Complete the following exercise to see if you have acquired a working knowledge of some of the terms we have provided.

1. Compose three short sentences using one of the following terms in each sentence: (a) cassette, (b) cash flow, (c) certification.

   _____

   _____

   _____

   _____

   _____

   _____

2. Continued nonattendance at work either deliberately or habitually is (a) punctuality, (b) perseverance, (c) absenteeism, (d) antagonism.

3. To join up with, or to associate one business with another in the business world, is to (a) affiliate, (b) separate, (c) communicate, (d) speculate.

4. The payment of income or an allowance over a fixed period of time in an insurance policy is a (a) stipend, (b) honorarium, (c) wage, (d) annuity.

5. The natural ability or talent to learn is a person's (a) ideals, (b) character, (c) aptitude, (d) interest.

6. The definition of the noun *cartel* is _____

   _____

7. Define the noun *certification.* _____

   _____

8. The meaning of the noun *chip* is _____

   _____

9. The noun *Centrex* refers to _____

   _____

REVIEW EXERCISE ON CHAPTERS 1–4

This exercise tests your knowledge on the contents of Chapters 1–4.

A. Indicate whether each statement is true or false.

_____ 1. Dictionaries usually identify the part of speech a word is.

_____ 2. A common form of business communication is the intraoffice memo.

_____ 3. *Supercede* is spelled correctly.

_____ 4. Homonyms have the same meaning.

_____ 5. A misspelled word in something you write will create a negative impression of you.

_____ 6. The addition of such prefixes as *de-, dis-, mis-, non-, re-, trans-,* and *un-* usually does not cause any alteration in the spelling of the word to which the prefix is added.

_____ 7. If you have a good vocabulary, you really do not need a dictionary because only a few words in English have more than one meaning.

_____ 8. Occasionally there will be more than one acceptable way to spell a word.

_____ 9. *Faint* and *feint* are homonyms.

_____ 10. Words that have opposite meanings are called *antonyms.*

_____ 11. *Personal* and *personnel* can be used interchangeably without any significant differences in meaning; therefore, they are synonyms.

_____ 12. *Stupify* is spelled correctly.

_____ 13. *Your* is one form of the several acceptable contractions of *you are.*

_____ 14. The following sentence is correct: "The principal of the school followed the principles established by the school board."

_____ 15. An unabridged dictionary is usually shorter than an abridged one.

_____ 16. Three words in the English language end in *-ceed: exceed, proceed,* and *succeed.*

_____ 17. *It's* is a contraction of *it is.*

_____ 18. A dictionary usually will not provide the correct spelling of common words.

_____ 19. *To, two,* and *too* are correctly used in this sentence: "The boss went *to* his club *two* times last week, *too,* just as he did this week."

_____ 20. You should make a list of words you regularly misspell.

_____ 21. *Seperate* is spelled correctly.

_____ 22. A *miner* is a person who has yet to attain legal age.

_____ 23. The words *big* and *large* are synonyms.

_____ 24. *Whose* is a contraction of *who is.*

_____ 25. *Between* should refer to only two items.

B. In each of the groups below, one word is spelled correctly. Put its letter in the blank at the left.

_____ 1. (a) advertising, (b) advertizing, (c) adverticing, (d) advertissing.

_____ 2. (a) wether, (b) whether, (c) wheather, (d) whethar.

_____ 3. (a) thief, (b) theif, (c) theaf, (d) theef.

_____ 4. (a) secratary, (b) secretery, (c) seccretary, (d) secretary.

_____ 5. (a) professar, (b) proffessor, (c) professor, (d) proffesser.

_____ 6. (a) ocured, (b) occured, (c) occurred, (d) ocurred.

_____ 7. (a) allready, (b) already, (c) alreaddy, (d) allreddie.

_____ 8. (a) bankrup, (b) bankwrupt, (c) bankrupt, (d) bankruped.

_____ 9. (a) committy, (b) committee, (c) comittee, (d) commitee.

_____ 10. (a) cortesy, (b) courtessie, (c) courtescy, (d) courtesy.

_____ 11. (a) developement, (b) developemant, (c) development, (d) devellopment.

_____ 12. (a) dout, (b) doubt, (c) doule, (d) dowt.

_____ 13. (a) goverment, (b) governmantt, (c) govermant, (d) government.

_____ 14. (a) syllible, (b) sylable, (c) syllable, (d) syllabble.

_____ 15. (a) sincerelie, (b) sincerel, (c) sincerely, (d) sinserly.

_____ 16. (a) prevalent, (b) prevalant, (c) prevlant, (d) prevlent.

_____ 17. (a) pairalel, (b) paralel, (c) paralell, (d) parallel.

_____ 18. (a) morgage, (b) mortgauge, (c) morgauge, (d) mortgage.

_____ 19. (a) loose, (b) loos, (c) looce, (d) locse.

_____ 20. (a) librarey, (b) libarry, (c) library, (d) librery.

_____ 21. (a) its', (b) it's, (c) it's', (d) i't's'.

_____ 22. (a) relevant, (b) revalant, (c) relevent, (d) revelent.

_____ 23. (a) intresting, (b) intristing, (c) interesting, (d) interisting.

_____ 24. (a) guidance, (b) guydance, (c) guydence, (d) guidence.

_____ 25. (a) grammer, (b) gramer, (c) gramar, (d) grammar.

C. Choose the correct word from within the parentheses and write it in the blank at the left.

_____ 1. It takes (to, too) long if you use that method.

_____ 2. Divide the proceeds (among, between) the two of them.

_____ 3. Monica enrolled in two (coarses, courses) this term.

_____ 4. The (cite, sight, site) of the new school has not yet been picked.

_____ 5. Does your cold (affect, effect) your work?

_____ 6. The work had (already, all ready) been completed by the time she arrived.

_____ 7. Suzanne was very (adapt, adept, adopt) at keeping accurate records.

_____ 8. Mark used company (stationary, stationery) to prepare the letter.

_____ 9. Isao (accepted, excepted) the bonus with grace and a sincere "Thank you."

_____ 10. His recommendation (implied, inferred) a lack of confidence.

_____ 11. The instructions in this memo (supersede, superseed, supercede) all previous instructions.

_____ 12. (Beside, Besides) typing, Ellen does superior bookkeeping.

_____ 13. (Their, There, They're) particularly busy at the Christmas season.

_____ 14. It is (alright, all right) with me if you come to work earlier in the summer months.

_____ 15. The judge in the company lawsuit was excellent; he maintained (a disinterested, an uninterested) attitude throughout the trial.

_____ 16. (It's, Its) cover makes the yearly report really stand out.

_____ 17. (Formally, Formerly), Watson worked in the shipping department.

_____ 18. Ms. Goldberg deposits the day's (receipts, reciepts) each night.

_____ 19. The company naturally does not want to (lose, loose) money on this venture.

_____ 20. The (personal, personnel) in the accounting department are the best paid in the entire company.

_____ 21. The (moral, morale) of the department is sure to be improved with the new salaries.

_____ 22. Please do the filing first and save the new typing until (later, latter).

_____ 23. No one who has not been given proper clearance may have (access, excess) to this room.

_____ 24. The boss gave his written (assent, ascent) to my getting two days off next month.

_____ 25. Sandra types better (than, then) Elaine.

D. In the following memo there are at least 25 errors. Find as many as you can and correct them by writing the preferred form immediately above the error.

TO: Mr. L. M. Oshio, District Manager

FROM: David Blaine, Sales Staff

DATE: October 29, 198_

SUBJECT: Sales Report from Southwest Region

You're request for a report on sales in this territory led to my

writting you this memo. As you know, we are understaffed in the

Southwest. Beside me their are only Monica Ball, whose really at

---

work only a few days each week because of her recovery from surgery, and Becky Klein, who's going to be a super salesperson, but is now having to except the fact that its not an easy job to learn.

Between the three of us, we try to acomodate the needs of our customers. There major need at the moment is for more advise on how to increase they're production. If we want to have a good affect on the future, we need, I believe, to take some time away from sales in order to give some council. We have been doing so and, thus, our sales are less then they were last year at this time. But its to early to tell for sure how this quarter will come out. I am hopping that we finish with some sales figures that show that we are suceding.

For now, than, please do not be too concerned. Latter I am sure the sales figures will increase. I am confidant that we will achieve our full compliment of orders and that our territory will show that it can adopt to new conditions and achieve an access of sales. Our sales curve, I promise, will show an assent.

Part Two
Parts of Speech and Parts of Sentences

Examine these sentences:

The sales manager divided the commission between José and I. [between José and me]

My sister she works in the accounting office. [My sister works]

She could of really went to the convention if she had completed her work. [could have . . . gone]

He gave Willie and I the most difficult territory. [Willie and me]

Working in Boston every summer, the cheapest places to buy clothes were well known to her.
[Working in Boston every summer, she knew the cheapest places . . .]

The report took hours, all the executives became bored. [hours. All the (or) hours; all the]

In the middle of the second paragraph where you have a comma. [This group of words is not a complete sentence.]

We have to get them advertisements ready at least a week before the sale. [those advertisements]

Of the two reports, Teresa's was clearly the best. [the better]

These kind of rules are broken in every factory. [These kinds]

Even if you make the kinds of mistakes illustrated in these sentences (and corrected in the brackets), the chances are good that no one will hate you or divorce you or fire you. But you may not get hired or promoted as quickly as you would if you avoided errors. Indeed, you might not get hired or promoted at all.

Like it or not, people are judged by the language they use and especially by the mistakes they make. This is particularly true in the world of business. The secretary who uses the wrong verb form, the shipping clerk who makes a pronoun error, the receptionist who says "ain't" all reflect negatively both on themselves and, of more importance to their employers, on the firms they represent. Simply stated, it is better to avoid errors.

But this judgment about your language goes beyond any errors you might make. People also examine the good aspects of your language, how well you string words together, how gracefully your sentences flow, how forcefully your paragraphs are created. Using English well marks you as a person who cares about language and about the impression you make. You want to look your best and that means more than clothing and grooming; it includes the effective use of language.

Happily, a better use of a language is something you can learn. You will not become the world's greatest novelist as a result of studying this book, but you can become a solid, effective speaker and writer who is an asset to any company.

Given a sentence like "Over the river and through the woods to grandmother's house we go," you could analyze it in a number of ways. You could, for example, count the number of letters or words. You could find the ratio of consonants to vowels or determine what letters appear most frequently. You could rearrange the words. Would it be better to begin with "We go"? Or should you put "we go" after "woods"?

These kinds of analyses are trivial or useless. They do not help us improve our skill with English. But two kinds of analyses are most helpful: (1) parts of speech (nouns, pronouns, adjectives, verbs, adverbs, prepositions, conjunctions, and interjections) and (2) parts of sentences (subjects, predicates, direct objects, indirect objects, and objects of prepositions). Thus, our sample sentence would look like this if analyzed by these two means:

Part of Speech	preposition	adjective	noun	conjunction	preposition	adjective	noun
	Over	*the*	*river*	*and*	*through*	*the*	*woods*
Part of Sentence	preposition	modifier	object of preposition	conjunction	preposition	modifier	object of preposition
	prepositional phrase				prepositional phrase		

Part of Speech	preposition	possessive noun	noun	pronoun	verb
	to	*Grandmother's*	*house*	*we*	*go*
Part of Sentence	preposition	modifier	object of preposition	subject	predicate
	prepositional phrase				

As you can see in this analysis, conjunctions and prepositions are identified by the same terms, whether the analysis is parts of speech or parts of sentences. But the adjectives, nouns, pronouns, and verbs are classified under different headings for parts of speech than they are for parts of sentences. The reason for this distinction will become clear as we go through the next seven chapters. Study those chapters carefully. Work the exercises thoughtfully. We believe that, after such studying and thinking, you will be more skilled with language and more self-confident as a result of that skill.

5 Parts of Speech
Nouns and Pronouns

NOUNS

Nouns name persons, places, or things. *River, woods, grandmother* are all nouns. So are *book* or *bed* or *bagel, louse* or *mouse* or *house*. Note the number of nouns in the following short description:

> The *applicant* made a good *impression* on the personnel *manager.* He wore a carefully pressed *suit.* His *shoes* were shined. His *necktie* had a conservative *pattern.* But the most distinctive *characteristic* was his *speech.* He gave thoughtful *answers* with almost an eloquent *use* of *language.* He got the *job.*

CLASSIFICATIONS OF NOUNS

There are a number of classifications of nouns, but all of them are still names.

1. *Proper nouns.* These nouns name specific persons, places, or things and are always capitalized.

   Henry Ford   *The Chicago Tribune*   U.S. Steel   Indiana University   Rebecca Goldman

2. *Common nouns.* These nouns name general classes of persons, places, or things and are not capitalized.

   boys   canyons   factories   trees   ideas   rivers   books

3. *Concrete nouns.* These nouns name persons, places, or things that can be felt or tasted or seen or touched or heard (that is, discovered by the senses).

   lamp   dog   invoice   scent   sound   cinnamon

4. *Abstract nouns.* These nouns name a quality or an idea that is not concrete.

   love   beauty   freedom   fear   respect

5. *Collective nouns.* These nouns are singular in form but refer to more than one person, animal, or thing.

   faculty   class   crowd   jury   panel   audience   band   navy   board   group   committee

6. *Compound nouns.* These nouns are two or more words joined to name one person, place, or thing. Compound nouns are written either as one joined word, two or more hyphenated words, or two or more words with spaces between them. Since common usage may change the preferred format of compound nouns, refer to a current dictionary if you are in doubt.

   Joined Words

   headache   checklist   eyewitness   goodwill   timetable   trademark

   Hyphenated Words

   mother-in-law   runner-up   attorney-at-law   self-confidence

Words with Spaces

telephone operator   executive committee   board of trustees   trade name   air express

Note: If a word is used to *name* (even though in a different sentence that same word might have a different function), it is best thought of as a *noun.* ☑

PLURAL FORMS OF NOUNS

Most nouns simply add *s* or *es* to form their plural form. *Job* becomes *jobs. Watch* becomes *watches.* And usually you will know which of these is the appropriate form simply by saying the word to yourself. We could confuse you with many rules that attempt to explain why it is *radios* and *potatoes* (*s* or *es?*), *safes* and *lives* (*f* or *v?*), or *men* and *boys* (change vowel or add *s?*), but each of these rules has many exceptions. A better method is to refer to your dictionary. That valuable reference book will be especially helpful when you use words derived from foreign languages, such as *alumnus* or *criterion* or *datum.*

A few general guidelines, however, can help you form noun plurals with a degree of confidence.

COMMON NOUNS

Common nouns that end in *sh, ch, s, z,* or *x* form their plurals by adding *es* instead of *s*. As you can see, it would be difficult to pronounce the plurals without the short *e* sound.

ES Endings	**S Endings**
COMPARE wat*ches*	WITH clo*cks*
COMPARE bru*shes*	WITH co*mbs*
COMPARE bo*sses*	WITH employ*ers*
COMPARE ta*xes*	WITH l*aws*

COMPOUND WORDS

Form the plural of compound nouns by adding *s* to the most important part of the noun.

Self-Check Exercise 1

Determine your ability to recognize proper, common, concrete, abstract, collective, and compound nouns in the following paragraph. Underline every noun you can find. When you have completed the exercise, check your answers with the key at the end of the chapter.

The authors of *Communicating in Business* write that a major cause of communication breakdown in our society is inadequate listening. The good listener hears not only the facts presented, but also the feelings behind the stated facts. Our deep involvement with our problems, our goals, and our feelings makes it difficult for us to hear what is really communicated. If we will listen carefully with understanding and concern for the speaker, however, the message may come through very clearly.

Singular	Plural
runner-up	*runners*-up
mother-in-law	*mothers*-in-law
credit manager	credit *managers*
major general	major *generals*
editor in chief	*editors* in chief
passerby	*passers*by

NOUNS ENDING IN Y

Singular nouns ending *y* need special attention to form their plurals. Although this was discussed in the spelling chapter on page 45, a brief reminder is in order.

1. In a singular noun, if the final *y* is preceded by a consonant, change the *y* to *i* and add *es* to form the plural.

Singular	Plural
necessity	necessit*ies*
discrepancy	discrepanc*ies*
economy	econom*ies*
library	librar*ies*
secretary	secretar*ies*

2. If the final *y* is preceded by a vowel, leave the *y* and merely add *s* to form the plural.

Singular	Plural
toy	toy*s*
attorney	attorney*s*
delay	delay*s*

NOUNS ENDING IN O

Nouns that end in *o* preceded by a consonant form their plurals by adding either *s* (two*s*) or *es* (tomato*es*). If you are not certain whether a singular word ending in *o* preceded by a consonant ends in *s* or *es*, check your dictionary. Here are some examples showing this inconsistency:

S Endings		ES Endings	
memo	memo*s*	hero	hero*es*
auto	auto*s*	potato	potato*es*
photo	photo*s*	veto	veto*es*

Note: One helpful guideline is that such nouns pertaining to music consistently add just *s*.

Singular	Plural
piano	piano*s*
alto	alto*s*
concerto	concerto*s*
tempo	tempo*s*

Singular nouns ending in *o* preceded by a vowel consistently form their plurals by just adding *s*.

Singular	Plural
studio	studio*s*
ratio	ratio*s*
patio	patio*s*

FOREIGN NOUNS

Because familiar foreign words are taken directly from foreign languages, they do not follow English language principles in forming their plurals. you can see from the following list how many plural endings there are:

Singular	Plural
medium	medi*a*
datum	dat*a*
referendum	referend*a* or referend*ums*
criterion	criteri*a*
alumna	alumn*ae*
alumnus	alumn*i*
syllabus	syllab*i*
maître d'	maître d'*s*
appendix	appendix*es* or appendic*es*
analysis	analys*es*
basis	bas*es*
parenthesis	parenthes*es*

Note: Through the years some of the more popular foreign words have developed alternative English plurals that are accepted by many. When you are not sure which foreign word plural is preferred, refer to the dictionary you keep close at hand.

PROPER NAMES

Form the plural of surnames (last names) by adding *s* unless the surname ends in the sound of *sh, ch, s,* or *z,* in which case *es* is needed to assist in pronunciation.

S Endings	ES Endings
The Smiths	The Jones*es*
The Greens	The Gross*es*
The Jacksons	The Barnes*es*

Sometimes the plural of a surname ending in *s* is difficult to pronounce if *es* is added to it.

Surname	Incorrect Plural
Rogers	Rogerses
Andrews	Andrewses

With names such as Rogers and Andrews, the singular and plural are the same.

Singular	Plural
The car belongs to John Rogers.	The car belongs to the Rogers. (Mr. and Mrs. Rogers)
Take the gift to J. Andrews.	Take the gift to the Andrews. (Mr. and Mrs. Andrews)

IRREGULAR NOUNS

Although most nouns form their plural by adding an *s* or *es,* irregular nouns, like those in the list that follows, form their plural in many ways. Some change their consonants or vowels. Some add endings other than *s* or *es.* Some even have the same form for singular and plural. Look at these examples:

Singular	Plural
child	children
man	men
ox	oxen
mouse	mice
foot	feet
life	lives
half	halves
news	news (no change)
apparatus	apparatus (no change) ☑

Self-Check Exercise 2

Select the correct answers in the following exercise. Then check your selection with the key at the end of the chapter.

1. The spa provided (pedometers, pedometeres) for some of its jogging members.

2. Jonathon and Mary were (runner-ups, runners-up) in the husband-and-wife Sunday marathon.

3. The Labeque sisters owned twin grand (pianoes, pianos).

4. Have you seen the many (trademarks, tradesmark) the artist has been working on?

5. What (necessitys, necessities) are to be stored in the basement of the Salem Boys' Club?

6. Both my cousins expect to be practicing (attorneys, attorneyes, attornies) in New Orleans by September.

7. The space (heroes, heros) were honored at the annual formal dinner of the association.

8. Ms. Hwa opened two art (studios, studioes) in Quebec last year.

9. The (datas, data) collected by the researcher were very helpful to the journalist.

10. The congregation of the French (maître ds, maître d's) caused quite a commotion at the Hotel René.

POSSESSIVE FORMS OF NOUNS

One persistent problem in English is the possessive form of nouns. Specifically, the problem is where to place the apostrophe. (Curiously, this problem occurs only in written English. In spoken English your listener does not know if you have used the apostrophe properly. Indeed, one can make a good case that the apostrophe will not be around a hundred years from now except in the most formal writing.)

Yet the apostrophe that shows possession remains a problem, and you should study it. To help you gain confidence in the proper use of this mark of punctuation, we introduce a few helpful guidelines here. Then in Chapter 14, a punctuation chapter, the overall use of the apostrophe will be reemphasized and fully explained. This double-barreled approach will help you in writing the possessive forms of both singular and plural nouns.

1. To form the possessive of a *singular noun* that does not end in *s* or *z*, add an apostrophe and *s* (*'s*).

Singular	Singular Possessive	Example
attorney	attorney*'s*	the attorney's practice
employer	employer*'s*	the employer's firm
analyst	analyst*'s*	the analyst's records
computer	computer*'s*	the computer's keyboard

2. To create the possessive of a *singular noun* that does end in *s* or *z,* add an apostrophe and *s* (*'s*) only if the pronunciation of the possessive forms a smooth new syllable.

Singular	Singular Possessive	Example
boss	boss*'s*	the boss's desk
Jones	Jones*'s*	Mr. Jones's suit
hostess	hostess*'s*	the hostess's duties
Buzz	Buzz*'s*	Buzz's computer
Ross	Ross*'s*	Ross's books

Note: If the pronunciation of the possessive creates an awkward-sounding new syllable, just add an apostrophe (*'*) to the singular noun ending in *s* or *z.*

Athens' neighboring islands [not hard-to-pronounce Athens's]

Texas' Stetson hats [not Texas's]

Loretta Jergens' research paper [not Jergens's]

Bill Rogers' old automobile [not Rogers's]

3. To form the possessive of a *regular plural noun* (one that ends in *s* or *es*), add only the apostrophe (*'*).

Plural	Plural Possessive	Example
girls	girls*'*	the girls' assignments
companies	companies*'*	the companies' profits
Kleins	Kleins*'*	the Kleins' condominium

4. To form the possessive of an *irregular plural noun* (one that does not end in *s* or *es*), add the apostrophe and *s* (*'s*).

Plural	Plural Possessive	Example
men	men*'s*	men's uniforms
children	children*'s*	children's rights
women	women*'s*	women's fashions

Note: You should show possession by means of an apostrophe or by using the word *of.*
USE *the worker's responsibility* OR *the responsibility of the worker.*
USE *the women's reports* OR *the reports of the women.*

What you should *not* do is use both the apostrophe and the *of.* That is incorrect.
USE either the *employers' role* OR *the roles of the employers* BUT NOT *the roles of the employers'.* ☑

PRONOUNS

Pronouns are words that take the place of nouns or other pronouns. Consider how foolish the absence of pronouns makes these sentences in a letter of recommendation:

Maria Soto is an excellent worker. Maria comes to the office on time and Maria works steadily once Maria is there. Maria has a good understanding of Maria's job and does Maria's work without extensive supervision. Maria is being considered for a promotion by Maria's supervisor. Maria's friends agree that Maria deserves the promotion.

As you can see, pronouns are very useful little words. But they also cause some big problems in English, both as parts of speech and, as will be shown later, as parts of sentences.

As parts of speech, pronouns are expected to agree in number and gender (male or female) with the nouns for which they are substituting. These nouns are called the *antecedents* of the pronouns. *A pronoun should agree with its antecedent in number and gender.* Normally this rule does not present a problem, as the following sentences indicate.

Sally typed *her* report. [*Her* agrees with Sally.]

After Herb cleaned the store windows, *he* began stocking the shelves. [*He* agrees with Herb.]

Because Tom and Elena worked together on the sale, *they* want to share the commission. [*They* agrees with Tom and Elena.]

Occasionally problems do occur with this rule. Consider the following sentences:

Every student took *his* seat. [Clearly the writer means that all the students took their seats, yet this wording requires *his or her* if the rule is to be strictly adhered to. A better phrasing might be to say, "All the students took their seats."]

Each one of the saleswomen changed *her* dress before dinner. [Why not say, "All the saleswomen changed their dresses"?]

Self-Check Exercise 3

The following paragraph contains errors in the punctuation of possessive nouns. Make the needed changes, then check the key at the end of the chapter to see if your answers are correct.

Herbert Barsons office was in Pittsburghs new Grant Building. He furnished the office with his fathers desk, his one cousins leather couch and chairs, his one neighbors slightly worn but attractive oriental rug, and the antique desk chair belonging to his two French cousins. Barsons office was quite elegant compared with his three partners offices down the hall.

And then there is what is referred to as *sexist* language. Consider this sentence:

Each secretary must take care of *her* boss's daily schedule. [Why *her*? Are there not some male secretaries?]

But is this any better?

Each secretary must take care of his or her boss's daily schedule so that he or she can tell the boss in a minute what is scheduled for the day. [Too much "he or she" can become cumbersome and awkward.]

It is not advisable to use *he* (or *him* or *his*) when you are unsure of the sex, for this practice is offensive to many people. It may be best to try to avoid the dilemma altogether by using a plural form: "All secretaries should take care of their bosses' daily schedules." Thus, you should modify this rule about pronouns and antecedents to avoid confusing, awkward, or sexist expressions.

Now let us look at the classifications of pronouns.

PERSONAL PRONOUNS

NOMINATIVE FORM

In Chapter 9, you will study the use of pronouns as subjects of sentences. Now, however, it is important to review a few particulars about the *nominative* case. Traditionally, the nominative forms of a pronoun are used as follows:

1. As the subject of a verb.

   He is an attorney.
   They purchased a word processor.
   We shall audit the books.

2. As a predicate nominative that follows a linking or "being" verb.

   This must be *she*.
   It is *I*.
   The leaders should be *they*.

Here are the nominative forms of the most common personal pronouns:

SINGULAR

Person	Pronoun	Example
First (the one speaking)	I	*I* am going.
Second (the one spoken to)	you	*You* may call.
Third (the one spoken about)	he/she/it	*He* has left. *She* is working. *It* is blue.

Note: Who and *whoever* are also nominative forms. (*Who* are they? *Whoever* answers the telephone will get the message.) See discussion of *who* and *whoever* later in this chapter.

PLURAL

Person	Pronoun	Example
First (the ones speaking)	we	*We* shall attend.
Second (the ones spoken to)	you (plural)	*You* are all correct.
Third (the ones spoken about)	they	*They* tested well.

OBJECTIVE FORM

Of equal importance is a review of the objective form of personal pronouns. The objective form is used as follows:

1. As the object of a verb.

    They respect *her.*
    The team members applauded *them.*
    Our accountants selected *him.*

2. As the object of a preposition.

    I am attending the conference with *them.*
    The story was about *them.*
    The package is behind *her.*

3. As the subject or object of a verb infinitive.

    The vice president encouraged *me to study* this.
    You ought *to visit him* this weekend.
    Jane wanted *him to run* for the presidency.

Objective forms are usually quite easy to recall if you precede the pronoun with a preposition such as *to.* Consider these examples:

SINGULAR

Person	Pronoun	Example
First	me	Give the book to *me.*
Second	you	I will give the book to *you.*
Third	him/her	It belongs to *him.*
		It belongs to *her.*

*Note: **Whom** and **whomever** are also objective forms. (To **whom** does that belong? **Whomever** he nominates I will support.) Discussion of **whom** and **whomever** appears later in this chapter.*

PLURAL

Person	Pronoun	Example
First	us	Share the newspaper with *us.*
Second	you (plural)	I will give the test to *you.*
Third	them	A card came from *them.*

POSSESSIVE FORM

These pronouns are simply a type of personal pronoun that is used to show possession or ownership. Study the following:

PERSON	PRONOUN	EXAMPLE
	Singular	
First	my	*My* book is on the desk.
	mine	The book is *mine.*
Second	your*	*Your* clock has stopped.
	yours	The clock is *yours.*
Third	his	*His* notes are missing.
		The notes are *his.*
	her	*Her* mother is visiting.
	hers	That pen is *hers.*
	its**	*Its* color is fading.

*Not *you're,* which is a contraction of *you are.*

**Not *it's,* which is a contraction of *it is.*

Plural

First	our	*Our* knives were sharpened.
	ours	The computer is *ours.*
Second	yours (plural)	The coats are *yours.*
	your (plural)	*Your* coats are on the bench.
Third	their	*Their* pool is empty.
	theirs	Those packages are *theirs.*

Note: Whose is also a possessive form. (*Whose* are those? *Whose* papers were lost?) For further review of the nominative, objective, and possessive forms of common personal pronouns, see the chart on page 213 in Chapter 9.

WHO AND WHOM

When should you use *who* (nominative form) rather than *whom* (objective form) in a sentence? This decision puzzles many writers who are otherwise quite confident in their writing skills. A careful review of the following section should be helpful.

• *USED AS A SUBJECT*

The nominative form *who* is the correct choice when a subject of a verb is needed. *Who* is used whenever the nominative form personal pronouns such as *I* or *we* or *they* could be substituted. For example:

Who are here?	*They* are here.
Who had left?	*We* had left.
Who is in the room?	*I* am in the room.

Note: From the examples just given, you can see that *who* and *whom* can be either singular or plural. Here are some additional examples supporting this point:

Singular

Mary Snyder is *the speaker who* will impress you the most.

Mary Snyder, whom we are pleased to welcome, is an expert on office automation.

Plural

Mary Snyder and Ruth Scott are the *speakers who* will impress you the most.

Mary Snyder and Ruth Scott, whom we are pleased to welcome, are visitors from our Dallas branch.

• *USED AS A PREDICATE NOMINATIVE*

The nominative form *who* is used to follow a linking or "being" verb. Note these examples:

Your cousin is *who*?	Your cousin is *she.*
The leaders are *who*?	The leaders are *they.*

• *USED AS A DIRECT OBJECT OF AN ACTION VERB*

Here you need the objective form *whom. Whom* is your choice whenever the objective forms of the personal pronouns such as *him, them,* or *me* could be substituted. Note the following:

Whom will you visit tomorrow?	You will visit *me.*
Whom have you chosen?	You have chosen *them.*
Whom did you see on Saturday?	You saw *him.*

• *USED AS AN OBJECT OF A PREPOSITION*

The objective form *whom* is used as an object of a preposition. Here are some examples:

This receipt is for *whom*? [For *her.*]

About *whom* were you just speaking? [About *him.*]

You said I should give the tickets to *whom*? [To *them.*]

The lawyer about *whom* we talked will lead the debate. [We talked about *her.*]

> Whenever you need a nominative form, select *who*; an objective form, select *whom.*

WHOEVER AND WHOMEVER

> *Whoever,* like *who,* is the nominative form. It may be used as the subject of a verb and as a predicate nominative. Here are some examples:

Whoever is selected will be supported by the members.   *He* is selected.

They plan to select *whoever* volunteers.   *She* volunteers.

Whoever will bring the package will be invited to lunch.   *They* will bring the package.

> *Whomever,* like *whom,* is the objective form. It can serve as a direct object of a verb or an object of a preposition. Note these examples:

Whomever he chooses will receive the bonus.   He will choose *him.*

They will award *whomever* they find.   They will find *them.*

I will speak with *whomever* you designate.   You designate *her.*

Whomever he interviewed yesterday impressed him.   He interviewed *him.*

> When you make your selection between the nominative forms (*who* and *whoever*) and the objective forms (*whom* and *whomever*), test the accuracy of your selection by substituting *he* for *who* and *him* for *whom.* Although this substitution device cannot be used for *whoever* and *whomever,* remember that *whoever* is used as a subject or predicate nominative and *whomever* is used as an object.

INTENSIVE PRONOUNS

> A compound pronoun form is frequently used to provide *emphasis.* The words *self* or *selves* are added to a personal pronoun in the following way:

PERSON	PRONOUN	EXAMPLE
		Singular
First	myself	I *myself* wrote the book.
Second	yourself	Did you *yourself* bake that cake?
Third	herself	Kathy *herself* did the typing.
	himself	He *himself* saved her.
		Plural
First	ourselves	We *ourselves* built the doghouse.
Second	yourselves	You *yourselves* deserve the credit.
Third	themselves	Paul and Helen *themselves* made the window display.

REFLEXIVE PRONOUNS

Like intensive pronouns, reflexive pronouns are formed with *self* or *selves,* but are used to provide a later reference, a *reflexive* look. The pronoun reflects back to a noun or pronoun that appears before it in the sentence. Note these examples:

We found *ourselves* to be the only ones promoting the change. [*Ourselves* reflects back to *we.*]

Tina gave *herself* a raise. [*Herself* reflects back to *Tina.*]

If the two of you want to do the work *yourselves,* it's all right with me. [*Yourselves* reflects back to *two of you.*]

They have insured *themselves* against flood loss at the seashore. [*Themselves* reflects back to *they.*]

Note: You should not use pronouns ending with *self* or *selves* unless you want them to intensify or reflect back on a previous noun or pronoun. Do not make the *self* pronouns do the work of the personal pronouns. Careful writers and speakers avoid the following uses:

Hugh and myself prepared the report. [USE *Hugh and I.*]

Send the proceeds to Carolyn or myself. [USE *Carolyn or me.*]

Note: Hisself, theirself, and *theirselves* are incorrect expressions and should not be used.

INTERROGATIVE PRONOUNS

These pronouns are used in formulating questions. They are *who, whose, whom, which,* and *what.* Note the following:

Pronoun	Example
who	*Who* are they?
whose	*Whose* are these?
whom (objective form)	To *whom* did you give this?
which	*Which* one do you want?
what	*What* is that?

RELATIVE PRONOUNS

These pronouns "relate" whole groups of words, called clauses, to other parts of the sentence. Examples are *who, whom, which,* and *that.*

My sister Elaine, *who* moved to California recently, is a CPA.

Dr. Jardins, *whom* I have just met, recently received a Ph.D. in computer science.

The coats *that* were donated to the Salvation Army were worth $100 apiece when they were new.

My car, *which* is very old, still runs well.

Note: The following guidelines will help you select the correct relative pronoun:

Who refers to people, not things. [My sister Elaine, *who* . . .]

Whom refers to people, not things. [Dr. Jardins, *whom* . . .]

Which refers to things, not people. [My car, *which* . . .]

That can refer to either people or things. [The coats *that* . . .]

As for animals, it depends on how the animal is regarded by the speaker. If you feel your dog is "just like a member of the family," you will probably say, "My dog, *who* . . ."

DEMONSTRATIVE PRONOUNS

These pronouns (*this, that, these,* and *those*) point out *specific* persons, places, things, or ideas. Look at these examples:

FUNCTION	PRONOUN	EXAMPLE
	Singular	
Showing nearness	this	*This* is the book I referred to.
Showing distance	that	*That* videocassette has been on the market since July.

Plural

Showing nearness	these (plural of *this*)	*These* are her blouses.
Showing distance	those (plural of *that*)	*Those* are his tennis racquets.

INDEFINITE PRONOUNS

Indefinite pronouns refer in *general* terms to people, places, things, or ideas. Examples: *all, any, both, each, few, many, one, several, some,* and *most.* Note their use. ☑

Many will attend.	*Several* are missing.	*Any* left?
Few will be absent.	*One* has already left.	*Each* has had her turn.
Both are correct.	*All* are suitable.	*Some* of them remain.

SUMMARY

As the preceding pages indicated, there is a lot to remember about the various classifications and uses of nouns and pronouns. You may want to refer to the examples many more times before moving on to Chapter 6.

Of course, one way to see if you need a further review is to complete some or all of the Application Exercises that follow. Another way is to go back to page 111 and rewrite the paragraph about Maria Soto. Use pronouns to improve the description of Maria's accomplishments.

Self-Check Exercise 4

Underline all the personal, possessive, intensive, reflexive, interrogative, relative, demonstrative, and indefinite pronouns that you find in the following paragraph. Your answers may be checked with the key at the end of the chapter.

All the supervisors gave themselves a rest by watching the president himself play tennis in the tournament. He won his games and celebrated by taking them out to dinner at his expense. That proved to them he was a friendly executive. Who else would have treated the employees so generously? Only presidents who fully appreciate their supervisors reward them with expensive dinners at elegant restaurants.

APPLICATION EXERCISES

A. Use the material in this chapter to complete the sentences or answer the questions below. Write the answers in the blanks at the left.

_____ 1. *Niagara Falls* is what kind of noun?

_____ 2. The plural of *mother-in-law* is *mother-in-law's*. True or false?

_____ 3. Which of these is an abstract noun: (a) tree, (b) lake, or (c) beauty?

_____ 4. *Eyewitness* is an example of (a) an abstract noun, (b) a proper noun, or (c) a compound noun.

_____ 5. What one word in this sentence is a noun: "The expensive new computer worked silently, steadily, and efficiently"?

_____ 6. True or false: *Hisself* is useful only in the most formal kinds of correspondence.

_____ 7. In English, the "first person" refers to (a) the person speaking, (b) the person spoken to, (c) the person spoken about.

_____ 8. Which of these forms is a possessive pronoun: (a) there, (b) they're, (c) their?

_____ 9. Interrogative pronouns are used in (a) identifying persons, (b) asking questions, (c) replacing adjectives.

_____ 10. "She herself flew the plane." What kind of pronoun is *herself* in this sentence?

B. Most nouns form their plurals by adding *s* or *es,* as in *book/books* or *tax/taxes.* But other nouns have varied endings to form plurals. Use your dictionary to form the correct plural for each of the following nouns.

_____ 1. child

_____ 2. supply

_____ 3. life

_____ 4. motto

_____ 5. deer

_____ 6. dish

_____ 7. editor in chief

_____ 8. sister-in-law

_____ 9. ox

_____ 10. valley

_____ 11. attorney

_____ 12. agency

_____ 13. tomato

_____ 14. businessman

_____ 15. handkerchief

_____ 16. piano

_____ 17. zero

_____ 18. woman

_____ 19. trade-in

_____ 20. foot

_____ 21. analysis

_____ 22. series

_____ 23. key

_____ 24. watch

_____ 25. stimulus

C. In each of the following sentences one pronoun is italicized. Write the antecedent of that pronoun in the space at the left.

_____ 1. Sally and Julio are good workers. *Both* received bonuses.

_____ 2. Richard purchased the supplies *he* needed from us.

_____ 3. Agnes studied diligently because *she* wanted to do well in school.

_____ 4. The guidelines provided the union members with the facts *they* needed to determine whether to sign the new contract.

_____ 5. Does each employee have to sign in whenever *he* or *she* leaves?

_____ 6. Mario and Anita completed *theirs* yesterday.

_____ 7. Tyrone *himself* put the stock in the storeroom.

_____ 8. If you really want good pastries for the office party, *those* are the best we have.

_____ 9. Tom and Henry are co-workers, but *neither* likes the other.

_____ 10. Neither Tom nor Roberto wore *his*. [Hint: Be careful on this one.]

D. For each sentence, determine the case of the pronoun required (nominative, objective, or possessive) and write that in the next column. Then refer to the pronoun requested and complete the sentence.

Sentence	**Case**	**Pronoun**

Examples:

_____You_____ are kind and cooperative. ___nominative___ 2nd person singular

Give the report to ___them___ . ___objective___ 3rd person plural

1. _____ voted for her. _____ 1st person singular

2. Give the ballots to _____ . _____ 3rd person plural

3. _____ must turn off the power. _____ 2nd person singular

4. _____ new text-books have arrived. _____ 1st person plural

5. _____ watch is slow. _____ 2nd person singular

6. That project is for _____ to consider. _____ 1st person plural

7. _____ is the man you are to look for. _____ 3rd person singular

8. Have you seen our new material? _____ quality is outstanding. _____ 3rd person singular

9. The man's coat belongs to _____ . _____ 3rd person singular

10. That equipment is _____ . _____ 3rd person plural

11. The perfume you spilled was _____   3rd person singular

    _____ .

12. I will give the latest news to _____   2nd person plural

    _____ .

13. She lent _____ her   _____   1st person singular
    newest album.

14. _____ will attend   _____   1st person plural
    the concert.

15. The presents are   _____   2nd person plural

    _____ .

E. Insert the requested intensive pronoun in each sentence.

Pronoun   **Sentence**

 1. First person singular   I _____ voted for him.

 2. Third person plural   John and Betty _____ decorated both
                                     trees.

 3. Second person singular   Was that you _____ who put out the
                                     fire?

 4. Third person singular   The toddler _____ put the puzzle
                                     together.

 5. First person plural   We _____ prepared the itinerary.

 6. Second person singular   Was that afghan designed by you _____ ?

 7. Second person plural   Did you _____ decorate the gym?

 8. Third person plural   They _____ arranged the surprise
                                     party.

 9. First person singular   I _____ believe he is guilty.

10. Third person singular   She _____ is responsible for the
                                     breakage.

F. Write the possessive of the following nouns into the corresponding sentences.

Noun   **Sentence**

 1. company   The _____ budget was revised by the
                                     accountant.

2. party   Are you familiar with the highlights of the Democratic

_____ platform?

3. doctor   Their _____ speech was profound.

4. salesperson   A _____ salary may fluctuate depending upon his or her arrangement with the company.

5. funds   The money market _____ interest rates varied.

6. companies   The _____ buildings in the industrial park are structurally sound.

7. Gaines   Melissa _____ textbook was found by her classmate.

8. foremen   Our _____ salaries were raised.

9. dictionary   The new _____ format is the same as that of the last edition.

10. doctors   Several _____ opinions are needed.

G. Insert the correct pronouns in the following sentences:

1. (Who, Whom) _____ are the award winners?

2. The computer programmer (who, whom) _____ Walter mentioned was the keynote speaker at the data processing conference.

3. Charles Ferguson knew (who, whom) _____ his supervisor chose.

4. (Who, Whom) _____ do you plan to select?

5. (Who, Whom) _____ is assigned the role of acting recorder?

6. The office managers teach (whoever, whomever) _____ they hire to input data on the computers.

7. (Whoever, Whomever) _____ made that error should confess.

8. Mail a copy of the workbook to (whoever, whomever) _____ requested it.

9. Mail a copy of the workbook to (whoever, whomever) _____ Gerald listed.

10. John Lacy, (who, whom) _____ just enrolled in my Spanish class, plans to spend the summer in Mexico.

Challenge Exercise

Write a short creative sentence using the following nouns and pronouns.

1. cinnamon _____

_____

2. freedom _____

_____

3. panel (noun) _____

_____

4. eyewitness _____

_____

5. court-martial (noun) _____

_____

6. passersby _____

_____

7. discrepancies _____

_____

8. attorneys _____

_____

9. heroes _____

_____

10. concertos _____

_____

11. alumnae _____

_____

12. the Rogers' (belonging to a husband and wife) _____

_____

13. halves _____

_____

14. computer's _____

_____

15. Athens' _____

_____

16. yours _____

_____

17. its _____

_____

18. ourselves _____

_____

19. whom _____

_____

20. myself _____

_____

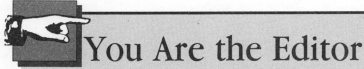

You Are the Editor

The primary errors in the following memo involve its nouns and pronouns. Encircle all errors and write the corrected spelling above the circles.

TO: J. Landings

FROM: B. Brett

DATE: February 3, 198_

SUBJECT: Fall Foliage in New England

John, as a free-lance photographer, you yourself will want to take photograph's of the beautiful scenic fall folage in Massachusetts.

Not only do Betty and myself admire your talent, but we ourself do not have the right camera equipment or skill to capture the colorful hues in our park's. We are hoping that you will agree to visit us one of the weekend's this October to spend time snapping pictures of our neighborhood and our attornies mother-in-laws farm. You may also want a picture of the Andrewses country home to be occupied beginning September 10.

Let me know if your new companies budget can withstand the cost of a trip to New England.

Key to Self-Check Exercises

Exercise 1

1. authors
2. *Communicating in Business*
3. cause
4. breakdown
5. society
6. listening
7. listener
8. facts
9. feelings
10. facts
11. involvement
12. problems
13. goals
14. feelings
15. understanding
16. concern
17. speaker
18. message

Exercise 2

1. pedometers
2. runners-up
3. pianos
4. trademarks
5. necessities
6. attorneys
7. heroes
8. studios
9. data
10. maître d's

Exercise 3

1. Barson's
2. Pittsburgh's
3. father's
4. cousin's
5. neighbor's
6. Barson's
7. partners'

Exercise 4

1. All (indefinite)
2. themselves (reflexive)
3. himself (intensive)
4. He (personal nominative)
5. his (possessive)
6. them (personal objective)
7. his (possessive)
8. That (demonstrative)
9. them (personal objective)
10. he (personal nominative)
11. Who (interrogative)
12. who (relative)
13. their (possessive)
14. them (personal objective)

A DYNAMIC BUSINESS VOCABULARY

Here is a new list of vocabulary terms to study. Learn their spelling, definitions, and use in sentences. Be sure to refer to your dictionary if you are uncertain about their pronunciation.

COBOL

Acronym for *CO*mmon *B*usiness-*O*riented *L*anguage. A highly technical computer language used by specialists.

The data-processing students mastered BASIC before undertaking COBOL.

Codicil

A written modification, or appendix, to a will.

The judge ruled that the handwritten codicil to Mr. Worthington's will was valid.

Collate

To assemble or combine several items to form a complete set in numerical or alphabetical order.

It took over three hours to collate the final examination for two classes.

Commodity

Anything that can be of commercial value or use.

Although wheat is a vital commodity, we have never shipped that particular grain to any of our accounts.

Conglomerate

The collection of several organizations, as in a merger, to form a more sound business organization.

The conglomerate was made up of plastics, lumber, and steel companies.

Consolidate

To bring together many parts, businesses, or agreements to form one.

Danny will consolidate all his notes into one notebook instead of three.

Consumer

Anyone who buys, consumes, or uses goods.

Although American consumers complain about inflation, their standard of living is the highest in the world.

CPU

The *C*entral *P*rocessing *U*nit, which consists of a core memory, a calculation function, and an operating control component. It controls what the computer does.

When the CPU malfunctioned, the class computer was of no use to the students.

THE ABC'S OF BUSINESS VOCABULARY

This exercise will test your knowledge of the business vocabulary you have studied thus far. Answer these questions as quickly and accurately as you can.

1. The definition of *CPU* is _____

   _____

2. Define the noun *commodity.* _____

   _____

3. The meaning of the noun *conglomerate* is _____

   _____

4. The acronym *COBOL* refers to _____

   _____

5. Compose three short sentences using one of the following words in each: (a) codicil, (b) collate, (c) analysis.

   _____

   _____

   _____

   _____

   _____

   _____

6. To bring together many parts, businesses, or agreements to form one unit is to (a) appoint, (b) consolidate, (c) conceal, (d) raze.

7. Anyone who buys or uses goods is a/an (a) employee, (b) shareholder, (c) consumer, (d) trader.

8. A person who receives benefits, funds, and the like from a will, insurance, or other form of settlement is a/an (a) executor, (b) executrix, (c) plaintiff, (d) beneficiary.

9. Economic periods of alternating prosperity, depression, or stability are called (a) business cycles, (b) seasons, (c) depressions, (d) recessions.

6 Parts of Speech
Verbs

In any analysis of sentences using the parts-of-speech method, you should pay particular attention to the verbs, for they carry the sentence, serve as its quarterback, and give it meaning and direction. Consider these five sentences, alike in all ways except for the verbs:

The employer *praised* the office staff.
The employer *blamed* the office staff.
The employer *paid* the office staff.
The employer *disliked* the office staff.
The employer *fired* the office staff.

FUNCTIONS OF VERBS

Verbs typically perform one of three functions in a sentence:

1. They express a condition or state of being, as in "My uncle *is* the boss." These kinds of verbs are called *nonaction* verbs.

2. They express action, as in "The receptionist *answered* the telephone." These kinds of verbs are called *action* verbs.

3. They help other verbs, and with these other verbs form verb phrases, as in "Juanita Clark *has been* working overtime." These kinds of verbs are called *helping* verbs.

Every written sentence must have a verb. In later chapters, when you study parts of sentences, you will discover that verbs are called *predicates*. For now, remember that we are focusing on parts of speech.

NONACTION VERBS

There are two main types of nonaction verbs. One is known as the "state-of-being" verb, frequently referred to as the verb *to be*. The second category is made up of a few verbs that refer to a condition or pertain to the senses. Some examples of these are *feel, look, taste, appear, seem,* and *become*. Nonaction verbs are also called *linking* verbs.

Condition or sense verbs in the following sentences link the subjects with *adjectives* (descriptive word):

The baby *seems* happy.   The actor *looks* pleasant.
His student *appears* disappointed.   My fingers *feel* warm.
That pizza *tastes* delicious.

The verb *to be* has several forms. The forms denote present, past, or future state of being and are widely used in writing. Selecting the proper form of the verb *to be* is second nature to successful writers. Here is a quick overview of their use in sentences.

AM, IS, ARE, WAS, WERE

PRESENT TENSE	**PAST TENSE**
Singular	

I *am* delighted.	I *was* sad.
You *are* pretty.	You *were* dejected.
He *is* shy.	He *was* lost.
She *is* assertive.	She *was* embarrassed.
It *is* cold.	It *was* sunny.

Plural

We *are* pleased.	We *were* surprised.
You *are* outstanding.	You *were* unhappy.
They *are* silly.	They *were* cooperative.

BE *WITH A HELPER*

I *shall be* pleased.	She *must be* ill.
They *can be* convinced.	You *should be* ashamed.
He *may be* agreeable.	I *would be* glad.
You *will be* miserable.	They *might be* willing.

BEEN *WITH A HELPER*

You *have been* wonderful.	It *has been* gradual.
They *had been* glum.	

BEING *WITH A HELPER*

You *were being* uncooperative.	He *is being* bratty.
I *am being* optimistic.	You *are being* bold.

ACTION VERBS

Action verbs take objects and adverbs and move sentences along, giving them vitality. Using many action verbs in your business writing can lead to vivid and exciting communications. Note how action verbs, accompanied by objects, adverbs, or both, bring life to the following sentences: ☑

She *sang* the opening song beautifully.

John *laughed* heartily.

The word-processing operator *keyboarded* speedily and accurately.

The athlete *swam* four laps quickly.

The executive *dictated* her correspondence skillfully.

HELPING VERBS

A *verb phrase* consists of one or more helping verbs followed by a main verb.

will be taught   am lecturing   might have known

The last verb in a verb phrase is the principal, or main, verb. Here are some additional examples:

	Helping Verb(s)	Main Verb	
He	has	squandered	his allowance.
She	was	walking	the dog.
He	is	singing	a ballad.
They	have been	watching	carefully.
We	might have been	driving	all night.
I	should have	thought	of that.

Note that the first three sentences have only one helping verb followed by a main verb. Of the remaining sentences, two have two helping verbs and one has three.

Note: Helping verbs, you must remember, must have a verb to help. Otherwise, they must be classified as *nonaction* or *action* verbs. Look at the difference:

Self-Check Exercise 1

Having reviewed this section on verbs, you are now ready to complete the following exercise accurately and speedily. Which function do the italicized verbs perform in the following sentences? Do they express *action, condition,* or *state of being*? Select one function for each sentence. Remember to check your answers with the key.

1. The guidesheet *provides* a detailed description.

2. You will *learn* techniques for selecting verbs.

3. The Jones Company *manufactures* oversized cartons.

4. I *was* very delighted.

5. This meat *tastes* undercooked.

6. The merit scholarship winner *was* always confident.

7. Please *accept* my sincere congratulations on your promotion.

8. He has never *been* proud of his accomplishments at work.

9. The cashier *reimbursed* the customer.

10. Her back *felt* strained after exercising.

11. Miriam *was* here before you arrived.

12. This *is* our professor's textbook.

He *has spent* his money. [Helping verb *has.*]
He *has* money. [Action verb *has.*]
He *was taking* a nap. [Helping verb *was.*]
He *was* the captain. [Nonaction verb *was.*]
They *had left* early. [Helping verb *had.*]
We *had* a good time. [Action verb *had.*] ☑

ONE LAST LOOK AT VERB HELPERS

To show some of the many forms a verb can take, we have listed 21 ways of using the verb *talk*. For easy reference, they are in alphabetical order.

can talk	have talked	talk
could talk	is talking	talked
did talk	may talk	talks
do talk	might talk	was talking
does talk	must talk	will be talking
had talked	should be talking	will talk
has talked	should talk	would talk

Self-Check Exercise 2

Encircle the main verbs in the following sentences, and underline any verb helpers that precede them. The answers can be found in the key at the end of the chapter.

1. Since he had not studied, he failed the examination.

2. They participated in the square dance.

3. The students observed the computer operator at work.

4. She might have been more cooperative with her peers.

5. Partying is a fun activity on Friday nights.

6. I am lecturing to a group of Temple University professors.

7. We should have spoken to the travel agent last week.

8. Although we cannot hire you now, we will keep your application on file for future consideration.

9. Her management professor is attending a lecture in Dallas.

10. I have helped my supervisor each weekend since the first of May.

11. They were trying to leave as early as eleven o'clock.

Note: Adverbs such as *surely, not, just, always, only, never,* and *certainly* are not part of a verb, though they may appear so in some sentences. Look at these examples:

I *could* not *cook.* [*Not* is an adverb, not a verb helper.]

He *should* always *look.* [*Always* is an adverb, not a helper.]

They *would* certainly *ask.* [*Certainly* is an adverb.]

You *had* surely *noticed.* [*Surely* is an adverb.]

They *had* never *smoked.* [*Never* is an adverb.]

He *has* just *seen* it. [*Just* is an adverb.]

USE HAVE, *NOT* OF

An important note about verbs concerns one of the most easily corrected common errors in English: the incorrect use of *of* for *have* in verb phrases.

USE could *have* gone   NOT could *of* gone
    might *have* learned   might *of* learned
    could *have* taught   could *of* taught
    might *have* arrived   might *of* arrived

Experts attribute the mix-up to the common contractions *could've* and *might've.* When they are spoken in informal dialogue, they sound like the incorrect *could of* and *might of.* They are, of course, contractions for *could have* and *might have.* If you remember that *of* is a preposition and has no place in a verb phrase, you will be sure to use *have* instead.

Study the following correct sentences:

She *could have* finished the project in time.

He *might have* called this morning.

They *could have* sold more if they had tried.

We *might have* participated in the program if we had been asked.

REGULAR AND IRREGULAR VERBS

A part of using proper English is avoiding bad English. Your listeners and readers will notice the mistakes you make. One common area of mistakes in English is in the use of verbs, especially *irregular* verbs. First, though, let us consider *regular* verbs.

REGULAR VERBS

Verbs have six tenses:

- *Present* tense (meaning now).

- *Past* tense (meaning before now).

- *Future* tense (meaning after now).

- *Present perfect* tense (meaning continuous action from the past to the present: "I have voted in every election since 1970."

- *Past perfect* tense (meaning starting one time in the past and continuing to the more recent past: "I had voted in every election since 1970."

- *Future perfect* tense (meaning starting in the past and extending into the future: "I will have voted in every election since 1970."

To form the different tenses, use different forms of the verb.

Use the present form for the present tense *(walk)*.

Use the past form for the past tense *(walked)*.

Use the present form with *will* to form the future tense *(will walk)*.

Use the past participle form with *have* or *had* or *will have* to form the perfect tenses *(have walked; had walked; will have walked)*.

These forms, called *principal parts,* can usually be easily recognized by inserting the appropriate form of the verb in these sentences:

First principal part: I (talk) today. [Present form]

Second principal part: I (talked) yesterday. [Past form]

Third principal part: I have (talked) many times. [Past participle form]

Regular verbs form the *past* and *past participle* by adding *ed* to the present form. These are examples:

Present	Past	Past Participle
call	called	called
paint	painted	painted
type	typed	typed
dictate	dictated	dictated
manage	managed	managed
perform	performed	performed

COMPARE:

I *perform* today.	I *performed* yesterday.	I *have performed* many times.
I *paint* today.	I *painted* yesterday.	I *have painted* many times.
I *type* today.	I *typed* yesterday.	I *have typed* many times.

Occasionally a slightly modified spelling is needed when the present form ends in *y*, but such verbs are still considered regular. For example:

study	studied	studied
carry	carried	carried

IRREGULAR VERBS

Irregular verbs are called by that term because they form their past tense or past participle irregularly. They do not simply add *ed* to the present form to form the past tense or past participle. Some irregular verbs change substantially in their past tense or past participle forms.

Present	Past	Past Participle
do	did	done
go	went	gone
ring	rang	rung
take	took	taken
choose	chose	chosen

COMPARE:

I *do* that today.	I *did* that yesterday.	I *have done* that many times.
I *go* today.	I *went* yesterday.	I *have gone* many times.
I *ring* it today.	I *rang* it yesterday.	I *have rung* it many times.
I *take* it today.	I *took* it yesterday.	I *have taken* it many times.
I *choose* today.	I *chose* yesterday.	I *have chosen* many times.

Remember, the past tense does not use a helper such as *has* or *have* or *had,* but, the past participle always has a helper.

There are a number of irregular verbs in English, and if you are in doubt about the proper form to use, consult a dictionary. Errors in verb form may brand you as a careless or ineffective writer. To help you avoid that label, we include here some common irregular verbs with their present, past, and past participle forms. The present participle form is merely the present form plus *ing* (beginn*ing*, bit*ing*, blow*ing*, break*ing*).

COMMONLY USED IRREGULAR VERBS

Present	Past	Past Participle
am, are, is	was, were	been
begin	began	begun
bite	bit	bitten
blow	blew	blown
break	broke	broken
bring	brought	brought
buy	bought	bought
catch	caught	caught
do	did	done
draw	drew	drawn
drink	drank	drunk
drive	drove	driven
eat	ate	eaten
fall	fell	fallen
fly	flew	flown
forget	forgot	forgotten
freeze	froze	frozen
get	got	got (gotten)
give	gave	given
go	went	gone
grow	grew	grown
hide	hid	hidden
hold	held	held
hurt	hurt	hurt
keep	kept	kept
know	knew	known
lay	laid	laid
leave	left	left
lend	lent	lent
lie	lay	lain
pay	paid	paid
ride	rode	ridden
ring	rang	rung
rise	rose	risen
run	ran	run

see	saw	seen
set	set	set
shake	shook	shaken
sing	sang	sung
sit	sat	sat
speak	spoke	spoken
steal	stole	stolen
swim	swam	swum
take	took	taken
teach	taught	taught
tear	tore	torn
throw	threw	thrown
wear	wore	worn
write	wrote	written ☑

Self-Check Exercise 3

Write the past tense and past participle of each of the following verbs. You will want to check your answers against those in the key.

1. tear   I _____ it yesterday.   I have _____ it many times.

2. pay   I _____ yesterday.   I have _____ many times.

3. leave   I _____ yesterday.   I have _____ many times.

4. tape   I _____ it yesterday.   I have _____ it many times.

5. wear   I _____ it yesterday.   I have _____ it many times.

6. travel   I _____ yesterday.   I have _____ many times.

7. telephone   I _____ yesterday.   I have _____ many times.

8. clean   I _____ yesterday.   I have _____ many times.

9. write   I _____ yesterday.   I have _____ many times.

10. sing   I _____ yesterday.   I have _____ many times.

11. teach   I _____ yesterday.   I have _____ many times.

12. cook   I _____ yesterday.   I have _____ many times.

TROUBLESOME VERBS

There are a few verb pairs and combinations that pose particular problems for writers. We shall examine four. Knowing when to use each of them will help you make your writing more precise and easier to understand.

SET VERSUS SIT

Set means to place an object somewhere; *sit* means to be seated.

Present	Past	Past Participle	Present Participle
set	set	set	setting
sit	sat	sat	sitting

USE I *set* the table today.
Yesterday I *set* the table.
I *have set* the table every Thanksgiving.
I *am setting* the table.

Set is a transitive verb—it requires an object.

USE I *sit* down every day.
Yesterday I *sat* down.
I *have sat* on that bench every day this week.
I *am sitting* down.

Sit is an intransitive verb—it does not take an object. The *i* in *sit* will remind you that it is intransitive. Intransitive verbs do not take objects.

LAY VERSUS LIE

Lay means to put down; *lie* means to rest in a prone position.

Present	Past	Past Participle	Present Participle
lay	laid	laid	laying
lie	lay	lain	lying

USE I *lay* the parcels down carefully.
I *laid* the parcels down carefully yesterday.
I *have laid* the parcels down carefully always.
I *am laying* the parcels down now.

Lay is a transitive verb; it requires an object.

USE I *lie* down every afternoon.
Yesterday I *lay* down early.
I *have lain* down daily.
I *am lying* down at presnt.

Lie is an intransitive verb. The *i* in *lie* will help you remember that it is intransitive. It does not take an object.

RAISE VERSUS RISE

Raise means to lift; *rise* means to get up.

Present	Past	Past Participle	Present Participle
raise	raised	raised	raising
rise	rose	risen	rising

USE I *raise* the flag every day.
Yesterday I *raised* the flag.
I *have raised* the flag every day for the past week.
I *am raising* the flag.

Raise is a transitive verb, requiring an object.

USE The sun *rises* early.
Yesterday it *rose* later.
I *have risen* early to see the sunrise.
I *am rising* earlier these days.

Rise is an intransitive verb; it does not require an object. The *i* in *rise* will help you remember this.

BOUGHT VERSUS BROUGHT

Bought means purchased; *brought* means carried.

Present	Past	Past Participle	Present Participle
buy	bought	bought	buying
bring	brought	brought	bringing

USE I *buy* my food at the market.
Yesterday I *bought* V-8 juice.
I have *bought* new shoes.
I *am buying* an antique desk.

The above sentences refer to *purchasing*. The following sentences refer to *carrying*.

USE I *bring* regards from your cousin to you.
Yesterday I *brought* the data with me.
I have *brought* my textbooks with me.
I *am bringing* up this matter because of its importance. ☑

SUMMARY

We have reviewed many verb characteristics. We explained that *nonaction* verbs express a condition or a state of being. *Action* verbs express action, of course, and *helping* verbs combine with other verbs to form verb phrases. Then the principal parts of regular and irregular verbs were explained, and the pitfalls of using helpers with past tense forms pointed out. Lastly, we reviewed common trouble spots in the selection of verbs—incorrectly using *of* instead of *have* or mixing up *lay/lie, sit/set, raise/rise,* or *bought/brought.*

Why devote an entire chapter reviewing verbs? Because, as you learned on the first page of this chapter, verbs are very important; they give your writing meaning and direction. Their precise use must be mastered by all who aspire to be effective writers.

Fortunately, you will have another opportunity to reinforce your correct use of verbs. In Chapter 9 we shall study verbs as *predicates*; this parts-of-sentence analysis will be equally helpful.

Self-Check Exercise 4

Select the correct one in each pair of troublesome verbs in the following sentences. The correct answers appear in the key.

1. _____ the books on the left-hand corner of the shelf. (set, sit)

2. I will _____ down on the couch for a short nap. (lay, lie)

3. Please do not _____ your voice in front of the children. (raise, rise)

4. Alton was glad that he had _____ his school supplies while they were still on sale. (bought, brought)

5. Don't worry! I will be able to _____ while I am waiting for you. (set, sit)

6. The chicken _____ her eggs yesterday. (laid, lay)

7. The water on the riverbank _____ as a result of the recent heavy rainfall. (raised, rose)

8. They had _____ attention to their cause by picketing the food market. (bought, brought)

APPLICATION EXERCISES

A. Put *true* or *false* in the blank at the left of each sentence.

_____ 1. Past tense verbs should always be preceded by a *helping* verb.

_____ 2. The third principal part of the verb is its *past participle*.

_____ 3. Verbs give meaning and direction to sentences.

_____ 4. The word *of* is often an acceptable substitute for *have* in verb phrases like *could of done*.

_____ 5. Irregular verbs form the past by adding *ed* to the present form.

_____ 6. One function of a verb is to express state of being.

_____ 7. *Has* can be both a helping verb and an action verb.

_____ 8. All written sentences should have a verb.

_____ 9. Helping verbs do not always need to have a verb to help.

_____ 10. One example of a *to be* verb is *could*.

B. Complete the following table of principal parts of verbs.

Present	Past	Past Participle
1. _____	did	_____
2. go	_____	_____
3. rise	_____	_____
4. _____	_____	eaten
5. _____	blew	_____
6. _____	_____	paid
7. _____	swam	_____
8. ring	_____	_____
9. sing	_____	_____
10. bring	_____	_____
11. _____	fired	_____

12. _____ _____ chosen

13. _____ _____ called

14. study   _____ _____

15. has   _____ _____

16. _____ _____ grown

17. _____ took   _____

18. hurt   _____ _____

19. _____ broke   _____

20. _____ designed   _____

21. _____ caught   _____

22. _____ rode   _____

23. hide   _____ _____

24. _____ gave   _____

25. _____ froze   _____

C. Pick out the helping verbs in the following sentences, and write them on the line. If there are no helping verbs, write *none* on the line.

1. The local high school can clinch the title. _____

2. There have been more than 30 heart transplants locally. _____

3. The nurse had gone out of her way for her aged patient. _____

4. Some descendants of Massachusetts settlers have traced their roots. _____

5. I am budgeting an extra $2,000 for next year. _____

6. John Moore might be unanimously voted in. _____

7. Toll Brothers had complained about the competition. _____

8. The stockbrokers were not at Tuesday's meeting. _____

9. Geraldine Brooks had the flu and a pulled muscle at the same time. _____

10. The new technology should be helpful. _____

D. In the following sentences you will find some errors in verb form. Encircle the errors in the sentences and write the corrections on the corresponding lines. If there is no error, write *C* on the line.

1. I choose the members of the team last week.   _____

2. Was that the telephone that rung?   _____

3. They claim that they seen every Diane Keaton film.   _____

4. I was carried away from the scene by a fireman.   _____

5. He had went to Florida before the semester started.   _____

6. She could of won that contest easily.   _____

7. He lays on the couch to take a nap.   _____

8. The stock prices raised yesterday.   _____

9. She is lying down to test our new mattress.   _____

10. The temperature should be rising gradually.   _____

11. I have sat the kitten in her litter box.   _____

12. She is setting the cleaning supplies on the shelf.   _____

13. I have bought my textbooks here to study.   _____

14. He could of failed to submit the bids on time.   _____

15. I know I should of went when I had the chance.   _____

16. Jeremy had wore his new sweater to the fraternity party.   _____

17. The secretaries thrown out the party favors.   _____

18. The sun had risen about 6:30 a.m.   _____

19. I swum that pool in record time.   _____

20. Last week I bought the data to the statistician.   _____

21. I have rose early to see the sunrise.   _____

22. They had paid $50 for the appliance.   _____

23. George Blank had forgot Mary Bergen's first name   _____

24. She certainly has grown.   _____

25. They have broke their promises to their parents.   _____

Challenge Exercise

Write a concise sentence for each of the following verbs.

1. hurt (past tense) _____

   _____

2. might not have _____

   _____

3. drive (future tense) _____

   _____

4. shall do _____

   _____

5. would translate _____

   _____

6. will be keyboarded _____

   _____

7. might have been _____

   _____

8. catch (past participle) _____

   _____

9. begin (present participle) _____

   _____

10. should have known _____

    _____

11. must be _____

    _____

12. were being _____

_____

13. feel (action verb) _____

_____

14. have (action verb) _____

_____

15. could have managed. _____

_____

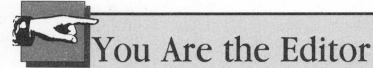

You Are the Editor

In the letter that follows there are some errors you should try to correct. Many of
them involve verbs, but watch for errors involving nouns and pronouns, also.

HOWARD INDUSTRIES, INC.

82 FRONTAGE ROAD   FAIRFIELD, CONNECTICUT 06437   (203) 480-6995

December 1, 198_

Mr. Richard Clark
2386 Overton Drive
Stamford, CN 06903

Dear Mr. Clark:

It must of seemed especially careless when you did not receive an

answer to you're letter of October 3. Its company policy to answer

such letters as soon as possible, and I apologize for not answering

your's. I suspect that your letter must of went to the wrong

department instead of directly to Mr. Carlos Alvarez, who should of

answered it hisself. Mr. Alvarez and myself will answer it now.

Your letter concerns the two part's you ordered for your lawn mower.

The larger of these two parts is, you had wrote, still too small to

fit your machine. This problem would not of occurred had you bought

your machine to our plant--Fairfield is only a few miles from

Stamford--or if one of our servicemen could have drove to your

house.   Then we could of done the work ourself and saved you the
trouble.

You see, Mr. Clark, we made two models like the one you own.   The
smaller of these two models is the one that fit the replacement
parts.   Those parts, however, are too small for your mower, which is
the larger of the two model's.   If you will return those parts, we
will have the correct ones sent to you immediately.

Cordially,

E. L. Langston, President

Key to Self-Check Exercises

Exercise 1

1. action
2. action
3. action
4. state of being
5. condition
6. state of being
7. action
8. state of being
9. action
10. condition
11. state of being
12. state of being

Exercise 2

Main Verb	Helper(s)
1. studied	had
failed	
2. participated	
3. observed	
4. been	might have
5. is	
6. lecturing	am
7. spoken	should have
8. hire	cannot
keep	will
9. attending	is
10. helped	have
11. trying	were

Exercise 3

	Past Tense	Past Participle
1.	tore	torn
2.	paid	paid
3.	left	left
4.	taped	taped
5.	wore	worn
6.	traveled	traveled
7.	telephoned	telephoned
8.	cleaned	cleaned
9.	wrote	written
10.	sang	sung
11.	taught	taught
12.	cooked	cooked

Exercise 4

1. Set
2. lie
3. raise
4. bought
5. sit
6. laid
7. rose
8. brought

A DYNAMIC BUSINESS VOCABULARY

Here is a new list of vocabulary words. Study their definitions and uses in sentences.

CRT

An abbreviation for cathode ray tube, which is similar to a display screen and usually accompanies a keyboard through which information is entered into a computer.

Many help-wanted ads call for experienced CRT operators to perform data-entry functions.

Cursor

A blinking indicator on a CRT that shows the user where the next character will be inserted.

To revise her printed copy, the word-processing operator had to move the cursor down seven lines.

Data

Information gathered for analysis or presentation; information given to or received from a computer. (*Data* takes a plural verb.)

In preparation for year-end analysis, data were collected for examination by the accountants.

Data base

A collection of similar or related information (data).

The data base includes the sales figures for 1985–87.

Debt

A financial obligation, as in money owed to someone.

The firm's debt became so large, we felt an investment in the organization would not be wise.

Decision making

The process of reaching decisions on the basis of facts, figures, and experience.

Accurate decision making is absolutely vital if a manager is to advance in his or her firm.

Deed

A written document that establishes ownership of property.

When Glen bought his first home, he was handed a deed to his property.

Defalcation

A form of embezzlement in which an individual cannot account for money that was left in his or her keeping.

The defalcation of funds was so large, we had no recourse except to prosecute him.

THE ABC'S OF BUSINESS VOCABULARY

Test your knowledge of the business terms you have studied thus far by completing the following exercise. If a refresher is needed, refer to the previous Dynamic Business Vocabularies.

1. Compose three short sentences using the following terms: (a) CPU, (b) deed, (c) affidavit.

_____

_____

_____

_____

_____

_____

2. A form of stealing in which people cannot account for money for which they are responsible is (a) thievery, (b) defalcation, (c) absconding, (d) burglary.

3. A blinking indicator on a CRT that shows where the next character will appear is a/an (a) asterisk, (b) arrow, (c) cursor, (d) plus sign.

4. To make payment over a specified period of time on a loan is to (a) amortize, (b) distribute, (c) scatter, (d) solidify.

5. An impartial party attempts to settle differences between other people at what type of hearing? (a) debate, (b) arbitration, (c) lecture, (d) official.

6. The definition of the noun *debt* is _____

_____

7. The meaning of the noun *data* is _____

_____

8. Define the adjective *bankrupt*. _____

_____

9. The noun *budget* means _____

_____

7 Parts of Speech
Adjectives and Adverbs

ADJECTIVES

Adjectives are words that modify nouns or noun substitutes. *Modify* means "change," "describe," or "define." Note how different adjectives change the word *job*:

| an *exciting* job | an *important* job | a *tedious* job |
| a *boring* job | a *new* job | a *challenging* job |

Adjectives usually tell one of three things about the nouns they modify:

1. They tell *which*: *this* job, *those* promotions, *either* approach.

2. They tell *how many*: *four* reports, *many* copies, *few* returns.

3. They tell *what kind*: *new* appointment, *rapid* advancement, *superb* plan.

SOME SPECIAL ADJECTIVES

ARTICLES

The words *a, an,* and *the* are adjectives that are usually referred to as *articles. The* is placed before a noun to designate that the noun is specific, rather than general.

The boy [a specific boy]
The box [a specific box]
The school [a specific school]

A is placed before a noun to designate that the noun is general, rather than specific.

A computer [not any one in particular]
A telephone call [not a specific one]
A report [not any one in particular]

For ease in pronunciation, *a* changes to *an* when it precedes a noun or noun substitute that begins with the sound of a vowel.

a unique situation [*unique* begins with the sound of the consonant *y.*]
a unit [*unit* also begins with the sound of the consonant *y.*]
a unified decision
an honorable person [*honorable* begins the sound of a vowel since the *h* is silent.]
a humorous person
a lively child
an inkling
an ordinary man

Note: The words *that, those, this,* and *these* also function as adjectives when they are used as definite articles before nouns to call attention to specific persons or things. Consider the following:

that book   *this* word processor
those people   *these* records

NOUNS AND PRONOUNS USED AS ADJECTIVES

When words such as *Philadelphia, secretary,* and *Mary* precede and describe other nouns, they serve as adjectives instead of nouns. Sometimes they assume a slightly different appearance:

Mary's blouse is attractive. [possessive adjective]

She has a *Philadelphia* accent. [*Philadelphia* is an adjective here.]

The *secretary's* job is different. [*Secretary's* is an adjective.]

Philadelphia's Society Hill has been restored. [*Philadelphia's* is an adjective.]

The possessive pronouns *my, your, his, her, its, our,* and *their* serve as adjectives when they precede and describe nouns:

That is *my* assignment.

Where was *its* cover?

Do you know *our* problem?

Is *her* project completed?

By now you may have discovered that the same word can be used as more than one part of speech. Note these examples:

Lynn's *concrete* suggestions helped greatly. [adjective]
Lynn works in a plant that makes *concrete.* [noun]

Her problem is oversupply. [adjective]
The manager fired *her.* [pronoun]

Those invoices are incomplete. [adjective]
Those are incomplete. [pronoun]

Be especially careful with pronouns that can be used as adjectives. Note these examples:

Those books are fine. [adjective]   *Those* are fine. [pronoun]

The boss liked *her* work. [adjective]   The boss liked *her.* [pronoun]

If a noun is being modified (those books, her work), it is safe to consider the modifier an adjective. Shifts from one part of speech to another, although confusing, should not cause you any communication problem.

COMPARISON OF REGULAR ADJECTIVES

Regular adjectives have a characteristic called *degree.* Consider these examples:

Positive Degree (describes one thing)	Comparative Degree (describes two things)	Superlative Degree (describes three or more things)
big box	*bigger* of the two	*biggest* of all
quick recipe	*quicker* of the two	*quickest* of all
beautiful baby	*more beautiful* than the other one	*most beautiful* of all

beautiful scenery	*less beautiful* than the other	*least beautiful* of all
efficient worker	*more efficient* than the other one	*most efficient* of all
conscientious student	*less conscientious* than the other one	*least conscientious* of all

The change in the form of adjectives is called *comparison*. On what basis do you select the positive degree? the comparative degree? the superlative degree?

When describing one item, use the positive degree.

When describing two items, use the comparative degree. [*-er* or *more* OR *-er* or *less*]

When describing three or more items, use the superlative degree. [*-est* or *most* OR *-est* or *least*]

Thus:

a *sound* proposition [one item]

the *sounder* of two propositions [two items]

the *soundest* of three propositions [three or more items]

Or:

Mark is *smart*. [one person]

Helen is *smarter* than Toby. [two people]

Gretchen is the *smartest* girl in the class. [three or more people] ☑

HELPFUL GUIDELINES

To make wise decisions about the use of *-er* or *more* for comparing two items and *-est* or *most* for comparing three or more items, follow these guidelines:

WITH ONE SYLLABLE
Most adjectives of *one syllable* use *-er* and *-est*, rather than *more* and *most*.

Positive Degree (one thing)	Comparative Degree (two things)	Superlative Degree (three or more)
loud noise	*louder* of two noises	*loudest* of all
soft cloth	*softer* of two cloths	*softest* of all
fast race	*faster* of two races	*fastest* of all
slow turtle	*slower* of two turtles	*slowest* of all

WITH THREE OR MORE SYLLABLES
Most adjectives of *three or more syllables* use *more* and *most*, rather than *-er* and *-est*.

Positive Degree (one thing)	Comparative Degree (two things)	Superlative Degree (three or more)
punctual student	*more punctual* than another	*most punctual* of all
irresponsible relative	*more irresponsible* than he	*most irresponsible* of all
responsible worker	*more responsible* than he	*most responsible* of all
reliable carpenter	*more reliable* than he	*most reliable* of all

WITH TWO SYLLABLES

Adjectives with *two syllables* use either *-er* and *-est* or are preceded by *more* and *most*. Select the combination that sounds the more natural to you; check your dictionary if in doubt.

Positive Degree	**Comparative Degree**	**Superlative Degree**
forthright statesman	*more forthright* than another	*most forthright* of all
greedy youngster	*greedier* than another	*greediest* of all
pleasant nurse	*more pleasant* than another	*most pleasant* of all
lively dance	*livelier* than another	*liveliest* of all

AN OVERALL LOOK

COMPARE WITH	*clean* room *reasonable* reply	*cleaner* of the two *more reasonable* of the two	*cleanest* of all *most reasonable* of all
COMPARE WITH	*sweet* fudge *permanent* job	*sweeter* of the two *more permanent* of the two	*sweetest* of all *most permanent* of all
COMPARE WITH	*tall* building *reputable* firm	*taller* of the two *more reputable* of the two	*tallest* of all *most reputable* of all

Self-Check Exercise 1

Examine the following sentences and underline all the adjectives. The answers appear in the key.

1. The table lost its leg when Abel fell on it.

2. Once a motivated person learns to study, he or she will continue studying for life.

3. A summary of ideas is what an ambitious manager needs.

4. Ms. Johnson's report was sent to the vice president.

5. Their branches lost their colorful leaves in early fall.

6. The museum offered $5,000 for the oil painting.

7. My aunt's vase is an antique.

8. Mary and John Ross's daughter is a brilliant pianist.

9. Where is your budget?

10. That computer is a help to the accountants in Brian Scott's office.

AVOIDING DOUBLE COMPARISONS

Do not combine *more* and *-er* in comparative degree. Use one or the other, but do not use both forms together. ☑

DON'T SAY	USE
more better	better
more sweeter	sweeter

Also, do not combine *most* and *-est* in superlative degree. Select one or the other, but do not use both forms together.

DON'T SAY	USE
most loudest	loudest
most safest	safest

IRREGULAR ADJECTIVES

Certain comparisons are *irregular*; that is, they do not conform to the usual pattern of adding *-er* or *more* for comparative and *-est* or *most* for superlative. Consider this list:

Self-Check Exercise 2

Circle the correct word(s) from each pair in the following sentences. The key provides the answers.

1. There is apt to be (an, a) union decrease before long.

2. They requested (an, a) humble opinion from the pastor.

3. The pastor preferred to offer (an, a) honest opinion on the matter.

4. Elwood Blackwood is (an, a) heir to his uncle's estate.

5. They will televise the debate in (an, a) hour.

6. That tool is the (most handiest) (handiest) (more handier) (handier) of the two.

7. That was clearly the (most hard, hardest) exam I have ever taken.

8. My feelings were (more intense, most intense) than hers.

9. She was (most frightened, more frightened) when she had to present the speech than when she submitted the paper to the panel.

10. She is the (most pleasant, pleasantest) nurse in the clinic.

good statement	*better* than another	*best* of all
bad apple	*worse* than another	*worst* of all
little amount	*less* than another	*least* of all
many items	*more* than another	*most* of all
much pepper	*more* than another	*most* of all

Note: To form the comparisons of some regular adjectives, it may be necessary to alter the spelling slightly. Consider these examples:

big	bigger	biggest
lucky	luckier	luckiest
far	farther	farthest

Consult your dictionary if you have questions about the spelling.

ABSOLUTE ADJECTIVES

Some adjectives do not have degrees as they are already at the limit of their potential quality. Examples are *perfect, square, complete, unique, full,* and *round.* How can one thing be more perfect than another if perfection means "the best something can be"? With words like these, we often use the terms "more nearly" and "most nearly." Examples include the following:

Her plan is the *most nearly perfect* of the many submitted.

That yard is *more nearly square* than the one next door.

This diamond is *more nearly round* than that one.

Jack's project is *more nearly complete* than mine.

My clothes hamper is *more nearly full* than Jan's.

PLACEMENT OF ADJECTIVES

Finally, adjectives usually appear directly before the nouns or pronouns they modify:

The *new fast-food* restaurant was a *surprising* success.

Four typing errors in a *short* letter disqualified her.

Of all the *tennis* players, he is the *fastest* (one).

But sometimes adjectives are better used *after* the words they modify. Consider these sentences:

Nelson's memorandum—*forceful, persuasive,* and *articulate*—made us all consider our work.

Nelson's memorandum was *forceful, persuasive,* and *articulate.* It made us all consider our work.

Note: The adjectives in the second sentence are called *predicate adjectives,* a term we shall explain in the section on parts of sentences.

Which sentence you favor is largely a matter of personal preference. You should, though, think of moving adjectives around for emphasis and variety. ☑

ADVERBS

Like adjectives, adverbs modify or describe. An adverb describes an action verb, an adjective, or another adverb. Typically, an adverb answers one of the following questions:

1. How? He typed the report *correctly.*

2. When? He typed the report *yesterday.*

3. Where? He typed the report *here.*

4. How often? He typed the report *twice.*

5. To what extent? He typed the report *extremely* rapidly. [Frequently adverbs that tell *to what extent* are used to modify other adverbs; in this instance, *extremely* modifies *rapidly.*]

Note: Most adverbs end in -*ly* but not all of them. On the other hand, a few adjectives (e.g., brother*ly,* cost*ly,* time*ly*) end in -*ly.*

Note the -*ly* endings in the following adverbs:

Adjectives	**Adverbs**
stylish dress	She dressed *stylishly.*
intelligent answer	He answered *intelligently.*
articulate speech	They spoke *articulately.*

Self-Check Exercise 3

Complete the following exercise to test your ability to recognize correct adjective forms. Your answers may be checked with the key.

1. She is the (thinner, thinnest) of the two girls.

2. The three boys are the (most happy, happiest) children I have ever seen.

3. He is the (more capable, most capable) of her two brothers.

4. This is the (baddest, worst) predicament I have ever experienced.

5. I would like the (littlest, least) amount.

6. She is the (littlest, least) girl in the kindergarten class.

7. In comparing the two projects, this one is (more complete, more nearly complete).

8. Katrina's suitcase was (fuller, more nearly full) than Elvis's.

9. Of the four jobs available, this one is the (more interesting, most interesting) of them all.

10. That is the (more pointless, more nearly pointless) of the two suggestions.

USES OF ADVERBS

TO MODIFY ACTION VERBS

The following sentences illustrate the use of adverbs to modify action verbs. Remember that adverbs are *not* used after linking verbs. *Adjectives* follow linking verbs.

I will calculate this *correctly*. [How?]
[*Calculate* is the verb; *correctly* is the adverb.]

He should arrive *early*. [When?]
[*Should arrive* is the verb; *early* is the adverb.]

They are skiing *here*. [Where?]
[*Are skiing* is the verb; *here* is the adverb.]

John has written *twice*. [How often?]
Has written is the verb; *twice* is the adverb.]

TO MODIFY ADJECTIVES

In the following sentences there are adverbs that modify adjectives:

The cake he baked was *very* good. [To what extent?]
[*Very* is the adverb modifying the adjective *good.*]

She was *quite* assertive. [To what extent?]
[*Quite* is the adverb; *assertive* is the adjective.]

Our meeting was *purely* coincidental. [To what extent?]
[*Purely* is the adverb modifying the adjective coincidental.]

This model appears to be *slightly* smaller. [To what extent?]
[*Slightly* is the adverb modifying the adjective *smaller.*]

TO MODIFY OTHER ADVERBS

Adverbs frequently modify other adverbs. Note these examples:

The soprano sang *very* beautifully. [To what extent?]
The adverb *very* modifies the adverb *beautifully.*]

She did her work *too* quickly. [To what extent?]
[The adverb *too* modifies the adverb *quickly.*]

TO ACCOMPANY VERB PHRASES

Occasionally an adverb is found in the middle of a verb phrase. Often students incorrectly designate the adverb as a verb helper instead of realizing that it is an adverb used with verb phrases. Note these examples:

Adverb	Verb Phrase Plus Adverb	Verb Phrase Alone
never	have *never* smoked	have smoked
always	had *always* visited	had visited
rarely	have *rarely* participated	have participated
already	has *already* ordered	has ordered

COMPARISON OF ADVERBS

Like adjectives, adverbs can be compared with positive, comparative, and superlative degrees. Look at the following:

Positive	Comparative	Superlative
closely knit	*more closely* knit than another	*most closely* knit of all
	less closely knit than another	*least closely* knit of all

clearly written	*more clearly* written than another	*most clearly* written of all
arrive soon	arrive *sooner* than another	arrive *soonest* of all
acted *greedily*	acted *more greedily* than another	acted *most greedily* of all
typed *fast**	typed *faster* than another	typed *fastest* of all

Note: Just like adjectives, some adverbs show comparison by using -*er* and others are preceded by *more.* Also, some superlatives use -*est* and others are preceded by *most.* Use your judgment to select the most natural form. ☑

SPECIAL ADVERBS

ALMOST

Do not confuse the adverb *almost,* which means *very nearly,* with the adjective *most,* which means *a majority of:*

We are *almost* finished. [very nearly]

They *almost* finished their work. [very nearly]

Most of the book is finished. [a majority of]

Almost all the book is completed. [very nearly]

Self-Check Exercise 4

Underline the adverbs in the following sentences. Then indicate which of the following questions the adverbs answer: how? when? where? how often? to what extent?

1. The tenor sang very forcefully.

2. The attorney was quite right.

3. Marshall plans to attend the meeting soon.

4. The committee members met here.

5. Lana presented her case once before the panel.

6. Don't wait for me; I will eat later.

7. The new accountant audited the books very carefully.

8. They always complain.

9. The photographer's prints were clearly developed.

10. Let's discuss this matter tomorrow.

*The word *fast,* of course, functions as an adjective as well as an adverb. He is a *fast* worker. [adjective] He typed the report *fast.* [adverb]

SURELY

Do not confuse the adverb *surely*, which means *certainly*, with the adjective *sure*, which means *positive*:

> We will *surely* finish the book. [certainly]
>
> *Surely*, you can understand that. [certainly]
>
> Are you *sure*? [positive]

REALLY

Do not confuse the adverb *really*, which means *very*, with the adjective *real*, which means *genuine*.

> We are *really* pleased with the results. [very]
>
> He is *really* thin. [very]
>
> Is this *real*? [genuine]

ONLY

Exercise care in your use of *only* as an adverb, making sure that you use it as logically as you can. Consider these two sentences:

> Wilson *only* has four sales.
>
> Wilson has *only* four sales.

Clearly, the position of *only* in the second example is preferred, as it is nearer the adjective it modifies (*four*). Another reason to be careful with your placement of *only* in a sentence is that it can alter the meaning you convey. Consider these sentences:

> *Only* I prepared the material for the advertisement. [No one else helped me. I did it alone.]
>
> I *only* prepared the material for the advertisement. [I did not do other things, such as calling the paper to arrange for the date the ad would be placed.]
>
> I prepared *only* the material for the advertisement. [I did not prepare anything else.]

When you use *only*, be careful where you place it in a sentence.

VERY

Very is a very overworked word in the English language. Very many people very often cannot write very much without using this word very extensively. Although this practice is not very wrong, it can be very annoying and can make your writing appear very immature and very unpolished.

You get the point.

BADLY

Many people also tend to use the adverb *badly* incorrectly, especially with the verb *feel*. If *feel* were an action verb describing the act of sensing with your fingers, then *badly* would correctly describe how inept your sensing was. Of course, this is rarely what we mean when we use the word *feel*. The common use of *feel* is in sentences such as these:

> I feel bad about her illness.
>
> I feel bad about her moving.
>
> I feel bad about her misfortune.

These sentences are correct; *feel* functions as a linking verb, which takes an adjective (*bad*), not an adverb (*badly*).

NEVER OR NOT

Both *never* and *not* are adverbs that denote a negative situation, but they should not be used interchangeably. Use *not* in short-term negative instances; use *never* when *not ever* is meant:

> I have *never* smoked. [not ever]
>
> She has *not* arrived. [not yet]
>
> The politician says that Ronald Jameson will *never* be elected. [not ever]
>
> Maureen had *not* met the company comptroller. [not yet]

NOUNS USED AS ADVERBS

In this chapter we have already discussed how certain words can function as more than one part of speech. As a matter of fact, it is not unusual for nouns to be used as adverbs. Consider the following sentences:

> Diane worked *yesterday*. [*Yesterday* both names a time and tells *when*.]
>
> Tom went *home*. [*Home* both names a place and tells *where*.]
>
> They were skiing *Saturday*. [*Saturday* both names a day and tells *when*.]

Self-Check Exercise 5

Select the correct adjective or adverb to complete each of the following sentences, and then check your solutions with the key.

1. Mary said, "At the flea market, you can get a (real good, really good) bargain."

2. It appears to me that he (reads slowly, reads slow).

3. Don't talk so (quick, quickly).

4. He stared (suspiciously, suspicious) at the newcomers.

5. He loved his parents (deep, deeply).

6. Please do your work (silently, silent).

7. We felt (bad, badly) about her unsuccessful heart surgery.

8. The committee members had (never, not) arrived by ten o'clock.

9. The new typist works (good, well).

10. The doctors have finished (most, almost) all their rounds by now.

APPLICATION EXERCISES

A. Use the material in this chapter to answer the questions below.

_____ 1. *Three* is an adjective that answers what question?

_____ 2. What is the comparative form of the adjective *big*?

_____ 3. The superlative form of adjectives is used to describe (a) one, (b) two, (c) three or more nouns.

_____ 4. True or false? *Very* is an adverb that many ineffective writers overuse.

_____ 5. Adverbs have no comparative degree. True or false?

_____ 6. Can nouns ever function as adverbs?

_____ 7. Do most adjectives end in *-ly*?

_____ 8. What is the comparative form of *many*?

_____ 9. What is the superlative form of the adjective *round*? (Be careful.)

_____ 10. *Least* is always the superlative form of *little*. True or false?

B. Put the correct form of the adjective in parentheses in the blank.

_____ 1. Toni's commission on the sale was (large) than Jennifer's.

_____ 2. I believe that the tax situation is the (bad) I have ever seen.

_____ 3. Juanita has told me that she is feeling much (good) than she felt yesterday.

_____ 4. The drawing submitted by John is certainly (beautiful) than the one Sammie turned in.

_____ 5. There were several ways to get to the convention, but the bus was the (cheap).

_____ 6. The firm enjoyed a (huge) increase in sales.

_____ 7. Certainly Sharon did (perfect) typing than Janice. (Be careful.)

_____ 8. Alfonso's absence from the office is the (little) of my many worries. (The answer is *not* "littlest.")

_____ 9. He is the (exasperating) employee the firm has ever had.

_____ 10. Rhonda completed (many) worksheets than any other typist.

C. In the following sentences the adverbs are italicized. In the space after each sentence, write the word it modifies and whether it tells *how, where, when* or *to what extent*. Study the sample sentence.

Sentence	Word Modified	What Adverb Tells
Example: Jones typed *quickly*.	typed	how

1. You must work *tomorrow*.

2. He was *exceedingly* brave.

3. Susan left *home*.

4. Irene worked *slowly*.

5. Alfredo struggled *mightily*.

6. I had seen the report *before*.

7. Come *early* to get a good seat.

8. Your project is *quite* expensive.

9. Speak *softly* during a job interview.

10. He left *there* in a huff.

D. Find all the adjectives in the following sentences. Then tell which words the adjectives modify and what questions the adjectives answer (which, how many, what kind). Again, study the example.

Sentence	Adjective	Word Modified	Question Answered
Example: The store hoped for few returns.	the few	store returns	which how many

1. This itinerary will keep the salesman out of town for three weeks.

2. Those records should be duplicated for our accountant.

3. Give the proctor your finished math test.

4. A computer was first on her Christmas list.

5. Can you name someone whom you consider to be an honorable person?

6. He delivered the report pages with great speed.

7. Adam Henderson has spoken on that topic many times.

8. This situation is truly unique.

9. The security guard yearned for an unusual development in the job.

10. The audience thought they were forceful and inspiring.

E. In the space above each italicized word, tell what part of speech it is.

Both *Julio* and Rita *believed* that Carson Electronics was an *ideal* place for *them* to work. Julio *liked his* position in the *shipping* department. There *he* took charge of most of the recordkeeping about the *products* Carson *shipped daily.* The work *required skill,* but *it* was *very* rewarding. Rita *worked* in the *secretarial* pool. *She* was an *extremely efficient typist* and *knew* that her future with the company was a *bright* one. Together, Julio and Rita *formed* a *fine team* for Carson. *They hoped* to be able to remain with *Carson Electronics* until they were able to retire.

Challenge Exercise

Use the following adverbs and adjectives in short sentences.

1. bad (superlative) _____

_____

2. good (comparative) _____

_____

3. deteriorating _____

_____

4. complete (superlative—absolute adjective) _____

_____

5. full (comparative—absolute adjective) _____

_____

6. efficiently _____

_____

7. technical _____

_____

8. totally _____

_____

9. financial _____

_____

10. temporarily _____

_____

11. former _____

_____

12. industrial _____

_____

13. slyly _____

_____

14. improperly _____

_____

15. immediate _____

_____

You Are the Editor

The following letter has 26 errors, all of them underlined. Insert your corrections above the errors.

Wilson Plumbing
423 Center Street   Birmingham, Alabama 35203   (205) 427-8375

January 24, 198_

Mr. Carlos Rivera

651A San Ranch Drive

Birmingham, AL 35203

Dear Mr. Rivera:

We are in receipt of your courteous letter of January 16 about <u>ours</u> work on your house on January 7. The records of our <u>servicemen's</u> indicate that <u>there</u> efforts to fix your plumbing were the <u>better</u> ones of all our work that day. In fact, I was one of the <u>servicemen's</u> who worked on your house. Bob Nielsen was the other man <u>which</u> worked.

<u>Its</u> not <u>more correct</u> that we did not work on the pipes in the upstairs bathroom until after we worked in the kitchen. We went to the upstairs bathroom first because we knew water had leaked into the music room below and had damaged the two <u>pianoes</u> you have there. The pipes in that bathroom were the <u>most hardest</u> to repair. Bob and <u>myself</u> tried to fix <u>they're</u> leaks, and we believe we did the

perfectest job possible. When we finished, Bob hisself said that he thought our work was the better he had ever seen, and he has seen many jobs.

The kitchen pipes were not as seriously in need of repair, although Bob and I both shocked ourself when we failed to check the electrical cutoff before cleaning the water. (Its a good thing that plumber's, like cats, have nine lifes.) But we did fix the pipes and I think you will discover now that you have the efficientest plumbing system available to you.

That is why we are concerned about you're letter that complains about the work and it's cost. We discussed the matter with Mr. Jone's legal services, and he believes a more quicker solution can result if we discuss this with our lawyer and your's. Therefore, we shall place our file and your letter in the hands of our attornies'.

Cordially,

P. J. Wilson

Key to Self-Check Exercises

Exercise 1

1. The   its
2. a   motivated
3. A   an ambitious
4. Ms. Johnson's   the
5. Their   their colorful   early
6. The   the oil
7. My   aunt's   an
8. Mary   John Ross's   a brilliant
9. your
10. That   a   the   Brian Scott's

Exercise 2

1. a
2. a
3. an
4. an
5. an
6. handier
7. hardest
8. more intense
9. more frightened
10. most pleasant

Exercise 3

1. thinner
2. happiest
3. more capable
4. worst
5. least
6. littlest
7. more nearly complete
8. more nearly full
9. most interesting
10. more nearly pointless

Exercise 4

1. very (to what extent?)   forcefully (how?)
2. quite (to what extent?)
3. soon (when?)
4. here (where?)
5. once (how often?)
6. later (when?)
7. very (to what extent?)   carefully (how?)
8. always (how often?)
9. clearly (how?)
10. tomorrow (when?)

Exercise 5

1. really good
2. reads slowly
3. quickly
4. suspiciously
5. deeply
6. silently
7. bad
8. not
9. well
10. almost

A DYNAMIC BUSINESS VOCABULARY

To improve your vocabulary, study the spelling of these words, their definitions, and their use in sentences. In addition, check their pronunciation by referring to your handy dictionary.

Default

The failure to make payment on a debt

Donna and Mark were three months in default on their payment.

Defendant

A person who is sued by another (usually the plaintiff in the case).

Mike was the defendant in the divorce proceedings.

Deficit

The amount of money lacking in a financial obligation.

His account reflected a deficit of almost $10,000.

Defraud

To swindle someone out of what is his or hers.

Her effort to defraud the bank was quickly discovered.

Delinquent

Normally made in reference to a financial obligation that is overdue.

Joe Cannon's account was now delinquent.

Deposition

A written statement, as in testimony, to be used in court.

The deposition that was taken from the plaintiff was presented in court.

Depreciation

The reduction of purchasing power or value of property because of age.

The depreciation on the property came to almost $5,000 by the fifth year after purchase.

Depression

A failing economic condition characterized by unemployment, a lessening of buying power, and decreasing business activity.

The Great Depression caused thousands of small firms to go out of business.

THE ABC'S OF BUSINESS VOCABULARY

Check your knowledge of business vocabulary words by completing this exercise as quickly and accurately as you can.

1. A person who is sued by the plaintiff in a court case is the (a) subject, (b) complainer, (c) victim, (d) defendant.

2. The reduction of purchasing power or the value of property because of age is (a) shrinkage, (b) depreciation, (c) liability, (d) asset.

3. A legal action undertaken by one or more plaintiffs on behalf of themselves and all other persons having an identical interest in the alleged wrong leads to what kind of legal suit? (a) claim, (b) class-action, (c) defendant, (d) arbitration.

4. Rules and regulations governing an organization are (a) bylaws, (b) principles, (c) guidelines, (d) practices.

5. The definition of the noun *depression* as it pertains to business is _____

_____

6. The meaning of the adjective *delinquent* as it pertains to business is _____

_____

7. Define the noun *data base*. _____

_____

8. The noun *default* means _____

_____

9. Compose three short sentences using one of the following words in each sentence: (a) deficit, (b) data (plural noun), (c) collate.

_____

_____

_____

_____

_____

_____

8 Parts of Speech
Prepositions, Conjunctions, and Interjections

The remaining parts of speech to be examined are prepositions, conjunctions, and interjections. Interjections do not appear frequently in business communications, but the others are worth considerable study.

PREPOSITIONS

A preposition is a connecting word that is linked to a noun or pronoun to form a phrase. Though prepositions are typically small and easily overlooked, they create major differences in meaning. Consider these three sentences, exactly alike except for their prepositions:

John came to work *at* six o'clock.
John came to work *before* six o'clock.
John came to work *after* six o'clock.

The list below contains most of the commonly used prepositions. Refer to it frequently, as knowledge of prepositions can pay dividends in your ability to analyze sentences, write well, and avoid errors.

about	by	on
above	concerning	over
after	during	through
among	except	to
around	for	toward
at	from	under
before	in	until
below	into	up
beside	like	upon
between	of	with
but (meaning *except*)	off	without

Sometimes a group of words will function as a single preposition. Note the following examples:

on account of her illness   *in spite of* John's vacation
along with my report   *in regard to* the latest technology

Prepositions always introduce phrases, with a noun or noun substitute (such as a pronoun) serving as the *object* of the preposition, as in the following:

between us [*Between* is the preposition; *us* is the object.]
in the desk [*in* is the preposition; *desk* is the object.]
on the desk [*on* is the preposition; *desk* is the object.]
over the counter [*over* is the preposition; *counter* is the object.]
above the shelf [*above* is the preposition; *shelf* is the object.]

The noun or noun substitute is frequently modified by adjectives. Consider:

> on the student's desk [The preposition is *on*; the adjectives *the* and *student's* modify the noun *desk*.]
>
> in the mahogany box [*In* is the preposition; *the* and *mahogany* are the adjectives that modify the noun *box*.]

In the first phrase—*on the student's desk*—the preposition *(on)* plus its object *(desk)* plus the modifiers of that object *(the student's)* form the entire prepositional phrase. Likewise, in the second phrase—*in the mahogany box*—the preposition *(in)* plus its object *(box)* plus the modifiers of that object *(the mahogany)* form the prepositional phrase.

In the sentences that follow, the prepositional phrases are italicized:

> *After lunch* Robert filed the letters *from Durrell/in the yellow folder.* [This sentence has three prepositional phrases, each beginning with a preposition and ending with a noun.]
>
> *In spite of her misgivings,* Ruth hired the applicant *from the downtown employment agency/on Central Street.* [Three prepositional phrases.]
>
> *Over the river* and *through the woods/to Grandmother's house* we go. [Again, three prepositional phrases—each begins with a preposition and ends with a noun.] ☑

PROBLEMS WITH PREPOSITIONS

Certain prepositions have been known to cause problems. If you commit the following rules to memory, you can avoid making many errors.

Self-Check Exercise 1

Indicate the part of speech of every word in the following prepositional phrases. The key at the end of the chapter should be checked after you complete the exercise.

1. without cinnamon

2. until tomorrow

3. through the maze

4. into that showroom

5. during an executive board meeting

6. between the new computers

7. beside the circle

8. around a secretarial cubicle

9. below the small zero

10. above this conference room

BETWEEN, AMONG

Between is a preposition to be used to connect two—and only two—nouns or noun substitutes to the rest of the sentence. If you have three or more nouns or noun substitutes, use *among*. Note these examples:

The territory was divided *between* Helen and Susan, the two top salespersons. [two people]

Because all three had worked on the project, the bonus was divided *among* George, Carol, and Ramon. [three people]

You may recall that these two prepositions, *between* and *among,* were listed in Chapter 4 as words frequently misused.

OF

Be careful about routinely tacking on *of* after other words. Sometimes it belongs; sometimes it does not. Study these guidelines and the examples.

Inside, outside, top

Place the garbage *inside the container.* [Omit *of* after *inside.*]

She does extra work *outside the office.* [Omit *of* after *outside.*]

Place the Nelson file on *top of the filing cabinet.* [Correct use of *of.* It is correct to use *of* after *top.*]

All, both

Use *of* after *all* or *both* if the *of* is followed by a pronoun.

All *of* them are visiting us. [*Them* is a pronoun.]

Both *of* them are visiting us.

Omit *of* after *all* or *both* if the *of* is followed by a noun.

All the girls are visiting us. [NO *of*]

Both the girls are visiting us.

IN, INTO

In refers to position. *Into* refers to motion.

After the executive walked *into* the office, she looked *in* the file drawer.

I am going *into* the garage to look *in* the metal cabinet.

BESIDE, BESIDES

Beside means "next to" or "by the side of." *Besides* means "in addition to."

The clerk left his empty coffee pot on the table *beside* his desk. [next to]

The stock boy placed the milk coupon *beside* the cereal boxes. [next to]

Besides you, how many clerks will want to be off that day? [in addition to]

Who is attending the word-processing meeting *besides* you? [in addition to]

AT OR TO AFTER WHERE

Even careful speakers often say, "Where are you going to?" or "Where's it at?" *Where to* and *where at* expressions should not be used.

Where did the boss go *to*? [The *to* should be omitted as it is not needed.]

Where should I deliver the boxes *at*? [The *at* is incorrect.]

WITH REGARD TO, IN REGARD TO, AS REGARDS

Any one of these prepositions is correct. The problem with them occurs because careless speakers or writers use *regards* with *with* or *in,* as in this incorrect expression: "In regards to your request for a loan . . ." Remember: use *regards* only with *as.* You can remember this easily by noting that both words end in *-s*: a*s* regard*s*.

> *With regard to* this project, it should be finished soon.
> *In regard to* this project, it should be finished soon.
> *As regards* this project, it should be finished soon.

All three sentences are correct; therefore, any one of them could be included in an effective communication. You may use "with regard to" or "in regard to" or "as regards" in your writing.

OVER

People frequently say or write, "I can't wait to get this job over *with.*" The *with* is unnecessary. "*Over with*" should be avoided.

> I can't wait to get this job over. [NO *with*]
> When this job is over, I will be pleased. [NO *with*]

UP

Careless speakers frequently add *up* to other words, especially verbs, when it is unnecessary. Note these incorrect sentences:

> I will connect up this week's sales figures with last week's. [Omit *up.*]
> Hurry up! [Omit *up.*]

PREPOSITIONS WITH OTHER WORDS

Sometimes other words, usually verbs, require prepositions. Through frequent use, specific prepositions have been paired with specific words. Unfortunately, this popular usage brands someone who deviates from the norm as an incorrect writer or speaker.

Perhaps some day there will be more tolerance and flexibility in the pairing of prepositions with other words. For the time being, however, study the following items with their examples, and use them in your communications.

1. Agree *to* (rules or procedures): The owners agreed to the demands of the workers.
   Agree *upon* (a plan): The workers agreed upon the proposal they would submit.
   Agree *with* (a person): The chief negotiator agreed with the workers.

2. Angry *at* (a situation or condition; not a person): Clemmons was angry at the decline in profits.
   Angry *with* (a person): Clemmons was angry with the sales force.

3. Deal *in* (a service): Nielson and Company deals in uncut diamonds.
   Deal *with* (a person): Nielson and Company deals with most jewelers in the city.

4. Differ *with* (a person or an opinion): Sheila differs with Anthony about the campaign to utilize staff better.
   Differ *from* (another object): Rossi's plan for staff utilization differs from Nixon's plan.

5. Different *from,* NOT different *than*: This form is *different from* ours.

6. Discrepancy *in* (the object of the preposition is *singular*): *There is a discrepancy in* John's statistical report.
   Discrepancy *between* (the object of the preposition is *plural*): There is a *discrepancy between* Sheldon's and Joel's studies.

7. Identical *with*, NOT identical *to*: This form is *identical with* ours.

8. *Like*, NOT *like for*: We would *like* you to use the form that is identical with ours.

9. Part *with* (give up something other than a person): Reluctantly, Chris *parted with* her favorite personal computer.
   Part *from* (a person): Chris *parted from* her fellow workers at a retirement party held in her honor.

10. Plan *to* NOT plan *on*: I certainly *plan to* discuss this with my supervisor.

11. Retroactive *to*, NOT retroactive *from*: Our contract indicates that we will get a 9 percent salary increase *retroactive to* last September.

12. Talk *with* (two or more people talk together): The office workers *talked with* each other about their new employer.
    Talk *to* (only one person talks): The irate parent *talked to* her wayward teenager.

Refer to this section often to gain confidence in using prepositions correctly. ☑

CONJUNCTIONS

Conjunctions are words used to connect words, phrases, or clauses. Note the conjunctions in the following sentences:

Marilyn worked hard, *but* Faith didn't.
Both Hines *and* Goldberg were promoted.
Juan knew *when* the shipping room was behind schedule.
Since she came into the office, the work has been efficiently completed.

There are three kinds of conjunctions: *coordinate, correlative,* and *subordinate.* First we shall look at coordinate conjunctions.

COORDINATE CONJUNCTIONS

If your remember the acronym FANBOY, you will remember all the coordinate conjunctions.

F	A	N	B	O	Y
for	and	nor	but	or	yet

These kinds of conjunctions join words, phrases, and clauses of equal grammatical rank. (We shall define and explain phrases and clauses in the section on parts of sentences.) *Equal grammatical rank* means that the sentence elements joined are the same kind of element, such as prepositional phrases or nouns or verbs or adjectives or independent clauses. Note this incorrect use of coordinate conjunctions:

Sharp runs the store ably *and* with the highest degree of efficiency. [*Ably* is an adverb; *with the highest degree of efficiency* is a prepositional phrase.]

Here are two ways to correct the sentence so that *and* will join items of equal grammatical rank:

Sharp runs the store ably *and* efficiently. [*And* joins two adverbs.]
Sharp runs the store with ability *and* with efficiency. [*And* joins two prepositional phrases.]

Which sentence do you prefer?

Self-Check Exercise 2

Indicate your knowledge of prepositional use by correcting the following sentences.

1. The pistachio nuts were divided between the four boys.

2. The potato chips were divided among the two boys.

3. Don't go inside of that room until I give you permission.

4. Outside of the school is a playground that is fully equipped.

5. All of the students studied for the quiz.

6. Both of the students earned their tuition last summer.

7. I am looking into the drawer to find my stapler.

8. Beside that, I couldn't go anyway.

9. Where should I mail the brochures to?

10. In regards to the final examination, study pages 1–125.

11. The student said, "I will not be satisfied until this term is over with."

12. I do not agree with the stipulations in the bylaws of their club.

13. I am angry at my neighbors.

14. Our Vanguard program differs with their Encore program.

15. The teacher talked with the class about punctuality and absenteeism.

16. "He is different than all the rest," said the young girl.

17. Your attaché case is identical to mine.

18. I would like for you to visit when you have an opportunity.

19. He received a salary raise retroactive from January.

Selecting the appropriate coordinating conjunction to join two independent clauses sometimes creates a problem for a writer. (See page 000 for further discussion of dependent and independent clauses.) The guidelines that follow should help you choose the correct coordinating conjunctions.

1. *And.* Generally use *and* to connect words or groups of words when you mean *in addition to.*

    Harry is a good mechanic, *and* Bob is a good worker at the gas pumps.

2. *But.* Use *but* when your meaning is *contrasting.*

   Harry is a good mechanic, *but* Bob is a better one.

3. *Or.* Use *or* to give the reader *a choice.*

   Use Harry to complete the job, *or* use Bob to finish it.

4. *For.* Use *for* when the second independent clause explains the first independent clause in a sentence.

   Be sure to hire Bob *for* he is a competent worker.

5. *Nor.* Use *nor* with a negative.

   I did not agree to the arrangements, *nor* did Sam agree to them.

6. *Yet.* Use *yet* in a negative or opposing situation. [Similar to *but*]

   She wanted to pass the CPA examination, *yet* she found it difficult to do so.

   If you want to remember the coordinate conjunctions, simply remember FANBOY. ☑

Self-Check Exercise 3

Insert the appropriate coordinating conjunctions (FANBOY) in place of the question marks. The correct answers appear in the key.

1. It is one of nature's rarest ? most exquisite phenomena.

2. He desires wealth ? lacks the opportunity to amass it.

3. Janet needed six fillings ? she rarely brushed her teeth.

4. Laura completed law school first ? she then enrolled in medical school.

5. I wanted to work for my uncle this summer ? the summer positions were all filled.

6. He is retiring very early ? he had two serious heart attacks.

7. You can make your appointment for Wednesday ? you can make it for Thursday.

8. My mother may prepare dinner at home ? we may all go to a restaurant.

9. Madeline will write the article first ? the book second.

10. The vice president was depressed ? sales had decreased.

CORRELATIVE CONJUNCTIONS

Correlative conjunctions are used mainly for emphasis. There are four sets:

both . . . and   either . . . or
neither . . . nor   not only . . . but also

As you can see, the correlative (pronounced kə-'rel-ət-iv) conjunctions are coordinate conjunctions paired with other words. The initial word permits you to emphasize two elements equally. (Like coordinate conjunctions, they join words, phrases, and clauses of *equal grammatical rank*.)

Both Anita *and* Mary applied for the new position.

Not only Anita *but also* Mary applied for the new position.

Neither Anita *nor* Mary had much chance of attaining the new position. [Use *neither . . . nor* when expressing a negative situation.]

Either Anita *or* Mary would handle the new duties well. [Use *either . . . or* when expressing a positive situation.]

SUBORDINATE CONJUNCTIONS

Subordinate conjunctions join clauses of *unequal* grammatical rank:

After finishing the semester, the professor traveled to the Orient.
The professor traveled to the Orient *after* finishing the semester.

Note that the subordinate conjunction begins the dependent (or subordinate) clause. We shall focus on the use of subordinate conjunctions in the parts-of-sentences chapters. For now, simply become familiar with this list of subordinate conjunctions:

after (*after* we finished the semester)

although (*although* we couldn't attend)

as (*as* we were leaving work)

as if (*as if* we could do anything about it)

as though (*as though* it would make any difference)

because (*because* it didn't matter)

before (*before* we left for work)

if (*if* we had known)

in order that (*in order that* we could watch)

provided (*provided* we were permitted)

since (*since* it was inconvenient)

that (*that* we were able to finish the project)

COMPARE:

though (*though* we do not all agree)

unless (*unless* all of us agree)

until (*until* we all agree)

when (*when* we all agree)

where (*where* it is impossible for us all to agree)

whether (*whether* we can all agree)

while (*while* we may all agree)

Familiarize yourself with the 19 subordinate conjunctions.

PROBLEM SPOTS

If you will remember that coordinate conjunctions join elements of equal rank and subordinate conjunctions join elements of unequal rank, you will generally select the appropriate conjunctions. There are two trouble spots, however, that you should avoid:

1. Using *being that* as a subordinate conjunction. *Being that* is not a subordinate conjunction.

   Unacceptable

   Being that I am sick, I cannot participate in the meeting.

   Acceptable

   "Since I am sick, I cannot participate in the meeting.

   "Because I am sick, I cannot participate in the meeting.

   "While I am sick, I cannot participate in the meeting.

2. Using *like* as a subordinate conjunction. *Like* is either a verb (I *like* him.) or a preposition (This puppy looks *like* hers.); it is not a subordinate conjunction and should not be used as one.

   Unacceptable

   Like you were told at the meeting, the new software arrived yesterday.

   Acceptable

   As you were told at the meeting, the new software arrived yesterday.

Don't use *being that* or *like* as subordinate conjunctions. ☑

INTERJECTIONS

Interjections are words that express strong emotion and have no grammatical relationship to other words in the sentence. Typically they stand alone. Note these examples:

Great!   Wow!   Super!   Ouch!   No!

As you can see, such words are usually punctuated with an exclamation point. They are, after all, exclamations.

Only in rare instances would you have use for interjections in business communications. Possibly you could use one in an informal memo in which you wanted to express strong feeling to a coworker. Note the following sentences, which could have been part of a memo from an employer to an employee: "Sam, your sales campaign was great. I think it will work. Super!"

Self-Check Exercise 4

Insert an appropriate conjunction in place of the question mark in each sentence. This exercise will test your ability to use correlative and subordinate conjunctions. The solutions are in the key.

1. ? Laura completed law school, she enrolled in medical school. [subordinate]

2. ? did Laura complete law school ? she ? completed medical school. [correlative]

3. ? we no longer have any summer openings, we shall keep your application for next year. [subordinate]

4. ? summer jobs ? part-time fall jobs are available for the students. [correlative]

5. ? he had two serious heart attacks, he retired from work. [subordinate]

6. ? his two serious heart attacks ? his migraine headaches convinced him to retire from his job. [correlative]

7. We will have to disband our team ? it is impossible for us all to agree. [subordinate]

8. ? Jackson ? Doreen had an opportunity to take a vacation. [correlative]

9. ? our meeting, we had to prepare and mail out the agenda. [subordinate]

10. ? our junior partner ? Archibald Jones went to Cleveland to audit their books. [correlative]

APPLICATION EXERCISES

A. Write *true* or *false* in the blank at the left of each sentence.

_____ 1. Generally interjections are inappropriate in business communications.

_____ 2. *Because* is a coordinate conjunction.

_____ 3. With two objects, *between* is the appropriate preposition; with more than two, use *among*.

_____ 4. One should agree *with* a person.

_____ 5. Coordinate conjunctions connect words, phrases, and clauses of equal grammatical rank.

_____ 6. Careful speakers and writers avoid putting *at* at the end of a sentence beginning with *where*, as in "Where is my order blank at?"

_____ 7. One parts *with* an object, but *from* another person.

_____ 8. *Beside* and *besides* mean the same thing.

_____ 9. When Johnny talks *to* Miriam, Johnny does almost all the talking.

_____ 10. *Into* is used correctly in this sentence: "Mr. Jones walked into the conference room from his office."

B. There is at least one prepositional phrase in each of the following sentences. Draw a circle around each and underline the preposition.

1. After lunch Maggie hurried to the steno pool for another stack of correspondence.

2. Part of the problem in the record business lies in the loss of profits because of shoplifting.

3. In the end, the campaign worked and the company saved millions of dollars in advertising costs.

4. Between you and me, Larry's manner at the interview with Mr. Clark seemed brusque and inappropriate.

5. In spite of her serious illness in the last quarter of the fiscal year, Maria still completed the project in record time.

6. Throughout the convention, the publishers worked behind the scenes with prospective purchasers of their books.

7. A sense of organization and a commitment to excellence exist within every successful executive.

8. Since September, seven people have been hired by the production department.

9. She walked across the room, stopped at the filing cabinet, withdrew the Hedges file, and took it into the boardroom with her.

10. During every month but the last, the sales of hamburgers increased over the sales of the corresponding month in the previous year.

C. In each sentence below there is a preposition or conjunction error. Correct the error in the space above it.

1. Rosa is an able secretary, and Ruby is more efficient.

2. Martin permits his office staff to accept employment outside of the office.

3. I certainly felt the money for the suggestion should have been divided between Charles, Harold, and Ken.

4. When he is on vacation, Bill likes both swimming and to play golf.

5. The boss became angry at him for not following through on the account.

6. Put the new dresses besides the blouses that are on sale.

7. Where is the typed copy of the invoice at?

8. Alexander differs from Robinson on the best way to redesign the outer office.

9. We need to ask the treasurer to link up the sales report and the profit statement.

10. In regards to the proposed merger, Smith and Randolph want to present an opposing viewpoint.

D. Underline all coordinate, subordinate, and correlative conjunctions in the following sentences, and indicate in the space to the right which type each conjunction is.

Sentence	Type
Example: The space program has been fairly successful, but it has had its share of tragedy.	*coordinate*

1. Neither the lawyer nor the accountant kept their appointments.

2. Fifty-five were municipal court cases, and eight were heard in Common Pleas Court.

3. Before the class began, the students congregated outside the door.

4. The graduate student applied for a summer job, but she was told that there would be no summer openings.

5. An auction record was broken when an 18th-century table sold for $1,045,000.

6. Not only Streep but also Redford are popular with today's movie audiences.

7. Both a vacation and a few days away from work can be relaxing.

8. I wanted to buy a new car, yet I knew that my budget would not allow it.

9. Since Bermuda's weather is springlike in the winter, I shall wear medium-weight clothing.

10. He refused to lend his brother a car, for he knew his parents would disapprove.

Challenge Exercise

Indicate the parts of speech of all italicized words in the following:

We *are pleased* that you *have selected* AAA Life Insurance Company to provide your *insurance* protection. We know that you *will be satisfied with* our annual *premium rate and* with *the* service extended *by our* employees. In addition, *you have* the *opportunity* to buy *added* insurance *without* a *medical examination until November 23. For additional* information *call our toll-free* number appearing *on your policy. In* addition, be sure to tell *your friends and family about our* extensive *insurance offerings.*

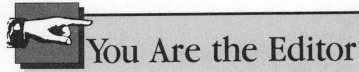

You Are the Editor

Correct all the errors you find in this memo.

TO: Staff on Watson Soap Account

FROM: Theo Nelson

DATE: January 16, 198_

SUBJECT: Upcoming Promotion Campaign

This is simply an informal note to let you know that its not too early to begin thinking about ways to connect up the Watson Soap account with the Watson Food account. As you know, Watson makes many product's beside food, and soap is one of them. Mr. Allan and myself have been successful in luring the soap account away from one of our competitors, and I think that we should make every effort to come up with a campaign that Watson will agree with.

Mr. Allan believes we could of failed in the negotations for the new account. What saved us was the willingness of Watson hisself to change agencies. He could have went to other agencies, but he has chose us, and we must hurry up and prepare our program for his' company.

In regards to where we place ads at, both newspapers and television seem appropiate. Television is probably the best choice. Its both available at a cost we can afford and an exciting medium in which to work in.   I am dividing the initial responsibility for devising a prospectus equally among Jameson and Andrews, but all of you must of been thinking about this, so talk to each other and share your ideas. I will be happy when this project is over with.

Key to Self-Check Exercises

Exercise 1

1. without (prep.)   cinnamon (n.)
2. until (prep.)   tomorrow (n.)
3. through (prep.)   the (adj.)   maze (n.)
4. into (prep.)   that (adj.)   showroom (n.)
5. during (prep.)   an executive board (adjs.)   meeting (n.)
6. between (prep.)   the new (adjs.)   computers (n.)
7. beside (prep.)   the (adj.)   circle (n.)
8. around (prep.)   a secretarial (adjs.)   cubicle (n.)
9. below (prep.)   the small (adjs.)   zero (n.)
10. above (prep.)   this conference (adjs.)   room (n.)

Exercise 3

1. and
2. yet OR but
3. for
4. and
5. but
6. for
7. or
8. or
9. and
10. for

Exercise 2

1. among
2. between
3. inside that room (no *of*)
4. Outside the school (no *of*)
5. All the students (no *of*)
6. Both the students (no *of*)
7. in the drawer
8. Besides that,
9. the brochures? (no *to*)
10. In regard to
11. over." or "is ended."
12. agree to
13. angry with
14. differs from
15. talked to
16. different from
17. identical with
18. like you (no *for*)
19. retroactive to

Exercise 4

1. After, before, though, OR when
2. Not only   but   also
3. Since, although, as, though, OR while
4. Either   or, Neither   nor, OR Not only   but also
5. After, because, before, since, OR when
6. Either   or, Neither   nor, OR Not only   but also
7. If, since, as OR because
8. Not only   but also OR Neither   nor
9. Before
10. Not only   but also, Either   or, OR Neither   nor

A DYNAMIC BUSINESS VOCABULARY

Here are eight more business vocabulary terms to study, define, and use in sentences. Remember to check their pronunciation in your dictionary if you have the slightest doubt how to pronounce them.

Devaluation

The reduction in value of currency by the lowering of its gold equivalency.

The devaluation of the dollar caused real problems for American tourists abroad.

Disk (Disc)

Magnetic-coated material in a record-like shape on which information and programs are stored for computers.

The students' lab fee was raised to cover the cost of computer disks.

Dividend

The share of profits spread among stockholders.

Interestingly enough, the firm has paid a stock dividend each year since its founding in 1925.

Edit

To revise written material to make it acceptable for publication.

If you will edit the report for clarity and conciseness, we shall publish it.

Electronic Keyboard

A typewriter keyboard that operates electronically and, therefore, silently.

The secretary found the new electronic keyboard difficult at first.

Electronic mail

Communications transmitted in digital code between distant locations and reproduced in paper format at the destination.

The state community colleges have invested a considerable sum in the installation of an electronic mail system.

Embargo

An official prohibition against imports to or exports from a port.

The U.S. placed an embargo on the shipment of wheat to Russia.

Embezzlement

The taking of money or property left in an individual's care for personal gain.

Mr. Kelly was sentenced to jail for the embezzlement of bank funds.

THE ABC'S OF BUSINESS VOCABULARY

Test your knowledge of the business vocabulary you have studied by completing the following exercise.

1. Compose three short sentences using one of the following words in each sentence: (a) dividend, (b) embargo, (c) embezzlement.

   _____

   _____

   _____

   _____

   _____

   _____

2. Define the noun *disk (disc)*. _____

   _____

   _____

3. *Electronic mail* refers to _____

   _____

   _____

4. An important characteristic of an *electronic keyboard* is _____

   _____

5. The noun *deposition* means _____

   _____

6. Lowering the value of currency by lowering its gold equivalency is called (a) devaluation, (b) interest, (c) charge, (d) penalty.

7. A failing economic condition characterized by unemployment or a lessening of buying power and decreasing business activity is (a) inflation, (b) retribution, (c) depression, (d) deflation.

8. The failure to make payment on a debt is (a) reneging, (b) default, (c) avoidance, (d) omission.

9. To revise written material to make it acceptable for publication is to (a) edit, (b) denigrate, (c) eliminate, (d) revoke the material.

REVIEW EXERCISE ON CHAPTERS 1–8

A. Write the letter for each business vocabulary term before its definition.

	Definition	**Term**
_____	1. Rules and regulations governing an organization	a. affidavit
_____	2. A written statement authenticating a document, fact, or promise	b. cartel
_____	3. A list, outline, or plan of things to be considered or done at a meeting	c. bylaws
_____	4. A computer language that uses common English words and mathematical symbols to perform problem-solving operations.	d. debt
_____	5. The hearing and determination of a dispute by an impartial party	e. aptitude
_____	6. A list of expenditures or income itemized for a certain period of time	f. deposition
_____	7. A highly technical computer language used by specialists.	g. agenda
_____	8. A written document that lists ownership of property	h. cassette
_____	9. The reduction of purchasing power or value of property because of age	i. BASIC
_____	10. A written statement, as in testimony, to be used in court	j. embezzlement
_____	11. A statement written and sworn to in the presence of a notary public	k. arbitration
_____	12. The ability to learn and retain information; a natural ability	l. certification
_____	13. The taking of money or property left in an individual's care for personal gain	m. COBOL
_____	14. The collection of several organizations, as in a merger, to form a more sound business organization	n. acronym
_____	15. To bring together many parts, businesses, or agreements to form one	o. conglomerate

———— 16. A small plastic cartridge containing magnetic   p. budget
tape, used in dictation and word-processing
equipment

———— 17. A group of independent businesses set up to   q. deed
regulate the pricing, production, and marketing
of products

———— 18. A financial obligation, as in money owed to   r. edit
someone

———— 19. A word formed from the first letter of words or   s. depreciation
parts of a word in a term, title, or name

———— 20. To revise written material to make it acceptable   t. consolidate
for publication

B. Select the correct word from each pair in parentheses, and write it on the line to the left.

————————— 1. (Let, Leave) me give you some help.

————————— 2. He reached (in, into) the desk drawer.

————————— 3. From the tone of their discussion, I (implied, inferred) that
they were all dissatisfied.

————————— 4. South Florida's winter climate can be very (healthy,
healthful).

————————— 5. (Can, May) I practice my keyboarding skills on your
computer?

————————— 6. (Beside, Besides) her Spanish skills, Maureen also speaks
French fluently.

————————— 7. The thought of taking a driving test made her very (anxious,
eager).

————————— 8. (Most, Almost) all my friends are professionals.

————————— 9. Don't (aggravate, irritate) me with your petty remarks.

————————— 10. (Your, You're) welcome any day of the week.

————————— 11. (Who's, Whose) textbook is this?

————————— 12. I have no intention of (waiving, waving) my rights.

————————— 13. Did the hardware section carry the (vice, vise) you need?

————————— 14. Her scholastic average has (risen, raised) gradually.

————————— 15. What is the (principal, principle) textbook used in your class?

_____ 16. Dr. Simon (proceeded, preceded) Dr. Marchesano as president of our organization.

_____ 17. In making our decision, we referred to (precedence, precedents) already set by other cases.

_____ 18. They will (plane, plain) the unfinished desk for a smoother finish.

_____ 19. The (plaintiff, plaintive) in the case was out of town.

_____ 20. They are not looking at it from the right (perspective, prospective) in this situation.

C. Some of the following sentences have errors in the spelling, hyphenation, possessive form, or use of various parts of speech. Write the corrections on the lines at the left. If no corrections are needed, write OK.

_____ 1. My father in law will join us at the meeting.

_____ 2. They attended the conference made up of many editor in chiefs.

_____ 3. You will be surprised to see so many discrepancys in the column totals.

_____ 4. My cousins from St. Louis are both attornies.

_____ 5. The company uses two art studioes.

_____ 6. Her school folders have a number of course syllabuses.

_____ 7. Select the correct word in the parenthesis.

_____ 8. The Smith's cars were both parked on the school lot.

_____ 9. How many grapefruit halfs have you eaten today?

_____ 10. Our companies' profits are sizable considering that the company was formed two years ago.

_____ 11. Whomever you are you still cannot see Mr. Johnson without an appointment.

_____ 12. This file belongs to whomever left it on my desk last week.

_____ 13. Who are here?

_____ 14. The Blazing Brothers are the acrobats whom will impress you the most.

_____ 15. Whom have you chosen?

_____ 16. Gerald himself finished the project.

_____ 17. Those are her files on this desk.

_____ 18. The choir had sang the opening hymn.

_____ 19. They will chose the most senior member to write the report.

_____ 20. The superintendent rung the bell three times.

_____ 21. Yesterday my fingers nearly frozed in the snowstorm.

_____ 22. It had began before we arrived.

_____ 23. Susan lay the presents on the table yesterday.

_____ 24. They have forgot to bring the agenda with them.

_____ 25. We could of adhered to the company's policy.

_____ 26. You may sit the typewriter on this table.

_____ 27. Because of my illness, I have lain down every afternoon this week.

_____ 28. Have you bought your textbook with you?

_____ 29. The astronaut appeared to be a honorable person.

_____ 30. The parcel I am mailing is the biggest of the two.

D. Use the following words correctly in concise sentences.

1. louder _____

_____

2. most reliable _____

_____

3. more permanent _____

_____

4. least _____

_____

5. better _____

_____

6. more nearly round _____

_____

7. intelligently _____

_____

8. very _____

_____

9. has rarely participated _____

_____

10. surely _____

_____

E. Select the correct word or phrase from within each set of parentheses, and write it on the line to the left.

_____ 1. The figures were computed (correct, correctly).

_____ 2. When my cousins were in the neighborhood, they (had visited always, had always visited).

_____ 3. This report is the (more clearly, most clearly) written of all.

_____ 4. Her photograph was the (most perfect, most nearly perfect) of the three.

_____ 5. Because of his diet, he is (real, really) thin.

_____ 6. They felt (bad, badly) about her accident.

_____ 7. She (never, has not) arrived.

_____ 8. (In regards to, As regards) the new technology, we find it to be fascinating.

_____ 9. He tries not to work (outside, outside of) his home office.

_____ 10. (All of the, All the) girls have met their teammates.

_____ 11. Where is (it, it at)?

_____ 12. They will be happy when this project is (over with, over).

_____ 13. Have you agreed (upon, to) the plan?

_____ 14. The employees were angry (at, with) their unfair supervisor.

_____ 15. George's plan differs (with, from) Rosa's plan.

_____ 16. There is a decided discrepancy (in, between) the two conclusions.

_____ 17. This suggested format is identical (with, to) ours.

_____ 18. Ms. Andrews would (like for, like) you to arrive by noon.

_____ 19. I am not happy to part (with, from) my relatives after a holiday dinner.

_____ 20. Please (plan to discuss, plan on discussing) your new project.

9 Parts of Sentences
Subjects and Predicates

Knowing parts of sentences will help you communicate more effectively for three reasons. First, if you know parts of sentences, you know what you are doing when you write. You are in control. Certainly you can talk or write intelligibly, perhaps even elegantly, without knowing parts of sentences, but there is comfort in knowing what you are doing, what sentence tools you are using.

Second, knowing parts of sentences will help you avoid errors. We stress again and again in this text that one way to appear to be a good user of English is not to appear to be a bad user. In other words, avoid errors. Consider the errors in the following sentences:

Bob and me organized the office party. [It should be *Bob and I...*]

Each of the salespersons were late in sending the monthly reports. [It should be *Each... was...*]

Being late for work, the shipment was not unloaded by him until 2:30. [It should be *Because he was late for work, he did not unload...*]

Let's you and I clean the typewriters this time. [It should be *Let's you and me...*]

The full-page advertisement was canceled by the manager that was scheduled for Friday's paper. [It should be *... advertisement that was scheduled for Friday was canceled...*]

It could have been her who got the promotion. [It should be *... could have been she...*]

In all these instances, a knowledge of parts of sentences would help the writer avoid errors.

Finally, a knowledge of parts of sentences can help you dress up your writing, give it some flair. Consider these sentences:

John got a promotion and Rita received a sales bonus.

Although John got a promotion, Rita received a sales bonus.

John's getting a promotion came at the same time as Rita's receiving a sales bonus.

John, with a promotion, and Rita, with a sales bonus, were pleased at their good fortune.

These sentences convey the same ideas, but they do so differently, with differing emphases. If you have a good grasp of parts of sentences, you can create sentences like these or any others. You will have options. You will be able to decide, for instance, if you want to modify a noun with a simple adjective, a participial phrase, or an adjective clause. Note these samples:

He read the *edited* version.

He read the version *edited by Clark.*

He read the version *that had been edited by Clark.*

You will be able to determine if one sentence pattern has been overused in your writing, if you need to combine sentences, if you need to use more verbals. (You may be worrying at the moment about some of these terms—*verbals, participles, adjective clauses.* You will soon know them and know them well.)

So there you have them—some good reasons for knowing parts of sentences. Let us begin.

THE SUBJECT

THE COMPLETE SUBJECT

The *complete subject* of a sentence is that part of a sentence about which something is being said. It tells what (or whom) you are talking about. Note the italicized subject in each of the following examples:

> *Linda* types.
>
> *Shirley, who sits at the desk near the window,* does most of the filing.
>
> *The invoices printed on the copier* were sent to the field staff.
>
> *Few of our European salesmen* visit the United States.

THE SIMPLE SUBJECT

The *simple subject* is the main word in the complete subject that indicates what the sentence is about. It is almost always a noun or noun substitute. (So far the only noun substitute you have studied is the pronoun. In the chapters that follow, other noun substitutes will be introduced.) Note the italicized simple subjects in these examples:

> Concerned about the diminishing sales, the *manager* planned an extensive advertising campaign.
>
> A financial *audit* revealed a deficit of several thousand dollars.
>
> *Luis* deserves the promotion.
>
> *Working* in an emergency room is quite stressful.

COMPOUND SUBJECTS

A *compound subject* is two or more simple subjects connected by a coordinate conjunction.

> *Roosevelt Johnson* and *Irene Grier* were the top applicants.
>
> Neither *Kelly* nor *Isaac* presented good reports.
>
> The *systems analyst* or the *computer programmer* can help you with BASIC.

THE PREDICATE

THE COMPLETE PREDICATE

The *complete predicate* is that part of the sentence that says something about the complete subject. Whatever is not in the complete subject makes up the complete predicate. Note the italicized complete predicate in each of the following sentences:

> Harriet, the bookkeeper, *was able to balance everyone else's books but not her own checkbook.*
>
> *Did* you *hire him?*
>
> Nelson, who works in shipping, and Sanchez, who works in accounting, *put together an excellent suggestion for keeping closer track of our current inventory.*
>
> *Over the river and through the woods to Grandmother's house we go.*

THE SIMPLE PREDICATE

The *simple predicate* is the main verb in the complete predicate. Often it is called simply the *verb* of the sentence, thus borrowing its name from parts of speech. Note the italicized simple predicates in these sentences:

Both stenographers *ate* their lunches rapidly.

As a direct consequence of her employer's memo, Elena *changed* her habits of dress and timeliness.

Muhammed Farenci *has been gone* from the office for over an hour.

Louis *is* the most creative writer on the staff.

COMPOUND PREDICATES

Compound predicates consist of two or more verbs (with the same subject) connected by a coordinate conjunction. Note the italicized examples in these sentences:

Larson *fussed* and *fumed* about the air conditioning in the reception area.

Sue *came* to work, *punched* the time clock, *uncovered* her typewriter, and *began* a letter—all by 9:05.

Marshall *took* a spelling test, *typed* a letter, and *solved* ten math problems as part of the screening process for the job.

FINDING PREDICATES

As you will see, it is helpful to be able to identify simple predicates of sentences. Typically, finding the simple predicate is not difficult, especially if you follow these guidelines:

1. Ignore the contents of all prepositional phrases when you search for the simple predicate.

2. Look for the main verb showing action or state of being in the rest of the sentence.

3. Remember that the main verb gives the sentence its essential meaning, as it denotes action or state of being.

Example 1

In the local newspaper, Charlton Snieder experienced widespread support.

Discounted prepositional phrase: In the local newspaper

noun   *verb*   *adjective*   *noun*

Rest of sentence: Charlton Snieder experienced widespread support
Simple predicate (verb): experienced

Example 2

Under the supervision of her coordinator, Delores Gomez mastered word processing and other computer skills by the end of the year.

Discounted prepositional phrases: Under the supervision/of her coordinator/by the end/of the year

noun   verb   noun   conj. *adj. noun or adj./noun*

Rest of sentence: Delores Gomez mastered word processing and other   computer skills

Simple predicate (verb): mastered

Example 3

Under the shelf but over the desk, you will find the new wall lamp.

Discounted prepositional phrases: Under the shelf/over the desk

conj. pro.   *verb*   *adjectives*   *noun*

Rest of sentence: but you will find the new wall lamp

Simple predicate (verb): will find

FINDING SUBJECTS

Finding the subject can be a little more challenging, partly because we are accustomed to thinking that the subject is always the first word in the sentence. These tips will help.

1. Find the simple predicate (or verb), then ask yourself who or what does or is whatever the verb is talking about. The subject of a sentence, like its verb, is never in a prepositional phrase. Note these examples, with the prepositional phrases in parentheses.

    Henry bought the policy. [*Bought* is the verb. Who bought? Henry. Therefore, *Henry* is the subject.]

    (In the preparation) (of the company handbook), Arlene worked overtime every night (for a week). [*Worked* is the verb. Who worked? Arlene. Therefore, *Arlene* is the subject.]

    Clint is the new employer. [*Is* is the verb—a state-of-being verb. Who *is*? Clint. Therefore, *Clint* is the subject.]

    (In the local newspaper), Charlton Snieder experienced widespread support. [*experienced* is the verb. Who experienced? Charlton Snieder. Therefore, *Charlton Snieder* is the subject.

    (Under the supervision) (of her coordinator), Delores Gomez mastered word processing and other computer skills (by the end) (of the year). [*mastered* is the verb. Who mastered? Delores Gomez. Then *Delores Gomez* is the subject.

    (Under the shelf) but (over the desk), you will find the new wall lamp. [*will find* is the verb. Who will find? You. *You* is the subject.]

    The staff (in the dilapidated offices) (on the fourth floor) (of the Goddard Building) still did their work efficiently and cooperatively. [*did* is the verb. Who *did*? The staff did. *Staff* is the simple subject.]

    (Over the river) and (through the woods) (to Grandmother's house) we go. [*go* is the verb. Who goes? We go. *We* is the subject.]

Note: Now you can see why it is mandatory to be able to recognize prepositions. With that ability, you can quickly discard the contents of prepositional phrases as you try to find the simple subject of a sentence.

2. If the sentence is a question, one way to find the subject is to turn the question into a statement.

Did Smathers complete the travel vouchers? [Change this to "Smathers did complete the travel vouchers," and you can more easily see that *Smathers* is the simple subject and *did complete* is the simple predicate.]

Have you sent them your annual report? [Change this to "You have sent them your annual report," and it is apparent that *you* is the simple subject and *have sent* is the simple predicate.]

Could the students join the alumni at the football game? [Change to "The students could join the alumni at the football game." Now you can see that *students* is the simple subject and *could join* is the simple predicate.]

3. Another way to find the subject in a question is to analyze the first three or four words. Frequently the first word in a question is a verb helper; the second word (with any adjectives), the subject; and the third word, the main verb.

    Let us take another look at the questions in the second tip:

Did Smathers complete the travel vouchers? [First word *(did)* is a verb helper. Second word *(Smathers)* is the simple subject. Third word *(complete)* is the main verb.]

Have you sent them your annual report? [First word *(have)* is a verb helper. Second word *(you)* is the simple subject. Third word *(sent)* is the main verb.]

Could the students join the alumni at the football game? [First word *(could)* is a verb helper. Second and third words *(the students)* are an adjective and a simple subject. Next word *(join)* is the main verb.]

4. Words like *there, here,* or *it* sometimes begin sentences and appear to be the subjects, but frequently—almost always in the case of *there* or *here*— they are not. Usually the subject is the first noun or noun substitute following the first verb. Look at these examples:

There is a good reason for my decision about employing Monica. [*There* in this sentence is called an *expletive,* which is simply a word that gets an inverted sentence started. *Inverted sentences* are ones in which the verb appears before the subject. *Is* is the verb. The first noun is *reason. Reason* is the subject.]

Here are the sales figures. [*Here* in this sentence can be considered either an expletive or an adverb indicating where. *Are* is the verb. *Figures,* the first noun, is the subject.]

There are roses and violets in the imported Chinese vase. [*There* is an expletive; *are* is the verb. The first and second nouns *(roses/violets)* represent a compound subject.]

Note: The last example clearly indicates that you do not want to eliminate the possibility of a compound subject (two or more nouns or noun substitutes) following the verb in an inverted sentence. Be on the alert! ☑

PRONOUNS AS SUBJECTS

REVIEW

In some languages, nouns are spelled with one ending when they are used as subjects and with another ending when they are used as complements. (*Complements* will be explained in the next chapter.) These different endings are called *case forms.* In English, nouns are spelled the same whether they function in the sentences as subjects or as complements. They do not, in other words, have different case forms.

Pronouns, however, do have different forms, as we learned previously. Study these examples:

He did the typing.   *His** typing is good.   The typing pleased *him.*

**His* in this sentence can be considered a pronoun or an adjective. For his discussion we shall consider it a pronoun.

Self-Check Exercise 1

Underline the *simple or compound subjects* in each of the six sentences that follow. The answers appear in the key at the end of the chapter.

1. The stenographers and typists who work in our office have excellent skills.

2. Behind the chairs was the trunk to be sent to overnight camp.

3. Walter and Nancy are students studying at the University of Pennsylvania.

4. One's thoughts are sometimes private.

5. Anybody's ideas are acceptable in this brainstorming session.

6. The invoices printed on the copier were sent to the field staff yesterday.

Underline the *simple or compound predicates* in each of the six sentences that follow.

7. My employer carried the new self-correcting electronic typewriter.

8. Ice cream and pie is my very favorite dessert.

9. She sang and danced and jumped for joy when she heard of her new promotion.

10. Georgia and Georgette are participating in the identical-twins contest.

11. Over half the folders were damaged in the explosion.

12. The library, including its check-out system, shelving, and tables and chairs, has been completely renovated this year.

Underline the *complete subjects* and encircle the *complete predicates* in the following sentences.

13. The engineers who moved to our Fort Washington branch are much happier in this new location.

14. Above the piano was a portrait of our hostess.

15. We know that you are very competent.

16. Have you seen the latest film on that subject?

17. Aggressive Tom and assertive Thelma stormed into the conference room and lectured the group.

18. The tennis players are hoping to win this year's tournament.

In these examples the italicized words are pronouns, all referring to the same single male, yet each is formed differently. Each has a different *case,* depending on its function in the sentence. These cases are nominative, possessive, and objective.

Pronouns also have *number.* That is, they have different forms to indicate whether they are singular or plural.

As explained in Chapter 5, pronouns have *person.* First person indicates the person speaking, second person the person spoken to, and third person the person spoken about.

Pronouns in the third person singular also have different forms for *gender* to indicate if they are masculine, feminine, or neuter.

All these forms are summarized here for your review.

Forms of Personal Pronouns

Number	Nominative Case Singular	Nominative Case Plural	Objective Case Singular	Objective Case Plural	Possessive Case Singular	Possessive Case Plural
First person	I	we	me	us	my (mine)†	our (ours)
Second person	you	you	you	you	your (yours)	your (yours)
Third person						
Masculine	he	they	him	them	his	their (theirs)
Feminine	she	they	her	them	her (hers)	their (theirs)
Neuter	it	they	it	them	its‡	their (theirs)

PRONOUN PITFALLS

Pronouns used as subjects take the nominative case.

I did the typing. [NOT *Me* did the typing.]

She opened the account. [NOT *Her* opened the account.]

They used the new accounting procedures. [NOT *Them* used the new accounting procedures.]

Few English speakers or writers would be guilty of the errors in the sentences above. But many are guilty, especially in spoken English, of the kind below.

Bob and *me* did the typing.

Barbara and *her* opened the account.

The managers and *them* used the new accounting procedures.

Do you see the difference? In the first set of examples, the subjects are not compound. In the second set, they are. People often make errors when they are using compounds, and these errors cause those people to be labeled careless or even incompetent users of English. Be sure to avoid these errors.

Fortunately, there is an easy way to learn how to handle the problems of compound subjects. Simply separate them and deal with each element individually. Note the following illustrations.

---

*†The forms in parentheses indicate the pronoun that is used without an accompanying noun to show possession. (*Mine* pleases me.) (It is *yours.*)

‡*Its,* a possessive pronoun, *does not* have an apostrophe.

Example 1

Tyrone and (he, him) arranged the interview.

Assume these two sentences:

Tyrone arranged the interview. He arranged the interview.

Then put the sentences together:

Tyrone and he . . .

Example 2

Benjamin and (I, me) checked the account.

Assume these two sentences:

Benjamin checked the account. I checked the account.

Then put them together:

Benjamin and I . . . ☑

Self-Check Exercise 2

Complete the following exercise to test your knowledge about the use of pronouns. Select the correct answers. After finishing the assignment, compare your answers with those in the key.

1. Mitchell and (me, I) undertook the project for (they, them) to expedite matters.

2. My mother and (she, her) opened separate accounts.

3. The supervisor and (them, they) attended the annual records management conference with (him, he).

4. Matilda and (he, him) will handle the overload very conveniently.

5. The professor and (her, she) received certificates for their excellent contributions.

6. Betty, Dorothy, and (I, me) have made arrangements for the party.

7. Mr. Kelly and (I, me) were selected.

SUBJECT-VERB AGREEMENT

Another reason for identifying the subject of a sentence is to be sure that your subjects and predicates agree in number. That subject and predicate must agree is a basic rule of English grammar and an area in which speakers and writers make numerous errors. Study the rules in this section. Remember—the third-person singular pronoun (*he, she,* or *it*) or any noun or noun substitute meaning *he, she,* or *it* requires a singular verb that ends in *s* when the present tense is used.

AGREEMENT IN NUMBER

Verbs must agree in number with their subjects. Do not be confused by words or groups of words that are between the subject and the verb. Study these examples:

> The typist with several years of training types better. [typist . . . types]
>
> The two typists with several years of training type better. [typists . . . type]

AGREEMENT IN AN INVERTED SENTENCE

If sentences are inverted, it often helps to put them in normal order before attempting to make subjects and verbs agree.

> Among Barbara's many good characteristics is her exciting personality. [*Personality* is the subject; *is* is the verb.]
>
> In the accompanying envelope are three proposals. [*Proposals* is the subject; *are* is the verb.]

When a sentence is introduced by an expletive (*there, here,* or *it*), the subject will typically appear after the verb. Still, subject and verb must agree.

> There are seven people interested in this position. [*People* is the subject; hence, *are* is the correct plural verb.]
>
> Here, among your papers, is the report. [*Report* is the subject; hence, *is* is the correct singular verb.]

SPECIAL SINGULAR WORDS

The following words are usually thought of as singular, so they take a singular verb: *everyone, someone, anyone, everybody, somebody, anybody, nobody, each* (one), *either* (one), and *neither* (one). In the following examples, the subjects and verbs are italicized.

> *Neither* of the two boys *was* hired. [Neither one . . . was]
>
> *Every one* of the secretaries *works* hard during National Secretaries Week. [Every one . . . works]
>
> *Each* of the four applicants *makes* an impressive appearance. [Each one . . . makes]

SPECIAL PLURAL WORDS

The following words are usually thought of as plural, and hence take a plural verb: *both, several, many,* and *few.* In these examples, the subjects and verbs are italicized:

> *Both* of the members from the temporary staff *look* helpful. [Both . . . look]
>
> *Many* of the members of his class at the business school *were employed* during their school years. [Many . . . were employed]

"PART" EXPRESSIONS

"Part" expressions such as "some of the cooking" and "some of the cakes" depend on the noun or pronoun that follows to determine the kind of verb required. In other words, the key word is the object of the preposition *of.* If the object of the preposition is singular, use a singular verb. If it is plural, use a plural verb. (*Part expressions* are those in which the subject expresses only a part of something.)

> Some of the typing *has been completed.* [*Typing* is singular; hence, a singular verb is required.]
>
> Some of the reports *have been typed.* [*Reports* is plural; hence, a plural verb is required.]
>
> Most of the alteration *has been made.* [COMPARE WITH Most of the changes *have been made.*]
>
> All* the copies *were* carefully *made.* [COMPARE WITH All the copying *was* carefully *done.*]

A NUMBER, THE NUMBER

When used as subjects, the expression *a number* is considered *plural* and the expression *the number* is considered *singular.* (The plural nature of the noun following *of* in these sentences does not determine the correct verb.)

> A *number* of complaints *come* to our attention every day. [plural verb]
>
> The *number* of complaints *has* decreased since last quarter. [singular verb]
>
> A *number* of accountants *attend* the yearly meeting. [plural verb]
>
> The *number* of accountants *is* on the rise. [singular verb]

COMPOUND SUBJECTS

Singular compound subjects joined by the coordinate conjunction *and* take plural verbs.

> Martha and Jim *deserve* the award for their work.
>
> Tom, Jodi, and Elena *work* the evening shift.

When the two or more elements of a compound are commonly thought of as one unit, a singular verb is appropriate.

> Ham and eggs for breakfast *starts* the day right. [one dish]
>
> Pie and ice cream *is* a delicious dessert. [one dish]

When the two or more elements of a compound subject are modified by *each* or *every,* a singular verb is required. (A good way to remember this is to recall that *each* [one] and *every*[one] also require singular verbs.)

> *Each* typist, secretary, and receptionist *is* expected to be at work by 8:30.
>
> *Every* word and sentence and paragraph in the prospectus for the new factory *has been* carefully *considered* by the lawyers.

Singular compound subjects joined by the coordinate conjunctions *or* and *nor* take singular verbs:

> Tracy or Helena *seems* to me the ideal person for the work.
>
> Neither Kelly nor Toni *is lacking* in personality or beauty.

If one element of a compound subject is singular and the other is plural and they are joined by the coordinate conjunctions *or* or *nor,* the verb should agree with the *nearer* subject.

All is considered a part expression word even though, technically, *all* of something is not *part* of it.

Neither Gregory's two sisters nor *Gregory is* interested in working. [singular]

Neither Gregory nor his two *sisters are* interested in working. [plural]

The secretaries or their *supervisor is* permitted to sign for them. [singular]

The supervisor or her *secretaries are* permitted to sign for them. [plural]

NAMES OF FIRMS
Names of firms or businesses are usually considered singular.

Wilcox, Fallett, and Eliot *is* the biggest insurance firm in town.

McGill Brothers *makes* excellent accounting forms.

Nielsen, Grey, and White *handles* negligence cases for our community.

AN AMOUNT
An amount, though plural in form, takes a singular verb if it is thought of as a single entity.

Fifty pounds *is* the ideal weight for that material.

Fifty dollars *is* an excellent gift for a college student ☑

Self-Check Exercise 3

Select the correct form of each verb to show that you understand subject-verb agreement.

1. There (are, is) a speaker and an introducer on the platform.

2. There (are, is) speakers on the stage.

3. The house, together with its furnishings, (are, is) a very good buy.

4. Some of the report (are, is) completely finished.

5. Some of the reports (are, is) ready to be mailed.

6. Each of us (has her; have our) dress cleaned and pressed and ready to go.

7. Everybody (has, have) to wear an academic robe at graduation.

8. Neither of his remarks (were, was) pleasant.

9. A number of suggestions (was, were) offered.

10. The number of suggestions (has, have) increased since the bonus plan went into effect.

11. Neither the student nor her professors (was, were) satisfied with her academic standing.

12. Neither Jane's professors nor Jane (was, were) happy with her final grades.

13. A rose and a geranium (was, were) placed in the bud vase.

14. Bacon and eggs (are, is) a delicious way to start the weekend off.

15. William or Charles (was, were) responsible for last month's sales figures.

16. A. J. Smythe Brothers (print, prints) executive's stationery and business cards.

APPLICATION EXERCISES

A. Put *true* or *false* in the blank at the left.

_____ 1. "Bob and me will attend the game together" is an acceptable use of the first-person singular pronoun.

_____ 2. Pronouns used as subjects must agree in number with their verbs.

_____ 3. The simple subject is usually the last word in a complete subject.

_____ 4. The third-person, singular, nominative, feminine pronoun is *she*.

_____ 5. *A number,* when used as a subject, takes a singular verb.

_____ 6. *There* in a sentence like "There is a good reason for that" is an expletive.

_____ 7. Words such as *someone, anyone, somebody, nobody, each, either,* and *neither,* when used as subjects, take plural verbs.

_____ 8. Most singular verbs in the present tense end in *-s* or *-es.*

_____ 9. Possessive pronouns include *him, her,* and *them.*

_____ 10. When two singular subjects are joined by *or,* they take a plural verb.

B. In each of the following sentences, underline the simple subject once and the simple predicate (the verb) twice. (Be careful of compound subjects and predicates and of inverted sentences.)

1. The carpeting company on Fourth Street created an outstanding advertising campaign.

2. Either Marcia or Mary will answer the correspondence.

3. In addition to his other fine qualities, Klein shows a real sensitivity for his fellow workers.

4. Did you include the brochure on the new development?

5. I designed the plan and found the financing for it.

6. With the exception of Maria Ortiz, Roberta and I are the only experienced manicurists in the shop.

7. There is no substitute for intelligence in a chief executive or, for that matter, in a custodian.

8. Humphrey believes in accuracy in his work.

9. Charlotte and Ruth assembled the pages, stapled the report, and put an attractive cover

on it.

10. Over the river and through the woods to Grandmother's house we go.

C. In five of the following ten sentences, pronouns are used incorrectly. Correct the errors by putting the appropriate pronoun immediately above the incorrect form.

1. Henry and she completed the planning last night.

2. Me and him had some disagreement about the pay.

3. In the interests of harmony, Bob and me will not apply for the promotion.

4. Cliff and I know the new procedures.

5. Both he and she were members of the union.

6. You or I can complete the work after closing time.

7. Neither Mary nor him had the right qualifications.

8. The women in the outer office and them in the shipping department formed an outstand-

ing bowling team.

9. Carlos and I planned the documentary.

10. In the final analysis Morgan or me should be the only ones considered for the promotion.

D. Underline the correct form of the verb in parentheses in each of the following sentences.

1. Both Clark and Watson (is, are) coming to the sales meeting.

2. Three fourths of the shipment (has, have) been sent to the manufacturer.

3. Neither the supplier nor his representatives (is, are) attending the meeting.

4. The number of accountants in the sales office (is, are) increasing each year.

5. Each of the three secretaries (types, type) the interoffice memos for Mr. Cunningham.

6. All the workers (knows, know) the rules of the game.

7. The subject of his memo and her reaction to it (is, are) the chief topic of conversation at the water cooler.

8. Thirty dollars (is, are) the right amount for that item.

9. Bob or Sid (is, are) dependable.

10. Few of the pieces of equipment at the college for barbers (was, were) insured.

Challenge Exercise

First compose an original sentence according to the instructions. Then underline the simple or compound subject once and the simple or compound predicate twice in each sentence.

1. Compose a sentence with a compound subject and a compound predicate.

   _____

   _____

2. An inverted sentence beginning with the expletive "Here." _____

   _____

3. A sentence that includes the name of a company. _____

   _____

4. A sentence containing the part expression "Some of the." _____

   _____

5. A sentence beginning with the subject "The number." _____

   _____

6. A sentence using the words "always stressing excellence" between the subject and verb.

   _____

   _____

7. A sentence beginning with the subject "A number." _____

   _____

8. An inverted sentence beginning with the expletive "There." _____

   _____

9. A sentence with singular compound subjects joined by "or." _____

   _____

10. A sentence beginning with "Everyone," "Nobody," or "Somebody." _____

   _____

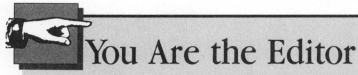

You Are the Editor

Correct all the errors you find in the following memo by writing the proper form above the error. Some errors will be in verb forms, adjectives, or other items covered in earlier chapters.

TO: Emco Sales Staff

FROM: Art Collins, Emco Sales Division

DATE: November 16, 198_

SUBJECT: Sales Efforts in the Next Quarter

As you know, the managers of the sales division is determined to try to improve sales. They have wrote all the division managers to tell us.

I have discussed our plan with my assistant, Betsy Erving, and she and me feel that there is a number of suggestions we can make. First of all, when you or one of your associates calls on potential customers, please give them our new brochure. Each of you have an ample supply of these. Betsy and myself believes that this brochure will help you make a good impression.

Next, be certain to tell the customer about our new products. Every one of them have full descriptions in our new catalog, and the customers theirselves will know that most of our products is fully guaranteed.

Finally, if you could of gone to the national meeting, you would of picked up this idea there. Call the customers the next day after you're visit. This is a affective technique.

Lets hear from you when it is convenent. Send your reports to Betsy or myself. Either her or I will study them and try to offer you more clearer suggestions about your next move. Good luck.

Key to Self-Check Exercises

Exercise 1

1. stenographers   typists
2. trunk
3. Walter   Nancy
4. thoughts
5. ideas
6. invoices
7. carried
8. is
9. sang and danced and jumped
10. are participating
11. were damaged
12. has been renovated
13. The engineers who moved to our Fort Washington

   branch

   (are much happier in this new location.)

14. A portrait of our hostess

   (was above the piano.)

15. We

   (know that you are very competent.)

16. You

   (have seen the latest film on that subject.)

17. Aggressive Tom and assertive Thelma

   (stormed into the conference room and lectured the)

   (group.)

18. The tennis players

   (are hoping to win this year's tournament.)

Exercise 2

1. I   them
2. she
3. they   him
4. he
5. she
6. I
7. I

Exercise 3

1. are
2. are
3. is
4. is
5. are
6. has her
7. has
8. was
9. were
10. has
11. were
12. was
13. were
14. is (considered as one dish)
15. was
16. prints

A DYNAMIC BUSINESS VOCABULARY

Here is another list of important business words for you to study, define, and use in sentences. Should you be uncertain about the pronunciation, be sure to consult your dictionary.

Empathy

The ability to understand the thoughts, feelings, and needs of others without being told.

The empathy he displayed for his subordinates' problems was a major factor in their job commitment.

Encumbered

Handicapped by a legal claim (applied to property).

The home was encumbered by a $10,000 second mortgage.

Endorsement

Approval or support.

Her endorsement of the product was enough to ensure its success when it was brought on the market.

Endowment

That portion of an organization's funds that produces income.

The endowment produced enough funds to pay the director's salary.

Entrepreneur

An individual who organizes and operates a business.

Ralph was an outstanding entrepreneur.

Facsimile

An exact copy or reproduction of a document.

My copy of the deed is a facsimile of the one the bank has.

Feedback

Return of information by a machine or an individual.

Feedback received from customers can tell how efficiently our sales personnel are doing their jobs.

Finance

To raise money for; economics; a branch of economics.

It will take almost $5 million to finance the building.

THE ABC'S OF BUSINESS VOCABULARY

To test your memory of the many business words and terms that we have introduced, complete the following quiz. If the answers elude you, restudy the business vocabulary lists.

1. The definition of the noun *embargo* is _____

   _____

2. The meaning of the verb *edit* is _____

   _____

3. Define the adjective *encumbered.* _____

   _____

4. The verb *defraud* means _____

   _____

5. Compose three short sentences using one of the following words or terms in each sentence: (a) finance, (b) endowment, (c) endorsement.

   _____

   _____

   _____

   _____

   _____

6. The ability to understand the thoughts, feelings, and needs of others without being told is (a) pathos, (b) humility, (c) empathy, (d) appreciation.

7. The return of information from a machine or an individual is (a) feedback, (b) backtalk, (c) inventory, (d) printout.

8. An exact copy or reproduction of a document is a (a) cassette, (b) facsimile, (c) photograph, (d) videotape.

9. An individual who organizes and operates a business is a/an (a) comptroller, (b) entrepreneur, (c) employee, (d) corporate officer.

10 Parts of Sentences
Complements and Appositives

The most common sentence pattern is not simply subject plus verb, but subject plus verb plus completer (which is usually called a *complement*). By using completers, you can add meaning and variety to your writing, and these qualities will enrich your communication skills.

Consider the following sentences:

He left.

New ideas abound for the development of the product.

Janice types beautifully.

In these sentences there are no loose ends. They are complete in themselves. Contrast them with these sentences:

The boss hired . . .

Tom is . . .

After a thorough search in the filing drawer, he found . . .

She sells . . .

In these sentences more is needed to complete the thought, to *complement* or *add on* to the subject and verb. Note the complements in these sentences:

The boss hired *Abbie.*

Tom is *the new foreman.*

After a thorough search in the filing drawer, he found *the Wilcox and Jones Insurance Company file under "C" for company.*

She sells *seashells by the seashore.*

COMPLEMENTS

The word *complement* has several meanings. Two are particularly applicable to our study of standard English:

1. Something that fills up, completes, or makes perfect, or

2. An added word or expression by which a predicate is made complete.*

The words *president* and *beautiful* in "They elected him president" and "He thought her beautiful" are examples of complements.

*From *Webster's Ninth New Collegiate Dictionary* (Springfield, MA: Merriam-Webster Inc., 1985), p. 269.

We know from these definitions that complements are *completers*. They complete the meaning of the sentence that is begun by the subject and predicate. In the following pages we shall focus on six kinds of complements:

> Direct objects
> Indirect objects
> Objective complements
> Objects of prepositions
> Predicate nominatives
> Predicate adjectives

DIRECT OBJECTS

A *direct object* is a noun or noun substitute that follows an action verb and answers the question *what?* or *whom?* that the subject and verb raise. Study these examples:

> The cabinetmaker finished the executive's bookcase on time. [What is the subject? *Cabinetmaker.* What is the verb? *Finished.* Finished what? *Bookcase. Bookcase* is the direct object.]

> Sally typed the report. [*Sally* is the subject, *typed* is the verb, and *report* is the direct object because it answers the question *what?* after the subject and verb.]

> Because of the tremendous loss of income in the last two months of the fiscal year, management changed its policies about advertising on television. [*Management* is the subject, *changed* is the verb, and *policies,* because it answers *what?* after the subject and verb, is the direct object.]

Note: Like the subject and verb, the direct object is never in a prepositional phrase. If you remove all the prepositional phrases in the previous example, all you have to consider is "Management changed its policies." It is far easier to pick out elements of sentences like subjects or direct objects from a few words than from many.

> They placed the computer on the sideboard. [The discounted phrase is *on the sideboard.* The rest of the sentence is *They placed the computer. They* is the subject. *Placed* is the verb. Placed *what? Computer. Computer* is the direct object.]

> The manager employed a new accountant. [*Manager* is the subject, *employed* is the verb, and *accountant,* because it answers *whom?,* is the direct object.]

> I will be substituting my cousin's services for my vacationing salesman's services. [The discounted phrase is *for my vacationing salesman's services;* the rest of the sentence is *I will be substituting my cousin's services; I* is the subject; *will be substituting* is the verb. Substituting *what? Services. (My cousin's) services* is the direct object.]

COMPOUND DIRECT OBJECTS

Like other parts of sentences, direct objects can be joined with coordinate conjunctions (*and* or *or*) to form compound direct objects. Note these examples, with the compound direct objects italicized:

> The new procedure helped *Mary* and *Sue.* [Helped *whom?*]

> The firm sold *pots* and *pans.* [Sold *what?*]

> Enrico earned a *salary,* a *commission,* and a *bonus.* [Earned *what?*]

> We bought an *IBM PC* and a *MacIntosh* to replace our dedicated word-processing machines. [Bought *what?*]

Note: Remember that coordinate conjunctions join words of equal grammatical rank. They join subjects, verbs, direct objects, or other equal grammatical elements.

INDIRECT OBJECTS PLUS DIRECT OBJECTS

An *indirect object* is a noun or noun substitute that *receives the action* the verb makes on the direct object. It answers the questions of *to whom? to what? for what?* and *for whom?* pertaining to the action of the main verb.

In looking for the indirect object, remember these guidelines:

1. An indirect object cannot appear without a direct object.

2. An indirect object cannot appear in a prepositional phrase.

3. If there is an indirect object, it will always precede a direct object.

4. Indirect objects always possess the direct object literally or figuratively.

5. An indirect object is usually a person rather than a thing.

Note these examples:

Samantha sent her editor three revised chapters. [The subject is *Samantha.* The verb is *sent.* Sent *what? Chapters. Chapters* is the direct object. To *whom? Her editor. Her editor* is the indirect object.]

She mailed him a letter. [*She* is the subject; *mailed* is the verb. Mailed *what? A letter. A letter* is the direct object. To *whom? Him. Him* is the indirect object.]

The radio announcer gave us the latest weather report. [*Announcer* is the subject; *gave* is the verb. Gave *what? Report. Report* is the direct object. To *whom? Us. Us* is the indirect object.]

In response to the demand of the second vice president, the office staff gave the new method a second try. [This sentence is more difficult. *Staff* is the subject. *Gave* is the verb. Gave *what? A second try. Try* is the direct object. What word receives the action of *gave* and comes before the direct object *try?* The answer is *method. Method* is the indirect object.]

Note: This example is more difficult because the indirect object is a *thing,* not a *person.*

Prepositions like *to* or *for* are clearly implied in these sentences:

Sarah wrote (to) her recommendation.

Sarah did (for) her a favor.

If the prepositions appear, there is no indirect object, even though the meaning may be exactly the same. Consider these examples:

She gave Sam her typewriter.

She gave her typewriter to Sam.

The first sentence has an indirect object, *Sam.* In the second sentence *Sam* is the object of the preposition *to* and is not an indirect object.

Indirect objects may, of course, be compound. ☑

He gave *Mary and Claudette* their five-year pins.

OBJECTIVE COMPLEMENTS

In English sentences, occasionally a noun or noun substitute or an adjective is required *after* the direct object to complete its meaning. Study these sentences:

The office staff elected Maria president [*Maria* is the direct object, but additional information is provided by the word *president.*]

Self-Check Exercise 1

Underline the *direct object* in the following sentences. The correct answers are in the key at the end of the chapter.

1. Her secretary transcribed ten letters in one hour.

2. Because of the new company policy, the division director changed his plans for the year.

3. The CPA hired a new assistant.

4. The union contract encouraged the part-time teachers to complain.

5. E. L. Robinson Co. sells the finest luggage.

6. She earned interest on her checking account balance.

Underline the *indirect object* in the following sentences.

7. We sent them the antique vase to be appraised.

8. His past employer gave him a fine compliment.

9. The neighbors granted her what she requested.

10. Mitchell gave Simon foreign stamps to expand his collection.

11. The coach tossed Verdette and Bea the remaining tennis balls.

His boss considered him outstanding. [*Him* is the direct object, but *outstanding* gives additional meaning.]

We call nouns used as *president* is used or adjectives used as *outstanding* is used *objective complements*. To locate objective complements in a sentence, just follow these guidelines:

1. Refer to the main verb. Not many verbs in English take objective complements. Those that do usually mean "consider" or "make." Here are a few examples:

   elect (make)   *appoint* (make)   *think* (consider)

2. If the verb means "consider" or "make," find the direct object in the sentence.

3. An objective complement appears after the direct object and has special reference to it. It may rename it, as *president* does, or describe it, as *outstanding* does.

verb	*dir. obj.*	*obj. comp.*
elected	Maria	president

verb	*dir. obj.*	*obj. comp.*
considered	him	outstanding

4. You can usually insert *to be* between the direct object and the objective complement without changing the meaning of the sentence.

> The office staff elected Maria (to be) president.
>
> His boss considered him (to be) outstanding.

Note how *make* or *consider* could be substituted for the verbs in the following sentences. The objective complement in each sentence is italicized.

> His association appointed him *parliamentarian*. [*Made* him parliamentarian.]
>
> Her signature rendered the lease *official*. [*Made* the lease official.]
>
> They thought the procedure *stupid*. [*Considered* the procedure stupid.]

Note: It is worth repeating that subjects, verbs, direct objects, indirect objects, and objective complements never appear in prepositional phrases.

OBJECTS OF PREPOSITIONS

Another kind of object in our study of parts of sentences is the *object of a preposition* in a prepositional phrase. Objects of prepositions are nouns or noun substitutes that follow prepositions and are linked by them to the rest of the sentence.

When looking for the object of a preposition in a prepositional phrase, remember to do two things:

1. Look for a noun or noun substitute that follows the preposition; discount all adjectives that may be between the preposition and the noun.

2. This time restrict your search to prepositional phrases.

Study the following sentences, in which the prepositional phrases are enclosed in parentheses and the objects of the prepositions are italicized.

> (In the shipping *department*) Mason works (on the loading *platform*) (beside *Kowalski*).
>
> You will find the auditor's report (on my *desk*), (in my top file *drawer*), or (in your tickler *file*).
>
> (Over the *river*) and (through the *woods*) (to Grandmother's *house*) we go.

COMPOUND OBJECTS OF PREPOSITIONS

Like other objects, objects of prepositions may be compound, connected with coordinate conjunctions (*and* or *or*). ☑

> We worked overtime (for *him* and *her*).
>
> The commission was divided (between *Sam* and *Eric*).
>
> Julio was asked to work (with *Clark* and *Estelle*).

PRONOUNS AS OBJECTS

Examine the following sentences, all of which contain pronoun errors. The errors are italicized.

> José hired *he*.
>
> She sent *I* the check.
>
> George worked with *I* on the project.

Self-Check Exercise 2

Underline the *objective complements* in the following sentences. Remember that objective complements are nouns or adjectives that appear after the direct object in a sentence; they complete the meaning of the direct object. Your answers may be checked with the key.

1. The senior class elected Bob treasurer.

2. His family considered them inefficient.

3. Her experience in presenting seminars made the workshop professional.

4. They deemed the project successful.

Underline the *objects of the prepositions* in the following sentences.

5. In the building John is the maintenance supervisor over twelve workers.

6. Those two books are on the shelf; the other two are on the chair.

7. The responsibilities are divided between the two girls.

8. The fruit-fly spraying occurred over the cluster of six houses.

9. Thomas and Anya waited for the train for one hour in the snowstorm.

10. Her grandparents did not want to part with their collection of family memorabilia.

Few writers or speakers of English make these kinds of errors. They offend the ear, causing us to notice that something is wrong and in need of correction. The following kinds of errors, however, are not uncommon:

José hired Marge and *he*.

She sent Elena and *I* the check.

George worked with Larry and *I* on the project.

You must avoid these kinds of errors if you are to be an effective user of English. Here are some hints to help you.

1. Recall from the table in the last chapter that some pronouns are in the nominative case, some are in the possessive case, and some—the ones we are concerned with here—are in the objective case. There are eight objective case pronouns:

me	us
you	you
him, her, it	them

Add to this list *whom* and *whomever.*
     Pronouns used as objects are in the objective case. Hence, all the examples in the previous sentences should be objective case pronouns.

José hired Marge and *him.*

She sent Elena and *me* the check.

George worked with Larry and *me* on the project.

2. There is an easy way to handle any problems you have with compound objects when one or more of them is a pronoun. Simply deal with each element of the compound singly, determine what it should be, and then put the sentence back together. Study these examples:

Shirley hired Marge and (I, me). [Break this sentence into two: *Shirley hired Marge* and *Shirley hired me.* Then put them back together into *Shirley hired Marge and me.*]

Roberto gave (he, him) and (I, me) the bonus. [Break this sentence into two: *Roberto gave him the bonus* and *Roberto gave me the bonus.* Then put them back together into *Roberto gave him and me the bonus.*]

Carla worked with you and (he, him). [Break this sentence into two: *Carla worked with you* and *Carla worked with him.* Then put them back together into *Carla worked with you and him.*]

Note: In the last example the *you* is no problem, as *you* is the same form whether it is in the nominative case or, as in this example, in the objective case.

BETWEEN

The word *between* creates a special problem and contributes to what are surely among the most common errors made in English. Take the sentence *He divided the money between you and (I, me).* To use the procedure in which you break the sentence into two parts does not work, as it yields nonsense sentences like *He divided the money between you* or *He divided the money between me.* Another method is required. One way to handle pronouns used with *between* is to remember that *between* is a preposition and that pronouns used as objects of prepositions take the objective case. Another method, perhaps more useful, is to try to drill yourself to use the objective case by memorizing the following six phrases:

between you and me	between her and me	between you and him
between him and me	between him and her	between you and her

If you can learn these, you will make fewer mistakes than many of your fellow users of English. ☑
Note: A reminder—use *between* with two objects; use *among* with three or more.

PREDICATE NOMINATIVES

Study these sentences:

My boss *is* the tall *fellow* on the left. [*Is* is the verb.]

John McCarthy *is* a modern *painter.* [*Is* is the verb.]

She *was* an outstanding *secretary.* [*Was* is the verb.]

In each of these sentences the verb is some form of the verb *to be.* This verb does not take direct objects (and hence cannot take indirect objects or objective complements). Rather, it usually serves to *link* the subject with a noun or noun substitute in the predicate. This kind of verb, as you learned earlier, is called a *linking verb.*

Self-Check Exercise 3

Select the correct *pronouns* in the following sentences; then check your answers with the key.

1. Roberts and (her, she) selected (him, he) for the job.

2. The payroll department sent (I, me) the overdue compensation.

3. Anne worked with (him, he) on the Apollo program.

4. The personnel director selected Maria and (him, he) for the two job openings.

5. The payroll department sent Madge and (I, me) our overdue wages.

6. Anita and (she, her) worked with Luis and (him, he) last weekend.

7. The budget director and (them, they) divided the remaining monies between (he, him) and (she, her).

The noun or noun substitute linked to the subject by a linking verb is called a *predicate nominative*. The predicate nominative renames the subject after a linking verb. Look at these examples:

> Collins was the most successful salesperson. [*Salesperson* renames *Collins,* the subject, after the linking verb *was;* hence, *salesperson* is a predicate nominative.]

> Beverly will be my first choice for the position. [*Choice* renames *Beverly,* the subject, after the linking verb *will be;* hence, *choice* is a predicate nominative.]

PRONOUNS AS PREDICATE NOMINATIVES

Because predicate nominatives rename the subject, they are in the nominative case. Therefore, when pronouns are used as predicate nominatives, they must be in the nominative case. There are eight nominative case pronouns:

I	we
you	you
he, she, it	they

Add to this list *who* and *whoever.*
Study these examples:

The winner is *she.* [*She* is a predicate nominative.]

The new employers will be *they.* [*They* is a predicate nominative.]

It is *I.* [*I* is a predicate nominative.]

To determine if a pronoun is being used as part of a compound predicate nominative, use the separation method previously discussed.

The leading candidates are Thurmond and (him, he). [The leading candidate is *Thurmond.* The leading candidate is *he.* Since *he* renames *candidate(s),* it is a predicate nominative and takes the nominative case.

The winners are Barbara and (she, her). [Divide the sentence into two parts: *The winner is Barbara* and *The winner is she.* Since the pronoun *she* renames the winner, it must be a nominative case pronoun *(she).*]

PREDICATE ADJECTIVES

Another kind of complement is a predicate adjective. In the following sentences, which have linking verbs, the predicate adjectives are italicized:

Clark has been *useful.*

Maria will be *helpful.*

The manager is *considerate.*

Just as with predicate nominatives, in each of these sentences the verb is some form of the verb *to be.* However, in these sentences the verb links descriptive words (adjectives) with the subject, instead of nouns or noun substitutes. An adjective linked to a subject by the verb *to be* is a *predicate adjective.*

The predicate adjective modifies or describes the subject, usually with an adjective that tells *what kind.* Study the predicate adjectives in these sentences:

Adela is extremely competent. [*Competent* is an adjective that modifies *Adela,* the subject, after the linking verb *is;* hence, *competent* is a predicate adjective.]

Reynolds will be helpful. [*Helpful* is an adjective that modifies *Reynolds,* the subject, after the linking verb *will be;* hence, *helpful* is a predicate adjective.]

Predicate adjectives can be a little tricky, so be careful. Study these examples and the accompanying explanations:

Reynolds will be a helpful worker. [Here *helpful* is an adjective modifying the predicate nominative *worker.* Because it does not modify the subject, it is not a predicate adjective.]

Reynolds will be helpful. [*Helpful* is a predicate adjective linked to the subject *Reynolds* by *will be,* the linking verb.]

She is going. [*Going* is part of the verb phrase *is going,* in which *is* is a helping verb, not a linking verb. *Going* is *not* a predicate adjective.]

Note: Predicate nominatives and predicate adjectives are sometimes called *subjective complements,* as they complete the subject and predicate. ☑

APPOSITIVES

Appositives are nouns or noun substitutes that rename other nouns or noun substitutes, usually ones immediately preceding them. Study the italicized appositives in the following examples:

Wilson, the *bookkeeper,* was sick last week. [The appositive *bookkeeper* renames the subject *Wilson.*]

He is Wilson, the *bookkeeper.* [The appositive *bookkeeper* renames the predicate nominative *Wilson.*]

The boss fired Wilson, the *bookkeeper.* [The appositive *bookkeeper* renames the direct object *Wilson.*]

The boss gave Wilson, the *bookkeeper,* a raise. [The appositive *bookkeeper* renames the indirect object *Wilson.*]

Self-Check Exercise 4

Underline the *predicate nominatives* in the following sentences. As you know, predicate nominatives are nouns or noun substitutes linked to subjects by linking verbs. The answers appear in the key.

1. She is the blonde model posing for the photographer.

2. The manager said, "She was an efficient employee."

3. Roberts is a vice president of Northeast Banking Company.

4. Bill's collections proved that he was a successful credit manager.

5. Sarah is my selection for the position.

Underline the *predicate adjectives* in the following sentences. Remember that predicate adjectives are adjectives linked to subjects by linking verbs.

6. The laboratory aide has been extremely helpful.

7. The computer will be quite useful in expediting our work.

8. Linda is definitely capable and well suited for her job.

9. The pocket calculator is valuable to the accounting student.

10. The Grand Canyon is scenic and interesting.

Note: Appositives should not be confused with predicate nominatives, though both sentence parts do rename. Predicate nominatives rename only the *subject* and are separated from that subject by a linking verb.

When a pronoun serves as an appositive, it takes the case of the noun or noun substitute it renames. It can be in either the nominative or objective case, depending on how the noun it renames is used in the sentence. Study these examples:

My relatives, *Jonathan Germain* and *she,* are likely candidates for awards. [*She* is an appositive renaming the subject *relatives;* hence, the nominative case is required. Note that in this example there is also a predicate nominative: *candidates.*]

Yes, my college roommates, *Geoffrey* and *he,* will be joining me in Vermont. [*He* is an appositive renaming the subject *roommates;* the nominative case is required.]

Management employed two new accountants, *Margo* and *her.* [*Her* is an appositive renaming the direct object *accountant;* hence, the objective case is required.]

Give the printouts to my partners, *Rosa Jefferson* and *her.* [*Her* is an appositive renaming the object of the preposition; it must be in the objective case.]

LET'S (LET US)

A common error in both spoken and written English involves the expression "Let's you and I . . . " Though this expression sounds correct, it is not. Objective case pronouns—*you* and *me*—are required because they actually serve as appositives to *us*. *Us* is part of the contraction *let's*, which stands for *let us*. Here is a correct sentence: ☑

> Let's you and me study the applications. [Meaning "Let us, you and me, . . . "]

SENTENCE PATTERNS

In this chapter and Chapter 9 you have studied subjects, predicates, complements, and appositives—virtually all the basic sentence parts. These parts of sentences fit into certain patterns, and though the English language is infinitely varied, the number of *common* sentence patterns is small. Here are some common patterns with examples of each:

Self-Check Exercise 5

Underline the *appositives* in the following exercise. An appositive is a noun or noun substitute that renames another noun or noun substitute that comes before it in the sentence. The answers are in the key.

1. Ming Toy, the adorable shaggy dog, learned several new tricks.

2. He is Stephen Jeffries, the world-renowned traveler.

3. The teacher praised Suzanne, the class valedictorian.

4. The supervisor gave Walter Smith, the computer programmer, extra vacation time.

5. The two jewelry salespeople, Alan and she, traveled to Germany for precious stones.

6. Trans Scope Corporation hired two consultants, Colleen Ormes and Doris Watson, to replace the two who had been promoted.

7. The assistant buyers, Clarence Thomas and Hilda Warrick, attended the retail buyers' conference in Puerto Rico.

8. We have selected John Tate, a successful insurance salesman, to represent us at the convention.

1. Subject + Verb

   Maria won.

   Over the river and through the woods to Grandmother's house we go.

2. Subject + Verb + Direct Object

   Tyrone got the job.

   In the middle of the sales campaign, Joe earned a bonus.

3. Subject + Verb + Indirect Object + Direct Object

   Dorothy sent me a letter.

   Cliff gave Tom and me a lecture about appropriate language in interoffice communication.

4. Subject + Verb + Direct Object + Objective Complement

   Bruce made me president.

   After the conflict over the merger, they considered her intelligent.

5. Subject + Verb + Predicate Nominative

   He is the boss.

   She will be the person in the middle of the squabble between Jones and him.

6. Subject + Verb + Predicate Adjective

   They are creative.

   Undoubtedly the new invoices are better for our handling of dead accounts.

7. Expletive + Verb + Subject

   There are the books.

   Here are two reasons for going over the office procedures.

Note: In this pattern the verb precedes the subject. We call this kind of sentence an *inverted order* sentence.

REVIEW

Let's take one more brief look at the complements and appositives introduced in this chapter.

Name	Part of Speech	Precedes	Follows
Direct object	Noun or noun substitute	—	Action verb
Indirect object	Noun or noun substitute	Direct object	—
Objective complement	Noun or noun substitute or adjective	—	Direct object
Object of preposition	Noun or noun substitute	—	Preposition and modifiers
Predicate nominative	Noun or noun substitute	—	Verb *to be*
Predicate adjective	Adjective	—	Verb *to be*
Appositive	Noun or noun substitute	—	Another noun or noun substitute

In the next two chapters we shall add phrases and clauses; you will then have the tools of grammar to create virtually any kind of sentence you need to communicate effectively.

APPLICATION EXERCISES

A. In the blank at the left write *true* or *false* before each of the following sentences.

_____ 1. A sentence can have an indirect object without having a direct object.

_____ 2. A sentence can have an objective complement without having a direct object.

_____ 3. A sentence can have a direct object without having either an indirect object or an objective complement.

_____ 4. Appositives are nouns or noun substitutes that rename.

_____ 5. "Between you and I" is incorrect usage.

_____ 6. Pronouns used as predicate nominatives are in the objective case.

_____ 7. Linking verbs link predicate nominatives and predicate adjectives with the subject.

_____ 8. *There + verb + subject* is an example of a normal-order sentence pattern.

_____ 9. Pronouns used as objects of prepositions are in the objective case.

_____ 10. In the sentence "The supervisor made me the foreman," *foreman* is an objective complement.

B. Using the abbreviations below, label each italicized word by writing the appropriate abbreviation immediately above it.

S = subject	OP = object of preposition
V = verb	PN = predicate nominative
DO = direct object	PA = predicate adjective
IO = indirect object	APP = appositive
OC = objective complement	

1. In the bitter argument between *him* and *me,* I said only one *word: no.*

2. The shipping *costs* were extraordinarily *high* for the month of June.

3. The manager gave *José* a *raise* in salary after six *months.*

4. Timothy and Sam *appointed Helen* the general *manager* of the Tallahassee branch office.

5. In a properly written memo, you *should be careful* of the length.

6. *Computers are* really the most expensive *items* in the office.

7. *Willie,* the office *worker* with the most *seniority,* and *Alice,* the *one* with the best attendance *record,* gave speeches at the company banquet.

8. Let's *you* and *me* decide on an alternate filing *procedure.*

9. Of the three of *us*—Ted, Norm, and Lois—Lois *was* certainly the most *efficient.*

10. His typing *skills* and general office *sense* both *impressed us* and *excited* us.

C. Underline the direct object in each sentence.

1. The Los Angeles City Council passed a resolution pertaining to political activists.

2. The court had rejected the main evidence.

3. Back in 1945, the U.S. Navy put the first digital computer through its paces.

4. Some women's organizations have fewer complaints.

5. The Reagan Administration applauded the formation of the federation.

    Underline the indirect object in each sentence.

6. The prime minister passed him the secret files.

7. Give her the formula for the math problem.

8. The Nobel Committee awarded them the 1986 Peace Prize.

9. A lover of animals, Charles bought his son a new puppy.

10. She reluctantly lent Walter the latest computer printout.

D. Complete the following fragments by writing concise sentences using either a predicate
nominative or a predicate adjective.

1. Word processing is _____

_____

2. Cooperative Education has always been _____

_____

3. Using a home message machine was _____

_____

4. A career in computer science seems to be _____

_____

5. Without a doubt, Margaret Thatcher is _____

_____

6. You might have been _____

_____

7. Large institutions have rarely been _____

_____

8. *Nova,* a PBS television program, could have been _____

_____

9. Harvard University Law School is _____

_____

10. The London stockbroker was _____

_____

Challenge Exercise

In the space at the left write the correct abbreviation for the pattern of each sentence. Use the abbreviations listed below:

S + V = Subject + verb

S + V + DO = Subject + verb + direct object

S + V + IO + DO = Subject + verb + indirect object + direct object

S + V + DO + OC = Subject + verb + direct object + objective complement

S + V + DO + OP = Subject + verb + direct object + object of preposition

S + V + PN = Subject + verb + predicate nominative

S + V + PA = Subject + verb + predicate adjective

EX + V + S = Expletive + verb + subject

_____ 1. There are numerous reasons for her failure at that job.

_____ 2. Leshaun named Irene her secretary for the project.

_____ 3. He is truly a remarkable leader for the company.

_____ 4. Despite his success with the Nelson account and his marvelous work in Omaha, nobody respects him.

_____ 5. Between you and me, the manager gave her too much responsibility.

_____ 6. For an office with limited personnel, Margarita would be outstanding.

_____ 7. After a particularly heavy period of investment, the analysts relax for a week or two.

_____ 8. Here is an exciting possibility for you in the fast-food business.

_____ 9. They found the office clean.

_____ 10. Over the river and through the woods to Grandmother's house we go.

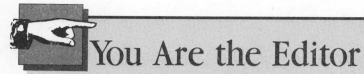

You Are the Editor

Correct all the mechanical errors in this letter.

2121 Firth Street
St. Louis, MO 63102
October 6, 198_

Mr. Carlos Soto
Personnel Manager
DeWing Supplies, Inc.
Box 45611
St. Louis, MO 63102

Dear Mr. Soto:

Since you know my mother, I am sending you the personnel information you requested.

My mother and myself moved to St. Louis when her was widowed and I was a child. We could of moved to Chicago, but St. Louis seemed preferable at the time. Just between you and I, I think Mom and me would have faired better in Chicago, but the manager of an apartment building here gave Mom and I comfortable living facilities at low-cost rental.

I graduated from Brookhaven High in St. Louis. Their was a number of good business courses at Brookhaven, and I tried to take as many as possible to improve my clerical and basic business knowledge. I also developed fast and accurate data-entry skills.

After high school I worked for Sloan Company as a data-entry operator for six months. My cousin Heather worked with my brother and I, but neither our supervisor nor her assistants was very helpful. It weren't a very good company to work for.

I recently decided to leave Sloan Company, hoping to have a chance to fill one of your available data-entry position. If you need an employment recommendation, my supervisor has agreed to send you one. Please write to me at you're convenence.

Sincerly,

Edna Price

Key to Self-Check Exercises

Exercise 1

1. letters
2. plans
3. assistant
4. teachers
5. luggage
6. interest
7. them
8. him
9. her
10. Simon
11. Verdette and Bea

Exercise 2

1. treasurer
2. inefficient
3. professional
4. successful
5. building   workers
6. shelf   chair
7. girls
8. cluster   houses
9. train   hour   snowstorm
10. collection   memorabilia

Exercise 3

1. she   him
2. me
3. him
4. him
5. me
6. she   him
7. they   him   her

Exercise 4

1. model
2. employee
3. vice president
4. manager
5. selection
6. helpful
7. useful
8. capable   suited
9. valuable
10. scenic   interesting

Exercise 5

1. dog
2. traveler
3. valedictorian
4. programmer
5. Alan and she
6. Colleen Ormes and Doris Watson
7. Clarence Thomas and Hilda Warrick
8. salesman

A DYNAMIC BUSINESS VOCABULARY

To improve your vocabulary, study the spelling of these words, their definitions, and their use in sentences. In addition, check their pronunciation by referring to your dictionary.

Fiscal

Pertaining to finance, a government's finances, or monetary policies.

The fiscal policy of the new administration was viewed with alarm by almost all banking leaders.

Flowchart

A form or diagram that indicates the various steps or processes required to complete a project.

The senior analyst instructed her two assistants on the preparation of company flowcharts.

Fluctuation

The rise and fall of prices or financial levels.

The fluctuation of the stock market results from lack of faith in our economy.

Forecasting

The estimation or calculation of future events.

No one has ever devised a successful formula for forecasting fluctuations of the stock market.

FORTRAN

An algebraic and logical language used for programming computers—an acronym for FORmula TRANslation.

One of the first high-level computer languages was FORTRAN.

Franchise

Permission granted to a person or group by an individual or organization to distribute or sell a product or service.

Most gas stations are franchises of major oil companies.

Fraud

Deliberate deception to realize personal gain.

Once the audit was completed, it was obvious how the fraud had been carried on.

Fringe benefits

A benefit given an employee in addition to the basic salary or wages.

Many fringe benefits, such as dental insurance and retirement payments, are accorded to Marshall's employees.

THE ABC'S OF BUSINESS VOCABULARY

Test your ability to answer questions that relate to the words and terms listed in this book. Complete the following exercise as quickly and as accurately as you can.

1. Compose three short sentences using one of the following in each: (a) FORTRAN, (b) flowchart, (c) franchise.

   _____

   _____

   _____

   _____

   _____

   _____

2. The definition of the verb *amortize* is _____

   _____

3. *Fringe benefits* refer to _____

   _____

4. Define the verb *adjudicate*. _____

   _____

5. The noun *fraud* means _____

   _____

6. A word that is formed from the initial letters of words in a term, title, or name (e.g., NASA, FORTRAN) is a/an (a) substitute, (b) alias, (c) nickname, (d) acronym.

7. The estimation or calculation of future events is (a) ESP, (b) magic, (c) mental telepathy, (d) forecasting.

8. An individual qualified to analyze rates and systems to determine future situations, usually involving financial matters and time, is a/an (a) rater, (b) actuary, (c) analyst, (d) financier.

9. That portion of an organization's funds that produces income is its (a) endowment, (b) savings, (c) interest, (d) bonds.

11 Phrases

One positive characteristic of good writers is that their writing has variety. Not every sentence is subject plus verb plus direct object, with a few modifiers like adjectives or adverbs thrown in here or there. Instead, good writers blend sentence patterns (as well as *sentence types* and *sentence purposes,* two items you will study in future chapters. They use vivid words, especially verbs. On this last point, consider the power that variety gives your writing. Study these sentences, all ways of writing "He said":

He mumbled.	He stuttered.	He prayed.
He asserted.	He argued.	He shouted.
He exclaimed.	He pleaded.	He whispered.

When you can use alternative words, you can give your writing flavor and variety.

Similarly, when you can use *phrases,* you also can add variety to your writing. So far what you have studied is parts of speech like nouns or pronouns and parts of sentences like subjects or direct objects. These are usually single-word elements. But in English, clusters of words frequently function together. Consider these sentences, paying attention to their explanations:

She wanted *to earn the bonus.* [Do you see how the italicized expression functions as one word—in this case as a direct object answering the question *what?* after an action verb?]

Earning the bonus was her chief desire. [Note how this italicized expression functions as one word—in this case as the subject.]

Earning the bonus, she thanked her employers. [This italicized expression functions as one word, a modifier, to tell you more about the subject, *she.*]

The bonus, *earned last week,* has been spent. [Again, the italicized expression functions as one word, this time also as a modifier to tell you more about the subject, *bonus.*]

All these expressions are phrases, the chief topic of this chapter.

CHARACTERISTICS OF PHRASES

Phrases can be defined by three characteristics:

1. A phrase contains two or more related words.

2. A phrase does not contain a subject or predicate.

3. A phrase can serve as three parts of speech:

   a. A noun (*Swimming a mile a day* is my objective.)

   b. An adjective (My supervisor, *tired from working overtime,* took a day's personal leave.)

   c. An adverb (Rebecca played the organ *with great skill.*)

We shall look closely at four kinds of phrases that appear in business writing:

1. Prepositional phrases (on the boat   in the water),

2. Gerund phrases (knitting a sweater   walking a mile),

3. Participial phrases (tired from jogging   eaten by the dog),

4. Infinitive phrases (to wash the floor   to drink apple cider).

PREPOSITIONAL PHRASES

In earlier chapters we described the prepositional phrase as a preposition plus its object (a noun or noun substitute) plus any modifiers (usually adjectives) that describe that noun or noun substitute. What remains is to look at these groups of words to see how they function as phrases, that is, as one part of speech. Study the following sentences, in which the prepositional phrases have been italicized:

> The file *by the window* holds the letters *of the applicants*. [Do you notice how these prepositional phrases serve as adjectives? They answer the question *which?* about the nouns *file* (the subject) and *letters* (the direct object).]

> The secretary sent the letter *to the president*. [In this sentence the prepositional phrase functions as an adverb, modifying the verb *sent*. It answers the question *where?*]

Prepositional phrases function in two ways:

1. As *adjectives,* they modify nouns and noun substitutes.

    > As coordinator *of the committee,* you should write a progress report. [*Of the committee* explains more about the noun *coordinator.*]

    > Joseph had a coat *of many colors*. [*Of many colors* describes the noun *coat.*]

2. As *adverbs,* they modify verbs, as well as adjectives and adverbs on occasion.

    > Place the extra chair *between you and me*. [Place (verb) where? *Between you and me.*]

    > The accountant mailed the report *at six o'clock*. [Mailed (verb) when? *At six o'clock.*]

GERUND PHRASES

A gerund is a form of a verb ending in *-ing* that is used as a noun. It is a verbal noun. To form a gerund, add *-ing* to the first principal part of the verb, with occasional spelling modifications. Look at these examples:

First Principal Part of Verb	Gerund
be	being
work	working
drive	driving
swim	swimming

Because they function as nouns (or noun substitutes), gerunds can be used in the same ways nouns can be used, that is, as subjects, direct objects, objects of prepositions, indirect objects, objective complements, predicate nominatives, or appositives. Study these illustrative sentences:

Typing is fun. [The gerund *typing* is the subject of the sentence.]

He likes *typing*. [*Typing* is a direct object.]

They gave *typing* the top priority. [*Typing* is an indirect object.]

Her task is *typing*. [*Typing* is a predicate nominative.]

She filed letters after *typing*. [*Typing* is an object of the preposition.]

Her task—*typing*—consumes most of her time. [*Typing* is an appositive.]

Note: It is unlikely that you will have a sentence in which a gerund is used as an objective complement.

Because they are part verb, gerunds can do what verbs can do: take complements, or completers, especially direct objects or indirect objects plus direct objects. Study these sentences and their explanations:

(*Typing* the letter) was a chore. [The gerund is *typing;* its object is *letter,* which is modified by *the.* The entire group of words in parentheses is the *gerund phrase,* and the entire phrase, used as a single part of speech, is used as a noun and serves as the *subject* of the sentence.]

He hated (*typing* the letter). [In this sentence the gerund phrase serves as *direct object.*]

Her task is (*typing* the letter). [In this sentence the gerund phrase is a *predicate nominative.*]

Of course, you can have a gerund with both an indirect object and a direct object:

(Typing *him* the letter) occupied her time. The gerund is *typing.* Its direct object is *letter. The* is an adjective modifier. *Him* is the indirect object. The whole gerund phrase functions as a noun and serves as the subject of the sentence.

Similarly, a gerund can take a direct object and an objective complement:

They considered (making Terry the manager). The gerund is *making.* Its direct object is *Terry. The* is an adjective modifier. *Manager* is an objective complement. The whole gerund phrase functions as a noun and serves as a direct object of the verb *considered.* Considered what? *Making Terry the manager.*

Frequently you will want to emphasize the gerund in a gerund phrase by modifying it or indicating its ownership. You can do this by using the noun's or pronoun's possessive case. Note these examples: ☑

My going to the office is important. [NOT Me going to the office.]

Rick's paneling the room enhanced the impressiveness of the office. [NOT Rick paneling the room.]

Sally's doing the work helped all of us. [In this sentence the gerund *doing* is emphasized with the word *Sally's.* The entire gerund phrase is the subject of the sentence.]

I liked *his chairing the session.* [*Chairing* is the gerund and it is emphasized with *his.* The entire gerund phrase is the direct object of *like.*]

PARTICIPIAL PHRASES

A participle is a form of the verb used as an *adjective.* There are two kinds of participles: present and past. The present participle is the first principal part of the verb plus *-ing.* Here are some examples:

First Principal Part of Verb	Present Participle
be	being
do	doing
run	running
close	closing

Self-Check Exercise 1

Underline the *prepositional phrases* in the following sentences. A prepositional phrase begins with a preposition and ends with a noun or noun substitute. It also may have modifiers (usually adjectives) describing the noun. The answers may be found in the key at the end of the chapter.

1. The plant on the table was originally placed on the shelf over the piano.

2. The president's memo was sent to the trustees, to the faculty, and to the students.

3. Behind the bookcase and under the table, you will find your school notes.

4. They are going to the seashore this summer.

5. You can find the poem in this new anthology.

Underline the *gerund phrases* in the following sentences. A gerund phrase is a group of related words that begins with a gerund.

6. Writing the memo was the comptroller's responsibility.

7. She liked piloting the airplane.

8. Her job is watering the plants and feeding the dog.

9. Giving him instructions takes time.

10. Winding the clocks is fun for the owner of E. Z. Clock Shoppe.

Select the correct *nouns* or *pronouns* in the following sentences.

11. (Me, My) writing the report took all day Sunday.

12. (Bill's, Bill) mowing the lawn prevented us from picnicking on July 4.

13. (Us, Our) planning to renovate the kitchen meant that we could not spend money on a winter vacation.

14. (Your, You) doing that for us was extremely helpful.

15. (Steven, Steven's) traveling to England meant that our buyer did not have to attend the fashion show

Yes, you are correct: the form of the present participle and the form of the gerund are exactly alike. Remember, however, that the gerund is used as a *noun* and the participle is used as an *adjective*.

The past participle is the third principal part of the verb, the verb form customarily preceded by *have* or *had*. Here are some examples:

First Principal Part of Verb	**Past Participle**
drive	driven
hide	hidden
close	closed
go	gone
bring	brought
file	filed
type	typed

A participial phrase is two or more words functioning as an *adjective*. The phrase modifies nouns or noun substitutes. Examine these examples:

The dinner table (set by Ramona) was very inviting. [*Set* is a past participle modifying the subject *table*. The whole phrase serves as an adjective.]

The work (completed by Sally) is best. [*Completed* is a past participle modifying the subject *work*. The entire phrase serves as an adjective.]

The executive liked the work (completed by Sally). [*Completed* is a past participle modifying the direct object *work*. The participial phrase functions as an adjective.]

Participles are part verbs. Therefore, they can have all the completers that verbs can have: direct objects, indirect objects plus direct objects, etc. Study these examples:

(Completing her work), Sally took a break. [*Completing* is the present participle; *work* is the direct object of the participle. The entire group of words within parentheses is a participial phrase that functions as an adjective. The phrase modifies the subject, *Sally.*]

Note: A participial phrase that introduces a sentence is called an *introductory participial phrase* and is separated from the subject, *which it must modify,* by a comma.

Calculating the statistics, Charles realized that his math skills were rusty. [*Calculating* is the present participle; *statistics* is the direct object of *calculating*. The entire participial phrase serves as an adjective modifying the subject, *Charles.*]

TELLING PRESENT PARTICIPLES FROM GERUNDS

Study these sentences:

1. (*Doing* the bookwork) was Marty's main job.
2. (*Doing* the bookwork), Marty used a new method.
3. After (*doing* the bookwork), Marty began a letter.

What are the italicized words—gerunds or participles? To find out, you have to examine how they are used in sentences. In sentences (1) and (3) *doing* is a gerund because it functions as a noun, in (1) as the subject of the sentence, in (3) as the object of a preposition. In (2), however, *doing* is an adjective modifying *Marty;* hence, it is a participle.

Another method is to use the "something" test. For a gerund phrase you can usually substitute the word *something* and the sentence will still make structural sense:

Something was Marty's main job.

After *something,* Marty began a letter.

In place of a participle, however, *something* will seem awkward, structurally unsound:

Something, Marty used a new method.

(We shall return to the "something" test in the next chapter, on clauses.)

INFINITIVE PHRASES

Another kind of verbal phrase is the *infinitive phrase,* in which the key word is an infinitive. An infinitive is the first principal part of the verb preceded by the word *to.* These are infinitives:

Principal Part of Verb	Infinitive
go	to go
type	to type
have	to have
write	to write

Infinitives are used as nouns, adjectives, and adverbs. Because it is part verb, an infinitive can, like a gerund and a participle, take complements; an infinitive and any complements form the *infinitive phrase.* Study these examples:

To get the job was John's first priority. [*To get the job* is an infinitive phrase used as a noun and serving as the subject of the sentence. *Job* is the direct object of the infinitive *to get.*]

John wanted *to get the job.* [Here the same infinitive phrase is used as a direct object.]

The job *to get* is in the supply room. [The infinitive *to get* functions as an adjective modifying the noun *job,* which is the subject of the sentence.]

Getting a job is hard *to do.* [*To do* is an infinitive used as an adverb and modifying the predicate adjective *hard.* Note that in this sentence the subject is the gerund phrase *getting a job.*]

To do the work himself was John's goal. [In this sentence the italicized infinitive phrase is used as a noun and serves as the subject.]

Infinitives must not be confused with prepositional phrases that begin with *to.*

1. Infinitive phrases begin with *to; to* is followed by a verb.

2. Prepositional phrases begin with *to,* followed by a noun or noun substitute and any modifiers.

Here are some examples:

Infinitive	Prepositional Phrase
to communicate	to Wanamaker's store
to swim	to dinner
to write	to them
to order	to Chicago
to go	to Mary

If a pronoun serves as the subject of the infinitive, the subject is in the *objective* case because it is the object of a preceding verb.

> Robert asked *him* to clean the deck. [*Him* is the subject of *to clean* and the object of *asked.*]

> The vice president told *her* to begin her vacation next Saturday. [*Her* is the subject of *to begin* and the object of *told.*]

You will recall, of course, that phrases were defined as groups of related words that do not contain subjects or predicates. The *subject of the infinitive* is the only exception to that rule. ☑

Self-Check Exercise 2

Underline the *participial phrases* in the following sentences. The answers can be found in the key.

1. The girl dressed in her new suit was well received by the interviewer.

2. George Hurst admired the report written by the new junior accountant.

3. Finishing the job, Harold looked forward to his vacation.

4. She completed the course taught by her favorite professor.

5. Michael, finished for the day, left his office briskly.

Underline the *infinitive phrases* in the following sentences.

6. To sing that operatic aria is an easy task for Luciano Pavarotti.

7. Enrico will be happy to complete that project.

8. Amelia planned to walk to the college library.

9. The interns were eager to leave the hospital.

10. Do you wish to order Chinese food for dinner?

VERBALS AND ADVERBS

Because verbals—gerunds, participles, and infinitives—are part verbs, they can be modified by adverbs. The adverb is a part of the *verbal phrase*.

> *Typing quickly* creates errors. [*Typing quickly* is a gerund phrase used as the subject; *quickly* is an adverb modifying *typing.*]

> *Typing quickly,* Marcia soon finished the letter. [In this sentence *typing quickly* is a participial phrase modifying *Marcia. Quickly* modifies *typing.*]

Some years ago one of the unforgivable sins in English was the "split infinitive": *to quickly type.* You should be aware that, though most people no longer consider this error quite so monumental, some will still note it if you make it. It is better to be on the safe side and avoid split infinitives.

Avoid	Use
to carefully prepare	to prepare carefully
to accurately keyboard	to keyboard accurately
to quickly begin	to begin quickly
to generously donate	to donate generously

Another reason to avoid split infinitives is that they frequently lead to awkward-sounding constructions.

DANGLING VERBALS

A far more grievous and confusing error is the *dangling verbal.* Usually this is a verbal phrase that introduces a sentence but does not modify or relate to the subject of the sentence in a logical and clear manner. These sentences contain errors:

> Hurrying out of the office door, a collision seemed inevitable. [Was the collision doing the hurrying?]

> After sorting the mail, the coffee was made. [Did the coffee sort the mail?]

> To type clean letters, a new ribbon is needed. [Does the ribbon do the typing?]

Now examine these correct forms:

> Hurrying out of the office door, you should watch out for collisions. [Here the participial phrase *hurrying out of the door* modifies the subject *you.*]

> After sorting the mail, William made the coffee. [The gerund phrase *sorting the mail* serves as the object of the preposition *after.* The phrase tells when William made the coffee.]

> To type clean letters, you will need a new ribbon. [The infinitive phrase *to type clean letters* serves as an adverb modifying the verb *will need. You* will be doing the typing.]

PARALLEL STRUCTURE

Elegant sentences can often be written using verb phrases, but you must take care to use them correctly. This is especially true if you use phrases in coordinate ways. Coordinate conjunctions connect words, phrases, and clauses of equal grammatical rank. If they connect phrases, the phrases must be alike. Connecting items of equal grammatical rank creates *parallel structure.* In the case of phrases, if the phrases are not alike, parallelism does not exist. In these examples, note first the faulty parallelism and next its correction:

Wrong (Not Parallel)	Correct (Parallel)
The executive liked fishing and to swim.	The executive liked fishing and swimming. OR The executive liked to fish and to swim.
After winning the promotion and when he took his new job, Jones became elated.	After winning the promotion and taking his new job, Jones became elated. OR When he won the promotion and took over his new job, Jones became elated.
The procedure is: a. To arrive by 8:45 a.m. b. Sitting at your desk by 9:00 a.m. c. A break from 10:15 to 10:30. d. Work should be finished by noon.	The procedure is: a. To arrive by 8:45 a.m. b. To sit at your desk by 9:00 a.m. c. To take a break from 10:15 to 10:30. d. To finish your work by noon.

We will return later to parallel structure. It can be an important help in developing your writing skill. ☑

Self-Check Exercise 3

Select the correct answers in the following exercise. You will want to check your answers with those in the key.

1. I plan (to speedily type this, to type this speedily).

2. Be sure (to accurately complete this, to complete this accurately).

3. He appears (to gradually improve, to improve gradually).

4. Fleeing out of the door, (the house keys were dropped, he dropped the house keys).

5. To read with understanding, (books must be well written, William must have well-written books available to him).

6. For relaxation, she preferred to bowl (and working on her embroidery, and to embroider).

7. Eating (and to drink, and drinking) were pastimes at the school picnic.

8. Her duties as an administrative assistant include supervising, dictating, and (scheduling, a look at the daily schedules).

9. (To clean the basement, Cleaning the basement) and (organizing the Boy Scouts' picnic, to organize the Boy Scouts' picnic) were the Scout leader's weekend chores.

10. Decorating the office complex, (the wall lamps fit in, the partners selected wall lamps).

REVIEW

This summary of the special characteristics of the phrases described in this chapter should be helpful for quick reference.

Type of Phrase	Format	Function
Prepositional	1. Phrase begins with preposition. 2. Preposition is followed by noun or noun substitute and any modifiers.	As adjective or adverb
Gerund	1. Phrase begins with gerund. 2. Gerund is first principal part of verb plus -*ing*. 3. Gerund is followed by one or more related words.	As noun or noun substitute
Participial	1. Phrase begins with present or past participle. 2. Present participle (like gerund) is first principal part of verb plus -*ing*. Past participle is third principal part of verb. 3. Participles are followed by one or more related words.	As adjective
Infinitive	1. Phrase generally begins with infinitive. 2. Infinitive is the present tense of verb preceded by *to*. 3. Infinitive is followed by one or more related words.	As noun, adjective, or adverb

APPLICATION EXERCISES

A. Put *true* or *false* in the blank at the left of each sentence.

_____ 1. A verbal is part verb and part some other part of speech.

_____ 2. Past participles are formed by putting *to* in front of the third principal part of the verb.

_____ 3. The subject of an infinitive, if a pronoun, is in the nominative case.

_____ 4. Gerunds can take direct objects and indirect objects plus direct objects.

_____ 5. A gerund, because it is part noun, can be used as a predicate adjective.

_____ 6. An introductory participial phrase typically modifies the subject of the sentence.

_____ 7. Infinitives may not take direct objects.

_____ 8. Because they can be used as nouns, infinitives can serve as appositives.

_____ 9. A phrase does not contain a predicate.

_____ 10. A participle may take a direct object.

B. In the following sentences there are 15 prepositional phrases. In the spaces provided, write each phrase and tell what word it modifies. The first sentence is completed for you.

1. After the sales program, George divided the bonus between you and me.
   1. (a) After the sales program
      (b) modifies *divided*
   2. (a) between you and me
      (b) modifies *divided*

2. The report on the desk near the window caught my eye during her presentation on office management.

3. Eggerston and O'Malley, the law firm in Sunningdale, called me about a switch in my insurance policy.

4. On Thanksgiving Day, he announced to his family that he planned to retire from the company.

5. Over the river and through the woods to Grandmother's house we go.

C. In the following sentences there are 11 gerund phrases. In the spaces provided, write each gerund phrase and tell how it functions in the sentence. (Remember that gerund phrases are noun substitutes. Therefore, they function as subjects, direct objects, indirect objects, objective complements, predicate nominatives, and appositives.) The first sentence is completed for you.

1. Winning the interoffice game after losing our best player was a real pleasure.

    1. (a) Winning the interoffice game
       (b) subject of sentence

    2. (a) losing our best player
       (b) object of preposition *after*

2. He tried fixing the copy machine himself.

3. Audrey's main task—doing the book work—was completed between typing her reports and filing the correspondence.

4. Mr. Smith's hobby was growing plants in his office.

5. Marcia and Lewis gave listening carefully a second chance after learning about its usefulness.

6. Doing your best work all the time is really an important aspect of successful work in any field.

7. She began studying the new office manual during her spare time. (Careful: *during,* you will recall, is a preposition.)

D. In the following sentences there are ten participial phrases. In the spaces provided, write each participial phrase and tell what word it modifies. Remember that present participles are the first principal part of the verb plus *-ing*. Past participles are the third principal part of the verb. Remember, too, that they are used as adjectives to modify a noun or noun substitute. The first sentence is completed for you.

1. Ordering the new merchandise, she used the computer purchased last month.

    1. (a) Ordering the new merchandise
        (b) modifies *she*

    2. (a) purchased last month
        (b) modifies *computer*

2. The clock, sitting on my desk and grinning its ugly grin, moves very slowly on Friday afternoons.

3. Copied first by hand and then by machine, the new printouts looked excellent.

4. Speaking for myself, I believe in the method employed by Turner and Wells and advocated by Richard Johnson.

5. The curtains, blowing gently in the breeze, added much to our enjoyment of the new headquarters.

6. Arguing for higher salaries, a task made more difficult by the decline in sales, exhausted Carlos. (Careful: There is also a gerund phrase in this sentence.)

E. In the following sentences there are nine infinitive phrases. In the spaces provided, write each infinitive phrase and tell what word it modifies or how it functions in the sentence. Remember that infinitives are the first principal part of the verb preceded by *to*. The first sentence is completed for you.

1. To get the best value for her money, she decided to buy a used file cabinet.

    1. (a) To get the best value for her money
       (b) modifies *decided*

    2. (a) to buy a used file cabinet
       (b) direct object

2. Thomas wanted to create the new logo for the stationery.

3. The receptionist had no time to waste.

4. His job, to train the new employees, was difficult.

5. His job was to train the new employees.

6. To get to work on time and to leave on time are two commands to obey.

Challenge Exercise

This exercise is called "Putting It All Together." In the sentences that follow are 13 verbal phrases—gerund, participial, and infinitive. For each sentence, write the phrases, tell what kind they are, and tell how they are used in the sentence. The first sentence is completed for you. (Remember that one verbal phrase can be a part of another.)

1. After doing good work, Clarice was glad to spend the raise given to her.

    1. (a) doing good work
       (b) gerund phrase
       (c) object of preposition *after*

    2. (a) to spend the raise given to her
       (b) infinitive phrase
       (c) adverb modifying *glad*

    3. (a) given to her
       (b) participial phrase
       (c) modifies *raise*

2. Wanting to succeed is a key element in every successful career.

3. Born 17 years apart, the two brothers functioned like twins in the office.

4. At every office party John tries to drink too much and embarrasses himself by making a fool of himself.

5. Shana's wish to earn enough money for a new car gave her an incentive.

6. He liked sweeping the office and watering the plants.

7. Knowing the way to put in a new ribbon, Kathy was always called on for that task.

You Are the Editor
Correct all the mechanical errors you find in the following memo.

TO: Office Staff, Women Especially

FROM: Claude Arnold

DATE: November 10, 198_

SUBJECT: Dress Code for Employees

Its not easy to write a memo like this one. Yet, Mr. Nelson and myself feel that some of the members of the office staff is dressing very poorly. Coming to work in these kind of clothes, the office looks bad. We do not mind you wearing slack's, though, between you and I, I don't think Mr. Nelson likes slacks too much. He don't say anything about them, but he could of said that they were alright and he has not done so.

I have already gone to the trouble of reminding some of you about your appearance. I just talked with Monica, for example. I told her to wear more simpler clothes. Mr. Nelson could of brung there dress styles' to the attention of the board, but he did not do so, and I hope he does not do so in the future.

For now, then, try to dress as appropriately as possible. I know that some of you likes wearing bright clothes and to dress in a flashy manner, but its going to be better for all of us if each of the workers try to dress well.

Thank you for you're attention to this matter.

Key to Self-Check Exercises

Exercise 1

1. on the table   on the shelf   over the piano
2. to the trustees   to the faculty to the students
3. Behind the bookcase   under the table
4. to the seashore
5. in this new anthology
6. Writing the memo
7. piloting the airplane
8. watering the plants   feeding the dog
9. Giving him instructions
10. Winding the clocks
11. My
12. Bill's
13. Our
14. Your
15. Steven's

Exercise 2

1. dressed in her new suit
2. written by the new junior accountant
3. Finishing the job
4. taught by her favorite professor
5. finished for the day
6. To sing that operatic aria
7. to complete that project
8. to walk
9. to leave the hospital
10. to order Chinese food

Exercise 3

1. to type this speedily
2. to complete this accurately
3. to improve gradually
4. he dropped the house keys
5. William must have well-written books available to him
6. and to embroider
7. and drinking
8. scheduling
9. To clean the basement   to organize the Boy Scouts' picnic OR Cleaning the basement   organizing the Boy Scouts' picnic
10. the partners selected wall lamps

A DYNAMIC BUSINESS VOCABULARY

Here are some additional business words and terms to learn. Study their spelling, definitions, and use in sentences. Refer to a dictionary for their correct pronunciation if you are in doubt.

Frozen asset

An asset that cannot be used because of legal action instituted.

Although the firm's sales were excellent, all its assets had been frozen by court order.

Garnishee

To take the property or income of an individual to satisfy a debt.

Whitman Department Store will begin to garnishee Steven's wages in three days.

Gratuity

A material gift, such as money, given in return for services, as in a tip.

The average gratuity given to a waitress is 15 percent of the bill.

Grievance

A complaint, either actual or supposed, regarded as a just cause for protest.

The grievance committee of the union will meet to review Mr. Compton's complaint against the company.

Gross

The total amount before deductions.
Steven's gross pay was $1,600 last month.

Guarantor

An individual who promises to assume responsibility for another.

Mr. Banks served as the guarantor for his son's loan.

Hardware

The physical equipment that goes into a computer system, consisting of the central processing unit plus all peripherals.

AT&T plans to compete with the leading computer hardware manufacturers for a sizable part of the market.

Holding company

A company that controls, either partially or completely, the interests of another company.

Standard Oil is the holding company of several smaller firms.

Name _____

THE ABC'S OF BUSINESS VOCABULARY

Do you remember the business words that have been introduced in each chapter to expand your vocabulary? Test your knowledge by answering these questions.

1. The definition of the noun *gratuity* is _____
_____

2. The meaning of *frozen asset* is _____
_____

3. The noun *gross* means _____
_____

4. A company that controls either partially or completely the interests of another company is a/an (a) holding company, (b) partnership, (c) associate, (d) corporation.

5. The raising of money or a branch of economics is (a) pharmacy, (b) sociology, (c) history, (d) finance.

6. The physical equipment that goes into a computer system, consisting of the CPU and all the peripherals is the (a) typewriter, (b) software, (c) hardware, (d) program.

7. Compose three short sentences using one of the following words in each sentence: (a) grievance, (b) fraud, (c) franchise.

_____
_____
_____
_____
_____
_____

12 Clauses

The difference between experienced and inexperienced physicians is not so much what they do, but what skills they bring to their tasks. Though both groups may diagnose or prescribe or operate, doctors who have been in the profession for some years choose techniques from a broader repertory; they have many options.

So is it with writers. Few beginning writers possess the sentence-manipulation practices their more experienced counterparts use. They lack skill in using a rich variety of verbs or complements or phrases. They especially lack skill in improving their writing with clauses.

HOW CLAUSES DIFFER FROM PHRASES

A *clause* is a group of related words that contains a subject and a predicate. A phrase, as was discussed in the previous chapter, is a group of related words that does not contain a subject or predicate and that functions as a single part of speech.

To refresh your memory, consider these phrases:

to his office [prepositional phrase]

winning the lottery [gerund phrase]

between you and me [prepositional phrase]

doing the book work [gerund phrase if used as a noun, participial phrase if used as an adjective]

ordering the paint and wallpaper [gerund phrase]

Now let's look at some clauses that contain subjects and predicates:

the doctor opened his office

when I arrive

who recently established a retail shoe business

as soon as college classes begin

that this winter the weather would be comparatively mild

INDEPENDENT VERSUS DEPENDENT CLAUSES

There are two kinds of clauses:

1. Independent clauses (frequently referred to as *main clauses*),

2. Dependent clauses (sometimes called *subordinate clauses*).

Independent clauses can stand alone as sentences; dependent clauses cannot.

The first clause above is an independent clause. *The doctor opened his office* could stand alone and serve as a complete sentence. The other clauses are dependent clauses; they have two distinctive characteristics:

1. Each one is a group of related words with a subject and predicate.

2. Not one could stand alone as a complete sentence, for each is an incomplete thought.

Consider the differences in these additional pairs of independent and dependent clauses:

When we went to work Friday morning [dependent clause]

We went to work Friday morning [independent clause]

In the first clause we need to know more. We need to know, for example, what happened Friday morning. The second clause could stand alone as a complete sentence.

A new method would help. [independent clause]

That a new method would help. [dependent clause]

In the second clause we need to know who said or wrote or thought that a new method would help. In the first clause we have a complete thought that could serve as a complete sentence.

Who began the project [dependent clause]

Tom began the project [independent clause]

In the first clause we need to know whether it was Tom or Sarah or Michael or someone else who began the project. That clause cannot stand alone as a sentence. In the second clause we have a complete thought.

In each of the three pairs above was an independent clause, which could stand alone as a sentence. When an independent clause by itself is a sentence, we often call it a *simple sentence*. When it is combined with other clauses, we call it an *independent clause*. You can see the difference in these examples:

Tom began the project. [This is a simple sentence.]

Tom, who is the second vice president, began the project. [In this sentence we also have a dependent clause, *who is the second vice president.* Hence, the clause *Tom began the project* is an independent clause.]

Although there was no longer a need for the forms, the accountant mailed the package to the Ocean City office. [In this sentence we have a dependent clause, *although there was no longer a need for the forms,* and an independent clause, *the accountant mailed the package to the Ocean City office.*]

USING DEPENDENT CLAUSES

You will want your business writing to have power and force. One good way to achieve this goal is to learn the uses of effective subordination by combining clauses in your sentences. Such knowledge will enable you to embed one idea in another, to avoid immature sentences, to have options. Consider these sentences:

Tom began the project.

Tom is the second vice president.

He began it last Friday.

On Friday it rained.

It was a perfect day to sell umbrellas.

Here is one possible revision that illustrates how a thought can be expanded through the proper use of clauses:

(When it rained last Friday) Tom (who is our second vice president) began the project (because he knew that it was a perfect day to sell umbrellas).

In this revision the dependent clauses are enclosed in parentheses. The independent clause is *Tom began the project*. Now let's take a look at the entire sentence correctly punctuated:

When it rained last Friday, Tom, who is our second vice president, began the project because he knew that it was a perfect day to sell umbrellas.

KINDS OF DEPENDENT CLAUSES

In this chapter you will study three kinds of dependent clauses. This will help you understand the special characteristics and uses of these important parts of sentences and help you use them effectively in your writing. The three categories are noun, adjective, and adverbial clauses. Before we look closely at the differences among these three kinds of clauses, let's consider their similarities:

1. All the clauses are groups of related words that contain subjects and predicates.

2. All the clauses are dependent clauses.

3. All the clauses relate to one or more words in their complete sentences and, subsequently, depend on those same words.

Now let's look at their differences and special characteristics.

NOUN CLAUSES

A *noun* clause has four characteristics:

1. It is a dependent clause that serves as a *noun*.

2. It is a group of related words containing a subject and a predicate.

3. These related words function as a noun functions in a sentence.

4. It can act as a subject, direct object, object of a preposition, predicate nominative, appositive, or indirect object or objective complement (rarely).

Let's examine the more common uses.

AS A SUBJECT

What Carmelita did bothered the other workers. [The noun clause, *What Carmelita did,* functions as the subject of the sentence. In the clause itself, *Carmelita* is its subject, *did* is its verb, and *what* is its direct object.]

That Stephanie typed the project surprised her instructor. [The noun clause, *That Stephanie typed the project,* functions as the subject of the sentence.]

AS A DIRECT OBJECT

Jodie knew *that Ed divided the work between him and her.* [The noun clause, *that Ed divided the work between him and her,* tells what Jodie knew. It functions, therefore, as a direct object of the verb *knew.*]

The lawyer thought *that her client's will should be updated.* [The noun clause, *that her client's will should be updated,* tells what the lawyer thought. It serves as a direct object of the verb *thought.*]

AS AN OBJECT OF A PREPOSITION

Jack awarded the bonus to *whoever sold the biggest order.* [The noun clause, *whoever sold the biggest order,* serves as the object of the preposition *to. Whoever,* a nominative case pronoun, serves as the subject of the noun clause.]

The family offered a reward to *whoever returned the lost stocks and bonds.* [The noun clause, *whoever returned the lost stocks and bonds,* serves as the object of the preposition *to.*]

AS A PREDICATE NOMINATIVE

Doreen's answer was *that she would take the position.* [The noun clause, *that she would take the position,* follows the intransitive verb *was* and functions as a predicate nominative.]

The computer programmer's reply will be *that she can no longer work overtime on the weekends.* [The noun clause, *that she can no longer work overtime on the weekends,* follows the intransitive verb *will be* and functions as a predicate nominative.]

AS AN APPOSITIVE

Karl's reason for not writing the office manual—*that he was already too busy*—did not please his supervisor. [The noun clause, *that he was already too busy,* refers to the noun *reason.* It serves as an appositive explaining what Karl's reason was. In this noun clause there are a subject *(he),* a verb *(was),* and a predicate adjective *(busy).*]

His New Year's resolution—*that he will complete all projects on time*—may be difficult to fulfill. [The noun clause, *that he will complete all projects on time,* refers to the noun *resolution.* It acts as an appositive in the sentence explaining what his resolution is.]

Noun clauses can often be recognized by using the "something" test described in the last chapter. If you substitute *something* for the noun clause, the sentence will make structural sense.

Something bothered the other workers.

Jodie knew *something.*

Doreen's answer was *something.*

Jack awarded the bonus to *some(one).*

ADJECTIVE CLAUSES

An *adjective* clause is all of the following:

1. A dependent clause that is used as an *adjective.*

2. A group of related words containing a subject and a predicate.

3. A group of related words that functions as an adjective functions in a sentence.

4. A clause that modifies or explains nouns or noun substitutes.

Study these examples:

Evelyn, *who does my typing,* is an outstanding secretary. [The adjective clause *who does my typing* modifies the noun *Evelyn,* the subject of the main clause.]

I am very fond of Lillian, *who works in my office.* [*Who works in my office* is an adjective clause, which modifies the noun *Lillian,* the object of the preposition *of.*]

The filing *that Linda did* was exceptionally well done. [*That Linda did* is an adjective clause modifying the noun *filing.*]

Adjective clauses often begin with the *relative pronouns: who, whom, whose, which,* and *that.* Sometimes these words are not expressed, but understood.

The work (that) he did was important.

Sometimes, too, a word like *where* will introduce an adjective clause:

The room *where they worked* was too cold.

Note: The same group of words could function as a noun clause or an adjective clause:

I wonder *who will order the new material.* [The italicized noun clause is used as a direct object. It answers the question I wonder *what?*]

The person *who will order the new material* is Donna. [The italicized words are an adjective clause used to modify the noun *person.*]

You can usually tell whether a clause is a noun or an adjective clause by applying the *something* test. If the words are a noun clause, substituting the word *something* for them will leave you with a sentence that is structurally sound. If the words are an adjective clause, substituting *something* for them will leave you with an awkward or nonsensical sentence:

I wonder *something* [Noun clause]

The staff person *something* is Donna. [Adjective clause]

ADVERBIAL CLAUSES

An *adverbial* clause can be described in five ways:

1. As a dependent clause that is used as an *adverb.*

2. As a group of related words containing a subject and a predicate.

3. As a group of related words that functions as an adverb functions in a sentence.

4. As a clause that modifies and explains verbs.

5. As a clause that on rare occasions modifies and explains adjectives or adverbs.

Here are some examples:

When you go to the office, you should dress well. [The adverbial clause *when you go to the office* modifies the verb *should dress.*]

If he can, Clark will prepare the agenda. [The adverbial clause *if he can* modifies the verb *will prepare.*]

As soon as the accountant can, she will finish the audit. [The adverbial clause *as soon as the accountant can* modifies the verb *will finish.*]

In each of the three examples above, note that the adverbial clause introduces the sentence. When the adverbial clause (dependent clause) precedes the independent clause, a comma is inserted to separate the two clauses. However, if the adverbial clause (dependent clause) follows the independent clause, usually no comma is needed.

Here are some examples in which no comma is needed:

> You should dress well *when you go to the office.* [No comma—the adverbial clause follows the independent clause.]

> Clark will prepare the agenda *if he can.* [No comma.]

> The accountant will finish the audit *as soon as she can.* [No comma]

> He writes better *than I do.* [The adverbial clause *than I do* modifies the adverb *better.*]

Most adverbial clauses begin with a conjunction called a *subordinating* or *adverbial conjunction.* Here is a list of common adverbial conjunctions with suggested clauses:

after she reads the will	*provided that* they do not have to work overtime
although she may hide the will	*since* she was promoted
as he was writing his will	*unless* we hear from you
as if he were an officer	*until* we hear from you
as though he were an officer	*when* she reads the will
because they were working overtime	*where* you would prefer to live
if they have to work overtime	*while* they were working overtime

Occasionally in writing and often in speaking, we do not complete an adverbial clause. Note the incomplete clauses in these sentences with the understood words in parentheses:

> Larson worked harder than Smith (worked).

> When (you are) typing, try to keep the margins properly aligned.

Note: Pronouns can be a source of problems in incomplete adverbial clauses. Study the choices in these sentences:

> She works better than (he, him). [*He* is correct because *he* is the subject of the implied adverbial clause *he works,* and subjects are in the nominative case.]

> George is shorter than (her, she). [*She* is correct. If complete, the sentence would read *George is shorter than she is.*]

Sometimes you are better advised to write out the clause completely. In this sentence, for example, two interpretations are possible:

> I admire Shirley more than Estella. [admires Shirley]

> I admire Shirley more than Estella. [more than I admire Estella]

Do I admire Shirley more than Estella admires Shirley, or more than I admire Estella? It is difficult to tell the meaning when the clause is incomplete. Now you can see why it is frequently better to write out the entire clause. ☑

PHRASES AND CLAUSES TOGETHER

Skilled writers blend phrases and clauses in their writing. You may recall that gerund phrases function as nouns. They can therefore function as subjects of sentences and also as subjects of dependent clauses. Similarly, one clause can be embedded in another. Study this example and the accompanying explanation.

> She knew that redoing the worksheets would be a big job. [In this sentence the noun clause, *that redoing the worksheets would be a big job,* is used as the direct object of *knew.* Embedded within that noun clause is a gerund phrase, *redoing the worksheets.* This phrase serves as the subject of the whole noun clause.]

Self-Check Exercise 1

Underline the *dependent noun clauses* in the following sentences. All answers to this exercise can be found in the key.

1. What Bobby cleaned helped the owner of the property.

2. Genevieve's views on bringing up children—that they should be seen and not heard—were unpopular with her family.

3. The social worker realized that the participants in the program would succeed.

4. The student's answer was that her home responsibilities came first.

5. The dean gave the award to whoever had the highest scholastic average that year.

Underline the *dependent adjective clauses* in the following sentences:

6. Diane, who serves as his secretary, has been ill this winter.

7. He is married to Mary Stewart, who is a partner in their law firm.

8. The picture that Suzanne drew won first prize in the sidewalk art contest.

9. The house where they lived has been sold.

Underline the *dependent adverbial clauses* in the following sentences:

10. When you go shopping, you should use your credit cards.

11. If he can, my grandfather will attend our business opening.

12. Although we have no job openings, we will hold your application on file.

13. Since you are unavailable, we will contact one of your colleagues.

14. We will not begin the project because we are unprepared.

Select the correct *pronouns* in the following sentences:

15. She types better than (he, him).

16. Our department earns less than (them, they).

17. He grew taller than (her, she).

18. That couple has traveled more than (us, we).

COMPLEXITY OF SENTENCES

We have already classified sentences according to their pattern of subjects, verbs, and so forth. You will recall the S + V + DO pattern (subject plus verb plus direct object) and the various other patterns. Another method of classification is to use the clause structure.* There are several categories of sentences. In the following discussion we shall examine simple, compound, complex, and compound-complex sentences.

SIMPLE SENTENCES

A *simple sentence* contains one independent clause and no dependent clauses. Here are four examples of simple sentences:

The professor critiqued the students' technical writing reports.

In the front section of the office, the boss has a large antique clock. [Two prepositional phrases precede one independent clause.]

Over the river and through the woods to Grandmother's house we go. [In this sentence three prepositional phrases precede the subject and predicate.]

The computer operators and systems analysts met and discussed the new computer installation. [Here we have a compound subject and compound predicate but only one independent clause.]

COMPOUND SENTENCES

A *compound sentence* differs from a simple sentence in that it contains *two or more* independent clauses (instead of one) and no dependent clauses. The multiple independent clauses are joined by coordinating conjunctions. Here are three examples:

Karen typed the letters and Cerise stuffed them into envelopes. [Two short independent clauses are joined by the conjunction *and.*]

George carefully considered the job, for he had been interested in returning to this field for a long time. [The two independent clauses are joined by the conjunction *for* preceded by a comma. Only in very short compound sentences is the comma omitted before the coordinating conjunction.]

First, pick up your luggage from the baggage area, and second, stand in the U.S. Customs line for luggage inspection. [The two independent clauses are joined by the conjunction *and,* which is preceded by a comma.]

Note: Remember that independent clauses can have compound subjects, compound predicates, or both. But a compound subject or compound predicate does not make a compound sentence. A compound sentence must have two or more independent clauses. Look at these examples:

Lorna and Bob are a practicing psychologist and practicing psychiatrist, respectively. [Simple sentence with compound subject. This is only one independent clause.]

The lawyer and accountant sat and waited for their clients, but the Jones brothers decided not to meet with them after all. [A compound sentence with two independent clauses joined by *but.* The first independent clause has a compound subject and predicate; the second independent clause has only one subject and predicate.]

COMPLEX SENTENCES

A *complex sentence* contains one independent clause plus one or more dependent clauses. Complex sentences may be written in two ways:

*Knowing the clause structure classification and being able to use alternative patterns or complexities will help you be a good writer.

1. With the dependent clause preceding the independent clause.

   If you cannot learn to run a computer, [dependent clause] the position will go to someone who can. [independent clause]

   When Carlos opened the mail, [dependent clause] he learned that he had been given a new title. [independent clause]

2. With the independent clause preceding the dependent clause.

   The position will go to someone who can [independent clause] if you cannot learn to run a computer. [dependent clause]

   Carlos learned that he had been given a new title [independent clause] when he opened the mail. [dependent clause]

Note: In a complex sentence when the dependent clause precedes the independent clause, separate the two clauses with a comma. Conversely, when the independent clause precedes the dependent clause, the comma is usually omitted.

COMPOUND-COMPLEX SENTENCES

Here we have a longer, more complicated type of sentence. Its special characteristics are:

1. It contains two or more independent clauses like a regular compound sentence.

2. It also contains one or more separate dependent clauses.

3. The combination of an independent clause and a dependent clause gives the sentence its resemblance, in part, to a regular complex sentence. Hence, it is called a *compound-complex* sentence.

Let's look at some compound-complex sentences:

Since he took the job, he has tried to do his best, but he has failed to do so, for he has been ill.

   Since he took the job [dependent clause]

   he has tried to do his best [independent clause]

   but he has failed to do so [independent clause]

   for he has been ill [independent clause]

Although we cannot accept you, our branch office may be able to use your services, and I suggest that you contact our branch manager before Monday.

   Although we cannot accept you [dependent clause]

   our branch office may be able to use your services [independent clause]

   and I suggest that you contact our branch manager before Monday [dependent clause]

REVIEW

Before ending this chapter, let's take one more look at the differences among the three types of dependent clauses: noun, adjective, and adverbial. ☑

Type	Primary Functions	Example
Noun	Subject Direct object Object of preposition Predicate nominative Appositive	*What the student keyboarded* pleased the instructor.
Adjective	Adjective that modifies nouns or noun substitutes	The professor was pleased with the student, *who keyboarded the assignment correctly and quickly.*
Adverbial	Adverb that modifies verbs, adjectives, or adverbs	The professor was pleased *when he saw the student's project.*

Self-Check Exercise 2

Can you correctly identify the type of sentences in this exercise? Indicate on the lines to the right whether the sentence is *simple, compound, complex,* or *compound-complex.* The key provides the answers.

1. Before he started to work in your office, he realized that the job would be a demanding one. _____

2. Any three-year-old economic recovery is vulnerable to a host of troubles. _____

3. Disney's three theme parks in the U.S. and Japan contributed $1.1 billion to company revenues, and France's new park will be another source of income. _____

4. While the society acknowledges that wild birds are in danger of extinction, it maintains that condors kept in zoos may not survive when they are eventually freed. _____

5. When Ms. Ferguson was hired, she believed that her advertising career was within her grasp, but now she realizes that her opportunities are few. _____

6. On Broadway, Dorothy Louden, Leslie Uggams, and Chita Rivera starred in Jerry Herman's *Jerry's Girls.* _____

7. The analyst prepared the summation report when he received the phone call from the company's controller. _____

8. In your writing, it would be false economy to sacrifice clarity and completeness for brevity. _____

9. The charge customers were invited to take advantage of the special sale now or to purchase the sale merchandise later. _____

10. Let's begin by studying in the library Friday evening, and then let's schedule a study group session for Saturday afternoon. _____

Name _____

APPLICATION EXERCISES

A. Put *true* or *false* in the space at the left of each statement below.

_____ 1. Dependent clauses contain subjects but not predicates.

_____ 2. An independent clause can stand alone as a sentence.

_____ 3. A noun clause can be used as a direct object.

_____ 4. Subordinating conjunctions often begin adverbial clauses.

_____ 5. A simple sentence contains an independent clause and no dependent clauses.

_____ 6. Adjective clauses modify verbs.

_____ 7. An adverbial clause could modify an adverb.

_____ 8. A gerund phrase could be the subject of a noun clause.

B. The following sentences contain noun clauses. In the spaces provided, write each clause and tell how it is used in the sentence. (Remember that noun clauses are groups of related words that contain subjects and predicates and are used as nouns in a sentence. That is, they are subjects, direct objects, objects of prepositions, predicate nominatives, or appositives.) The first one is completed for you.

1. After what happened to the Smith and Klein team, we felt that our office staff would win the bowling trophy.

    1. (a) what happened to the Smith and Klein team
       (b) object of the preposition *after*

    2. (a) that our office staff would win the bowling trophy
       (b) direct object of *felt*

2. His belief that foreign stamps were a good investment governed his money management.

3. That she was constantly late for work caused me to wonder if Helena would be a good employee. (An infinitive phrase can take a noun clause as its direct object.)

4. The fact is that Benson made the fewest mistakes of all the applicants for the secretarial position.

5. My opinion is that Ernst deserves the job.

C. The following sentences contain adjective clauses. In the spaces provided, write each clause and tell the word it modifies. (Remember that adjective clauses are groups of related words that contain subjects and predicates and are used as adjectives to modify nouns or noun substitutes.) The first sentence is completed for you.

1. Raymond, who works in the personnel department, reviews the appointments that Diana makes.

   1. (a) who works in the personnel department
      (b) modifies *Raymond*

   2. (a) that Diana makes
      (b) modifies *appointments*

2. Please put that folder in the place where it belongs.

3. To do the job that he had volunteered for, he had to create a new computer program for his boss. (Adjective clauses can modify nouns in infinitive phrases.)

4. That is the one I saw. (Careful: Some adjective clauses begin with an understood relative pronoun.)

5. The cookies, which I brought, and the punch, which Suzanne brought, made the surprise party for Linda, who is transferring to another office, a very pleasant gathering.

6. The ideas that she has are especially sound for someone who has so little training.

D. In the following sentences there are adverbial clauses. In the spaces provided, write each adverbial clause and tell what word it modifies. (Remember that adverbial clauses are groups of related words that contain subjects and predicates and modify verbs, adjectives, or adverbs.) The first sentence is completed for you.

1. Since Beverly wrote the manual, the office staff has functioned smoothly when problems have arisen.

   1. (a) Since Beverly wrote the manual
      (b) modifies *has functioned*

   2. (a) when problems have arisen
      (b) modifies *has functioned*

2. Because he has no choice, Max will make the retirement speech.

3. When the economist spoke to the class, the students asked him many questions.

4. Certainly Leroy was busier than Nina was.

Challenge Exercise

In the sentences that follow there are dependent clauses—noun, adjective, and adverb. For each sentence, write the clause, tell what kind of clause it is, and tell how it is used in the sentence. The first sentence is completed for you. (Remember that one dependent clause can be part of another.)

1. When Clark discovered the mistake, he told Mrs. King, who knew that it was not really serious.

    1. (a) When Clark discovered the mistake
       (b) adverbial clause
       (c) modifies *told*

    2. (a) who knew that it was not really serious
       (b) adjective clause
       (c) modifies *Mrs. King*

    3. (a) that it was not really serious
       (b) noun clause
       (c) direct object of *knew*

2. Until I learned that Howard would be an asset to the company, I was suspicious of him.

3. His opinion is that all workers who are on the retirement plan should contribute to it.

4. Mrs. Walters, who told Marie that she would be in charge of the new accounts, has been the best supervisor.

5. Following the procedure that she had helped to develop, Carla knew exactly what she was doing.

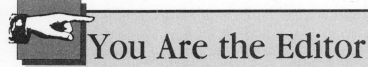

You Are the Editor

Correct all the errors you find in this intraoffice communication.

TO: Mr. Juan Suarez, District Manager

FROM: Dolores Brown

DATE: August 2, 198_

SUBJECT: Office Practices at Spenser Chemicals

You will recall that in your memorandum of July 9 you asked
Christie Allen and I to study the office practices at Spensers
chemicals Company. We have now, as of yesterday, wrote this final
report of our work, and Christie and myself believe that its important
that you read it as soon as possible.

Their is a lot of efficiency in the office procedures of Spenser
Chemicals. Each of the secretary's are well trained and do what is
required of them. Both Mrs. Clark, the office manager, and Mrs.
Gonzalez, the assistant office manager, appears to have a good grasp
of what is going on. Of course, we could of been shown only the best
side of things, but it don't seem likely since we arrived
unannounced.

Coming into the office from the left door, the copying machine is the
first thing you see. Besides it is the typewriters and the computer

terminals. Two-thirds of the office staff are able to work on the computers. A number of the newly employed staff is also knowledgeable about computers. Letters and other material flows from the computer to the secretaries and on to the two managers. (Just between you and I, Mr. Suarz, the procedure may be a little too efficient; their's a kind of impersonal air about the office, as

though everyone of the staff people are robots or something.) Neither Mrs. Clark nor Mrs. Gonzalez ever left their desk when Christie and I was there to see the operation.

In general, though, the office seems to be the most smoothest operation that we could of seen.

Key to Self-Check Exercises

Exercise 1

1. What Bobby cleaned
2. that they should be seen and not heard
3. that the participants in the program would succeed
4. that her home responsibilities came first
5. whoever had the highest scholastic average that year
6. who serves as his secretary
7. who is a partner in their law firm
8. that Suzanne drew
9. where they lived
10. When you go shopping
11. If he can
12. Although we have no job openings
13. Since you are unavailable
14. because we are unprepared
15. he
16. they
17. she
18. we

Exercise 2

1. complex
2. simple
3. compound
4. complex
5. compound-complex
6. simple
7. complex
8. simple
9. simple
10. compound

A DYNAMIC BUSINESS VOCABULARY

The following is another list of useful business words or terms.

Hypothesis

An unproved idea, thesis, or principle tentatively agreed upon to explain facts or ideas.

His hypothesis concerning the drop in sales seemed reasonable; however, we shall have to examine several areas before we can accept it.

Incentive

A factor used to influence, stimulate, or motivate for the purpose of accomplishing a specific purpose.

Many car dealers are giving cash rebates as an incentive to purchase a car.

Indemnity

Protection against a loss from damage.

The indemnity policy provides compensation in the event an explosion takes place.

Inflation

An increase in the amount of money in circulation resulting in a decline of monetary value and a concurrent rise in prices.

The rate of inflation in Mexico is beyond comprehension.

Inherit

To become an heir, as in obtaining possession or transfer of property.

Many private universities inherit the estates of wealthy alumni.

Injunction

A court order prohibiting the carrying out of an action.

The injunction was handed down by the court and effectively halted all production.

Innovation

A new method, custom, or way of doing something.

The recent innovation in direct mail has produced an 80 percent increase in sales.

Insolvent

With an inadequate quantity of funds to pay debts.

Many companies find themselves insolvent and must go out of business.

THE ABC'S OF BUSINESS VOCABULARY

Review your ability to recognize, define, and use the business vocabulary words included in these chapters. Complete the following exercise.

1. Write three short sentences using one of the following words in each sentence: (a) inflation, (b) incentive, (c) inherit.

   _____

   _____

   _____

   _____

   _____

   _____

2. A definition of the noun *consumer* is _____

   _____

3. The meaning of the adjective *fiscal* is _____

   _____

4. The amount of salary you earn *before subtracting deductions* is the (a) net amount, (b) gross amount, (c) petty cash amount, (d) interest amount.

5. A court order that prohibits the carrying out of an action is a/an (a) indemnity, (b) incentive, (c) grievance, (d) injunction.

6. An unproved idea, thesis, or principle tentatively agreed upon to explain facts or ideas is a (a) guess, (b) supposition, (c) hypothesis, (d) problem.

REVIEW EXERCISE ON CHAPTERS 1–12

Test your knowledge on the contents of Chapters 1–12 by completing this review exercise.

A. Put *true* or *false* in the space at the left.

_____ 1. All dictionaries have approximately the same number of words.

_____ 2. This word is spelled correctly: *supersede*.

_____ 3. A gerund is a form of a verb used as a noun.

_____ 4. A sentence cannot have an indirect object unless it also has a direct object.

_____ 5. A complex sentence contains no dependent clauses.

_____ 6. Dictionaries tell what part or parts of speech a word is.

_____ 7. The superlative form of *big* is *bigger*.

_____ 8. After the word *between,* pronouns should be in the objective case.

_____ 9. An infinitive phrase may be used as a noun, an adjective, or an adverb.

_____ 10. Pronouns used as predicate nominatives are in the nominative case.

_____ 11. The subject of a sentence and the predicate are often found in prepositional phrases.

_____ 12. A noun clause can be used to modify a verb.

_____ 13. The third principal part of the verb *write* is *wrote*.

_____ 14. This sentence has an indirect object: *He gave Mary the assignment.*

_____ 15. Subordinate conjunctions often introduce adverb clauses.

_____ 16. The present participle of the verb *see* is *seeing*.

_____ 17. The sentence *She is a truly efficient secretary* is an S-V-PN pattern.

_____ 18. *All right* is a correct spelling; *alright* is incorrect.

_____ 19. *A number,* when used as a subject, takes a plural verb.

_____ 20. The plural form of most nouns is created by adding an apostrophe and *s* to the singular form, as in *book* and *book's*.

_____ 21. Dictionaries generally provide pronunciations of words.

_____ 22. *Hisself* is an acceptable pronoun form.

_____ 23. Pronouns, gerunds, and noun clauses are all forms of noun substitutes.

_____ 24. An appositive may rename a predicate nominative.

_____ 25. *Liquefy* is spelled correctly.

B. Using the abbreviations below, identify the part of speech each italicized word is. Write the abbreviation above the word.

N = noun	ADV = adverb
PRO = pronoun	PREP = preposition
V = verb	CONJ = conjunction
ADJ = adjective	INTER = interjection

1. *Ricardo brought* a *new* excitement *to* the company.

2. If you can, divide the money *between you and* me.

3. She *took* the news of her dismissal *rather quietly.*

4. *Super!* Your *proposal* is *excellent.*

5. George *or* Lucille *will begin that* project in the morning.

6. *He is* a *stern but* fair *boss.*

C. Using the abbreviations listed below, identify the part of sentence each italicized word is. Write the abbreviation above the word.

S = subject	APP = appositive
P = predicate	EXP = expletive
DO = direct object	PN = predicate nominative
IO = indirect object	PA = predicate adjective
OC = objective complement	NA = noun used as adverb
OP = object of a preposition	

1. The firm made *Julian* the *secretary* to the *president.*

2. *Sandra gave him* the bonus in a sealed envelope.

3. Shirley and Margarita *are* the two main *contenders* for the new *position.*

4. Mr. Clark, the *president* of the company, personally *supervised* the *hiring* of the new *manager yesterday.*

5. *There* are several *reasons* for his strange behavior in the office.

6. *Tom,* the *son* of the president, *presented Susan* her five-year *pin.*

D. In the following sentences, ten phrases and clauses are italicized. Tell what kind of phrase or clause each is, and how it is used in the sentence.

Example: *Hurrying quickly,* he came through the office door.

(a) participial phrase
(b) modifies *he*

1. Larry threw the old invoices *into the wastebasket.*

2. *Keeping your desk neat and clean* is a good practice.

3. Juanita knew *that she would be given the promotion.*

4. Judy, *who is the best secretary in the plant,* completely restructured our filing procedures.

5. The job *begun last week* is now over.

6. *When you get a position in the Kyoto office,* you should feel proud.

7. I needed *to complete the ten reports for Mr. Jensen.*

8. The invoice *on my desk* is incorrect.

9. She used the copier, *which I had repaired.*

10. She did her task—*answering the telephone*—exceptionally well.

E. Each of the following sentences contains at least one error, and some contain several. Correct the errors by writing the corrections immediately above the errors.

1. Let's you and I reccommend a new procedure.

2. If he could of done the work hisself, its likely that it would have turned out alright.

3. Coming through the office door, the desk was in the way.

4. Each of the two workers are to receive a bonus.

5. Just between you and I, Sarah and me modified the managers orders to suit ourself.

6. Neither Mr. Ross nor his two associated is able to fix the typewriter which was broke in the earthquake last month.

7. Of the two applicants, I liked Sally best; Tom preferred Susan.

8. Him going to the storeroom for more supplies.

9. If it don't matter to you, I will send Perry and her to the new department.

10. These kind of problems gives Tom and I trouble.

11. The number of working days lost because of sickness among the employee's are alarming.

12. When working, a typewriter cover is helpful.

13. Carla is pleasanter than him.

14. I think I must of went over his letter ten times before I found this here little error.

15. Each of the women' in the office did their best work.

16. Me and him can do the work together, or he can do it hisself.

17. Fred and them was given the opertunities to create a new plan.

F. Write each of the following sentences.

1. Write an S-V-IO-DO sentence.

_____

_____

2. Write a sentence containing a compound predicate.

_____

_____

3. Write a sentence containing a gerund phrase used as the subject.

_____

_____

4. Write a sentence expressing an opinion.

_____

_____

5. Write a sentence containing a predicate adjective.

_____

_____

6. Write a complex sentence.

_____

_____

7. Write a sentence containing an introductory adverbial clause.

    _____

    _____

8. Write a sentence containing an appositive.

    _____

    _____

9. Write a sentence containing two prepositional phrases.

    _____

    _____

10. Write a sentence containing a correlative conjunction.

    _____

    _____

Part Three
Punctuation, Capitalization Numbers, and Putting It All Together

Now that you have completed the chapters on parts of speech and parts of sentences, you are ready for a refresher on the use of proper punctuation and capitalization. In addition, you will learn about the latest practices relating to the writing of numbers in business communications. The chapter on numbers will help you make intelligent selections when you use numbers in sentences such as the following:

The same error was made on pages (5, five) and (7, seven).
Our meeting is on (March 3, 1987; 3/3/87).
The payment is due on the (2, second, 2nd, 2d) of January.

Inserting proper punctuation, using capitals discriminatingly, and knowing when to spell out numbers and when to use numerals are three important skills. Once you decide what you want to express in your writing, you can affect its clarity by the way you say it. Your accurate vocabulary and use of phrases and clauses are important, but they will be ineffective without precision in the use of punctuation, capitalization, and number writing. The principles and examples in the chapters that follow will guide you in your selection of the correct answers in the following test.

Insert punctuation, such as commas, semicolons, colons, dashes, apostrophes, quotation marks, or parentheses, where needed in these sentences:

1. *I will go to Wanamakers Store first and then I will go to the Acme to buy my groceries.*

307

2. *Meanwhile I am writing my history report.*

3. *If it will be helpful to you I will coordinate the meeting next Thursday.*

4. *I will coordinate the meeting next Thursday if it will be helpful to you.*

5. *His accountant who used to be a neighbor of mine in Atlantic City visited me last week.*

6. *You Miss Dinnerman are one of our most valued customers.*

7. *Some of our secretaries take dictation from the officers other secretaries use transcribing machines.*

8. *I feel that one day Shelley will be very successful however I cant make the same statement for Dorothy.*

9. *Each person should bring the following equipment one sleeping bag hiking boots and heavy outdoor clothes.*

10. *You are both correct stated Betsy.*

11. *Here is an excellent textbook economical too.*

12. *The politician heard from only a few three of his many followers.*

13. *Our motto is Dont call us well call you.*

Select the correct answer in these sentences:

14. *It was a miserable night: (The, the) rain poured, the wind howled, and the electricity failed.*

15. *My instructor said that (All, all) assignments must be submitted by Friday.*

16. *He was coordinator for the special (Government, government) project, (operation overload, Operation Overload).*

17. *Her lunch consists of Campbell's (Chicken Soup, chicken soup) and Sanka (Coffee, coffee).*

18. *Martin was going to major in (Spanish, spanish) and (Accounting, accounting).*

19. *In Denver, I live at (One, 1) Raleigh Place.*

20. *The candy wasn't worth (sixty-five, 65) (cents, ¢).*

How confident are you that the answers you selected are correct? You will be able to check them as you study each of the remaining chapters and learn about up-to-date practices in the mechanics of English in today's business writing.

13 Punctuation
Periods and Commas

. , ; : " ? ( ) - ' — ! [ ] To the unfamiliar, these may be unimportant-looking characters, but the role they play in communication is very important. Correct punctuation enhances the effect of written communication. The importance of the role of punctuation is most obvious to the reader, for he or she relies on punctuation marks to correctly interpret written material.

While inflection, pauses, variations in voice level, and changes in the rate of delivery help give meaning to what we say to others, punctuation marks help clarify the ideas we attempt to convey in our writing. Note, for example, what the placement of the comma does to the meaning of the following statements:

> The instant the bullet hit, Francis Ferguson drew his gun.

> The instant the bullet hit Francis, Ferguson drew his gun.

You will find that the sound of the sentence will tell you not only where to place the mark of punctuation, but quite often which type of mark to use. A short pause between two ideas or a series of words usually calls for a comma; a longer pause or a stop indicates the possible use of a semicolon or a period.

An accurate way to use punctuation is to analyze the structure of the dialogue, the sentence, or the paragraph. Specific principles, based on sentence structure, should be followed to ensure accuracy in communication. When punctuation is used incorrectly or not at all, those who read what you write may not interpret your ideas as you intend.

In this chapter, our discussion of punctuation will cover periods and commas. In Chapters 14 and 15 we shall discuss the following:

Semicolons	Question marks	Hyphens
Colons	Parentheses	Brackets
Quotation marks	Dashes	Underlines
Exclamation points	Apostrophes	Ellipses

PERIODS

1. Use periods at the end of declarative sentences, mild imperative sentences, or indirect questions.

Declarative Sentence

> I feel it is now time for me to leave.

> We enjoyed your party very much.
> Placing periods at the end of complete sentences is an easy assignment.

Mild Imperative Statement

> You should really watch what you say.
>
> Be sure to come to my party.
>
> Return the damaged goods to us immediately.

Indirect Question

> He inquired how anyone could remain well in this weather.
>
> She asked if any of us knew the answer.
>
> The only question I have is whether he has the background to handle this project.

2. Use a period after a request phrased as a question (a "courteous request").

> Will you please call me in reference to an employment interview.

Even though the example is phrased as a question, the writer is politely requesting *action,* not an *answer.* When we want action instead of an answer, as in these examples, we use a period instead of a question mark.

> May I suggest that you revise this letter.
>
> Would you please stop in when you get an opportunity.
>
> May we hear from you within two weeks.

3. Use periods with most abbreviations.

p.m.	Dr.	Inc.
Mr.	C.O.D.	Sr.
Mrs.	a.m.	f.o.b.
Ph.D.	G. Robert Ryan	Ltd.

Note: The designation *Ms.,* frequently used as a female title, is an alternative to *Miss,* which signifies an unmarried status, and *Mrs.,* which signifies a married status. Although *Ms.* is not an abbreviation for a longer word, it is spelled with a period.

Familiar abbreviations are frequently accepted without periods. Current usage permits periods to be dropped in these cases:

IBM	NASA	TV
RSVP	UN	ESL
AFL	USAF	NATO
PC	PBX	CEO

In some offices the familiar letter notation *Enclosure,* frequently typed *Enc.* or *Encl.,* has now evolved into *enc*, with no capital and no period. This practice is not yet widespread, however. ☑

COMMAS

Commas are pesky little critters that act as road signs in our writing and help convey our meaning to our readers. They are placed *within* sentences and are the most frequently used marks of internal punctuation in the English language. The reason they are frequently misused or erroneously omitted is that there are so many rules governing their use. Many people do not take the trouble to learn the comma rules, preferring to depend on one or the other of these oft-quoted doctrines:

Self-Check Exercise 1

Since there are few important rules governing the use of periods, it is easy to remember them and to know how to apply them. Punctuate the following paragraph by adding periods where needed. Be sure to begin each new sentence with a capital letter. The key is at the end of the chapter.

"One of the most popular male stars today is Alan Alda he is a talented actor, writer, and director who comes by his talent rightfully Alan is the son of another famous Hollywood star, Robert Alda the younger Alda is frequently asked by his fans whether he prefers acting over writing or directing for your information, three of Alan Alda's major successes are *The Seduction of Joe Tynan, The Four Seasons,* and *MASH"*

1. When in doubt, insert commas.

2. When in doubt, omit all commas.

Amy Sterling is an example of a writer who follows Doctrine 1. Figure 13-1 shows a typical memo composed by Amy.

Compare this memo to George Plumton's communication. George followed Doctrine 2. Since he wasn't familiar with the comma rules, he preferred to omit all commas to be safe. Figure 13-2 shows what his memo looked like.

You wouldn't want your memos to resemble either Amy's or George's. The way to prevent it is to study the comma rules and their practical application to your writing.

Neither Amy nor George took the time to read, study, and apply the principles of comma use. They both perpetuated careless habits in their writing by illogically inserting or omitting commas. This practice detracts from clarity in their written communications. There is no question that their readers are at a disadvantage.

If you learn the following principles, you will have a decided edge on writers such as Amy and George.

A *comma* is used primarily to separate or set off elements in a sentence. It provides a short rest for the reader and can be used only as *internal punctuation.*

WITH INTRODUCTORY ELEMENTS IN SENTENCES

Commas are used after such introductory elements as words, phrases, or dependent clauses in a complex sentence. The introductory items precede the subject and verb in the main clause.

Introductory Words

Meanwhile, I am reading my French 102 assignment.

Yes, I will be attending the dinner meeting this Tuesday.

Hi, I'm not sure we have met before. [Interjection.]

Well, well, so we finally finished that project. [Interjection.]

Therefore, our meeting must be postponed [Transitional word referring to preceding sentence.]

Figure 13-1. Typical memo written by Amy—irrational insertion of commas.

TO: John Ormes

FROM: Amy Sterling

DATE: May 10, 198_

SUBJECT: The Lortz Account

Amanda Brown, Lortz's administrative assistant, promised to call us, as soon as her supervisor returned, from a week's vacation but, we have not yet heard from her. By contrast, on May 16 198_ a similar situation occurred but James Latino who was then Lortz's administrative assistant, followed through, on his promise.

Fortunately Ms. Brown's lackadaisical attitude does not reflect Charles Lortz's operation; therefore, I suggest, you call him directly. After all we do want to maintain, our reputation, of being responsive enthusiastic, and cooperative, when it comes to promoting our product. Let us not allow, Ms. Brown's seemingly irresponsible unconcerned behavior, to affect our sales record.

John you have my support. Call Charles Lortz, at 10 a.m. Monday and, arrange to fly to Cleveland, to see him shortly after.

Introductory Phrases

> While waiting for his plane, James Skidderman read the sports section of the *Inquirer.*
>
> Before running, he always exercised for ten minutes.
>
> On the other hand, it may be worth the two-day trip. [Transitional expression.]
>
> In most cases, a competent professor will listen carefully to students' questions.

Note: Phrases can end sentences as well as begin them; an ending phrase should also be separated from the rest of the sentence by a comma.

> Her tennis game is slipping, in my opinion.
>
> A competent professor will listen carefully to students' questions, in most cases.

Introductory Dependent Clauses in Complex Sentences

> Since we have no job openings now, we are not accepting applications for summer jobs.
>
> When I entered the crowded assembly hall, I immediately noted the presence of armed guards.
>
> If it is absolutely vital to you, I will insist that the meeting be held in the morning.
>
> After five years of concentrated study in the various art centers of the world, he felt sufficiently confident to permit his work to be exhibited.

Note: If the dependent clause follows the independent clause, the comma is usually omitted.

Figure 13-2. George's underpunctuation.

TO: John Ormes

FROM: George Plumton

DATE: May 10 198_

SUBJECT: The Lortz Account

Amanda Brown Lortz's administrative assistant promised to call us as soon as her supervisor returned from a week's vacation but we have not yet heard from her. By contrast on May 16 198_ a similar situation occurred but James Latino who was then Lortz's administrative assistant followed through on his promise.

Fortunately Ms. Brown's lackadaisical attitude does not reflect Charles Lortz's operation; therefore I suggest you call him directly. After all we do want to maintain our reputation of being responsive enthusiastic and cooperative when it comes to promoting our product. Let us not allow Ms. Brown's seemingly irresponsible unconcerned behavior to affect our sales record.

John you have my support. Call Charles Lortz at 10 a.m. Monday and arrange to fly to Cleveland to see him shortly after.

gp

We are not accepting applications for summer jobs *since we have no job openings now* [No comma.]

I immediately noted the presence of armed guards *when I entered the crowded assembly hall.* [No comma.]

I shall insist that the meeting be held in the morning *if it is absolutely vital to you.* [No comma.]

A primary exception to this principle involves the use of *although.* When the dependent clause starts with *although,* precede the dependent clause with a comma.

We are accepting resumes, *although we have no job openings at the present time.* [Precede *although* with a comma.]

I would accept balcony seats for the rock concert, *although we prefer to sit downstairs.* [Precede *although* with a comma.]

WITH INDEPENDENT CLAUSES IN COMPOUND SENTENCES

Commas precede coordinating conjunctions (*and, or, but, for, nor, yet*) that join independent clauses in compound sentences.

I shall go to the basketball game on Friday night, or I shall see the latest foreign film at the Cinema II.

Bob decided to drive to Las Vegas, and Marty flew to California.

I believe that we are all in this together, but those who live in Illinois can avoid the problem.

My parents had hoped that their three children would enter the family furniture business, but my two sisters and I decided to open a small boutique in New Hope.

Key management personnel in the large organization should be carefully selected, and all managers should be informed of their specific responsibilities.

Typists should become acquainted with computer operation, for computers are helpful information-processing tools.

Note: When the independent clauses are short, the comma is often omitted.

The wind blew and the rains fell. [No comma needed.]
Mary dictated the letter and John typed it. [No comma needed.]
Barry shouted and Carlotta turned. [No comma needed.] ☑

WITH NONESSENTIAL ELEMENTS

1. Use commas to set off *nonrestrictive* clauses or phrases. A nonrestrictive clause or phrase is not essential to complete the meaning of the sentence; it merely adds some information

Self-Check Exercise 2

Thus far you have studied the first group of comma rules. These rules pertain to the use of the comma after introductory words, phrases, and dependent clauses and before a conjunction joining clauses in a compound sentence. Can you correctly apply these principles? Complete the following exercise by inserting commas where they are needed and check your answers with the key.

1. I will go to the store and buy the food.

2. I will go to the store and I will buy the food.

3. I will go to Gimbels Department Store first and then I will go to Shop'N'Bag to buy the week's groceries.

4. After we left the party we went directly home.

5. We went directly home after we left the party.

6. Yes I will be able to attend the meeting.

7. If this were Friday I would be able to collect my paycheck.

8. I would be able to collect my paycheck if this were Friday.

9. Personally I would prefer to wait at least a month.

10. Before going to sleep I read several sections of the Sunday *New York Times.*

that could have been omitted. The nonessential quality of a clause or phrase can be tested by reading the sentence without it. If the sentence makes sense and is structurally sound, the clause or phrase is nonessential and should be set off by commas.

His accountant, who had been a neighbor of mine in Denver, stopped in to visit me. [The *who* clause is nonessential, so it is set off with commas.]

It really pleased Joan, who was a trained nurse, to see Tami read the booklets on health care. [Since the *who* clause is not essential in this sentence, it is separated from the rest of the sentence with commas.]

If the clause or phrase *is* essential in the sentence, it is *restrictive.* Commas are not inserted to set off *restrictive* items in a sentence.

Ask the woman who is a trained nurse to administer first aid. [No commas, for the *who* clause is essential. What woman? The one who is a trained nurse.]

I will go to my cousin who is a lawyer to revise my will. [No commas, for the *who* clause is essential. Which cousin? The one who is a lawyer.]

To reinforce this point, consider these sentences.

Young players, who now seem to dominate the major teams, receive salaries undreamed of ten years ago. [Nonessential.]

The baseball player who set a record for his team in home runs gets a top salary. [Essential—no commas.]

John Foreman, who was a dentist, frequently vacations in Canada. [Nonessential.]

The dentist who always vacations in Canada called us yesterday. [Essential—no commas.]

The new procedure, as we mentioned in our telephone conversation, will begin the first of next month. [Nonessential.]

The new procedure that we discussed yesterday will begin on Monday. [Essential—no commas.]

Dr. John Kelly, who taught philosophy for 25 years, received frequent commendations from students and faculty. [Nonessential.]

A professor who taught philosophy for 25 years is speaking to our class this Friday. [Essential—no commas.]

2. Use commas to set off parenthetical (nonessential) words or phrases. Note how the non-essential words or phrases interrupt the flow of the sentence.

The most important item on the agenda, I believe, is the discussion of word-processing equipment. [*I believe* is not essential.]

Let me say, at the very start, that you will find this lecture series helpful when taking your graduate examinations. [*At the very start* could be omitted.]

Bobbie is, as a matter of fact, an extremely competent young woman.

That, however, was not true of her sister Barbara.

Do you believe, or shouldn't I ask, that the sale of Japanese-made cars will continue to increase?

Note: Afterthoughts should also be separated from the rest of the sentence.

This footnote could confuse the reader, *perhaps.*

Mail your contribution to PBS, *please,*

3. When nonessential words precede the second independent clause of a compound sentence but follow the coordinate conjunction, the nonessential words should be treated like introductory words. A comma should be placed after them *but not before them.*

I will drive you to the clinic, or *if you wish,* to your neighborhood doctor. [*If you wish* is nonessential. Treat it as introductory and put a comma after it.]

We are inviting your neighbors to the opening celebration, and *should you desire,* your parents will also be welcome. [*Should you desire* is nonessential. Treat it as introductory and put a comma after it.]

WITH DIRECT ADDRESS

In order to be polite and use the *you attitude* in writing, writers often mention their reader's first name or entire name. Since the name is nonessential to the meaning of the sentence, it is set off with commas. ☑

Bob, it was a pleasure meeting you on Tuesday.

Mr. Barron, write me at your earliest convenience so that I may arrange a tour for your team.

Write me at your earliest convenience, Mr. Barron, so that I may arrange a tour for your team.

Write me at your earliest convenience so that I may arrange a tour for your team, Mr. Barron.

Self-Check Exercise 3

Group 2 pertains to the use of commas with nonessential elements in a sentence. Clauses, phrases, and words that are added to a sentence may not be needed for clarity. After you distinguish between the essential and nonessential elements in the following sentences, insert commas where they are needed. Complete this exercise and check your answers in the key.

1. I understand however that the management consultant disagrees with the comptroller of your company.

2. Mrs. Daniels carefully explained that the accident was unavoidable.

3. You Miss Carson are one of our most valued customers.

4. The accounting students who received B or higher in the midterm exam are excused from the final exam.

5. The most recent class of flight attendants which is made up of six women and three men begins flying this Monday.

6. You can be sure of course that we will contact him when we fly to Barcelona.

7. We apologize Ms. Harmon for any inconvenience this may have caused you.

8. The Better Boy tomato plants that were recently planted are already beginning to blossom.

9. They are without doubt the most cooperative group of interns the hospital has ever had.

10. We will be writing to James Smithers as soon as our project is finished Bob.

WITH COMMAS IN A SERIES

In a sentence, a series is made up of three or more items, either words or phrases. The items should be separated by commas, but remember—no comma is placed after the last item in a series.

Series of Words

The sofa was red, green, blue, and orange.

English 101, Business Communications I, and Psychology 100 are required courses for first-semester students.

The new employee was tall and handsome, articulate and knowledgeable, and concerned and sincere.

Series of Phrases

Secure a degree, get a job, make huge amounts of money, and join the American race to ulcers and heart attacks.

The sofa was clean and uncluttered, inexpensive but not cheap, and colorful but not gaudy.

Will the conferences be held in Spokane, in New Orleans, or in Philadelphia?

Note: Do not use a comma to separate the parts of one measurement or one weight.

It took him 1 hour 35 minutes 15 seconds to jog around the park.

The measurement you requested is 1 yard 2 feet 7 inches.

WITH WORDS OR PHRASES IN APPOSITION

Commas are used to set off phrases or words in apposition, including geographical items, dates, and addresses. Words in apposition explain nouns or pronouns that generally immediately precede them.

My professor, Dr. Robert Gieselman, is the executive director of the Association for Business Communication. [*Dr. Robert Gieselman* is an appositive that explains the noun *professor.*]

Mike Connolly, the congressman, was deeply involved in trying to get that piece of legislation passed. [*The congressman* explains who Mike Connolly is.]

Jogging, an exercise widely prescribed to improve cardiovascular function, has become a habit for a large percentage of the population. [Words in apposition explain *jogging.*]

The Sports Forum, located in Los Angeles, California, was dedicated on December 3, 1981. [*California* explains the location of Los Angeles; *1981* explains which December 3.]

He left for Monterey, California, on Friday, June 27, 1986, at 2 p.m. [*California* explains the location of Monterey; *June 27* explains which Friday; *1986* explains which June 27.]

My new graduate student, Manuela Ortega, is interested in doing an independent study on "Women in Management."

Mrs. Spear, fashion director for Century Clothes, was elected president of the Designers' Association.

His sister, Roberta Smith, teaches in a community college.

She lives at Hill House, 125 South Broad Avenue, Lansing, Michigan. [Each element explains the item in the address that precedes it.]

Note: Appositives that are only one word are not set off by commas.

My only brother-in-law John drives a Seville. [*John* explains *brother-in-law* but is only one word— no commas.]

Next month May is my very favorite. [Appositive *May* is only one word—no commas.] ☑

Self-Check Exercise 4

Group 3 includes rules for comma use in a series of three or more words or phrases and in words or phrases in apposition. To check your ability to apply these rules, insert commas *where needed* in the following sentences.

1. The very contemporary design had lines and patterns of red green blue yellow violet and white.

2. Corn and wheat are important crops in our country.

3. Corn wheat and soybeans are important crops in our country.

4. It will be September 19 1987 before there is a solar eclipse in our area.

5. Have you read his only article "The American Scene"?

6. I am taking English 098 History 102 and Mathematics 190 this semester.

7. My English 112 professor Dr. Ferraro gives us reading and writing assignments three times a week.

8. We will be traveling to San Diego California before we attend the business conference in Seattle Washington.

9. The wallpaper we selected for the lobby is bright gold and light green.

10. Monday January 6 1986 was the first day of the semester I was discussing with the dean.

BETWEEN ADJECTIVES, TO INDICATE OMITTED WORDS, IN NUMBERS, FOR CLARITY, AND FOR MISCELLANEOUS USES

1. Use commas when two or more adjectives separately modify a noun and a conjunction is omitted. When the word *and* would make sense between the two adjectives but is omitted, a comma should be inserted.

Our doctor is a kind, considerate, hardworking person. [*And* could have been inserted between *kind* and *considerate, considerate* and *hardworking*. Since the conjunction was omitted, the commas are inserted.]

My nephew is a tall, thin teenager. [Comma instead of conjunction *and*.]

Our college president is a talkative, competent person.

I have a dark blue suit. [Omit comma as *dark* explains *blue,* not *suit*. I *have a dark and blue suit* does not make sense.]

2. Use commas to indicate the omission of a word or words that are understood.

Buckingham Way has been renamed Washington Street; Devonshire Place, Adams Avenue; and Kavenough Way, Jefferson Street. [The words *has been renamed* are omitted twice in this sentence; thus, commas are needed where the words are omitted.]

Binswanger Realtors sold our home; Cross Realtors, our office building; and Johnson Realty Company, our apartment building.

3. Use a comma to indicate a quantity of thousands in numbers.

$5,000 $60,000 $425,000 $1,000,000
6,000 bags   50,000 bushels   425,000 pens

Note: An important exception is that commas are not inserted in the decimal part of a number.

COMPARE $5,000   WITH 0.05634 [No commas are inserted after the decimal.]

COMPARE $50,000   WITH 58,343.12345 [Again, no commas after the decimal.]

A few sources indicate that commas should be used only in numbers of five or more figures and should be eliminated in numbers with four figures. This practice, however, is not widespread. We suggest that commas be inserted in accordance with Rule 3.

4. Use commas to ensure clarity in a sentence. If commas were omitted in the following sentences, misunderstanding could arise.

Shortly after, the team left the hall to continue celebrating.

As you know, little can be done on this renovation until the first of next month.

To a conservative like Ronnie, Reagan was the perfect choice.

John, implied Bob, was drunk.

The instant the bullet hit Francis, Ferguson drew his gun.

5. Use commas before *etc.* in a series. Place commas before and after *etc.* in the middle of a sentence.

An accounting student should be familiar with working papers, profit and loss statements, balance sheets, etc.

A personnel interviewer judges skills, personality, work experience, etc., when offering employment to a job applicant.

6. Use commas before *Jr., Sr.,* and *Inc.* when the person or company prefers their use. If the abbreviation comes in the middle of the sentence, use commas before and after it. By studying the company letterhead or signature in question, you can observe the individual preference.

USE George S. Beers, Sr.   OR George S. Beers Sr.
USE Lloyd Rivers, Jr.   OR Lloyd Rivers Jr.
USE Fashion Arrival, Inc.   OR Fashion Arrival Inc.

7. Use commas to separate repeated words. The words are usually repeated for *emphasis.*

That was a *big, big* breakfast he devoured considering he is on a diet.

It will be a *long, long* time before I take another vacation this expensive.

Ebeneezer Scrooge was a *stingy, stingy* man. ☑

Self-Check Exercise 5

Insert commas where needed in the following sentences. The answers appear in the key.

1. She is an attractive intelligent woman.

2. A sincere courteous helpful letter cultivates goodwill.

3. She wore a light green skirt and jacket to the meeting.

4. The material had all the colors in the rainbow, red blue green etc.

5. Let's eat Grandfather before we go to the ball game.

6. Her salary is $19000 annually.

7. Dr. Smith teaches Spanish 101; Dr. Greenspan English 125; and Professor Henson Education 203.

8. They ordered 1100 packages of panty hose and 1350 pairs of sport socks to send to their branch stores throughout the country.

9. A navy blue suit is appropriate to wear to a wedding.

AVOIDING COMMON COMMA PITFALLS

Writers frequently make the same comma mistakes over and over again. There are times when no commas are needed, but writers insist on inserting them. Perhaps this is because there are so many comma rules to study and apply. If you follow the rules described below, you can avoid the more common pitfalls.

1. When conjunctions precede every item in a series, no commas are needed.

    I will arise at 7:30 a.m. *and* put on the coffee pot *and* set the table. [The insertion of *and* before the series items negates the need for commas.]

    For work, I will need a new briefcase *and* a silver Cross pen *and* a new leather-bound address book. [Omit commas when conjunctions *(and)* precede items in a series.]

2. Do not separate subjects from their verbs with commas.

    John and Patricia swim at their neighborhood spa. [No commas separate the subjects *John and Patricia* from the verb *swim.*]

    His shopping at the market helped her significantly. [The subject *His shopping at the market* is not separated from the verb *helped* by a comma.]

3. Do not use a comma to separate *two* words or phrases joined by a conjunction.

    The class will cover the first two chapters and will then write a 500-word essay. [The class will do only two things—no comma.]

This winter she plans to take skiing lessons and try out the nearest beginner's hill. [She will do only two things—no comma.]

Baking chocolate chip cookies and roasting chestnuts are two of my favorite cold-weather pastimes. [No comma.]

We hope that you will travel to Florida and have an opportunity to visit Key West. [No comma.]

4. Do not use a comma to separate two independent clauses that are not joined with a conjunction, as that would create a *comma splice*. A semicolon or a period is the correct punctuation.

   The weather was beautiful; it was 80° and sunny. [No comma.]

   It seems to be very crowded in Washington; the Smithsonian Institution is filled with visitors. [No comma.]

5. Omit commas between a month and a year when the exact date is missing.

   She started working in March 1985. [No comma.]

   She started working on March 23, 1985. [Exact date is given. Insert comma.]

   In September 1985 my parents celebrated their 25th wedding anniversary. [No comma.]

   On September 11, 1985, my grandfather was 100 years old. [Exact date is given. Insert commas before and after year.]

TIME FOR REVISION

Now that you have studied the important comma rules and their application, you are ready to insert commas correctly in Amy's and George's memos. Circle all the comma errors made by Amy in Figure 13-1, and then check your corrections with the revision in Figure 13-3. Here are the *reasons* for the revisions:

Amanda Brown, Lortz's administrative assistant, [appositive]

promised to call us as soon as her supervisor returned from a week's vacation, but we have not yet heard from her. [before a conjunction in a compound sentence]

By contrast, [introductory phrase]

on May 16, 19 __ , [apposition giving dates]

a similar situation occurred, but [conjunction in a compound sentence]

James Latino, who was then Lortz's administrative assistant, followed through on his promise. [the *who* clause is not essential to the meaning]

Fortunately, [introductory word]

Ms. Brown's lackadaisical attitude does not reflect Charles Lortz's operation; therefore, [introductory word beginning independent clause]

I suggest you call him directly. After all, we do want to maintain [for clarity—*after all we do* could be confusing]

our reputation of being responsive, enthusiastic, and cooperative [series]

when it comes to promoting our product. Let us not allow Ms. Brown's seemingly irresponsible, unconcerned [comma instead of a conjunction between two adjectives] behavior to affect our sales record.

John, you have my support. [direct address]

Call Charles Lortz at 10 a.m. Monday and arrange to fly to Cleveland to see him shortly after. [no commas]

Figure 13-3. Correctly punctuated memo.

TO: John Ormes

FROM: Amy Sterling

DATE: May 10, 198_

SUBJECT: The Lortz Account

Amanda Brown, Lortz's administrative assistant, promised to call us
as soon as her supervisor returned from a week's vacation, but we
have not yet heard from her. By contrast, on May 16, 198_, a similar
situation occurred; but James Latino, who was then Lortz's
administrative assistant, followed through on his promise.

Fortunately, Ms. Brown's lackadaisical attitude does not reflect
Charles Lortz's operation; therefore, I suggest you call him
directly. After all, we do want to maintain our reputation of being
responsive, enthusiastic, and cooperative when it comes to promoting
our product. Let us not allow Ms. Brown's seemingly irresponsible,
unconcerned behavior to affect our sales record.

John, you have my support. Call Charles Lortz at 10 a.m. Monday, and
arrange to fly to Cleveland to see him shortly after.

APPLICATION EXERCISES

A. In the spaces to the right, indicate where commas and periods belong in the following sentences. If no punctuation is required or the comma or period inserted is correct, write *C* in the space.

1. When I entered the room __ Mark __ the magician __ hurried out.

    a   b   c
         __ __ __

      a b c

2. Professor Tahashi delivered his first lecture _;_ however __ no one seemed very interested.
         __ __

      a b

3. The band played _;_ the audience applauded __
         __ __

      a b

4. The men had finished their assignment most carefully _;_ and the women were now ready to begin theirs.
         __

      a

5. I think you will agree __ by and large __ that my assessment of the situation was correct and that Parker's was not.
         __ __

      a b

6. When she smiled __ her face shone like a light.
         __

      a

7. The sun shone _;_ the children played.
         __

      a

8. The sun shone __ and the children played.
         __

      a

9. Rosa __ the group leader __ was an outstanding artist _;_ her paintings hang in several of the city's galleries __ and she received the Grand Award of New York last year.
         __ __ __ __

      a b c d

10. Since you were the one who began to evaluate the foreman __ we feel you should be on the qualifying committee.
          __

      a

11. Do you feel __ Marty __ that we should leave now _?_
          __ __ __

      a b c

12. I can't agree with Mr. Kolkowski _;_ and I feel his wife is just as incorrect as he is.
          __

      a

13. I'm inclined to agree __ however _,_ with Mr. Toshiba.
          __ __

      a b

14. He was about to walk through the garden _;_ consequently __ I took a shortcut through the house.
          __ __

      a b

B. Insert punctuation where needed.

_____

TO: Keli Foreman

FROM: Jose Sanchez

DATE: January 14, 198_

SUBJECT: Infraction of Company Policy #221

This will give you the information you requested in your memo of January 3 198_ which arrived on January 8.

The precise wording of the Illinois Agreement of July 1, 198_ states: "All employees who have been designated as Senior will receive a 15 percent increase; those designated as Junior will be eligible for a 10 percent raise Those employees who are absent more than five days per month and those who have been late more than five times per month (both in this calendar year) may be terminated for cause."

I hope this will give you the information you want; you may be sure that this office is always eager to assist in any way possible

Heidi and Gretchen your former assistants say "Hi!"

ls

_____

C. Insert commas and periods correctly in the following sentences.

1. Do you think that Dr Darte will accept the order if it is sent COD to his home?

2. His presentation before the UN was greeted with applause.

3. When he came home he quickly checked the mail to see if his check had arrived

4. His Ph.D degree was in the field of anthropology; hers was in astronomy.

5. If you agree George I will not complete the report for NASA

6. He was on the whole a well-adjusted young man.

7. Before jogging he always drank two glasses of water.

8. Although Mr Kelly decided to go to Las Vegas his wife chose to vacation in London.

9. Professor Green completed his research in June and Professor Farnsworth finished his book in July

10. He purchased milk butter steaks fruit and bread.

11. The fabric had an interesting design woven in brown and gold red and orange and gold and silver.

12. The boys shouted and the girls giggled.

13. Mrs Hollingsworth agreed to the change but her partner Mrs Fitch thought the cost was unreasonable.

14. He decided to register for accounting Spanish finance and marketing.

15. Professor Mendoza who received his degree in Mexico was the most competent instructor I had in my four years at the university.

16. No action was taken by the Personnel Committee of UNESCO.

17. When Bob walked into the room everyone stood.

18. He was the youngest MD assigned to the UN Commission on Health Care.

19. For no good reason she began to cry it was a reaction that astounded me.

20. Since Mandrel paid the entire bill his father was free to leave the restaurant as an honorable man.

21. Although the boys had completed the assignment the girls had not even begun.

D. Insert commas and periods correctly in the following sentences.

1. Well I'm not sure we would agree.

2. He worked all night but he was eager to play tennis at 8 a.m.

3. Mr Calcalli will vote in our favor and if we are fortunate Mrs Calacalli will cast her ballot the same way.

4. John called and Bozo responded

5. Taki's jacket was red orange green and yellow.

6. Manuel Rodriguez who was not born in the United States was surely one of the most devoted of all U.S. citizens.

7. Betty Korowski the group's leader recently celebrated her 39th birthday.

8. Indira Bohandi will as certain as the day is long give full credit to you for your efforts as a coordinator.

9. His goal was pleasure not job achievement.

10. This nevertheless was not a solution to the problem.

11. Ramon Rodriguez the chef worked for years as the director of food service.

12. The ten boys were all trained; however the girls in the troop were not so fortunate.

13. The ten boys were all trained but the girls in the group were not so fortunate.

14. Of the new states you named three should be eligible for grants.

15. Petrocelli the designer commanded attention.

16. I believe strongly and I think you will agree that Sally should be permitted to leave.

17. Theodore you should now be ready to take the bar examination.

18. Betsy the youngest was as mature as a much older individual.

E. The following sentences may have some punctuation errors. Insert commas and periods where needed and cross out any that are incorrect.

1. When Johanna entered the room Wagner's face broke into a smile

2. Wagner greeted Johanna warmly and then Wagner turned to the other members of the team.

3. If you will send copies of the legal papers to M Robert Melvin and me we will start the investigation, immediately.

4. Well I'm not sure I should attend but you may if you wish.

5. He reenlisted in the USAF and two years later he held the rank of captain.

6. I believe on the whole that his solution would not be accepted by his colleagues.

7. Bancroft the new clerk worked very well with all store personnel

8. When the door swung open I was sure that Chen, would stride into the room.

9. The rugs were swept the furniture polished the food arranged and the chairs set up—the youngsters had completed all preparations.

10. The time to act, is now.

11. In his younger days he was a high flyer. Who could do no wrong.

12. No I don't believe I will have the time.

13. The needed ingredients are eggs, and butter, and crackers, and milk

14. At the shopping mall I plan to buy a new battery for my Seiko watch, and purchase a jogging shirt to replace the one that is faded.

15. The Alps are truly beautiful in Italy in Switzerland and in Austria.

16. We will, probably, replace our Honda Accord, in March, 1987.

17. I bought a navy, blue suit and a white long-sleeved blouse with a tie, I'm getting ready to go on job interviews in Erie Pennsylvania.

 # Challenge Exercise

The following paragraph has errors in comma and period usage. First insert the correct punctuation; then rewrite the paragraph correcting all errors.

Labor Day weekend, was a complete disaster, I awoke late on Saturday, and discovered that I had misplaced the train schedule, and couldn't find the phone number of my visiting cousins. Naturally my best friend my cat who always returns for her Meow Chow chose all day Saturday to disappear, she didn't reappear until Sunday morning, I thought she had been catnapped. My out-of-town cousins somewhat chagrined because I hadn't called or taken the train to visit them at their hotel appeared at my doorstep on Saturday afternoon. They remained until midnight on Monday and while they were visiting they nearly emptied my refrigerator and pantry. Of course, I had to sweep the floors and wash the dishes. As you can imagine I was tired disgruntled and unproductive, when I returned to work on Tuesday. You can believe, that next year I plan to hibernate in Atlantic City New Jersey over the Labor Day weekend. All by myself.

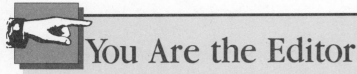

You Are the Editor

There are errors in punctuation in the following exercise. Cross out the incorrect punctuation and make all corrections directly in the letter.

THE PRINTING WORKS, INC.
6534 NORTH 17TH STREET
DRESHER, PA 19125
(215) 876-6032

August 3, 198_

Mr John Ferragami

1643 Broad Avenue

St Louis MO 61235

Dear Mr Ferragami:

We thank you for your pleasant concerned letter of July 15, it was a

very friendly gesture on your part.

Since we had not received any orders from you for over a year we were

doubly surprised to receive your kind letter. As a matter of fact we

thought for some reason our last order had displeased you. And we

would never hear from you again. Your letter of sympathy about the

death of our sales manager is sincerely, appreciated.

Of course Mr. Ferragami our fine products good service and low prices

continue despite our personnel change. Ms. Sally Kimberly our new

---

sales manager will be sending you a copy of our newest sales packet and latest catalogue, please feel free to call her collect if you wish any information, or if you wish to place an order.

Extend my very best personal regards to Samantha Agress your very talented partner.

Sincerely yours,

Robert J. Pressing

President

Key to Self-Check Exercises

Exercise 1

Alda. He

rightfully.   Alan

Alda. The

directing. For

MASH."

Exercise 2

1. no commas (not a compound sentence)
2. no commas (too short)
3. first, and
4. party, we
5. no commas
6. Yes, I
7. Friday, I
8. no commas
9. Personally, I
10. sleep, I

Exercise 3

1. understand, however,
2. no commas
3. You, Miss Carson,
4. no commas
5. attendants, which . . . men, begins
6. sure, of course,
7. apologize, Ms. Harmon,
8. no commas
9. no commas needed (*without doubt* seems needed in this sentence)
10. finished, Bob.

Exercise 4

1. red, green, blue, yellow, violet, and white.
2. no commas
3. Corn, wheat, and
4. September 19, 1987,
5. article, "The
6. English 098, History 102, and
7. professor, Dr. Ferraro,
8. San Diego, California, . . . Seattle, Washington.
9. no commas
10. Monday, January 6, 1986,

Exercise 5

1. attractive, intelligent
2. sincere, courteous, helpful
3. no commas
4. red, blue, green, etc.
5. eat, Grandfather,
6. $19,000
7. Dr. Greenspan, English 125; and Professor Henson, Education 203.
8. 1,100   1,350
9. no commas

A DYNAMIC BUSINESS VOCABULARY

Enrich your business vocabulary by learning the following words.

Inventory

An annual or periodic listing of all the goods, property, or stock of a business or organization.

Most department stores take inventory at the first of the year.

Invoice

A listing of all merchandise delivered to a destination and its prices; a bill.

The invoice that accompanied the shipment listed a 2 percent cash discount.

Job description

A written description of the duties and responsibilities of a specific job or assignment.

When interviewing for a position, always request a job description before accepting the job.

Joint venture

A business partnership formed by two or more individuals or entities to operate or finance a project.

The joint venture formed by the two firms worked out to their individual advantage.

Jurisdiction

The legal range of authority.

The Los Angeles Police Department has no official jurisdiction in Orange County.

Keypunch

A machine that punches holes in computer cards coded to represent information or data to be stored.

The keypunch operators had to work overtime to process all the orders.

Log sheet

A record kept in a word-processing center to monitor incoming and outgoing work.

The supervisor was congratulated by her department manager for keeping accurate, neat, and complete log sheets.

Logging

The process of entering incoming work on a sheet to control work flow.

Robert Barnes found that logging in the word-processing work assignments was a tedious and time-consuming job responsibility.

THE ABC'S OF BUSINESS VOCABULARY

Here is another short quiz to test your knowledge of the business words and terms presented.

1. The legal range of authority is known as (a) boundaries, (b) jurisdiction, (c) solvency, (d) territory.

2. A record kept to monitor incoming and outgoing work is a/an (a) inventory, (b) diary, (c) log sheet, (d) budget.

3. Protection against a loss from damage is known as (a) coverage, (b) premium, (c) indemnity, (d) collision.

4. A bill that lists merchandise delivered and its prices is a/an (a) log sheet, (b) draft, (c) charge, (d) invoice.

5. Compose three short sentences using one of the following words in each sentence: (a) keypunch, (b) inherit, (c) guarantor.

   _____

   _____

   _____

   _____

   _____

   _____

6. The meaning of the adjective *insolvent* is _____

   _____

7. The process of *logging* refers to _____

   _____

8. The noun *innovation* means _____

   _____

9. The noun *devaluation* refers to _____

   _____

 # Punctuation
Semicolons, Colons, Quotation Marks, and Apostrophes

SEMICOLONS

The proper use of the semicolon seems to be one of the mysteries of the world. Students who are quite knowledgeable about using other punctuation marks can find little use for the semicolon. Why all the mystery? The semicolon is a useful mark, and principles pertaining to its use are easy to learn.

Just remember, a semicolon is a "rest" mark that is stronger than a comma but weaker than a period. Study the following rules and their examples, and there won't be any mystery as far as you are concerned.

WITH COORDINATE INDEPENDENT CLAUSES

Use a semicolon between coordinate, independent clauses not joined by a coordinating conjunction *(for, and, nor, but, or, yet)*.

Betsy has a degree in communication arts; Roger's degree is in the fields of science and physical education. [A period could be used instead of a semicolon if the writer did not want to show a relationship between these two independent clauses.]

All men were accounted for; the march began. [Two short independent clauses.]

Mr. Stanowitz submitted his monthly report to the committee; it was accepted without comment.

Some of our secretaries take dictation from the officers; other secretaries use transcribing machines.

The senior faculty asked for the graduate classes; the junior faculty settled for the freshman classes.

WITH CONJUNCTIVE ADVERBS

Use a semicolon before a conjunctive adverb *(nevertheless, moreover, therefore, however)* joining two coordinate, independent clauses. In the following example, two independent clauses are separated by a semicolon:

I think that one day Shelley will be very successful; however, I can't make the same statement for Dorothy. [*However* introduces the second independent clause *(however, I can't make the same statement for Dorothy)*. A comma is placed after *however* as it is used as an introductory word in the second independent clause.]

Here is another example of two independent clauses separated by a semicolon:

Robin did not seem to work very hard; nevertheless, all household and office tasks assigned to her were completed competently and efficiently. [*Nevertheless* introduces the second independent clause *(nevertheless, all household and office tasks assigned to her were completed competently and efficiently)*. A comma is placed after *nevertheless,* for it is used as an introductory word in the second clause.]

Consider these examples:

I thought her report was much too long; therefore, I read only her summary of the findings. [A semicolon before *therefore* and a comma after it.]

My cousin graduated first in his law school class; moreover, he has enrolled for the fall term in Jefferson Medical College. [A semicolon before *moreover* and a comma after it.]

WITH LONG COMPOUND SENTENCES HAVING COMMAS

Use a semicolon before a coordinating conjunction *(for, and, nor, but, or, yet)* joining two independent clauses if the clauses are very long or have at least two commas in each clause.

When the race, which has been held every year since 1955, was scheduled, we had 22 contestants; but 5 additional entrants paid their fees to the official registrar, who immediately issued a qualifying certificate on March 10, 1986.

Each independent clause in this compound sentence has a nonessential clause within it, requiring commas to set off the clause. Because the compound sentence is long and each clause already has at least two commas, a semicolon should be placed before the conjunction *but* instead of another comma.

After studying business communications, public speaking, and organizational communications, James realized that effective written and oral communications are necessary for a successful business; and Susan Fletcher, his sales manager, agreed. [The sentence is long and each clause has at least two commas. Precede the coordinate conjunction *and* with a semicolon instead of a comma.]

I believe, and surely you agree from your years of experience, that a competent speaker always prepares carefully; and in addition, a competent speaker, when possible, also prepares his audience. [The sentence is long and both clauses have at least two commas.]

I asked you to mail me a check, the filled-in application form, and a copy of your report; and instead I received a memo giving me excuses, an illegible copy of a letter you had received, and a bill. [A semicolon precedes the conjunction *and* because each clause already has at least two commas.]

WITH A SERIES

Use a semicolon to separate a series when any of the items in the series already contain commas. ☑

Attending the ABC International Conference were Flora Wolk, executive director; Louise Finebaum, president; Ronald Charles, first vice president, and George Beers, journal editor.

My vacation itinerary includes stops at San Juan, Puerto Rico; Montego Bay, Jamaica, and Cancun, Mexico.

Note: The punctuation mark immediately preceding the conjunction *and* is a *comma,* not a semicolon.

COLONS

A *colon* is used infrequently in business writing, but it does serve a useful purpose. Seven important uses of the colon are explained in this section.

WITH A SERIES OF ITEMS

When the words "the following," "as follows," "are these," and similar expressions appear close to the end of a sentence introducing a series of items, you can assume that a colon is needed. Use a colon to introduce a series of items.

Each person should bring the following equipment: one sleeping bag, hiking boots, rainwear, a small shovel, and heavy outdoor clothes.

Self-Check Exercise 1

Now you should be ready to apply the four rules that pertain to the use of semi-colons in sentences. Complete the following sentences by inserting semicolons where needed. You can check your answers with the key at the end of the chapter.

1. The girls enjoyed their vacation however, their funds were badly depleted by the end of the second week, causing them to return home.

2. Those two books are on the reference shelf the others you asked about are not in the library.

3. A receptionist should not be too friendly actually, most employers prefer a little reserve.

4. They telephoned all the salesmen not one of them was in.

5. The television program was interesting moreover, it was educational.

6. The kits are not ready however, we can sell you another product.

7. United States does not have sufficient oil therefore, it has to import it from other countries.

8. Delays occurred throughout the delivery cycle consequently, the target date for announcing shipment had to be changed.

9. One merchant specializes in dishes from England another merchant sells only glassware from Sweden.

10. On cold days, Tom's hands are too cold to type on warm days, they are too hot.

11. Special orders are shipped if they total $50 or more this service is offered to charge customers only.

12. In our letter to your editor, James Johnson, we gave you a personal compliment but unfortunately, your assistant editor, Samantha Brown, did not include our kind remarks when publicizing your newly completed textbook.

13. Our itinerary includes Canton, Ohio Philadelphia, Pennsylvania Atlanta, Georgia, and Jacksonville, Florida.

The needlecraft skills that are necessary for this job are these: crewel stitchery, knitting, needle-point, and crocheting.

Remember to buy the following items for the salad: two heads of lettuce, six large tomatoes, one bag of carrots, and one pound of mushrooms.

WITH A LIST

The introductory sentence that precedes a list usually contains words such as "the following" or "are these." A colon should be placed before the list.

The following suggestions are important when typing a title page for a report:
1. Center each line.
2. Type the title of the report in capital letters and all the other lines in initial capitals.
3. Include the name of the writer, the date, the course, and the title of the report.

My favorite snack foods are these:
1. Pizza pie and soda,
2. Apple pie and coffee,
3. Cheese, crackers, and white wine.

WITH A LONG QUOTATION

Punctuation should separate words such as "Mary *said,*" "John *stated,*" or "Ms. Jones *asked*" from a quoted statement or question. When the quotation is short, the separating mark of punctuation is a *comma.*

Mary said, "I look forward to my summer vacation."

Ms. Jones asked, "Do you buy your business suits at a local department store?"

However, when the quotation is long, the separating mark of punctuation is a *colon.*

Dr. Lindman said: "My medical conference is in Chicago on May 19. I will attend that first, and then I will travel to Los Angeles to deliver my speech at the medical college."

Mary said: "I look forward to my summer vacation. First I plan to spend five days touring France, and then I will visit friends in Athens. Thinking of the delicious French food and Greek salads makes me *really* look forward to the trip."

WITH SPECIAL INDEPENDENT CLAUSES

Use a colon to separate two independent clauses when the second clause explains the first and a conjunction is omitted.

The painting was filled with images: the fire seemed to be the sun, the barren landscape could stand for poverty, and the smashed car was a reminder of his untimely death. [The second independent clause explains the first.]

John Casper frequently gave clear evidence of his malicious nature: he criticized the work of his colleagues, he purposely delayed the forwarding of departmental requests, and he often quoted individuals out of context.

Johnnie was an extremely negligent worker: he broke a turning rod, dropped a glass test kit, and tore a rubber protection sheet.

WITH A SALUTATION

Use a colon after the salutation in a business letter.

Dear Mr. Kaper: Dear Dr. Colton: Ladies and Gentlemen:

WITH TITLES

Use colons between the title and subtitle of a report or book.

Word Processing: Its Role in Information Processing

An Analysis of Organizational Communication: Assessing Employees' Feedback

The Banking Industry: The Role of the Loan Officer

WITH TIME DESIGNATIONS

Use colons in indications of time. ☑

If you feel that 11:30 a.m. is not a good time, we can switch to the original hour of 3:30 p.m.

On Saturday mornings I try to catch up on my sleep; I set my alarm for 9:30 a.m.

QUOTATION MARKS

It is easy to learn the principles that apply to the use of quotation marks in business writing. The following rules and examples will show you where quotation marks should be placed in sentences.

Self-Check Exercise 2

Do you know where to place the colons in the following exercise? Complete the exercise and check your answers with the key.

1. Are the following rights guaranteed by the Constitution the right to worship, the right to work, the right to privacy?

2. The following forms are needed an application, a contract, and an assignment sheet.

3. The three methods of filing used in our office are as follows alphabetic, numeric, and geographic.

4. Words frequently misspelled are these *convenience, accommodate,* and *separate.*

5. My interviews are scheduled at the following times 1000 a.m., 130 p.m., and 315 p.m.

6. Winter arrived with a sudden fury the temperature dropped to 15 degrees below zero, 6 inches of snow fell, and the wind howled violently.

7. The vacation you describe sounds very inviting the cost is low, the accommodations are comfortable, the mountain scenery is beautiful, and the fishing is the best in the Southeast.

WITH DIRECT QUOTATIONS

Use quotation marks to enclose all direct quotations.

> In *Future Shock,* A. Toffler wrote, "Organizations now change their internal shape with a frequency—and sometimes a rashness—that makes the head swim."

> Bill said, "People don't change; their basic characteristics remain the same throughout their lives."

> "I don't agree," replied Frances.

Note: Dialogue between individuals is set off in quotation marks, with each person's statements set off in separate paragraphs.

> Robin said, "Perhaps the most important principle is always be honest with yourself."

> "That may be so," replied Shelley, "but it is probably equally important to be honest with those around you."

> "You are both correct," Betsy declared.

When a quotation is interrupted by *replied Shelley* or *he said* or *stated Mr. Breen* or similar words, quotation marks are placed around the quoted section *before* the interrupting words and also around the quoted section *after* the interrupting words.

> "That may be so," replied Shelley, "but it is probably equally important to be honest with those around you." [This quotation is repeated here to show you an interrupted quote.]
>
>   "I may work on my business communications assignment tonight," said Jeremy, "or I may put it off until Sunday and go to the party instead."

WITH NONSTANDARD ENGLISH

Use quotation marks to enclose slang words or expressions to indicate that they are nonstandard English.

> I don't think that her "pad" is worth the monthly rental fees she is presently paying.

> He may or may not know the facts, but I notice he just "ain't sayin' nothin'."

WITH QUOTATIONS WITHIN QUOTATIONS

Double quotation marks (") are used to enclose a direct quotation; single quotation marks (') enclose a quotation within a quotation.

> Franklin D. Roosevelt stated, "We must fight for freedom, and as Winston Churchill said, 'We will all be slaves if that freedom is not secured.' " [The single quotation mark at the end shows the end of the quotation within a quotation, and the double quotation mark shows the end of the entire quoted statement.]

Note: A quotation within a quotation within a quotation follows the order of double, single, double quotation marks.

> Peter Fairington shouted, "I will not accept your conditions, for our leader has said, 'Every individual is a "giant" or a "midget." ' " [Find the quoted items using " ' ", in that order.]

> The professor said, "All groups have the same pleasure values, although Johnson disagrees with this when he says, 'Entertainment values are not the same for all age groups; a "trip" to some is attractive; to others, repulsive.' " [Find the three quoted items using " ' ", in that order.]

WITH SPECIAL TITLES AND NAMES

Use quotation marks to enclose titles or articles, chapters or sections of a book, lectures, essays, sermons, paintings, poems, and sculptures.

The article "Do You Listen When You Hear?" has been reproduced in several publications. [Omit commas before and after the title of the article because the title is *essential* in this sentence.]

Picasso's "Guernica" was shipped from the Museum of Modern Art to a museum in Madrid. [Work of art.]

The poet saw his finished work "The Light-Hearted Lass" in the *Ladies Home Journal.* [Poem.]

WITH DEFINITIONS

Use quotation marks to indicate terms being defined.

A "television addict" is someone who automatically turns the set on when waking up and leaves it on until nighttime when he or she goes to sleep.

A "principal" is the head of a school, while a "principle" is a rule or precept.

WITH WORDS TO BE SET OFF

Use quotation marks to set off words in a special situation.

Regardless of how you define "dignity," he does not possess it.

She is the perfect example of a true "humanitarian."

WITH OTHER PUNCTUATION MARKS

Use other punctuation marks with quotation marks as follows: ☑

1. Always place periods and commas *within* ending quotation marks.

   "I believe," said Dave, "that all men are created equal."

   "That may be," replied Joan, "but some of the creations turned out to be 'blockheads.' "

   "I will see you on Saturday," he said.

2. Always place semicolons and colons *outside* ending quotation marks.

   That is the "mark of Chicago": penetrating blasts of wind.

   I read the article "Proaction for Effective Communication"; now I must complete the assigned book, *Communicating in Business.*

   When I saw her, she said, "I will arrive at 10:30 p.m. on Tuesday"; however, she is still not here.

   Take the following books from the box marked "History 321": *Ancient Civilization, The Old World,* and *Egypt Versus Greece.*

3. When question marks and exclamation points apply to the quoted material, place them *inside* the ending quotation marks.

   Lester said, "Do you believe in life after death?" [The quote is a question.]

   They shouted, "Down with traitors!" [The quote is exclamatory.]

   Lester said, "Please read the article 'What's Happened to Employee Commitment?' " [The name of the article is a question.]

   Dr. Martinez asked, "Isn't that their usual performance?" [The quote is a question.]

   A voice exclaimed, "Stand up!" [The quote is exclamatory.]

Self-Check Exercise 3

Review the principles for placing quotation marks in sentences, and test your knowledge by completing the following exercise. Insert quotation marks where needed. The key provides the answers.

1. My teenager said it was a contemporary-style pad that he lived in.

2. Stevenson said, If we are to live in peace, we must, as the Israeli representative has indicated, Appreciate the dignity of all people at all times.

3. Thomas Carton wrote the article The Problems of International Finance, which recently appeared in *The Financial Quarterly.*

4. I just read Shirley Jackson's famous short story The Lottery.

5. Have you read the article The American Scene?

6. He asked, Can you attend our next meeting?

7. Alexander Solzhenitsyn in his 1970 Nobel lecture said, The salvation of mankind lies only in making everything the concern of all.

8. Have you traveled to Italy to see Leonardo Da Vinci's painting The Last Supper?

4. When question marks and exclamation points apply to the entire statement and not the quote, place them *outside* the ending quotation marks.

Did Lester say, "I believe in life after death"? [The statement is the question, not the quote.]

Did Dr. Martinez remark, "That is your usual performance"? [The statement is the question, not the quote.]

What a disgraceful example of "goofing off"! [The statement is exclamatory, not the quote.]

Don't work for that "Scrooge"! [The statement is exclamatory, not the quote.]

APOSTROPHES

Apostrophes are important punctuation marks. They perform two special functions:

1. To indicate the omission of letters in contractions (won't, didn't, isn't, can't, here's)

2. To indicate possession in nouns (girl's gloves, girls' gloves, people's applause, infant's cry, babies' bottles)

Apostrophes also play a role in indicating plurals (t's, M.D.'s).

The main rules governing the use of apostrophes in omission, possession, and plurals are listed below.

TO SHOW OMISSION

Use an apostrophe to indicate the omission of one or more letters in a contraction.

> Our motto is *"Don't* call us; *we'll* call you." [Do not, we shall.]
>
> *They're* going to Spain for the summer. [They are.]
>
> They *weren't* planning to travel together. [were not.]
>
> *It's* very hot in Majorca in the summer. [It is.]

Use an apostrophe to indicate the omission of one or more digits in a numeral.

> He *hasn't* been home since he graduated in *'70* [has not, 1970.]
>
> He belonged in the class of *'74*, but his sickness prevented him from graduating until *'75* [1974, 1975]

TO SHOW PLURAL NUMBER

While apostrophes usually indicate omissions in contractions and possession in nouns, they occasionally indicate plurals. Their role in forming plurals is limited to the following: To increase clarity, use the apostrophe and an *s* *('s)* to indicate the plural of lower case letters (t's, k's), capital letters (H's, J's), numerals (1979's, 6's), and abbreviations (Ed.D's).

> His *t's* were never crossed and his *i's* never dotted.
>
> She mispronounced all her *th's*.
>
> The *Ph.D.'s* were lined up in front of the *M.D.'s* for commencement exercises.
>
> The *1980's* have been profitable years for the firm.

TO SHOW POSSESSION

The possessive form of nouns was first presented in Chapter 5. We review it here to show more uses for the apostrophe.

1. To indicate possession if a *singular* noun does not end in an *s* or *z* sound, add an apostrophe and *s* *('s)* to the noun.

    > The woman's job was eliminated. [The job belonged to the woman.]
    >
    > The girl's coat was lime green. [The coat belonged to the girl.]
    >
    > He purchased a dollar's worth of candy.
    >
    > That was my aunt's car that was damaged.
    >
    > Mr. Brown's home was not damaged at all.

Note: In the case of inanimate objects (chair, table), possession can be indicated with an *of* phrase (rather than an apostrophe) or with omission of the possessive altogether. For example, use *leg of the table* or *table leg*, not *table's leg; arm of the chair* or *chair arm*, not *chair's arm; top of the sink* or *sink top*, not *sink's top*.

2. To indicate possession if a *plural* noun does not end in an *s* or *z* sound, add an apostrophe and *s* *('s)* to the noun.

    > The women's jobs were eliminated.
    >
    > The children's toys were everywhere.
    >
    > The people's voices were not heard clearly.
    >
    > The men's tools were left behind.

3. Add an apostrophe and *s* (*'s*) to an indefinite pronoun to indicate possession (*someone's*, *one's*, *somebody else's*).

One's time is often more valuable than money.

The result of the game is anyone's guess.

Note: Pronouns in the possessive case do *not* use an apostrophe to indicate ownership, as such words are already possessive (*its, our, his, hers, theirs.*).

The radio is *ours*. [No apostrophe.]

The car is *yours* but the boat is *ours*. [No apostrophe.]

Its surface was scratched, but *it's* [contraction of *it is*] really of no great importance.

4. When a *plural* noun already ends in an *s* or *z* sound, to show possession add an apostrophe (*'*) to the noun. Since most plural nouns end in an *s* or *z* sound, adding just an apostrophe to the noun is the most common way to form plural possessives. [See Rule 2 above for the exception.]

The ladies' coats and the babies' toys were in the closet of the guest room.

The Aviators' Association received its charter on June 1, 1945.

The girls' coats were lime green.

The three boys' jackets were stolen.

The Kleins' cars, a Chevrolet Celebrity and a Chevrolet Cavalier, were parked on our street.

You may use this section as a quick review.

Singular Nouns

girl   boy   lady   man   child

Plural Nouns

girls   boys   ladies   men   children

Singular Possessive Form Using Apostrophe and s

A *girl's* coat   a *boy's* jacket   a *lady's* sweater
a *man's* belt   a *child's* toy

Plural Possessive Form Using Apostrophe Alone

the *girls'* coats   the *boys'* jackets   the *ladies'* sweaters
the *men's* belts [a plural word not ending in *s*]
the *children's* toys [another plural word not ending in *s*]

Note: The last two examples indicate that plural words not ending in *s* must show possession with the addition of an apostrophe and *s* (*'s*). These irregular plural nouns have the same appearance as singular nouns and form their possessives the same way:

Singular Noun	*Singular Possessive*
child	child's toy

Irregular Plural Noun	*Irregular Plural Possessive*
children	children's toys

5. When two or more persons or objects own one or more items together, possession is indicated on the last-named owner only.

   That is Robin and Shelley's car. [Robin and Shelley own one car in partnership.]

   Bob and Dave's truck was big enough to accommodate all the furniture. [Joint ownership of one truck.]

   Bob and Dave's cars were all registered to the company. [Joint ownership of several cars.]

   Robin and Shelley's cars are on the used-car lot. [Robin and Shelley own more than one car in partnership.]

6. When two or more persons possess items individually, an apostrophe is used with each name.

   Robin's and Shelley's cars are parked outside. [Robin and Shelley own one car each.]

   Bob's and Dave's cars were blue and yellow, respectively. [Individual ownership.]

7. In compound words, an apostrophe is added to the final word to indicate possession.

   My brother-in-law's car was damaged in the accident. [Singular possessive.]

   My brothers-in-law's cars were all parked in front of the house. [Plural possessive. More than one brother-in-law.]

   You are using somebody else's dictionary. [Singular possessive.]

   My mother-in-law's car was bright red. [Singular possessive.]

   Anyone else's reaction would have been one of sorrow. [Singular possessive.]

8. Certain phrases involving time, which seem to express possession, use the apostrophe. Indicate a relationship between the *day, week, year* (or similar) and the noun that follows by inserting an apostrophe (and *s* if needed).

   A *month's pay* was granted. [Singular possessive.]

   Three hours' time is not adequate for the job. [Plural possessive.]

   His dream was to take *four weeks' vacation* in Bali. [Plural possessive. Alternative forms would be *a four-week vacation, a two-day vacation, a two-hour delay,* etc.]

   Tomorrow's game should be the best of the season. [Singular possessive.]

   A *week's wages* can easily be spent in *an hour's time* at the Paris Restaurant.

   Ten weeks' wages may pay for your vacation in England.

9. When writing a name with *Jr., Sr.,* or *Esq.,* indicate possession on the abbreviation, not the surname.

   Martin Casey, Jr.'s, coat was last year's model.

   Frank Barton, Sr.'s, phone was disconnected.

   Lawrence McDonald, Esq.'s, briefcase was stolen. [If this sounds awkward, delete *Esq.* and use *Lawrence McDonald's briefcase was stolen.*]

10. To indicate possession for names ending in *s* or *z*, practice varies. Either *'s* or simply an apostrophe can be added. Use *Mr. Jones's car* or *Mr. Jones' car, Mrs. Williams's car* or *Mrs. Williams' car, Ms. Ortiz' car* or *Ms. Ortiz's car.*

The Joneses' cars were all parked on the south side of the street. [More than one member of the Jones family owned cars.]

The Charleses' papers received identical scores. [Plural possessive.]

The Hamiltons' cars were part of the processing. [More than one Hamilton in the family.]

11. Where an appositive is used, possession is indicated on the appositive, rather than on the preceding noun.

Marcia Singer, the artist's, gloves were left in the car.

Note: Because this statement sounds awkward, it would be better to state,

The gloves of Marcia Singer, the artist, were left in the car. ☑

Self-Check Exercise 4

The use of apostrophes has been explained, and a number of examples have been given. Check your knowledge by inserting an apostrophe (') or an apostrophe and *s* (*'s*) where needed in the following exercise. The key provides the correct answers.

1. Ones thoughts are sometimes private.

2. Michael Kelly, Jr., tailor-made suit was ready to be delivered.

3. Anybodys ideas are acceptable in this brainstorming session.

4. Thomas Fonveille, Sr., store was sold.

5. The reunion of the class of 69 was held at the Aspen Inn.

6. Lindas attaché case was filled with her one clients records.

7. His portfolio held many clients records.

8. Our Christmas celebration is at my mother-in-laws house.

9. The boys coat was lost in the confusion.

10. The Buckmans cars were part of the parade.

11. This summer we are taking two weeks vacation in Spain.

12. All the students desks have arrived.

13. Do not separate the letter from its envelope.

14. You are using somebody elses dictionary.

15. Jack and Nells father is a policeman.

16. Theyre having trouble finding their place.

17. Mr. Smiths advice is always sound.

18. Have you seen the Davises new warehouse?

19. Its a good idea to answer the letters promptly.

20. Wouldnt you like to join us in their cafeteria?

APPLICATION EXERCISES

A. Use the following words as a possessive or as a contraction in a brief sentence.

1. Roberta _____

_____

2. It's _____

_____

3. Its _____

_____

4. They're _____

_____

5. Michele and Katy (who together own one item) _____

_____

6. Bob and Jess (who each own a separate item) _____

_____

7. Men _____

_____

8. Baby _____

_____

9. Babies _____

_____

10. Brother-in-law _____

_____

11. Teachers skills _____

_____

12. Bob, the attorneys, car (Bob is an attorney) _____

_____

13. Fathers-in-law coats _____

_____

14. Wendy and Cary Print Shop _____

_____

15. Mark Fores golf clubs _____

_____

16. Hers _____

_____

17. U.S. Governments buildings _____

_____

18. Corliss and Carpenter (name of a firm) cars _____

_____

19. Rolls Royce _____

_____

20. Everyone _____

_____

21. The effort of five weeks _____

_____

22. Theirs _____

_____

23. Thomas Ross, Jr. _____

_____

24. Ted Kellogg _____

_____

25. Mr. Ross _____

_____

B. Correct all errors that you find in the following memo. Strike out the incorrect punctuation marks and insert the correct ones. Also, add any marks that may be missing.

TO: All Section Chiefs

FROM: A. Moran

DATE: June 15, 198_

SUBJECT: Employees Responsibilities, Policy #221-3

This is in response to several employees questions about their responsibility for our companys' hand tools that they borrow for weekend use.

Company Policy #221-3 states: "Its the responsibility of each employee who borrows any Class #1 tools to insure that theyre returned in satisfactory condition. They may be used for a week's time with a vice presidents approval or 48 hours with a foremans approval. Those employees who wont or dont comply will be subject to administrative action."

Would all section chiefs please monitor their own section relating to this company policy.

ld

C. In the spaces provided in the margin, indicate the correct marks of punctuation for each letter. If no punctuation is required or the mark inserted in the sentence is correct, write C in the space.

1. You will need the following tools __;__ a hammer __,__ a crowbar __ a
           a   b   c

   file __ and a miter box.
        d

   __ __ __ __
   a b c d

2. Did Mary ask, __ Who is ready to join the club __ __
                 a   b c

   __ __ __
   a b c

3. You'll need the following components __;__ transistors __ resistors __   __ __ __ __
                                       a   b   c   a b c d

   and capacitors __.__
                     d

4. __"__ Now is the time to get __ plastered __ __ shouted Kurako __   __ __ __ __ __
   a   b   c d   e   a b c d e

5. "Do you feel we should go __ __ asked Marcia __   __ __ __
                           a b   c   a b c

6. "Now __ __ said Kelly __ __ we are prepared to attack __.__ __   __ __ __ __ __ __
        a b   c d   e f   a b c d e f

7. Mr. Morgan said, "I agree with Bradley's statement __ All govern-   __ __ __ __
                                                a   a b c d

   ment regulations should be abolished __ __ __
                                      b c d

8. Before I accepted __ his apology __ I made my feelings eminently   __ __
                        a   b   a b

   clear.

9. As I said earlier __;__ a background in accounting would be extremely   __ __
                       a   a b

   valuable to someone like Mr __ Oliver.
                                      b

10. If you can complete the contract today __ we shall all be very   __
                                          a   a

   indebted to you.

11. The game went into overtime __ as you can imagine __ the players   __ __
                                   a   b   a b

   were exhausted.

12. The cars were parked __ all the guests had arrived.   __
                              a   a

13. The cars were parked __ consequently __ I assumed all the guests   __ __
                              a   b   a b

   had arrived.

14. We agreed with Melinda __ the time had come to make a decision __   __ __
                                  a   b   a b

15. Do you think the article __ Report Writing for Results __ should be   __ __ __
                              a   b   a b c

   reproduced __
                    c

16. "I'm sure he is now __ flying high __ with excitement __ __ said   __ __ __ __
                               a   b   c d   a b c d

   Donna.

17. __ You are really a model for all our future Ph.D.'s __ __ said Chris-   __ __ __ __
   a   b c   a b c d

   tine __
         d

18. The days were endless __ consequently __ I began to weave reed   __ __ __
                                 a   b   a b c

   baskets __
          c

Name _____

D. Fill in the spaces with the correct marks of punctuation. If a mark is used incorrectly, strike it out and note the correction in the proper space. If it is used correctly write C.

1. His presentation was excellent __ it received the applause it
   a
   deserved.

   __
   a

2. __ I don't feel we are responsible __ __ said Petrocelli __
   a   b c   d

   __ __ __ __
   a b c d

3. Bob said __ __ My __ pad __ is available for a party at any time.__
           a b   c   d   e

   __ __ __ __ __
   a b c d e

4. __ The cases are all packed __ and the passengers are ready to leave
   a   b
   __ __ said Borcley with obvious satisfaction.
   c d

   __ __ __ __
   a b c d

5. I received a reprint of his article, __ Reports for Decision
                                        a
   Making __ __
          b c

   __ __ __
   a b c

6. Jones said, __ I haven't read it __ have you __? "
               a   b   c

   __ __ __
   a b c

7. Thompson called for a vote __ Bitterson objected strongly __
                              a   b

   __ __
   a b

8. __ That was a __ whopper __ of a tale __ " Coco said loudly.
   a   b   c   d

   __ __ __ __
   a b c d

9. Here is the tally __ 105 for Kindrick, 208 for Marsteller, 409 for
                     a
   Washington, and 995 for Steele.

   __
   a

10. __ We aren't always this lucky __ __ said Mrs __ Steele __
    a   b c   d   e

    __ __ __ __ __
    a b c d e

11. Foremen and Baxter led the field __ Tabishi and Sony came in
                                     a
    second __ .
           b

    __ __
    a b

12. When I said, __ All is well __ __ the group settled down __
                 a   b c   d

    __ __ __ __
    a b c d

13. Mr. Killet said, __ Please read the article __ Industry and Society __
                    a   b   c
    for our next class. __
                        d

    __ __ __ __
    a b c d

14. __ My way may be not your way, __ stated Mumford.
    a   b

    __ __
    a b

15. I can only tell you that Dave said, __Will she or won't she __ __
                                        a   b c

    __ __ __
    a b c

16. Did Dave say __ __ She would agree __ __
                 a b   c d

    __ __ __ __
    a b c d

17. Here are the ingredients __ eggs __ margarine __ bread crumbs __
                             a   b   c   d
    and yoghurt.

    __ __ __ __
    a b c d

18. __ I'm sure he is still __ down in the dumps __ __ " said
    a   b   c d
    Marcellino.

    __ __ __ __
    a b c d

19. __ Well __ I think you're badly mistaken __ __ replied Adagio.
    a   b   c d

    __ __ __ __
    a b c d

353

E. In the spaces provided, fill in the correct marks of punctuation. If a punctuation mark is used incorrectly in a sentence, strike it out and note the correction in the proper space. If it is used correctly, write C.

1. "Hi _,_ " said Bobbie, _ I believe it's high time we arrived _._ "
     a   b   c   a b c

2. The days were long and arduous _ waiting for our replacements
                         a   a b

    was a task I would not like to repeat _
                                b

3. _" That may be so, but wasn't it all worth the effort _?_ " said Dr.
   a   b   a b

    Greenberg.

4. _ I'm not sure it was _,_ _ responded Barry _,_ _ but you may be
   a   b c   d e   a b c d e

    correct in the long run."

5. Mark said _ _ I'm quite sure that all of us should appear before
            a b   a b c d e

    the court _ Surely that should satisfy the defense attorney _._ _
             c   d e

6. _ Where shall I go _ What shall I do _ _ Katrina wailed _
   a   b   c d   e   a b c d e

7. _ Well _ I'm sure I don't know _ _ her sympathetic husband
   a   b   c d   a b c d

    responded.

8. The following is a direct quote from *No Tomorrow* _ _ We were all
                                           a b   a b c d

    involved in the Yalta agreement _ _
                            c d

9. The outlook for dental technicians is an excellent one _ every
                                       a   a

    young person should consider the field seriously.

10. Kathy said _;_ "Will we survive this heat _,_ or will we die_._ "
            a   b   c   a b c

11. Here are the materials _ payment is due within 30 days.
                     a   a

12. They shouted in unison _ _ Never, never again _!_ "
                 a b   c   a b c

13. All the exercises were completed on time _ we were now free _
                               a   b   a b c

    or so I thought _ to leave on our vacation.
                 c

14. Sandra asked _ "Have you read the article _ Terrorism Curbs
              a   b   a b c

    European Travel _ ?
                 c

15. Did Mark state, _ No man is an island in today's complex
                a   a b c

    society _ _
          b c

16. __ Now __ __ doctor said, __ let's have a quick look at your throat __   __ __ __ __ __
     a   b c   d   a b c d e

    . "
    e

17. Here's the information __ we leave at dawn __   __ __
                           a   b   a b

F. Insert the correct marks of punctuation in the sentences that follow. If an incorrect mark
has already been used, strike it out, and insert the correct mark above it.

1. "Youre absolutely wrong?" he shouted.

2. "Will she live" Margarite asked.

3. The children were happy as could be they laughed loudly ate voraciously and ran around
   like little demons.

4. I feel we should leave immediately said Mr. Pushinski.

5. We are scheduled to arrive at 2 30 p.m.

6. Have you read the article Communication and Conflict Resolution

7. If I'm a blockhead as you say how come I was selected by Phi Beta Kappa and you were
   not

8. Carter stated I agree with the incoming President's comment We must strive for economic
   security.

9. Martin asked Do you agree with that point of view

10. Did Martin say Economic security is vital

11. It was a beautiful day the sun shone, the breeze was light and the sky was blue.

12. I cannot agree said Heidi for I worked in this dump before it was remodeled.

13. I do believe said Yoshi that the customs of your country and mine are drawing closer.

14. Will you please call Ray the car won't start.

15. The birds sang the dogs barked.

16. Please order the following items paint, plaster, tape, and brushes.

17. The days were long, sunny and beautiful as for the nights they were equally delightful.

18. The work was difficult and taxing the entertainment was fun and relaxing.

19. John played like a demon Mark expended almost no effort.

20. When I walked in I saw Coco the well-known dancer and for me the evening was now complete.

21. Coco was a magnificent entertainer however her partner Francois was barely acceptable.

22. Harry asked "Why can't we all go"

23. Should we set the table Betsy asked.

24. Margo asked, "What can we possibly do to save the situation?"

25. "I dont believe you will agree with my point of view said Wolfgang however you must in the final analysis do what you think is correct."

Challenge Exercise

Use the words listed as contractions or in statements indicating possession.

1. Hers _____

_____

2. Carillo and Morgan store (one store owned in partnership) _____

_____

_____

3. They're _____

_____

4. Mr. Glenn Williams car (the name is Glenn Williams) _____

_____

_____

5. Salary of one month _____

_____

6. An umbrella belonging to the tall woman _____

_____

_____

7. Three trucks belonging to Kelly and Tanaka (in partnership) _____

_____

_____

8. Weren't _____

_____

9. The coats of ten boys _____

_____

10. The home of Bobs mother-in-law _____

_____

_____

11. Ten Ph.D.s _____

_____

12. The decade of the 60s _____

_____

13. The record of NASA _____

_____

14. The skis of Shigeru Ozaki _____

_____

15. The watercolor by Carmen Frank the artist _____

_____

_____

16. Raniey Halstrom Jr. car _____

_____

17. The broken *rs* and *es* in the manuscript _____

_____

_____

18. Its _____

_____

19. Shouldnt _____

_____

20. Theirs _____

_____

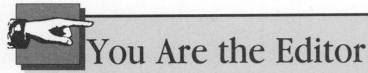

You Are the Editor

In the letter below, strike out errors and insert punctuation marks or other corrections where necessary.

 Electronics, Inc.

751 MacLean Avenue
Dallas, Texas 75223
(214) 804-9187

January 22, 198_

Mr. Taki Yamasuda

Gramercy Corp

1445 Wilshire Boulevard

Winnetka, IL 60093

Dear Mr. Yamasuda:

This is to acknowledge receipt of your request for the recent article; Electronic Components and Their Quality Control which appeared in a recent magazine.

On page 5 you will find the quotation to which you referred and on page 7 the following statement by Dr. Bernard,

> We can therefore expect a major increase in price because of the new U.S. Tariff Regulation #223 which states: "All items of this nature manufactured in Japan are subject to an 18 percent tariff computed on net selling price."

As to your question concerning our manufacturing facilities you are quite correct in your assumption that all electronic items are made in the US and all fasteners in our Hold Tight Line are made in our plant in Taiwan.

We have consistently been the leaders in the quality of electronic components, consequently our firm is now the leader in sales in North America However our prices are not always competitive. The bottom line is simply that companies will pay more for high-quality items.

I do hope I have answered all your questions and that you will receive an 'A' in your term paper; A Comparison of Quality in Domestic and Foreign Components.

Sincerely yours,

Robert K. Keller
Manager, Research Department

Key to Self-Check Exercises

Exercise 1

1. vacation; however,
2. shelf; the
3. friendly; actually,
4. salesmen; not
5. interesting; moreover,
6. ready; however,
7. oil; therefore,
8. cycle; consequently,
9. England; another
10. type; on
11. more; this
12. compliment; but
13. Ohio; Pennsylvania; Georgia, and

Exercise 2

1. Constitution: the
2. needed: an
3. follows: alphabetic,
4. these: *convenience,*
5. times: 10:00 a.m., 1:30 p.m., and 3:15 p.m.
6. fury: the
7. inviting: the

Exercise 3

1. contemporary-style "pad" that
2. said "If indicated, 'Appreciate times.' "
3. "The Finance,"
4. "The Lottery."
5. "The American Scene"?
6. "Can meeting?"
7. "The all."
8. "The Last Supper"?

Exercise 4

1. One's
2. Jr.'s,
3. Anybody's
4. Sr.'s,
5. class of '69
6. Linda's client's
7. clients'
8. mother-in-law's
9. boy's
10. Buckmans'
11. two weeks'
12. students'
13. correct
14. else's
15. Jack and Nell's
16. They're
17. Mr. Smith's
18. Davises'
19. It's
20. Wouldn't

A DYNAMIC BUSINESS VOCABULARY

Your business vocabulary will be enriched if you learn and use these words.

Memory typewriter
Electronic equipment that stores keyboarded material and plays it back automatically.

The office supervisor at the college requested a memory typewriter to help her complete her responsibilities quickly and efficiently.

Microcomputer
A piece of hardware that includes a microprocessing unit, keyboard for entering data, cassette recorder or disk for storing programs, and monitor.

The Computer Science Department placed an order for several microcomputers to be used by its freshmen.

Microfilm
A medium for permanently recording documents in a reduced form that requires optical magnifying devices for reading.

Copies of the *Journal of Commercial Education* were placed on microfilm.

Negotiable
Refers to an item of value that is transferable from one entity to another without further endorsement.

The bond was negotiable at its face value.

Negotiations
Process of reaching agreement by discussions and bargaining.

During final negotiations between the bank and the firm, the $1 million payment was agreed to by both parties.

Nepotism
Favoritism shown to relatives in business.

Most firms will not tolerate nepotism because of the negative effect it has on company morale.

Norm
A standard model for a group to follow.

We found that the norm for law students was to be 22 to 25 years of age, unmarried, and male.

THE ABC'S OF BUSINESS VOCABULARY

Complete the following exercise to test your knowledge of the business words and terms you have learned so far.

1. Compose three short sentences using one of the following in each sentence: (a memory typewriter, (b) microfilm, (c) negotiations.

   _____

   _____

   _____

   _____

   _____

   _____

2. Define the adjective *negotiable*. _____

   _____

3. The meaning of *joint venture* is _____

   _____

4. *Nepotism* refers to _____

   _____

5. The meaning of the noun *forecasting* is _____

   _____

6. A standard model for a group to follow is (a) mode, (b) median, (c) norm, (d) facsimile.

7. The rise and fall of prices or financial levels is (a) fluctuation, (b) stock market, (c) depression, (d) inflation.

8. Approval or support of a proposal or a product is (a) backing, (b) purchase, (c) endorsement, (d) statement.

9. An official prohibition against imports to or exports from a port or country is a/an (a) barricade, (b) barrier, (c) distribution, (d) embargo.

15 Other Marks of Punctuation

In addition to the period, comma, semicolon, colon, quotation marks, and apostrophe, which were discussed in the previous chapters, there are several marks of punctuation that are used less frequently. These marks, which also serve as road signs in your writing, are the exclamation point, question mark, dash, parentheses, brackets, ellipses, hyphen, and underline. Although they are not used as frequently as the marks in the previous chapters, they are still important to the clarity of written material. By learning the principles relating to these marks, you will be able to use them correctly and effectively.

EXCLAMATION POINTS

The exclamation point is used after a word, phrase, clause, or sentence to express a high degree of emotion. It is often used after an emphatic interjection (Wow! No! Phooey!). Exclamation points should be used sparingly so the few you do use are highly visible and effective. In business communications, exclamation points are used primarily in persuasive and sales letters.

> See our carpeting today!
>
> Remember! March 14 is our final sale day.
>
> Hush! She is working on her budget.
>
> "I won't obey the order!" he shouted.
>
> "Pull over now!" she yelled.
>
> Be quiet! They are recording.
>
> No! It isn't true!

QUESTION MARKS

1. Use the question mark after a direct question, but *not* after an indirect question. Consider the following examples:

   Direct Questions
   Do you believe that preparation for a job requires both education and experience?

   Have you completed your analysis of the Carter Company case?

   Are you coming to our dinner meeting?

   Indirect Questions
   He asked if we were coming to their dinner meeting. [No question mark.]

   They asked when our next meeting would be held. [No question mark.]

2. In a declarative sentence, use a question mark at the end of a quotation that asks a question. Place the question mark inside the ending quotation marks.

I don't know why Joan asked, "Should we prepare for trouble?" [The sentence is a statement, but the quotation is a question.]

"Should we prepare for trouble?" Joan asked. [Again, the sentence is a statement, but the quotation is a question.]

The client asked, "Is my case ready for suit yet?"

3. For emphasis, use question marks between the segments in a series of questions. The individual questions need not be complete sentences.

Were all the preparations for the meeting made? agendas mailed? visuals drawn? room reserved? lunch ordered?

Are you opening a branch office in Newark? in Albany? in Princeton?

Who is making the speech—the president? the dean? the business manager?

Note: Remember that, when a polite request for action is expressed as a question, a period, not a question mark, ends the sentence.

Will you call me as soon as possible.

May I hear from you tomorrow.

These courteous requests call for periods, not question marks.

DASHES

A *dash* sets off essential or nonessential elements within a sentence. It is used primarily to indicate a break in thought and to provide emphasis. Using a dash in place of commas or parentheses injects a touch of creativity into written material. There are three important principles to remember about the use of the dash. ☑

1. Use a dash to set off and emphasize nonessential material.

She stood alone—forlorn, frail, and defeated—and then walked through the doors of the institution.

Hal Rollins—you know he had worked for us since 1960—retired in August this year.

We plan to see that our faculty—some of whom have been with us since our college opened—receive cost-of-living raises in the next contract.

2. Use a dash to indicate when the idea in a sentence has been broken off sharply or to indicate a sudden change in thought within a sentence.

Can you believe that—

Here is an excellent textbook—economical, too!

Mario's eyes reflected compassion—or was it love?—when he spoke to Maria.

"Then we are agreed that—now what's the problem?" asked Jose.

Bob thinks we should move—but of course, Bob always thinks that plans made should be changed.

Do you believe that—no, I'm sure you would never accept it!

The spring meeting is at Indiana University in Bloomington, Indiana—or is it at Indiana State University in Pennsylvania?

3. Use a dash to precede a summarizing statement at the end of a sentence.

Good decision-making skills, excellent ability to communicate, and a strong desire to lead—those are the characteristics of our executive officers.

Compassion, competence, knowledge, and a desire to work hard—these are the qualities of our nurses.

Magazines were everywhere, the stereo was on, clothes were tossed helter-skelter, food disappeared quickly, laughter filled the air—the girls were home for the weekend.

PARENTHESES

Unlike dashes, parentheses are *not used* to set off *essential* words, phrases, or clauses. The role of parentheses is to deemphasize *nonessential* elements.

1. Parentheses are used to set off nonessential, supplementary words, phrases, or clauses within a sentence.

Self-Check Exercise 1

This exercise will challenge your knowledge of the correct use of the exclamation point, question mark, and dash. Insert these marks as needed in the following sentences. In addition, correct any punctuation that may need correcting in the exercise. Check the key at the end of the chapter.

1. "I will not" he shouted!

2. The repairman asked when the Multilith had been purchased?

3. Would you be interested in seeing a play or hearing a concert.

4. Mr. James asked if I had a good book on salesmanship.

5. Do you know the difference between a certified check and a bank check.

6. I can't believe it. She's fainted.

7. I'll most likely attend or maybe I won't let me think it over.

8. Lydia was a half hour late but of course, that was expected.

9. What are your plans for this summer!

10. Were all the supplies delivered the stationery the pens the folders the name tags.

11. His head was pounding, he found it difficult to concentrate, he could hardly stay awake he had been studying for his final exam all day.

There are some men who never seem to tire (Michael Yasuda is an example), but run for mile after mile after mile.

The politician heard from only a few (three) of his many followers.

I received a letter from Loretta Lawson (formerly Loretta Lyman) just last week.

Troilo's periodic reports (following the format recommended by the National Trade Council) were submitted by all department managers to the general superintendent.

John played tennis for the University of Southern California (varsity level). [Note that the period follows the ending parenthesis—see the following note.]

Note: When the items in parentheses appear at the end of a sentence, place the terminal mark of punctuation after the ending parenthesis.

Are your partners going to the Chicago conference (both Stephen and Jeffrey)?

We shall meet the next two Mondays (October 3 and 10).

When the element within the parentheses is inadvertently a complete sentence, do not capitalize the first word in the parentheses unless it is a proper noun or adjective, the pronoun *I,* or the beginning of a direct quotation.

Can your brothers join us (it has been a while)?

Please attempt to attend our next sales meeting (I'm strongly urging this).

Exception: If the material within the parentheses is intentionally treated as a separate, complete sentence, the closing mark of punctuation is placed within the second parenthesis and the sentence within the parentheses starts with a capital letter.

John was available to play tennis, as was Henry. (John was completely recovered from surgery.)

For your information, Jena Woodward will be tutoring in our student lab. (Didn't she attend your wedding?)

2. Use parentheses to enclose a numerical designation of a verbal statement of money—frequently found in legal documents.

The deposit of five hundred dollars ($500.00) will not be refunded except through court order.

The defendant owes the plaintiff the sum of two thousand dollars ($2,000.00).

3. Use parentheses to set off references and directions.

The information appears in the appendix (pages 280–283).

Because of the present renovations to our hospital (see the enclosed newsletter), we must postpone using your window-washing service until summer.

I notice that the ratio of part-time to full-time faculty (look at the attached) is being lowered.

4. Parentheses are used to enclose numerals or letters when a list is presented within a sentence.

Four basic factors must be considered before we move forward: (1) the amount of money needed, (2) the city permits for construction, (3) the completed contracts, and (4) the goodwill of the community.

The employment interview has four main parts: (a) the introduction, (b) the warm-up or relaxation period, (c) the question-and-answer session, and (d) the closing.

I plan to (1) visit my travel agent, (2) pick up my passport, and (3) call my relatives in Rome to tell them when I will be arriving.

BRACKETS

1. Use brackets to enclose editorial corrections or explanatory statements in quoted material.

    Henderson, a work-study student in 1986, had said, "Being paid the minimum wage [$3.35 an hour] prevents me from affording any luxuries."

    "I don't believe," said President Reagan, "that he [President Franklin D. Roosevelt] felt comfortable with the Yalta Treaty."

    In her article on political upsets, Stella stated, "Marvin was defeated in the election of 1966 [he was defeated in 1962], and this marked the end of 36 years of Democratic treasurers in Wade County."

    The newscaster stated, "The hostages were all safe [the local newspaper questioned the location of one hostage], according to the visiting diplomats."

    The statement on that issue, which appears in Canring's book *New America,* is:
    "All members of the Ardennes patrol were later charged with desersion [sic] and negligence of duty." [The word *sic* means "thus" or "this is the exact way the material appeared in the original statement."]

2. Brackets are used to enclose a small parenthetical (nonessential) statement within a larger parenthetical statement. The larger parenthetical statement has parentheses around it.

    Clara Carter left the television program because she was getting insufficient coverage. (However, the director stated [on March 23] that she has reconsidered her decision to leave.)

ELLIPSES

1. The ellipsis mark (three dots) is used to indicate the omission of a segment within a quoted passage. One typewriter space should separate each dot. ☑

    Entire Passage Without an Ellipsis
    I have spoken of the learning of Ligeia: it was immense—such as I have never known in a woman. In the classical tongue was she deeply proficient, and as far as my own acquaintance extended in regard to the modern dialects of Europe, I have never known her at fault.
    —Edgar Allan Poe

    Shortened Passage With an Ellipsis
    I have spoken of the learning of Ligeia: it was immense . . . I have never known in a woman. In the classical tongue was she deeply proficient, . . . I have never known her at fault.
    —Edgar Allan Poe

2. When the omission follows a complete declarative sentence, a period precedes the ellipsis.

    I have spoken of the learning of Ligeia: it was imense—such as I have never known in a woman. . . . I have never known her at fault.
    —Edgar Allan Poe

Note: When the omission is at the end of a sentence, use three periods for the ellipsis and then the proper terminal punctuation. (. . . . or . . . ! or . . . ?)

    Is anyone able to explain why . . . ?

    Wow! Did you see . . . ?

3. An ellipsis mark is used to indicate a pause or a deliberately unfinished statement.

    I agree in the case of Mr. Yamashika, but in the Cartright situation . . .

Note: A full line of spaced periods is used to indicate the omission of a paragraph or more in a prose quotation.

> As our Religion, our Education, our Art looks abroad, so does our spirit of society. All men plume themselves on the improvement of society, and no man improves.
>
> . . . .
>
> The civilized man has built a coach, but has lost the use of his feet. He is supported on crutches, but lacks so much support of muscle. He has a fine Geneva watch, but he fails . . .
> —Ralph Waldo Emerson

HYPHENS

1. Use a hyphen to divide a word at the end of a line. Since words are divided between syllables, words with only one syllable cannot be divided. Most words with two or more syllables, however, may be divided if the syllables have at least two letters. Words with more than two syllables can be divided even if one syllable contains only one letter if that syllable is not at the beginning or end of the word.*

Word	Number of Syllables	Division
consider	3	con- sider
bound	1	Cannot be divided.
proper	2	pro- per

Note: The primary use of word division is to maintain a reasonably straight right-hand margin. At no time, however, is it acceptable to hyphenate more than two line endings in a row. Also, remember you *should not* divide the last word of a paragraph or page and you *should* use word division sparingly, as it is not easy to read divided words.

> It is not enough to appreci-
> ate him; it is also necessary
> to appreciate his wife. Remem-
> ber this!

2. Hyphenated words may be divided only at the hyphen.

self-
assurance

well-
known

ex-
president

self-
portrait

3. Hyphens may be used to form compound nouns, verbs, and adjectives. Here are some examples of compound words that are presently hyphenated:

They advertised for a clerk-typist. [Compound noun.]

Mrs. Candelabreese was Tony's mother-in-law. [Compound noun.]

You should not have double-spaced that business letter. [Compound verb.]

*If you are not sure where syllables end in a word, refer to your dictionary to find the proper place for division.

Self-Check Exercise 2

Test your ability to correctly insert parentheses and brackets in the following sentences. Refer to the key when you complete the exercise.

1. This contract is unfair because it states, "Only five personal-use days we originally had ten are permitted."

2. He said, "Marie or Jane one or the other will deliver this package."

3. Florio, the gubernatorial candidate, met with a number eight of his staunchest supporters.

4. I received a telephone call from Cal Rutherford alias The Financier saying he was back in town.

5. Madrid a target of political terrorists was the site of the International Word Processing Conference in 1985.

6. Lyndon Johnson remarked, "He John F. Kennedy was an articulate speaker and a serious scholar."

7. You can stay with us we're close to the airport the night of the 13th.

8. The weatherman said, "Winds of 175 mph actually 190 mph winds were noted have been reported by the hurricane watchers in Miami."

Have you spot-checked your neighborhood? [Compound verb.]

He was a well-known speaker. [Compound adjective.]

Greens is a time-sharing resort. [Compound adjective.]

Do not write run-on sentences. [Compound adjective.]

THE UNDERLINE

The *underline* is also referred to as an *underscore*. In typewritten material, it is used for emphasis in place of *italics*.

1. When a foreign expression is unlikely to be familiar to the reader, use an underline to indicate that the expression is not part of the English language.

    There was a true spirit of gemütlichkeit at the family reunion. [Means cordiality.]

    The Israelis' greeting of shalom is a pleasant and friendly one. [Means hello.]

    The waiter wished us bon appétit. [Means good appetite.]

2. Use an underline to indicate titles of complete works that are published as separate items, such as books, pamphlets, magazines, newspapers, films, and plays. The names of pieces of sculpture and paintings are also underlined.

Note: Titles of complete works may be typed in all capital letters or underlined, but not both.

Every typist will find the handbook <u>Typing in Business</u> a necessary reference book.

OR

Every typist will find the handbook TYPING IN BUSINESS a necessary reference book.

The <u>Philadelphia Inquirer</u> has a very large classified section.

She is an avid reader of <u>Redbook</u> magazine.

He purchased a print of Rembrandt's <u>Portrait of a Lady With an Ostrich-Feather Fan.</u>

SUMMARY

You have just completed studying the most important principles governing the use of many punctuation marks. The examples in Chapters 13, 14, and 15 should have served as a refresher and helped you reinforce your mastery of these rules.

Use this textbook as a resource whenever a punctuation application rule slips your mind. When you want to check the punctuation in your writing, refer to the principles and examples provided here. Lastly, keep in mind that punctuation will help clear, concise writing, but will not improve poorly worded, illogical constructions. ☑

Self-Check Exercise 3

Check your ability to use the hyphen in the division of words. Determine where each of the following words could be divided (if at all) at the end of a line. Rewrite each word, inserting hyphens between syllables. You may refer to your dictionary.

1. incredulity

2. phrase

3. sentence

4. interjection

5. landlord

6. emphatic

7. committed

8. declarative

9. preparation

10. parentheses

In addition, insert a hyphen or underline where needed in the following sentences. All answers appear in the key.

11. Mrs. Lubicheck is my mother in law.

12. He was annoyed that I had double spaced the letter.

13. He is not a well known artist.

14. The self assured author wrote his first novel, The Heroes.

15. My stockbroker reads the Wall Street Journal religiously.

16. May I see your up to date records?

17. We recently adopted the business communication text Communicating in Business.

18. Do you understand the meaning of au revoir?

19. Jennifer Walsh, her attorney at law, has opened an office in Ames.

20. Public utilities offer high paying secretarial jobs.

APPLICATION EXERCISES

A. Insert the correct marks of punctuation in the sentences that follow. If an incorrect mark has already been used, strike it out, and insert the correct mark above it.

1. "Do you think no, I guess you just don't think," said Margo with great sarcasm.

2. Were all the ballots counted all the certificates signed all the permits recorded all the work completed.

3. "I don't believe well yes I do."

4. The accounting books there were a total of ten were all available for review.

5. "We will first attempt now what's your question" Yoshi asked irritably.

6. Some women and Bella Fire is one look beautiful in almost any clothes they wear.

7. He was the executive vice president of the bank (Bank of Mid-California)

8. John Greenberg was an officer (He was executive vice president of the Congressional Bank and Trust Company)

9. John Granowskis statement was, "We will seek to have the ruling of May 5, 1981 the correct date was May 15, 1981 overturned by the Supreme Court of the United States."

10. The quotation that appeared in the first edition was:
    We all agree that men are frail
    But there sic strength . . .

11. "My car exclaimed Cathy as she saw it go rolling over the cliff.

12. You can't possibly be serious?" said Featherstone

13. I certainly am Featherstone shouted.

14. "Well that means we've reached the end of the relationship Whippet said sadly.

15. "Halt!" Bob shouted!

16. "Are you going to the game," asked Toshiba.

17. Her illness has lasted for six months, consequently, our friends are feeling very low.

18. He left the building (the Burns Building at exactly 4:15 pm.

19. "Do you believe we should pay the ransom?" inquired Jack?

B. Use the following words as a possessive, a plural, or a contraction in a brief sentence.

1. Washington _____

_____

2. 1980's _____

_____

3. Six Ph.D.'s _____

_____

4. A Ph.Ds gown _____

_____

5. Theirs and ours _____

_____

6. Sister-in-law _____

_____

7. Brothers-in-law _____

_____

8. Galleys Garage _____

_____

9. A years collection _____

_____

10. Californias population _____

_____

11. José, Martel, and Katrina diplomas _____

_____

12. The Andrews car (family name is Andrews) _____

_____

13. Everybody books _____

_____

14. Kelly equipment _____

_____

15. Three hours time _____

_____

16. Baker Brothers annual sale catalog _____

_____

17. Its formula _____

_____

18. Koper and Arno shoe store always seemed busy _____

_____

19. The typewriters shift key was bent _____

_____

20. The patience of Ms. Kellogg _____

_____

21. Its _____

_____

22. France _____

_____

23. Illinois _____

_____

C. Insert the correct marks of punctuation where needed. If an incorrect mark has been used, circle it and indicate the correction.

1. "Do you believe Farincello," asked Maria.

2. More people are lost that way, greater care must be taken in checking medications.

3. Here is the list of items needed, large needles, heavy thread, a roll of canvas, and a large box.

4. He was really a, well, I guess he wasn't really.

5. Help, Margarite shouted.

6. The quotation read, "All vehicles will be . . . impounded if left unattended."

7. The deck was smooth and polished and the living quarters were in spotless condition.

8. When I inspected Anthony's craft I found a very different situation.

9. Will you therefore agree to be president.

10. He had lost his fortune therefore he took the position as company chairman.

11. Farmington said, "I don't agree with Truman's statement, "We must protect our citizens with any means possible."

12. Did Farmington also say, "The citizens welfare must come first?"

13. The "blockhead" kept misplacing his tools.

14. I don't think you should buy ready to wear clothes.

15. "I don't believe it should be purchased, said Rosa.

16. Martin secured 20 more shares he now had 250 which he added to his estate.

17. "I was about to say—now, let's see, what was I going to say" mumbled Garvey.

18. These are critical times, consequently, we must elect a strong leader.

19. "Holy smokes" he exclaimed.

20. The day was beautiful the sky was blue the breeze was warm and the flowers were in bloom.

D. This exercise tests your knowledge of apostrophes and hyphens. Insert the correct marks of punctuation in the sentences that follow. If an incorrect mark has already been used, strike it out and insert the correct mark above it. Also add the possessive *s* where needed.

1. The mans hat was designed by Fronicci.

2. The womens scarves were all Fronicci originals.

3. Joe home was demolished; Carlos auto was nowhere to be seen.

4. Mr. Green and Mr. Johnson store proved to be very successful.

5. Mr. Green and Mr. Johnson stores that they owned in partnership proved very successful.

6. Theyre going to issue a new edition.

7. Its leg was broken but its no great loss the chair had certainly seen better days.

8. Mike and Bob truck cost was figured as a business expense.

9. A months time can be given to the task.

10. A years salary can easily be spent in a nights gambling in a Las Vegas casino.

11. The cars tires (for all company cars) would be replaced at a cost of $5,000.

12. They havent arrived with Suikos package, but they have delivered ours.

13. The three attorneys notes were reproduced but the childrens records were lost.

14. The Joneses home was large and spacious.

15. It is everyones feeling that we will surely win.

16. The Kruzinskis song was certainly, "All Gods Children Got Wings."

17. His brother in law coat certainly did not fit Ted.

18. Moira and Kawa sweaters were gold and green respectively.

19. The three mothers in laws sons were all named—interestingly enough—Barclay.

20. The statement, "You Cant Go Home Again" is one we dont seem to take to heart.

21. "We arent free to return their deposit," said Marcia.

22. My brother in laws car was badly damaged.

23. Charles Hair Styling Shoppe wasnt as busy as I expected it to be.

24. Do you believe its best to leave well enough alone.

25. Although the case is hers, I dont believe that we should not have any jurisdiction over it.

E. This exercise tests your knowledge of many punctuation principles. Insert all necessary marks of punctuation in the sentences below.

1. The team members were somewhat shy and reticent it was the first time any of them had ever been in the presidential residence.

2. Wagner used the ceremony for the following purposes awarding medals presenting certificates and announcing his intention to run for office.

3. The conference accomplished all its objectives therefore, the Tuesday session was canceled.

4. Did Lou say, I think we have now completed our mission.

5. Harry replied, Do you really think this concludes our effort

6. One fact is clear, said Esmerelda, we really can't stonewall the situation any longer

7. The alarm was set for 815 a.m. however it never went off.

8. Joseph R. Sanchez Sr made an important suggestion for solving the problem it was contained in his Tuesday TV broadcast.

9. Barbara said, From what I can see all men are blockheads.

10. I do believe that all assignments have been completed we are now ready to begin signing the many construction contracts.

11. President Hoover said These are critical times but as Woodrow Wilson stated America's enormous resources will assure us of victory

12. Here is the solution to the problem pay each employee double his or her usual salary for a period of three weeks.

13. He may have been a high flyer said Michael but at our gatherings he was referred to as Stone Face.

14. I can't believe that's true responded Gary

15. Here are the results Kurowaki received a B McClintock was given an A and O'Malley scored a C.

16. Did you say One for all and all for one

17. Johanna replied If I win tomorrow will you accompany me to the state capital

18. Indira said, All students hit a low now and then in the course of the first semester.

19. Ouch he exclaimed

20. Did Sanchez say Mexico is the land of opportunity

21. Welcome home Mark shouted.

22. For many people this is the land of opportunity for others it is the country of despair.

23. My reaction is positive said Corona.

F. Insert the correct marks of punctuation in the sentences that follow. If an incorrect mark has already been used, strike it out, and insert the correct mark above it. Add the possessive *s* where needed.

1. He engraved all the Rs in English script.

2. He was coach of the Bulldogs 79 team.

3. The 1960s were memorable years on our college campus.

4. He could not seem to pronounce correctly the German *zevs.*

5. The M.D.s held a joint meeting with the D.D.S.s.

6. The *s were cracked on all ten typewriters keys.

7. He formed all his 7s in the European fashion by using a crossed line at midpoint.

8. I dont think he will agree, he hasnt in the past.

9. Although theyve lived in it for over a year Bob and Carol home is not yet completely furnished.

10. "Oh whats the difference Carol always said, its furnished by both of us."

11. The attorneys' offices were all located on the tenth floor of the building.

12. Robert R. Morales, Jr's certificate was turned over to his mother trust.

13. Conchita and Ruby apartment, which they have occupied since February, was furnished in good taste.

14. A years effort was expended on the project by Hermans children.

15. My brother in law basketball program was far ahead of its times.

16. Who knows what tomorrows sorrows will bring.

17. Do you feel that we shouldnt . . . no, I guess you rarely feel, said Perry.

18. The 1940s the War Years will be remembered by everyone who played some role in the worlds greatest military effort.

19. The womens and mens coats were all kept in the master bedroom.

20. We couldnt believe John's persistent efforts.

21. A weeks salary was lost because of their error.

22. My dentists car was damaged.

23. The boys and mens clothing department was located on the second floor.

24. Our familys Bibles cover was made of hand-sewn leather.

Challenge Exercise

The sentences that follow may have errors. Circle the errors and place the correct marks in the blanks. If there is no error, mark the sentence C.

_____ 1. If theyre ready, we will start the motor.

_____ 2. Did she say, "All men are equal?"

_____ 3. The runners were at the starting line, the crowd was restless, tense, and expectant.

_____ 4. "Now!" he shouted.

_____ 5. Its branches had all snapped off under the weight of the snow.

_____ 6. The uniforms were theirs; the baseball equipment was ours.

_____ 7. This however, is not the case to judge.

_____ 8. It seems to me, now, what was I going to say?

_____ 9. The ten M.D.'s gathered around the kings' bed for the consultation.

_____ 10. The UN's report on the armed action was held in abeyance.

_____ 11. Everyone of the _t_s' in the typesetting box was broken.

_____ 12. Having everybodys' vote was very important to me.

_____ 13. Although Korn and Kables' store was always busy, they consistently lost money.

_____ 14. My mother's-in-law car was bright red.

_____ 15. It wouldn't be the same without you; you must come and join Tess's party.

_____ 16. Tom's and Johns' coats were lying on the ground.

_____ 17. "You may believe what you want," stated Ralph, "but I know Im innocent."

_____ 18. "Thats good enough for me," said his attorney.

_____ 19. The 40's were critical war years for America.

_____ 20. "We're all set to—now what's your complaint," asked Bella.

Name _____

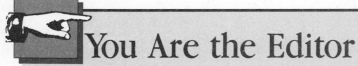

You Are the Editor

In the exercise that follows, use your pen to strike out errors. Insert corrections, including punctuation marks, where needed.

The Northern Company

806 Brunswick Road
Arlington, Illinois 60703
(312) 525-3020

November 15, 198_

Mr. Andrew Smith

Kelly and Smiths Book Store

1414 Dona Lee Dr.

Abington, PA 19001

Dear Mr. Smith

We received your recent request for a copy of Andrew Jacksons

statement before the Senate Committee. Its a pity we didn't hear

from you just a week earlier; we could have sent you a newly printed

copy. We double checked our records and found the following

statement,

     All citizens who lived in the floods path and sustained

     damage to personal property in excess of $500 it should

     have been $600 can make a citizens claim which will be

     honored in every countys' courthouse. Claims wont be

     honored after the first of January.

This quotation as you may be aware was first reproduced in Parker's and Bowers article, "Floridas Early History" which appeared in the out of print Collected U.S. History Monographs. It is interesting to note that Bower's son in law later wrote extensively on the history of the United States he dedicated all his works to his father's in law memory.

We hope this fills your request as our companys' founder said many years ago We try to please

Sincerely yours:

Markwell T. Marks

fr

Self-Check Exercise Key

Exercise 1

1. not!" he shouted.
2. purchased.
3. concert?
4. correct
5. check?
6. it! She fainted!
7. attend—or maybe I won't. Let
8. late—but of course,
9. summer?
10. delivered? the stationery? the pens? the folders? the name tags?
11. awake—he had been

Exercise 2

1. [we originally had ten]
2. [one or the other]
3. number (eight)
4. Rutherford (alias The Financier)
5. Madrid (a target of political terrorists)
6. He [John F. Kennedy]
7. us (we're close to the airport)
8. [actually 190 mph winds were noted]

Exercise 3

1. in-cre-du-li-ty
2. cannot divide
3. sen-tence
4. in-ter-jec-tion
5. land-lord
6. em-phat-ic
7. com-mit-ted
8. de-clar-a-tive (Divide after *a.* If a syllable is a single vowel, divide *after* it, not before it.)
9. prep-a-ra-tion (Divide after *a.*)
10. pa-ren-the-ses
11. mother-in-law
12. double-spaced
13. well-known
14. self-assured   novel, The Heroes
15. reads the Wall Street Journal
16. up-to-date
17. Communicating in Business or COMMUNICATING IN BUSINESS
18. meaning of au revoir
19. attorney-at-law
20. high-paying

A DYNAMIC BUSINESS VOCABULARY

Here is a new list of business vocabulary for you to study, define, and use in sentences. Be sure to check your dictionary if you have a question about the pronunciation of any of the terms.

Note

A signed statement promising to make payment on a specific date or dates.

When buying his car, Peter borrowed money from the bank and signed a note promising full payment within 26 months.

Personal computer

A microcomputer designed for personal record keeping, instructional use, or entertainment.

She was fascinated with the use of the mouse that accompanied the Apple MacIntosh personal computer.

Program

A series of instructions that causes a computer to perform an operation.

The DP 104 students learn how to write a computer program the first week of the semester.

Quantitative factor

A numerical factor that may influence a decision.

The quantitative factors indicated that 60 percent of the people would not shop before 10 a.m.

Questionnaire

A set of printed questions on a specific subject.

The response to the mail questionnaire was a very encouraging 75 percent.

Quota

An assigned allotment or level to be met.

Russell met his production quota for March, with a 10 percent surplus.

Scan

To examine quickly.

Paula will usually scan her notes before entering a board meeting.

THE ABC'S OF BUSINESS VOCABULARY

Review your ability to recognize, define, and use the business vocabulary words included in your textbook. Complete the following exercise:

1. Define the verb *scan.* _____

   _____

2. The meaning of the noun *incentive* is _____

   _____

3. *Quantitative factor* refers to _____

   _____

4. Give the definition of the noun *data.* _____

   _____

5. Compose three short sentences using one of the following in each sentence: (a) personal computer (b) note (business term) (c) debt.

   _____

   _____

   _____

   _____

   _____

   _____

6. An assigned allotment or level to be met is a/an (a) amount, (b) total, (c) quota, (d) share.

7. A series of instructions that causes a computer to perform an operation is a/an (a) hardware, (b) cursor, (c) data, (d) program.

8. A medium for permanently recording documents in a reduced form that requires optical magnifying devices for reading is a/an (a) slide, (b) snapshot, (c) picture, (d) microfilm.

9. A machine that cuts holes in computer cards to store information is a/an (a) electric scissors, (b) keypunch, (c) optical scanner, (d) Central Processing Unit (CPU).

16 Capitalization

What is the purpose of capitalizing the first letter of a word? Is it to indicate where a new sentence begins? Is it to emphasize the distinction of specific names or places? Is it to call the reader's attention to words the writer considers important? The answer is yes to all these questions.

There is no doubt that capitals "stand out" and thus should be used sparingly to ensure proper emphasis. The way to make sure that you capitalize correctly is to become acquainted with some of the basic guidelines for starting words with capitals.

This chapter provides many principles and examples relating to capitalization to help you in your business writing. Keep in mind, however, that should your company's preferences differ from the examples presented, you should follow your company's policy.

To see the importance of understanding capitalization, consider the letter of application in Figure 16-1. Does this letter indicate that the writer may lack at least one of the skills needed to fill a secretarial position? Let's hope you have answered yes. The errors in capitalization indicate that the writer could profit from the following instructive information on the use of capitals in business English.

FIRST WORDS

1. To indicate to the reader exactly where a new sentence begins, capitalize the first letter of the first word in each sentence.

   The inventory-control system was completely computerized.

   Up-to-date reports are placed on the executive's desk. [At the beginning of a sentence, capitalize the first element in a hyphenated word.]

   I must have the accounting information now! [The word *I* is always capitalized.]

   Where are your pamphlets?

2. Do you ever use an expression to replace a sentence? If so, capitalize the first word of the expression.

   Okay.   No way!   Not really.   Yes!   No!   Maybe!

3. Remember to capitalize the first word in a *direct* quotation.

   She asked, "Are you attending Friday's concert at the Arena?" [Direct quotation.]

   She asked whether you were attending Friday's concert. [Not a direct quotation.]

   He replied, "She is not attending the concert." [Direct quotation, so *She* is capitalized.]

   He replied that she was not attending the concert. [Not a direct quotation.]

Figure 16-1. Letter of application.

1590 van cortlandt terrace
teaneck, new jersey 07666
March 5, 198_

Mr. Timothy A. Jones
1919 south downy Road
trenton, NJ 08111

Dear mr. Jones:

I am applying for the position of Secretary that was advertised in the <u>daily</u> <u>post</u> on tuesday, march 3. my work experience and Education have prepared me for this job.

I have attached my résumé for your Referral. please call me at your convenience.

Very Truly Yours,

Frank M. Cucci

Note: Do not capitalize the second portion of a quoted sentence that is interrupted.

"Forty tons of material were hauled the first hour," said Glenn, "but only thirty tons the second."

"Many customers now use automatic bank machines," she stated, "instead of bank tellers."

4. Capitalize the first word of a complete sentence placed in parentheses.

Marty was late for the Board of Directors' meeting. (It is a fact that Marty has been late for every board meeting since 1977.) As usual, the sessions began without him.

Do not capitalize if the statement in parentheses is part of a larger sentence.

The English courses offered for next semester (see pp. 37–41 in the new catalogue) include an excellent one in business English.

5. You may write a complete sentence following a colon. When the complete sentence is used to state a rule or emphasize a statement, capitalize the first word of the sentence after the colon.

It was a miserable night: The rain poured, the wind howled, the lightning flashed, and the electricity failed. [The sentence that follows the colon emphasizes the statement that precedes the colon.]

Here is the principle we follow: Students with more than six unexcused absences cannot earn more than a D for the final grade in typing. [The sentence that follows the colon states a rule or principle alluded to in the statement that precedes the colon.]

6. Capitalize the first word in each line of a list or outline.

> We shall need the following:
> 1. Sketch pads,
> 2. Crayons,
> 3. Erasers.   [A list.]
> I. Two types of jobs
>   A. Accountants
>   1. Public
>   2. Private
>   B. Secretaries
>   1. Medical
>   2. Legal   [An outline.]

7. Normally capitalize each line of a poem.

> Surgeons must be very careful
> When they take the knife!
> Underneath their fine incisions
> Stirs the culprit,—Life!
> > Emily Dickinson

Note: In all situations, you are obligated to follow the poet's style precisely.

8. Salutations and complimentary closes are included in many business letters. Only the first word of the complimentary close is capitalized.

> Sincerely,   Sincerely yours,   Very truly yours,   Yours truly,

> In the salutation, capitalize the first word, the person's title, and the proper name.

> Dear Mr. Jones: Ladies and Gentlemen: Dear Personnel Director:

NAMES

TITLES OF WORKS

Do you know which words should begin with capitals in book, article, and film titles, songs, poems, and report headings? The answer is that all words should begin with capitals *except for* short conjunctions *(and, but, or),* articles *(the, a, an),* and prepositions of three or fewer letters *(in, at, on).*

> *War and Peace* [*And* is a short conjunction and is not capitalized.]

> *Communication for Management and Business* [*For* is a short preposition and is not capitalized.]

> *Gone With the Wind* [*With* is a preposition with four letters; *the* is an article.]

Note: Capitalize the first and last words in a title or heading even if they are articles, short conjunctions, or short prepositions.

> "Growing Up" [An article.]

> *As You Like It* [A play.]

> *The Creature From the Deep* [A movie title.]

> *To the Manor Born* [A television series.]

> *A Concise Guide for Writers* [A book title.]

Note: Capitalize the first word following a colon or dash in a heading or title. ☑

    Careers: *A* Look at Nursing

    Helpful Athletics—*And* Tennis Is for Me

PROPER NOUNS

Proper nouns, which are names of *specific* persons, places, or things, *should* be capitalized *(Dr. Lloyd Tucker, Rivoli Playhouse)*. Common nouns, which refer to *general categories* of persons, places, or things, *should not* be capitalized *(doctor, theater)*.

Self-Check Exercise 1

Thus far you have reviewed the use of capitals when beginning sentences; writing expressions and quotations; writing sentences in parentheses or after a colon; writing outlines, lists, or poems, and beginning salutations and complimentary closes. Do you understand the principles? Find and correct capitalization errors in the following items. Check your answers in the key. If any of your answers are incorrect, review the principles and do the Self-Check Exercise again.

1. the cure is simple.

2. Is your allowance sufficient? of course it is.

3. Pavlov wrote, "all my life I have loved and still love both intellectual and manual work."

4. My instructor said that All assignments must be submitted by Friday.

5. Here is what I plan to buy:
   1. stationery,
   2. business cards,
   3. expense book.

6. He ended his letter "Yours Very Truly."

7. The letter to the reservations clerk began, "Dear sir/madam."

8. Here is the beginning of my outline:
   I. history of banking
      A. in the United States
      B. in Pennsylvania

9. really? okay!

1. Capitalize proper names and nicknames of persons.

   My best friend in high school was Puddinhead O'Dell.

   Have you met Mean Rip Green, who terrorizes the neighborhood?

   Please visit my sister, Linda Grey.

2. Capitalize titles before proper names.

   President Reagan   Ambassador Baxter

   Have you met the course professor, Dr. Raigoza?

   The advanced seminar will be taught by Professor Abate.

   I feel Representative Anderson will take a very active role.

Note: Capitalize titles when they are used by themselves to refer to a specific, well-known individual.

   The Colonel [referring to Colonel Sanders] died on March 3.

   The President [referring to President Reagan] survived an assassination attempt.

3. Capitalize words used as proper nouns for individuals who are family members. Do not capitalize when the words are used as common nouns preceded by a possessive noun or pronoun (i.e, my uncle, his sister, Bill's mother).

   I agree with Mother in her evaluation of a college education. [*Mother* is used as a proper noun.]

   Let us visit Grandfather and my two uncles. [*Grandfather* is a proper noun; *uncles* is a common noun preceded by the possessive pronoun *my.*]

   Let us visit my grandfather. [*Grandfather* is a common noun preceded by the word *my.*]

   My brothers are much taller than I; however, my sister and I are exactly the same height. [*Brothers* and *sister* are both common nouns.]

4. Capitalize proper names of places. This includes streets, parks, bodies of water, cities, states, countries, buildings, etc.

   We are going to Great Britain. [Proper noun.]
   We are going to a foreign *country.* [Common noun.]

   The Fairmont Hotel is a new building. [Proper noun.]
   The *hotel* was recently built. [Common noun.]

   They picnic at Washington Park. [Proper noun.]
   They eat lunch at the *park.* [Common noun.]

   The Delaware River is overflowing. [Proper noun.]
   He rows on the *river* every Sunday. [Common noun.]

   We attend Bellville Baptist Church [Proper noun.]
   They try to attend *church* services frequently. [Common noun.]

5. Capitalize proper names of things, such as historical events (*Korean War*), companies (*Dupont Corporation*), documents (*Constitution of the United States*), organizations (*National Education Association*), schools (*Holmes Junior High School*), and periods in history (*Stone Age*).

   He had heard of the Treaty of Yalta. [Proper noun.]
   What *treaty* was referred to? [Common noun.]

He fought in the Spanish-American War. [Proper noun.]
He is a veteran of the last *war.* [Common noun.]

She is a vice president of Xerox Corporation. [Proper noun.]
She is the vice president of her *company.* [Common noun.]

They worked on the Scorpio Government Project. [Proper noun.]
They worked on the secret *government project.* [Common noun.]

COMMERCIAL PRODUCTS

Would you write *General Electric Appliances* or *General Electric appliances*? Normally, *General Electric appliances* would be correct because General Electric is the brand name. The common noun after the company name is not usually capitalized. ☑

Bufferin   Bayer aspirin   Oldsmobile Cutlass

Westinghouse refrigerator   Jordache jeans

PROPER ADJECTIVES

A proper adjective (*Spanish* food) is derived from a proper noun and is capitalized.

Easter bunny   French perfume   Egyptian history   Jewish food

Note: Because of common use, some proper adjectives are no longer capitalized:

india ink   venetian blinds   plaster of paris   chinaware

Self-Check Exercise 2

Complete the following exercise relating to the use of capitals in titles and headings and in proper nouns. Can you correctly apply the principles just presented?

1. When he was young, he saw his favorite movie, star wars, ten times.

2. I have not met our representative, ms. Claiborne.

3. Did you study the treaty of Paris?

4. He was coordinator for the special government project, operation overload.

5. The article in the magazine was entitled "what's happened to employee commitment?"

6. The City of Boston is near cape cod.

7. He will graduate from Benjamin Franklin high school.

8. The Republican national conference brought many visitors to new york.

POINTS OF THE COMPASS

Capitalize *north, south, east,* and *west* when the direction refers to a specific area.

> She hopes to visit the East Coast first and then go down South.
>
> Industry seems to be moving from the Northeast to the Sunbelt.
>
> Although he has spent the last ten years in the West, he still retained a New England accent.
>
> She is moving to 932 North Ford Road in Miami.

Do not capitalize these words when they indicate either direction or relative location.

> He had driven directly north for almost three days.
>
> They own a house south of Atlantic City.
>
> Many of our students live in the western part of our town.

COLLEGE OR UNIVERSITY

Capitalize the word *college* or *university* when it is part of a proper name of an institution.

> The University of Southern California   County College of Morris
>
> Community College of Philadelphia

Do not capitalize the words if they are common nouns and refer to an educational level.

> He will probably be sorry that he did not attend a college or university when he had the opportunity.

MONTHS, DAYS, HOLIDAYS, AND SEASONS OF THE YEAR

Are all words denoting months of the year, days of the week, holidays, or seasons of the year capitalized? No! Seasons of the year are not capitalized unless there is a specific designation attached. On the other hand, months, days, and holidays should always be capitalized. ☑

> Did you see our new spring merchandise?
>
> We shall attend the Stowe Winter Carnival. [Special designation.]
>
> Where will you be in the winter?
>
> We shall probably have an early and chilly fall this year.

Capitalize months, days of the week, and holidays.

> Next year the Fourth of July will fall on Thursday.
> Schools are closed on Good Friday and Rosh Hashana.
>
> We meet every Wednesday in February.

NATIONALITIES, RACES, RELIGIONS, AND LANGUAGES

> The student body was interracial—they were afro-americans, caucasians, and hispanics.

Should the ethnic groups or races referred to in the previous sentence be capitalized? Yes! Capitalize all nationalities, races, religions, and languages.

> The student body was interracial—Afro-Americans, Caucasians, and Hispanics.
>
> The teenagers studied Judaism, Christianity, and Buddhism in Comparative Religion 101.
>
> She majored in French and Chinese and also studied Sanskrit and Arabic.
>
> The American and Mexican students shared eight college dorms.

Self-Check Exercise 3

Correct capitalization errors in the following sentences. If any of your answers are incorrect, review the principles on the use of capitals in writing commercial products; proper adjectives; points of the compass; and months, days, holidays, and seasons of the year.

1. Her lunch consists of Campbell's Chicken Soup and Sanka Coffee.

2. I particularly like memorial day because it starts the vacation season.

3. I eat chinese fortune cookies for dessert.

4. The office worker frequently has the "monday blues."

5. Have you heard of the religious holiday passover?

6. The high school band marched in the veterans day parade.

7. She prefers tide laundry detergent to brand x.

DEITIES

Capitalize words referring to a deity. Pronouns that refer to a deity are capitalized only in biblical quotes or to avoid ambiguity.

> God   The Almighty   Lord   Allah
> God spoke to Moses and He said . . .

GOVERNMENT BODIES AND DEPARTMENTS

Capitalize the names of specific government bodies.

> He is being audited by the Internal Revenue Service.
> She is a member of the House of Representatives.
> The Federal Bureau of Investigation has been called in on this case.
> They are preparing the budgetary needs for the Department of Defense.
> He has applied for a supervisory position with the Illinois State Board of Education.

Note: Capitalize short forms referring to Congress and the Supreme Court, but not to other legislative bodies and courts.

> The House convened on Monday. [Refers to the House of Representatives.]
> The Senate voted on the motion. [Refers to the U.S. Senate.]
> The Court is in session. [Refers to the Supreme Court.]
> The legislature will reconvene next week.

MISCELLANEOUS

NOUNS WITH NUMBERS OR LETTERS

She referred to (Page, page) 3 in the book.

Which noun is correct? The correct form is *page* (without the capital). In most instances, however, a noun that is followed by a number or letter is capitalized.

He assigned Exercise 10 to the students.

Why do we have to read Chapter VIII?

May I see Chart 3?

Pay Invoice 163.

Exceptions to this rule are *line, paragraph, verse, size, page,* and *note* when they are followed by numbers. See these examples:

Read line 11 on page 64.

She wears a size 12 dress.

Refer to paragraph 12 on page 110.

COURSE TITLES

Capitalize course titles, but capitalize areas of study only if they are derived from proper names. ☑

Self-Check Exercise 4

By completing the following exercise, you can check your ability to use capitals when writing names of nationalities, races, religions, and languages; deities; government bodies and departments; nouns followed by numbers or letters, and course titles. Correct the capitalization errors in these sentences:

1. She resembles a japanese girl I once knew.

2. He studied catholicism in his religion course.

3. He was recently discharged from the french navy.

4. I took special courses in typing, economics, and english.

5. She was a computer analyst for the department of the budget in Washington, D.C.

6. The information came from Page 16, Line 10 in the History book.

7. They worship the almighty in their churches and synagogues.

Figure 16-2. Corrected letter.

1590 Van Cortlandt Terrace
Teaneck, New Jersey 07666
March 5, 198_

Mr. Timothy A. Jones
1919 South Downy Road
Trenton, NJ 08111

Dear Mr. Jones:

I am applying for the position of secretary that was advertised in the Daily Post on Tuesday, March 3. My work experience and education have prepared me for this job.

I have attached my résumé for your referral. Please call me at your convenience.

Very truly yours,

Frank M. Cucci

He registered for Finance 546.

He registered for a finance course.

Professor Barnes will teach two sections of Management 306.

Professor Barnes will teach two management courses.

Martin was going to major in Spanish and accounting. [Always capitalize languages.]

Martin was taking Spanish 100 and Accounting 101.

SUMMARY

Careful adherence to the basic guidelines for capitalization will help you emphasize the contents of your writing in the appropriate places. If the writer of the letter in Figure 16-1 had followed these guidelines, his letter would have looked like Figure 16-2.

There is little doubt that knowledge of proper capitalization can be extremely helpful to aspiring office employees and writers and all others interested in correct business English, regardless of their career choice.

Name _____

APPLICATION EXERCISES

A. Indicate the correct choice in the space provided.

_____ 1. He looked and talked like a (westerner, Westerner).

_____ 2. The (Middle Ages, middle ages) produced more advances than is commonly known.

_____ 3. Martin Carton, a (colonel, Colonel) took immediate command.

_____ 4. He registered for courses in (chemistry, Chemistry) and French.

_____ 5. I would say we are living in an (age of change, Age of Change).

_____ 6. The first Catholic (church, Church) built in Illinois was begun in 1644.

_____ 7. Vermont is a beautiful (State, state) in the autumn.

_____ 8. She was extremely proud of her (college, College).

_____ 9. Once Broadway branched off Highland (road, Road), it became a beautiful boulevard.

_____ 10. On Monday he will begin his job as junior accountant for the Philadelphia Gas (company, Company).

B. Indicate the correct choices in the blanks provided.

_____ 1. Our (senator, Senator), Mr. Tanaka, received all his formal education in the United States.

_____ 2. Will you vote for (senator, Senator) Tanaka in the next election?

_____ 3. The (northwest, Northwest) is probably one of the most beautiful parts of our nation.

_____ 4. The article appeared in the *(journal, Journal) of Higher Education.*

_____ 5. Do you feel that (thanksgiving, Thanksgiving) is a holiday that should be celebrated on the same date in each of our states?

_____ 6. General Motors (cars, Cars) may be found on roads everywhere in the world.

_____ 7. Because the (president, President) always flies on Air Force One, he does not have to use commercial aircraft.

_____   8. I would prefer to raise my children in the (west, West).

_____   9. You can reach your destination most rapidly by driving directly (west, West).

_____   10. We all referred to her as (aunt Sally, Aunt Sally).

C. Write a brief sentence using each of the following words correctly.

1. University _____

_____

2. university _____

_____

3. South _____

_____

4. south _____

_____

5. President _____

_____

6. president _____

_____

7. Theater _____

_____

8. theater _____

_____

9. Captain _____

_____

10. captain _____

_____

11. Accounting _____

_____

12. accounting _____

_____

13. Gainesville High School _____

_____

14. high school _____

_____

15. Corinth Corporation _____

_____

16. corporation _____

_____

D. In the following sentences, underline the words that should be capitalized.

1. Washington has many famous buildings that should be visited, such as the national gallery of art, the air and space museum, and the white house.

2. If we have a warm autumn, our business will probably decline 20 percent.

3. He drove down the only boulevard in the city and parked the car on lambert court.

4. The treaty of trent was a historical document.

5. Irish linen was an outstanding gift for the baxters' tenth wedding anniversary.

6. Although she had been an employee of northwest title and trust company for ten years, she was not promoted to the position of manager.

7. He carried the ball in almost every play the trojans made against the Washington huskies.

8. Many californians prefer skiing to swimming.

9. The battle of gettysburg was one of the most costly battles (in terms of lives) of the civil war.

10. Suddenly a strong northern wind sprang up.

E. If a word should be capitalized, insert the correction in the space provided. If the statement is correct, write C in the space.

_____ 1. He was given the title of state champion.

_____ 2. Susan was born in Illinois but grew up in Texas.

_____ 3. Although he was a member of the catholic church, he did not follow all the rules.

_____ 4. Because of her many years in great britain, she had acquired an English accent.

_____ 5. Do you believe that God will give his blessing on a union of that type?

_____ 6. Although he was the minister of the church, he was sometimes mistaken for the custodian.

_____ 7. I went to the park on broadway drive.

_____ 8. My aunt Sarah was a very generous person.

_____ 9. *Lust for Life* is one of the great biographies of our time.

_____ 10. The Spaniard Cortez was one of the great explorers of all time.

F. If you find a word in any of the following lines that should be capitalized but is not, circle it and write the correction in the space provided. If the statement is correct, write *C* in the space.

_____ 1. The atlantic ocean can be extremely rough, especially if you're in a boat as small as the *intrepid.*

_____ 2. It was my feeling, as we continued to drive east, that the weather was actually becoming warmer.

_____ 3. My aunt martha indicated that we should all gather at her home, which is near yosemite national park.

_____ 4. Many Americans in the midwest originally came from germany.

_____ 5. Did you register for Chemistry 104?

_____ 6. In the evening the southern wind was a welcome relief from the heat of the day.

_____ 7. The rabbi quoted the word of god in the prayer.

_____ 8. *Adventures in the south pacific* is a book you must be sure to read.

_____ 9. The U.S. Department of defense may well lose some major funding this year.

_____ 10. The battle of britain will be remembered as a major event in world war II.

_____ 11. The American civil war was one of our most costly wars in terms of lives lost.

_____ 12. Too often American Indians are "forgotten people."

_____ 13. I believe that president reagan will leave his mark on American history.

_____ 14. William martenson, the secretary of the club, will stand for reelection.

_____ 15. Do you feel that secretary of state acheson was one of america's outstanding statesmen?

Challenge Exercise

The following memo has many capitalization errors. Draw a diagonal line through incorrect capital letters to indicate that they should be lowercase. Where capitals are needed, insert corrections directly above the errors.

TO: Mr. Thomas Farrantino, president

FROM: Mrs. Dorothy Goldberg, vice president

DATE: August 17, 198_

SUBJECT: contributions To organizations

According to Company records, we have contributed well over

$10,000 to various Charitable Organizations in this Fiscal

Year.

An examination of the various Church groups, organizations

for the physically handicapped, Wildlife and Conservation

organizations, and religious organizations (jewish, english,

baptist, Catholic, italian, muslim, etc.) shows that we have

no fixed policies.

It is my recommendation that our contributions be based on specific policies so that the distributions are made on an equitable basis to Religious, conservation, and health care organizations, as well as to groups representing the Physically Handicapped. Please see the attached proposal, " Policies and practices for Charitable contributions," issued by the U.S. Department of commerce.

If you need any more Information on this matter, please call me before labor day.

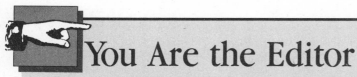

You Are the Editor

In the exercise below, strike out all capitalization errors. Insert corrections directly above the word or words incorrectly written.

mpi **MARTIN PRODUCTS, INC.**

1114 Wentworth Avenue
Ogden, North Dakota 58621
(701) 698-6946

October 29, 198_

Mrs. Shelley Wilkerson, R.n.

1382 north Glendon drive

Los Angeles, CA   90026

Dear customer:

We recently sent you one of our murphy-baxter blood pressure units. According to our records, your purchase was made over six months ago, in may of this year.

Because we value Your opinion highly, we would like to have you complete the questionnaire enclosed. Your findings, plus those of other Nurses, will give us information on the design of this piece of technical equipment.

Once all the data have been gathered, the results will be sent to you and other respondents, as well as to Hospitals, health care agencies, the U.S. department of public health, and Doctors.

We would appreciate your reply no later than November 10 of this
Year. You may be sure we appreciate your cooperation.

Sincerely yours,

John W. Armstrong, manager
Research and development Department

Key to Self-Check Exercises

Exercise 1

1. The
2. Of
3. "All
4. all
5. Stationery   Business   Expense
6. "Yours very truly."
7. "Dear Sir/Madam."
8. History   In the   In Pennsylvania
9. Really? Okay!

Exercise 2

1. , *Star Wars,*
2. Ms.
3. Treaty of Paris
4. Operation Overload.
5. "What's   Happened   to   Employee   Commitment?"
6. city of Boston   Cape Cod
7. Benjamin Franklin High School
8. Republican   National   Conference   New   York

Exercise 3

1. Campbell's chicken soup   Sanka coffee
2. Memorial Day
3. Chinese fortune cookies
4. "Monday blues."
5. Passover (Jewish holiday)
6. Veterans Day
7. Tide laundry detergent   Brand X

Exercise 4

1. Japanese girl
2. Catholicism
3. French navy
4. English
5. Department of the Budget
6. page 16, line 10 in the history book
7. Almighty

A DYNAMIC BUSINESS VOCABULARY

Here is a new list of business words and terms. Study their spelling, definitions, and their correct use in sentences.

Secretary, administrative

A person responsible for providing administrative support to more than one manager by handling correspondence, telephone calls, and record keeping.

The word-processing operator, tired of typing all day, applied for a job entitled "Administrative Secretary."

Secretary, corresponding

A word-processing specialist responsible for transcribing from rough drafts or dictation equipment, often using automated equipment to type letters, memos, reports, and other printed documents.

His 60-words-per-minute typing helped Mark Stone in his new job as a corresponding secretary for the telephone company.

Securities

Written proof of ownership of property, as in stock certificates.

The securities she received from her father were vital in her financing of the new business.

Shared logic system

A word-processing system in which a number of keyboard terminal operators use the powers of one computer CPU simultaneously.

The junior college's budget necessitated the purchase of a shared logic system for its new word-processing equipment.

Shareholder

A person who owns stock in a company or organization.

The shareholders' meeting was held on March 1 in Milwaukee.

Simulation

An imitation of an event, program, or series of transactions.

The computer simulation provided excellent training for the students who will one day be company managers.

Software

The programs used to control a computer's operations, run on the physical equipment known as hardware.

For the records management course, Miss Sparks hoped to obtain software for electronic filing and electronic mail.

Solvent

Able to pay one's debts.

It was agreed that Brown and Pearson, Inc., was solvent and able to continue selling its products.

THE ABC'S OF BUSINESS VOCABULARY

To test your knowledge of the business words and terms you have learned thus far, complete the following exercise.

1. An imitation of an event or program or series of transactions is a/an (a) role-play, (b) drama, (c) simulation, (d) replay.

2. Written proof of ownership of property as in a stock certificate is a/an (a) security, (b) bond, (c) advertisement, (d) fund.

3. Favoritism shown to relatives in business is called (a) bias, (b) prejudice, (c) nepotism, (d) gifts.

4. The process of reaching agreement by discussions and bargaining is (a) debate, (b) quarrel, (c) election, (d) negotiations.

5. Compose three short sentences using one of the following words in each sentence: (a) scan (verb), (b) software, (c) jurisdiction.

   _____

   _____

   _____

   _____

   _____

   _____

6. Define the noun *shareholder.* _____

   _____

7. The primary responsibilities of an *administrative secretary* are to _____

   _____

8. The noun *injunction* means _____

   _____

9. The definition of the noun *innovation* is _____

   _____

17 Using Numbers in Business English

Numbers are used in all types of communication, especially in business English. In correspondence there is frequent reference to quantities, invoice numbers, addresses, terms of sales, and dozens of other such items. In reports, proposals, and other longer communications, numbers are used extensively in tables and charts. In these instances, the numbers are also referred to in the text of the written communication. It is essential that clarity be retained.

For example, it might be quite simple to confuse the following: *3 5 volt transformers.* Does the writer mean *35-volt transformers* or *three 5-volt transformers?*

If the principles set down in this chapter are followed, you should be able to retain clarity in the use of numbers. These guidelines are used by most companies in the United States, so mistakes are reduced when they are followed.

Guidelines for expressing numbers involve *word style* and *numeral style.* Word style is generally used by writers of very formal and literary communications, whereas numeral style is used more frequently by writers of everyday business and technical communications. The principles outlined in this chapter follow the popular numeral style.

The memo in Figure 17-1 was dictated by Ms. Schneider to her secretary. The secretary was not familiar with her company's policy or current textbook principles that apply to the expression of numbers in business communications. She therefore made many errors—sometimes using numerals when she should have used words and sometimes using words when she should have used numerals. Can you find the eight errors in Figure 17-1?

Learning and remembering when to use numerals and when to use words is easy. Follow the principles in this chapter and test your knowledge using the Self-Check Exercises.

THE "TEN AND UNDER, ELEVEN AND OVER" RULES

1. When *quantity* numbers are ten and under, spell them out. When *quantity* numbers are eleven and above, use numerals. This rule applies to both exact and approximate numbers.

   She mailed five letters to the collection agency. [The number is ten or under.]

   I will need nine mailing envelopes now and two or three later. [All numbers are ten and under.]

   She mailed 15 letters to the collection agency. [The number is eleven or above.]

   As the city's purchasing agent, he has secured about 300 cars and about 1,000 trucks since he started to work in Chicago. [Approximate numbers eleven or over.]

   There were about eight Hispanic students at the English as a Second Language Conference. [Approximate number ten or under.]

2. When several numbers are used in a sentence and the numbers are all eleven and over, use numerals. If several numbers are used in a sentence and they are all ten and under, spell them out.

   The order called for 72 capacitors, 144 resistors, 288 BA transistors, and 36 Trenton cabinets. [All numbers are eleven and over.]

   We completed and shipped eight Trenton, three Kent, and ten Canterbury units. [All numbers are ten and under.]

Figure 17-1. The secretary's first memo.

TO: Miguel Cortez

FROM: Rose Schneider

DATE: 2-10-8_

SUBJECT: Departmental Request

Your memorandum of January twenty-third arrived on the 4 of February, and I completed the research you requested.

The records in our department indicate that one thousand, two hundred and sixty-four outdated files have been sent to our warehouse at Sixteen South 3d Street in Baltimore. I hope this information and the enclosed copy of Volume Twenty, No. IV, which you also requested, will be useful.

---

3. When some numbers are eleven and above, others are ten and below, and all are used in one sentence, you have a choice. Either spell them all out or use numerals for all. Just be consistent within the sentence.

    Her estate contained the following stock: five shares of General Electric, eight of General Motors, and seventy-five of Southern California Edison. [Seventy-five, which is above ten, is written out for consistency.]

    The inventory listed 75 pairs of shoes, 85 men's shirts, 8 men's suits, 10 boys' suits, 10 boys' jackets, and 25 boys' shirts. [Eight and ten are written in numerals to be consistent.]

4. If two unrelated numbers immediately follow each other, separate them by a comma to improve clarity.

    In 1990, 300 or more satellites should be operating in the stratosphere. [The year and the quantity are unrelated numbers.]

    On March 23, 11 new Chevrolets will be delivered to your showroom. [The date and the quantity are unrelated.]

    On page 16, 12 books are mentioned; all of them may be helpful. [Two unrelated numbers are separated by a comma.]

There are some exceptions to the "ten and under, eleven and over" rules.

1. When two or more numbers are used in different contexts in the same sentence, clarity and emphasis can sometimes be improved by spelling one or more out and writing one or more in numerals.

    The fifteen transformers in the warehouse were in the 300 series, and the eleven in the factory were in the 200 series.

    We found that twenty motors of 300 horsepower and sixty of 500 horsepower would cover our energy needs for the next three years.

2. If a sentence begins with a number, the number should be spelled out.

   Eight of the secretaries were treated to lunch on Secretaries' Day.

   Sixteen shrimp were placed on her dinner platter.

Note: Sometimes a sentence appears too cumbersome when it begins with a spelled-out number. If this occurs, revise the sentence by placing the number within the statement.

   Seventy-two capacitors, 144 resistors, 288 BA transistors and 36 Trenton cabinets were shipped on April 28. [Too cumbersome!]

   On April 28 we shipped 72 capacitors, 144 resistors, 288 BA transistors, and 36 Trenton cabinets. [Preferred.]

3. When one number immediately follows a related number, express the first number in words and the second in numerals.

   Carmelita secured seven 60-inch pieces of wool material for the class sewing project.

   All in all, seven 12-year-old girls were registered for the project.

Note: If the second number is significantly shorter than the first when it is spelled out, use numerals for the first number and words for the second number.

   Please get me 65 fifteen-foot boards. [Sixty-five is longer than fifteen.]

   I ordered 36 twelve-inch rulers for the class. [Thirty-six is longer than twelve.] ☑

Self-Check Exercise 1

Thus far you have studied general principles relating to the expression of numbers. Do you understand the "Ten and Under, Eleven and Over" guidelines and some of the exceptions to these guidelines? Test your knowledge by selecting the correct answers in the following exercise. When the exercise is completed, compare your answers with the key at the end of the chapter.

1. He purchased (five, 5) (fifty-nine-cent, 59-cent) notebooks for use in his classes.

2. In (1981 125, 1981, 125) tulips were planted at the south end of Longward Gardens.

3. We shipped (seventy-five, 75) chairs, (ninety, 90) tables, and (thirty-two, 32) pictures.

4. You have requested (two, 2) rugs, (three, 3) TV sets, and (eight, 8) area rugs.

5. (Fifteen, 15) students signed up for the Language Study Tour in Paris.

6. The scouts consumed (eleven, 11) chocolate cakes, (seven, 7) chickens, (eight, 8) quarts of milk, and (thirty-two, 32) bottles of soda.

7. She interviewed almost (one hundred, 100) job applicants last week.

414 Successful Business English

DATES

1. Express dates of months and years in numerals, and spell out names of months.

   April 28, 1988   OR   28 April 1988

   In North America the date *3/2/88* is read as *March 2, 1988,* but in Europe and Latin America it would be interpreted as *February 3, 1988,* with the second number representing the month, instead of the first number. To avoid a misinterpretation, write the date as follows:

   March 2, 1988   OR   2 March 1988 (not 3/2/88)

2. Use ordinals *(-d, -st,* or *-th)* with the day of the month when that day precedes the name of the month or stands by itself.

   Joan was married on the the 3d of August. [Date precedes name of month.]
   Joan was married on the third of August.
   Joan was married on August 3. [Date follows name of month; do not use ordinal form.]

   She became engaged on the fourth of January.
   She became engaged on the 4th of January. [Date precedes name of month.]
   She became engaged on January 4. [Date follows name of month.]

   Your invoice of the 2d did not reflect the discount due. [Month is omitted.]
   Your order of the first was processed immediately. [Month is omitted.]

3. Well-known years in history and references to class graduation years may appear in abbreviated form.

   The class of '51 was honored. [Class graduation year.]
   The blizzard of '88 was the worst storm of the century. [Well known in history.]

ADDRESSES

1. Express house or building numbers in numerals except for *one,* which should be written out.

   One East Broadway Place   BUT   2 East Broadway Place
   27 South Keyston Drive   272 West Market Street   2722 North Compton Avenue

2. Use words for street names from one to ten inclusive; use numerals for street names eleven and over. Ordinals may be used in street names that are written in numerals.

   4556 East Fifth Street [Fifth is ten or below.]
   2071 West Ninth Street [Ninth is ten or below.]
   4600 South 29th Street [29th is eleven or over.]
   2100 West 21st Avenue [21st is eleven or over.]

Note: The latest practice is to omit ordinals in addresses that have directions (South, West) separating house numbers from street names that are written in numerals.

   4600 South 29 Street   2100 West 21 Avenue   163 North 11 Road

3. If a number is used as a street name and a direction is not included, use a dash to separate the house number from the street name. For clarity, write the street name using ordinals or spell it out if ten or under. ☑

2100—20th Street	4545—21st Place
2100—Fourth Avenue	810—Second Street

AMOUNTS OF MONEY

1. Sums of money, domestic or foreign, should be expressed in numerals.

   Mr. Johnson's membership fee was $350.

   He paid $2,000 for the merchandise that arrived yesterday.

   You will have to convert the £350 into dollars before you pay Baxter. [English pounds.]

2. For sums of less than a dollar, follow the numerals with the word *cents*.

   The postage cost 22 cents.   The candy wasn't worth 65 cents.

Note: In a sentence with a series of amounts, some with cents and some without, use the dollar sign ($) with a decimal point (e.g., $.75) to indicate cents. This ensures consistency within the sentence.

   Thomas paid $.75 for the sponge ball, $5.00 for the baseball bat, and $14.95 for the baseball glove at the discount store. [Do not use 75 cents.]

   Spend up to $15.00 for the door prize, but only $.95 to $1.25 for the items in the small packages. [Do not use 95 cents.]

Self-Check Exercise 2

Several important principles were presented that explain the proper format for writing numbers in dates and addresses. Can you apply these principles to your writing? Test your ability by selecting the correct answers to the questions that follow. How many of your answers coincide with those in the key?

1. The graduation exercise is on (May 8, 1988; 5/8/88).

2. Please mail your check by March (28th, 28).

3. He moved to (123—19th Street, 123 19th Street).

4. In Atlantic City, I live at (One, 1) Raleigh Place.

5. My new business address is 610 South (Ninth, 9th, or 9) Street in Newark, New Jersey.

3. The symbol ¢ for *cents* is used in price quotations, technical communications, and statistical material.

    150 slats at 99¢   5 bags of cement at 98¢

4. When expressing dollar amounts that do not include cents, do not use a decimal and two zeros unless there are numbers with cents in the same sentence.

    Her fee was $250 a week for house and dogsitting. [Not $250. or $250.00.]

    He paid a monthly rental of $875 at the seashore in the winter. [Not $875. or $875.00.]

    She spent $200.00 for a suit, $39.95 for a blouse, and $45.50 for new black pumps. [For consistency, use decimal and zeros with $200.]

5. Large sums of money are frequently written in a combination of numerals and words, as they are easier to read that way.

    The deficit now stood at $45 billion. [This is easier to understand than $45,000,000,000.]

    The building sold for $1.5 million. [Not $1,500,000.]

6. In legal statements, the sum is often indicated by words and then numerals.

    The compensation we shall accept is thirty-five hundred dollars ($3,500), to be paid by January 5, 1989.

DECIMALS AND FRACTIONS

1. If a decimal begins with a number other than zero, precede the decimal with a zero to prevent the reader from overlooking the decimal point.

    0.234   0.1839

2. If a decimal begins with a *zero,* you may either add a zero to the *left* of the decimal point or omit the zero to the *left* of the decimal point.

    0.06781   OR   .06781
    0.00781   OR   .00781

3. Simple fractions should be spelled out for clarity.

    It took him one-half hour.

    We were about two-thirds finished when Baxter arrived.

    I have finished reading three-quarters of the book.

4. Mixed numbers (numbers composed of both a whole number and a fraction) may be expressed with a decimal or a fraction.

    It took him 1.5 hours to complete the job.   OR   It took him 1 1/2 hours to complete the job.
    The wall was 45.5 feet long.   OR   The wall was 45 1/2 feet long.

5. Spell out a mixed number only if it begins a sentence.

    One and one-half pounds of peanuts were eaten at the office party.
    Six and two-thirds of the pizzas were sold by noon. ☑

Self-Check Exercise 3

In business, it is important to know whether money, decimals, and fractions should be expressed in numerals or words. Have you mastered the principles that apply to these items? Select the correct answers in the following exercise, then compare your choices with those in the key.

1. Mrs. Rivera paid (two hundred dollars, $200) for the kitchen appliance.

2. The birthday card, which cost (sixty, 60) cents, was very appropriate for him.

3. At the drugstore, Maria paid $2.12 for toothpaste, $2.29 for hosiery, and (35 cents, $.35) for a bar of candy.

4. The two Broadway theater tickets cost them ($90.00, $90).

5. The college president requested ($11,000,000, $11 million) from the City Council to fund the next academic year.

6. I gave him (three-quarters, 3/4) of my weekly allowance.

7. It was (twenty-five and one-half, 25 1/2, 25.5) feet long.

TIME

1. Use numerals with a.m. or p.m. In business writing, use words with o'clock. *O'clock* is more formal sounding than *a.m.* or *p.m.*

   The train will leave at 5:15 p.m.

   We leave for work at 8:15 a.m.

   The train is due to arrive at ten o'clock. [Spell out the number before *o'clock.*]

   The opera began at seven o'clock on Saturday evening.

2. When expressing time on the hour without *a.m., p.m.,* or *o'clock,* spell out the hour.

   They prefer having dinner at seven. [Not 7.]
   My job begins at nine. [Not 9.]

Note: When expressing time on the hour using *a.m.* or *p.m.,* omit the colon and two zeroes.
   USE 10 a.m.   NOT 10:00 a.m.
   USE 1 p.m.   NOT 1:00 p.m.

3. References to periods of time in a nontechnical or statistical communication should be spelled out if the time period is one or two words.

   It will take twenty working days to complete this project.

   I have not seen her for twelve weeks.

   That took place 150 years ago. [Use numerals because *one hundred fifty* exceeds two words.]

MISCELLANEOUS SITUATIONS

Distance: Use numerals unless the total distance is less than a mile.

> It was about two-thirds of a mile to Don's home. [Less than a mile.]
>
> It is 12 miles to Ventura and 36 more miles to Santa Barbara. [More than a mile.]

Financial quotations: Use numerals for the whole number and also for the fraction if there is one.

> General Motors stock rose to 87 7/8.
>
> American Telephone and Telegraph hit 56 1/2 this afternoon.
>
> Brunswick seemed fixed at a solid 55.

Arithmetical expressions: Use numerals.

> José's home has approximately 3,300 square feet of living space.
>
> Multiply 70 by 44 to get your answer.

Weights and measures: Use numerals for emphasis and clarity.

> His farm never produced less than 200 bushels per acre.
>
> You will find to your dismay that 15 yards does not equal 15 meters.
>
> The barrel, which weighed 80 pounds, contained 55 gallons of oil.
>
> Add 2 teaspoons of salt to the 10 quarts of liquid. [Note that the numbers are ten or below.]

Identification numbers: Use numerals.

> The car's registration number was 38406175. [Registration number.]
>
> You will need Owner's Manual 225. [Manual or booklet.]
>
> Your code number will be 5007. [Code number.]

Linear dimensions: Use numerals with either × or *by* between them.

> The store measured 80 × 120 feet.
>
> The book's size was 7 1/3 by 11 inches.
>
> The room was 25 × 50 feet.

Age: Use numerals unless the reference is an approximation.

> On the day she turned 50, she became engaged for the first time. [Definite age.]
>
> My grandfather was about eighty when he died. [Approximate age.]
>
> Little Manuel is 4 years and 6 months old today. [Definite age.]

Government units: Spell out numbers used in titles or names of government units.

> He served in the Ninety-second Congress.
>
> She represented the Twenty-third Congressional District.
>
> She served as the representative from the Fourth Ward.

Book or magazine reference: In book and magazine references, major units such as *volume* are indicated by Roman numerals (I, XX), minor units such as *number* or *page* by Arabic numbers (1, 20). ☑

My article appeared in Volume XXV, No. 3, of the *Journal of Business Communication.* [*Volume* is a major unit; *No.* is minor.]

You will find Figure 8 and Table 5 on page 83 in Chapter 4. [All units are minor.]

It will not be necessary for you to purchase Volume II; all references may be found on pages 330–333 of Volume I. [*Volume* is major; *page* is minor.]

SUMMARY

The principles you have learned in this chapter can serve as guidelines for expressing numbers in your business writing. If Ms. Schneider's secretary had studied these principles, her memo would have been error free in the writing of numbers. It would have looked like Figure 17-2.

Try to remember the "Ten and Under, Eleven and Over" rules and the important exceptions to these rules. Refer to the examples in this chapter whenever you need a refresher.

Self-Check Exercise 4

Would you use numerals or words when writing sentences containing units of distance, financial quotations, arithmetical expressions, weights and measures, identification numbers, units of time, dimensions, ages, government units, and book or magazine references? Choose the correct answers in the following exercise, and check your answers with the key to see how well you have learned these principles.

1. The dimensions of the new room are (28 and 38 feet, 28 by 38 feet).

2. We will mail you our Procedures Manual (One hundred, 100).

3. It is important that you arrive at (6 o'clock, six o'clock).

4. Stephen graduated from high school when he was (seventeen, 17) years old.

5. He represented the (Tenth, 10th) Congressional District of his state.

6. Please refer to Volume (Twenty, XX) of the encyclopedia.

7. I read in the *Wall Street Journal* that Philadelphia Electric Company's common stock was selling at (twenty-one, 21).

Figure 17-2. The improved memo.

TO: Miguel Cortez

FROM: Rose Schneider

DATE: February 10, 198_

SUBJECT: Departmental Request

Your memorandum of January 23 arrived on the 4th of February, and I completed the research you requested.

The records in our department indicate that 1,264 outdated files have been sent to our warehouse at 16 South Third Street in Baltimore. I hope this information and the enclosed copy of Volume XX, No. 4, which you also requested, will be useful.

APPLICATION EXERCISES

A. In the following sentences, strike out any error in the expression of numbers and insert the correction in the space provided. If the sentence is correct, place a C in the space in the margin.

Example:

_____ eight _____   a. We bought 8 boxes of cereal.

_____ 1. The order listed 8 Johnson drills.

_____ 2. We shipped three motors and 4 heavy-duty saws.

_____ 3. You will need twenty boxes, 55 barrels, and 60 drums.

_____ 4. He sold 300 shares of IBM.

_____ 5. Five thousand students were enrolled the first year.

_____ 6. There were 25 lamps (all in the 500 series) which were damaged.

_____ 7. We were able to secure 5 48-inch-wide samples of the wool material.

_____ 8. Did the Johnson Corporation purchase the six 200-volt batteries?

_____ 9. You will find 55 large envelopes, 85 binders, and 7 cartons of clips in the box of office supplies.

_____ 10. Nissan sold over 5,000 cars in January in the Los Angeles area.

_____ 11. In 1990 45 representatives will be eligible for pension.

_____ 12. We were able to find 9 100-year-old-lamps in the shops we visited.

_____ 13. Please ship the merchandise no later than 2-4-87.

_____ 14. Do you think 8 chairs and our large table will fit in this dining room?

_____ 15. She was born on 30 April 1981.

_____ 16. The marriage was scheduled for the 5 of May.

_____ 17. We will expect your reply by May 21, 1987.

_____ 18. His new address was 1 South Oak Street.

_____ 19. He had resided at Seven North Oak Street.

_____ 20. I will not pay over $500 for the vase.

_____ 21. Please ship the vase to 2700 West Seventh Street.

_____ 22. It seemed to me that 50 British pounds was a high price for the Wedgwood bowl.

_____ 23. If you can sell them for six cents each, you will make money on the deal.

_____ 24. The Army budget for the year was over six billion dollars.

_____ 25. Our total defense budget was just under $40 billion.

B. Use each of the following items in a sentence. All items are spelled out, but that may or may not be correct. Follow the principles given in this chapter, converting words to numerals if necessary.

Example:

a. Four million dollars _____ Germany owed the United States $4 million. _____

1. Three million dollars _____

_____

2. Two boxes and five barrels _____

_____

3. Thirty-five cents _____

_____

4. Five-hundred-dollar fee _____

_____

5. Twenty-five hundred East Third Street _____

_____

_____

6. Seventy English pounds _____

_____

7. Forty-five inches _____

_____

8. Seven yards and twenty-one meters _____

_____

9. Forty thousand lira _____

_____

10. Thirteen hundred West Fifth Street _____

_____

11. Six telephones and eight lamps _____

_____

12. Two thousand dollars _____

_____

13. Fourteen north Sixty-Third Street _____

_____

14. Third of July of nineteen eighty-five _____

_____

15. The statement of the fifth _____

_____

16. Two hundred one-inch connectors _____

_____

17. Three twelve-year-old horses _____

_____

18. Three thousand gas stations _____

_____

19. Fifteen filters each in the fifty-gallon capacity _____

_____

_____

20. Three pens, four pencils, and one hundred ten pieces of chalk _____

_____

_____

21. Twenty-seven TVs, thirty-five radios, and nine tape decks _____

_____

_____

22. Ninety cents _____

_____

23. Thirty-eight logs _____

_____

24. One ten North Dexter Drive _____

_____

C. In the following sentences, strike out any error in the expression of numbers and write the correction above it.

Example:

                    .066

  a. The acceptable percentage was ~~0.066~~.

  1. That is Design 450.

  2. The room was 25.5 feet long.

  3. She drove almost six miles past the correct freeway turnoff.

  4. In France that would cost about ninety-five francs.

  5. He will be fortunate to secure 50 bushels per acre this spring.

  6. The security code number is one thousand five.

  7. The tolerance acceptable was plus or minus 0.0550 millimeters.

  8. The trim size of the manual was 11 by 7 and one half inches.

  9. Manny's plan was to arrive at 2 o'clock.

10. Bobby is exactly 5 years and 5 months today.

11. All her aunts and uncles lived well into their eighties.

12. Representative Bell, from the Twenty 3rd Congressional District, always voted with the Democratic majority.

13. The *Journal of Accounting,* Volume 25, will be mailed to you today.

14. Her temperature was well over 100.

15. Pages 3 to 40 in the text cover the entire topic.

16. The 50-gallon container was filled yesterday with exactly 12 pounds of explosives.

17. You will find Exercise 5 on page 83 of Chapter Four.

18. It was now 10 degrees below zero.

19. Her new address was One North 55th Boulevard.

20. The President rarely received the full support of the members of the 92nd Congress.

21. I should have sold the food stock when it hit 75½.

22. He ran the 26-mile marathon with ease.

23. The meeting was two-thirds completed when she arrived.

24. The Fox Company is legally liable for exactly $400.

25. Each surgeon received a fee of two thousand dollars.

D. In the following sentences, strike out any errors and insert the corrections in the spaces provided. If a sentence is correct, place a *C* in the space.

_____ 1. The total cost for all Lockheed planes was $75 million.

_____ 2. The booklets, in quantities of 1,000, cost $.75 cents each.

_____ 3. The lot was 250 by 300 feet.

_____ 4. The registration number of the truck was 3 thousand 60.

_____ 5. The freezer held at a consistent -3 degrees centigrade.

_____ 6. Our invoice did not carry a charge for the 25 saws, but it did list the fifty saw-blades.

_____ 7. She purchased 5 pounds of flour, 35 pounds of rice, and 50 pounds of sugar.

_____ 8. If we can sell 10,000 to 15,000 units each month, we shall have a profitable business.

————————————— 9. He walked ½ mile to Bob's home.

————————————— 10. She drove well over 200 miles in the morning and another one hundred in the afternoon.

————————————— 11. He had stock in National Conductor and U.S. Steel, which hit 58 and 68½, respectively.

————————————— 12. The warehouse has almost 18,000 square feet of storage area.

————————————— 13. His first oil well produced a surprising five hundred barrels per day.

————————————— 14. Her four children were 6, 17, 21, and 23 years of age.

————————————— 15. We shall leave on the stroke of ten o'clock.

————————————— 16. The Tenth District was made up of about 500 Asian-Americans.

————————————— 17. I'm not sure it was an authentic antique, although he said it was made about ninety years ago.

————————————— 18. You will find the quotation in Volume Five, No. 7, of the *Journal of Engineering.*

————————————— 19. Table 5 on page 50 is incorrect.

————————————— 20. The order included five door handles, 18 door locks, and 25 electrical outlets.

————————————— 21. She inherited almost 500 shares of stock.

————————————— 22. We should purchase the remaining twenty motors (each of 100 horsepower) that Merkle has in stock.

————————————— 23. It was a major order for us: 300 shovels and over seven hundred rakes.

————————————— 24. Please ship the entire order to Ten East Jackson Drive.

————————————— 25. The invoice for the merchandise will be mailed by the 10th of this month.

E. In the following sentences, strike out any errors and write the corrections in the spaces provided. If a sentence has no errors, write a *C* in the space.

————————————— 1. The lawyer's fee was $3,000; the doctor's was an even one thousand.

————————————— 2. The purchase price was $800.

————————————— 3. My gas tank held 20 gallons, which gave me a driving range of 400 miles.

_____ 4. American Airlines Flight 501 is due to arrive at 10:00 p.m.

_____ 5. The hall was exactly 150.5 feet from door to door.

_____ 6. Please mail the package to One North Fifteenth Street.

_____ 7. It was printed incorrectly on page 8, page 50, and page 85.

_____ 8. That topic is covered in Volume Two.

_____ 9. I can't imagine that it will cost more that $.50.

_____ 10. The temperature was minus 5 degrees.

_____ 11. The 10-kilometer race was scheduled for Friday.

_____ 12. The sheet is exactly 10 $\times$ 12 inches.

_____ 13. The big day will be the 13th of August.

_____ 14. We should therefore mail all invitations by July 20.

_____ 15. Her new address is 3500 West 3d Street.

_____ 16. The exact date of the shipment was 3/25/88.

_____ 17. In 1988 12 of our present executives will have retired.

_____ 18. I don't believe the value of the 3 cars and 20 trucks will pay off the firm's debt.

_____ 19. The cost of 10 billion dollars for the space shuttle does not seem unreasonable.

_____ 20. The stock rose to ninety on April 4, 1988.

_____ 21. I don't believe 5 cents is a high price for each plastic insert.

_____ 22. I would judge the clock was about seventy years old; however, it was in excellent condition.

_____ 23. Most new homes today have under 3,000 square feet of space.

_____ 24. A generation ago, the average home was about seven thousand square feet.

_____ 25. Lots zoned in the early 1900s were between two and 10 acres.

F. In the following sentences, strike out any error and indicate the correction in the space provided. If the sentence does not contain an error, write a *C* in the space provided.

_____ 1. On December 3 we shipped 48 refrigerators (#202), 24 electric stoves (#404), and 6 air-conditioning units (#808).

427

_____ 2. You will find that the fifteen industrial vacuum cleaners are all designed for two-twenty-volt current.

_____ 3. The wall will require 8 8-foot-high panels.

_____ 4. The payment is due on 2-3-88.

_____ 5. The payment is due on the 3 of February.

_____ 6. Please ship all the merchandise to our primary plant at One East Kelly Way.

_____ 7. The total cost of the car was $18,000.

_____ 8. Had the auto been purchased in England for eight thousand pounds, a significant amount could have been saved.

_____ 9. The monthly fee was $350 dollars.

_____ 10. The Department of Defense budgeted over $3 billion for aircraft purchases.

_____ 11. The charge per unit will be $.55¢ cents.

_____ 12. The capacitor had a thickness of 0.013 millimeters.

_____ 13. The room was 25.5 feet wide.

_____ 14. The distance was two-thirds of a mile to Bob's home, but over 35 miles to Phil's.

_____ 15. My stock dropped 15.5 points in just one hour.

_____ 16. Although her office appeared small, it contained over 600 square feet of space.

_____ 17. Each storage tank held 1,000 gallons of crude oil.

_____ 18. The motor's registration number was 363636.

_____ 19. All you need do is request Study 505, and you will receive exactly what you need.

_____ 20. The meeting is scheduled to end by two p.m.

_____ 21. The distance was precisely 2.5 centimeters.

_____ 22. It seemed to me that my grandfather was always about ninety years old.

_____ 23. The ballots from the 5th Ward were never found.

_____ 24. Please check Volume 25 of the *Journal of Business Communication*.

Name _____

_____ 25. You will find Table Five on page 28.

G. In the following sentences, strike out any error and indicate the correction in the space provided. If the sentence does not contain an error, write a *C* in the space provided.

_____ 1. It seems inconceivable that his temperature went to 105 degrees.

_____ 2. The same error was made on pages five, seven, and nine.

_____ 3. The 8 capacitors were all manufactured according to the specifications of our 500 Line.

_____ 4. I advise you to buy ten 36-inch-by-24-inch slabs of marble.

_____ 5. By 1990 500 units will have been manufactured.

_____ 6. You will find that it took place on 25 February 1985.

_____ 7. The shipment of the second did not arrive until the 9th.

_____ 8. The problem was caused by the incorrect address, which was listed as 4500 South 9th Avenue.

_____ 9. The charge was an even $500.

_____ 10. The total cost for land and building was $2.3 million.

_____ 11. It was certainly shorter than one-third yard.

_____ 12. In total, the order came to 35.5 yards.

_____ 13. It was exactly 435 miles to Vancouver from Belleville.

_____ 14. The stock dropped from ninety to 85½.

_____ 15. You will need about seven people to win the vote at our 6 o'clock evening meeting.

_____ 16. The annual report will be 8 × 11 inches.

_____ 17. The carton contained 25 cubic feet.

_____ 18. It is not possible to use the mixture if the temperature drops below 45° degrees.

_____ 19. Use page 29 of Volume 3 as a reference.

_____ 20. He was exactly thirty years old on the 5th.

_____ 21. The Twenty-first Congress was made up of many distinguished personalities.

_____ 22. Your alarm code number is 4555.

_____ 23. Ten miles is more than 10 kilometers.

_____ 24. The second bedroom was 14 × 16 feet.

_____ 25. You will get the best service from Model 205.

Challenge Exercise

If you find errors in the expression of numbers in this letter, strike them out and insert your corrections over them.

BAIN & KELLY REAL ESTATE

219 W. 35th Street
New York, New York 10052
(212) 645-2271

2-25-8_

Mr. Forest K. Farmer

Farmer Construction Company

Seventeen East 3rd Street

New York, NY 10052

Dear Mr. Farmer:

This is to secure your counsel and bid on the possible remodeling of the two residences at the following addresses:

    1345 North 29th Street

    210 South 2nd Street

Because these two homes are within three miles of each other, we thought you might like to bid on them as one job.

What we have in mind for the 29th Street home is the following:

1. Installation of a new fifty gallon water heater,

2. Construction of a 4-foot-high retaining wall approximately 35 feet long (4 x 8 x 8 inch concrete block construction),

3. New parquet oak wood floor installed in the dining room (two hundred twenty square feet).

The Second Street residence requires the following:

1. Installation of 4 forty watt fluorescent fixtures,

2. Four 4 x 8 foot walnut panels in the den area (east wall),

3. Construction of redwood fence on east side of property: sixty feet long, of 6 foot length standard quality wood.

You may inspect both homes and learn details of the job on either 3-3-8_ or 3-4-8_. Bids will be accepted up until midnight of March 10, 198_.

May we hear from you about this job, Mr. Farmer, and possibly work with you.

Sincerely yours,

Charles Lambert
Property Manager

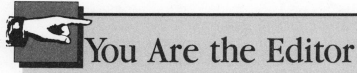

You Are the Editor

Strike out errors in the expression of numbers. Insert corrections directly above the errors.

TO: Robert Camero, Shipping Assistant

FROM: Jaime Villanova, Manager

DATE: 3-23-87

SUBJECT: Special Order

This is your written authorization to order these special items not requested in the requisition of 3-9-87, Number XXI.

We will need sixty feet of double-lead cable and 4 50-horsepower motors. In addition, 1 copy of the System Two Hundred Repair Manual and four standard bundles of forty pound-weight roofing shingles should be delivered. 300 square feet of Kentucky Blue grass sod is the last item to be requisitioned.

Bob, thank you for attending to this matter for me.

Key to Self-Check Exercises

Exercise 1

1. five 59-cent
2. 1981, 125
3. 75   90   32
4. two   three   eight
5. Fifteen
6. *Either*   11   7   8   32   *or*   eleven
   seven   eight   thirty-two
7. 100

Exercise 2

1. May 8, 1988.
2. 28.
3. 123—19th Street
4. One
5. Ninth

Exercise 3

1. $200
2. 60
3. $.35
4. $90
5. $11 million
6. three-quarters
7. 25½ *or* 25.5

Exercise 4

1. 28 by 38 feet.
2. 100.
3. six o'clock.
4. 17
5. Tenth
6. XX
7. 21.

A DYNAMIC BUSINESS VOCABULARY

Study the spelling of these words, their definitions, and their use in sentences to improve your vocabulary.

Station

An individual's workplace; a teletypewriter terminal in telecommunications.

Mary Hanson's work station was changed in the word-processing center.

Subsidy

Monetary assistance to individuals or private businesses with no payment expected.

Many U.S. farmers receive federal subsidies.

Tariff

A duty placed on imported and exported goods by a government or agency.

The tariff placed on Japanese cameras increased 20 percent.

Tax

A fee or contribution made for the support of government activities.

Is there still an extra tax on suitcases and leather handbags?

Telecommunications

The study of communication as it spans distances by radio, television, telephone, cable, and telegraphy.

The AT&T trainee hoped to become a telecommunications expert within five years.

Teleprinter (TELEX)

A keyboard machine operated by teletypists at distant locations to send and receive printed messages.

Three help-wanted advertisements for TELEX operators appeared in the local newspaper.

Tenancy

Living on or occupying property owned by someone else.

His tenancy in the apartment building was subject to the payment of a monthly rental.

Tenant

An individual who rents, leases, or uses property owned by another.

Thomas has been a tenant in the Fairmont apartment complex for twelve years.

THE ABC'S OF BUSINESS VOCABULARY

Test your knowledge of the business vocabulary you have studied by completing the following exercise.

1. An individual, firm, or entity that can pay its debts is said to be (a) insolvent, (b) bankrupt, (c) endangered, (d) solvent.

2. The programs used to control a computer's operations are called its (a) hardware, (b) printer, (c) software, (d) cursor.

3. A word-processing system in which operators at a number of computer keyboard terminals use the power of one computer's CPU simultaneously is called (a) memory typewriter, (b) keypunch machine, (c) facsimile, (d) shared logic system.

4. A word-processing secretary who is responsible for transcribing from dictation equipment or handwritten drafts is a/an (a) administrative secretary, (b) corresponding secretary, (c) mail secretary, (d) personal secretary.

5. Write three short sentences using one of the following words in each sentence: (a) station, (b) telecommunications, (c) teleprinter.

   _____

   _____

   _____

   _____

   _____

   _____

6. Define the noun *tenant*. _____

   _____

7. The meaning of *affidavit* is _____

   _____

8. Define the verb *collate*. _____

   _____

9. A *tariff* is _____

   _____

18 Writing Effective Sentences

In most textbooks one or two chapters are really pivotal. Master the material in those chapters and you have gone a long way toward mastering the basic objectives of the text. This is such a chapter. In it you should learn to avoid two of writing's most fundamental and noticeable errors—the sentence fragment and the run-together sentence. You will be asked to write many different sentences. While you may not be able to write correctly all the sentences we require, you should try. By trying, you will develop the increased confidence that comes from knowing you can produce effective and varied sentences. Work hard on this chapter. You will see the dividends in the sentences you write.

AVOIDING SENTENCE FRAGMENTS

A *sentence fragment* is a group of words that looks like a complete sentence but really is not. The fragment begins with a capital letter and ends with a period, but it is an incomplete thought. The sentence fragment, often a phrase or clause, needs additional words to become a complete sentence.

1. We know that you will be pleased with our linens. [Complete sentence.]

2. After you have a chance to study our catalog displays. [Sentence fragment.]

3. Give us a call to place your order. [Complete sentence.]

The fragment *After you have a chance to study our catalog displays* is a dependent clause and can be added to an independent clause to form a complex sentence. A *complex sentence* has at least one dependent clause and one independent clause.

For example, you could add the dependent clause to the first independent clause to form a complete *complex* sentence.

> We know that you will be pleased with our linens after you have a chance to study our catalog displays.

OR

> After you have a chance to study our catalog displays, we know that you will be pleased with our linens.

Fragments are errors you should try hard to avoid, as they reveal that you have basic problems in writing correct sentences. One common type of fragment is the *phrase fragment,* which is a phrase used alone. Note these italicized fragments and their corrections:

> Jeannie stood near the wall of the office. *By the water fountain.* [This prepositional phrase is a fragment.]
> *Correction:* Jeannie stood near the wall of the office by the water fountain.

> He completely overhauled the old typewriter. *Sitting on the desk in the storeroom.* [This participial phrase is a fragment.]
> *Correction:* He completely overhauled the old typewriter that was sitting on the desk in the storeroom.

Her work was hard. *Collating all those financial statements.* [This gerund phrase is a fragment.]
Correction: Collating all those financial statements was hard work.

The head secretary told Melissa what she had to do. *To avoid errors.* [This infinitive phrase is a fragment.]
Correction: The head secretary told Melissa that she had to avoid errors.

Another common kind of fragment is the *clause fragment,* which is a dependent clause used alone. Study these italicized fragments and their corrections:

When you work for Mrs. Barker. You really must use good English. [This adverb clause is a fragment.]
Correction: When you work for Mrs. Barker, you really must use good English.

Joan was transferred to the purchasing division last week. *Who is my friend.* [This adjective clause is a fragment.]
Correction: Joan, who is my friend, was transferred to the purchasing division last week.

I liked his ideas. *What he wanted to do.* [This noun clause is a fragment.]
Correction: I liked his ideas about what he wanted to do.

Sometimes fragments are acceptable. Certainly they are when we speak. Even the most careful speakers use fragments in their conversations. Occasionally fragments can be tolerated in writing:

You asked in your memo if I minded working overtime. *Not at all.*

Generally, however, you are well advised to avoid fragments in your writing. ☑

Self-Check Exercise 1

Underline the *phrase and clause fragments* in the following sentences. Check the key at the end of the chapter.

1. They plan to attend the business conference in Phoenix. If they can.

2. Christopher Reems and David Klein will meet in Washington, D.C. By the White House.

3. The repairman prepared to clean the Eureka vacuum cleaner. Standing among the broken sweepers.

4. His responsibilities were many. Administering to the vice president.

5. The professor helped her class. To gain its favor.

6. After you finish the Trial Balance. Begin the Profit and Loss Statement.

7. The attorney settled the case out of court. Who had recently passed the New York Bar Examination.

8. I admire his humanitarian deeds. What he does for the poverty-stricken senior citizens.

AVOIDING RUN-TOGETHER SENTENCES

Sometimes called "run-on sentences" or "comma splices," *run-together* sentences are another common error you should avoid. Usually a run-on sentence occurs when you let your sentences simply *run together,* joining two or more independent clauses with no punctuation or conjunction to separate them. Run-on sentences can be corrected in three ways:

1. By separating the independent clauses with a period.

    We appreciate your sincere interest we hope you will visit us soon with the controller of your company. [Incorrect.]

    We appreciate your sincere interest. We hope you will visit us soon with the controller of your company. [Correct.]

2. By separating short, related independent clauses with a semicolon.

    It is a pleasure to be of help enclosed is our latest booklet. [Incorrect.]

    It is a pleasure to be of help; enclosed is our latest booklet.

3. By joining two independent clauses with a coordinate conjunction preceded by a comma.

    There are a number of new private business schools in New York I am enclosing a list of 15 of them. [Incorrect.]

    There are a number of new private business schools in New York, *and* I am enclosing a list of 15 of them. [Correct.]

A *comma splice* occurs when two independent clauses are joined by a comma, rather than a period or semicolon. A comma is not strong enough to separate two complete thoughts unless it precedes a coordinating conjunction *(for, and, nor, but, or, yet).* A comma splice can be easily corrected in three ways:

1. By removing the incorrect comma and replacing it with a period or a semicolon when there are short, related independent clauses.

    Luis arrived at work earlier than he expected, Hector came too late to attend the meeting. [Incorrect.]
    Luis arrived at work earlier than he expected. Hector came too late to attend the meeting. [Correct.]
    Luis arrived at work earlier than he expected; Hector came too late to attend the meeting. [Correct.]

    She laughed at first about her bookkeeping errors, then she cried about them. [Incorrect]
    She laughed at first about her bookkeeping errors; then she cried about them. [Correct.]

    It wasn't long before she finished the word-processing project, she was then able to think about her weekend plans. [Incorrect.]
    It wasn't long before she finished the word-processing project. She was then able to think about her weekend plans. [Correct.]
    It wasn't long before she finished the word-processing project; she was then able to think about her weekend plans. [Correct.]

2. By adding a coordinate conjunction after the comma.

    Dolly fixed the typewriter, then she typed the letters. [Incorrect.]
    Dolly fixed the typewriter, *and* then she typed the letters. [Correct.]

    Yes, I would like to offer you summer employment, there are no jobs available. [Incorrect.]
    Yes, I would like to offer you summer employment, *but* there are no jobs available. [Correct.]

3. By eliminating the comma and integrating the ideas of one of the independent clauses into the other. ☑

   Linna took the dictation, then she transcribed it. [Incorrect.]

   After Linna took the dictation, she transcribed it. [Correct.]

   A suit on sale cannot be returned, it may not be the right purchase for you. [Incorrect.]

   Since a suit on sale cannot be returned, it may not be the right purchase for you. [Correct.]

   A suit on sale may not be the right purchase for you since it cannot be returned. [Correct.]

WRITING VARIED SENTENCES

So far we have studied sentences from the viewpoint of their patterns—that is, the arrangement of their subjects and verbs and completers—and from the viewpoint of their complexity—that is, the clauses they contain. A quick review may help.

PATTERNS OF SENTENCES

   Subject (S) + Verb (V): He slept.
   Subject (S) + Verb (V) + Direct Object (DO): She paid the bill.
   Subject (S) + Verb (V) + Indirect Object (IO) + Direct Object (DO): Mary sent Tom the check.
   Subject (S) + Verb (V) + Direct Object (DO) + Objective Complement (OC): They elected her president.
   Subject (S) + Verb (V) + Predicate Nominative (PN): She is the boss.
   Subject (S) + Verb (V) + Predicate Adjective (PA): He is efficient.
   Expletive + Verb (V) + Subject (S): There are two methods.

COMPLEXITY OF SENTENCES

A sentence is a group of words that represent a complete thought; it has a subject and predicate and accompanying modifiers and completers. It may have just one independent clause, two or more independent clauses, or a combination of independent and dependent clauses.

SIMPLE

A *simple sentence* is made up of only one independent clause.

   She hurried through her work.

   You may be interested in reading our publication.

   Mary, Bill, and John will be attending Purdue University.

   At his summer home, Jeremy likes to write poetry, jog on the beach, and barbecue ribs and chicken.

COMPOUND

A *compound sentence* is made up of at least two independent clauses joined by a coordinating conjunction.

   She typed the report as quickly as possible, and he proofread each page slowly and deliberately.

   He is looked upon as the primary spokesperson for the organization, and he must play that role at all times.

   They were invited to see *Cats* on Broadway, but they were unable to fly to New York in October.

Self-Check Exercise 2

Correct the following run-on sentences by *inserting a semicolon between the independent clauses.*

1. He began the seminar she finished it.

2. Learn to read quickly then practice composing paragraphs.

3. Your written communications have improved your oral communications are better, also.

4. Select your favorite record let us enjoy it, too.

5. Duplicate this report collate it on the machine to save time.

Correct the following comma-splice sentences by creating two separate sentences.

6. She was interviewed by the department head, now she was ready for the decision.

7. Retailing was his major in college, sailing was his primary interest.

8. Jot your ideas down on paper, we know how clever you are.

9. Philadelphia has my favorite symphony orchestra, Washington, D.C., has my favorite ballet company.

10. In the summer of 1985, he listened to music on his radio, he missed the broadcasts of the baseball games.

Correct the following comma-splice sentences by *inserting the appropriate coordinating conjunction (for, and, nor, but, or, yet) after the comma.*

11. I will enroll in the Secretarial Science curriculum, there are many secretarial openings for skilled people.

12. Alex wanted to take his vacation in May, company policy did not permit this in his department.

13. He accepted the job because of the higher beginning salary, he also approved of the fringe-benefits package.

14. In September I will enroll in the state-supported university, I will register at the local community college.

15. She wanted to attend the EBEA conference in San Juan, she knew that the air fare was prohibitive.

COMPLEX

A *complex sentence* consists of at least one dependent clause and one independent clause. The more important point is placed in the independent clause; the less important, in the dependent clause.

When their work was completed, Helen and Paula went home. [Dependent and independent clauses.]

Helen and Paula went home when their work was completed. [Independent and dependent clauses.]

COMPOUND-COMPLEX

A *compound-complex sentence* contains two independent clauses and one or more dependent clauses.

Roberto left after he had finished his work, and he went home. [Independent, dependent, and independent clauses.]

I will try to earn an *A* in my research report, but if I do not succeed, I hope you will not be disappointed in me. [Independent, dependent, and independent clauses.]

PURPOSE OF SENTENCES

There is still another way to describe sentences. Sentences may be classified according to their *purposes.* Here are some purposes, with an example of each:

Cause-Effect: If you let the water leak out of your car radiator, you will ruin the motor.

Comparison: Arthur types faster than Penny.

Contrast: The mornings go quickly in the office, but the afternoons drag on and on.

Definition: A thesauraus is a collection of synonyms.

Listing: The firm promoted Jamie, Ken, Helen, and her to assistant office managers.

Opinion: In my judgment, the new method of distributing the paychecks is superior.

Problem-Solution: You were in danger of getting fired until you began coming to work on time.

Procedure: First thread the machine; then check the bulb; finally turn on the sound.

Summary: All in all, Beth is a fine candidate.

Transition: Another issue is the low rate of pay.

There are, of course, numerous overlaps and omissions in this listing, but its intent is not to be exhaustive. Rather, you should study this list to see the different kinds of sentences you can write.

Given these three classifications—patterns, complexity, and purposes—you should understand how powerful and varied your writing can become. Let us assume for a moment that, as the office manager, you have been asked to recommend Kathy for a promotion. Believing her to be a fine worker, you want to recommend her highly. Note these options you have.

Patterns

S + V: Kathy works well with anybody.

S + V + DO: Kathy does excellent work.

S + V + IO + DO: Kathy will give you good service.

S + V + DO + OC: Kathy does her work well.

S + V + PN: Kathy is a good worker.

S + V + PA: Kathy is fantastic.

Expletive + V + S: Here is an able employee.

Complexity

Simple: Of all the staff members in my office, Kathy is the best.

Compound: Kathy works hard, but she never complains.

Complex: Since Kathy is an outstanding worker, she should receive a promotion.

Compound-Complex: Kathy works hard, and when the occasion demands it, she will work overtime.

Purposes

Cause-Effect: If you ask her to, Kathy will work on Saturdays.

Comparison: Kathy works harder than anyone else in the office.

Contrast: All the staff members work hard, but Kathy works harder.

Definition: Kathy is a good example of an outstanding worker.

Listing: Kathy listens well, writes sensibly, and talks intelligently.

Opinion: I believe that you will be pleased with Kathy.

Problem-Solution: If you need someone to bring some stability to your office, Kathy will do the job smoothly.

Procedure: Kathy sorts the mail, first by departments, then by individual employee.

Summary: In closing, Kathy is too valuable a worker for us not to promote her at the earliest opportunity.

Transition: A second thing you will like about Kathy is her punctuality.

Enough—maybe too much—about Kathy. You get the point: Knowing sentence patterns, complexity, and purposes provides you with the tools to create good sentences of your own.

APPLICATION EXERCISES

Some of the application exercises that follow may require you to return to the most recent chapters. Doing so, however, will be a good review for the Review Exercise that follows this chapter.

A. Write *true* or *false* in the blank to the left of each sentence.

_____ 1. A fragment can be a complete sentence.

_____ 2. A compound-complex sentence contains no dependent clauses.

_____ 3. Gerund phrases can be noun substitutes in a compound sentence.

_____ 4. "Cindy wrote Tom a letter" is an example of an S-V-IO-DO pattern.

_____ 5. A run-together sentence is made up of two or more independent clauses run together as one.

_____ 6. If a sentence has a compound subject, a compound predicate, or both, it is a compound sentence.

_____ 7. In a sentence beginning with an expletive, the verb will probably appear before the subject.

_____ 8. In a compound sentence in which the two independent clauses are connected with a coordinate conjunction, a comma should precede the coordinate conjunction.

B. Correct the fragments in the spaces provided by adding words to make them complete sentences. Put *complete* in the spaces if the sentences are already correct.

1. In the middle of the dictation that he gave to Ms. Warner. _____

    _____

    _____

2. Somehow it worked. _____

    _____

3. Coming in second place in the company golf tournament. _____

    _____

    _____

4. Just after you get to the elevator. _____

    _____

    _____

5. Shauna knew that her work was especially satisfactory to Ms. Carlyle, who headed the department. _____

_____

_____

6. When they completed the check of the purchasing procedures. _____

_____

_____

7. That she would do a really effective piece of work for the company. _____

_____

_____

8. To do the required work in the shortest possible amount of time. _____

_____

_____

9. When her request for a raise was formally denied, Lori decided to look for a different position. _____

_____

_____

10. In order to get the merchandise to you as soon as we can. _____

_____

_____

C. Correct the run-together sentences in the spaces provided in one of the following ways: (a) make two sentences, (b) separate the independent clauses with a semicolon, (c) separate the independent clauses with a coordinate conjunction preceded by a comma, or (d) put the idea of one independent clause into a dependent clause. The sample sentence is improved using all four ways. In your corrections one way will be sufficient. Mark the correct sentences *correct*.

Sample:

Carlos cheated on his application, he lied about his work experience. [Incorrect.]

(a) Carlos cheated on his application. He lied about his work experience.

(b) Carlos cheated on his application; he lied about his work experience.

(c) Carlos cheated on his application, and he also lied about his work experience.

(d) Carlos, who cheated on his application, also lied about his work experience.

1. Louise did most of the filing for the company, she likes that sort of work.

_____

_____

_____

2. Alan felt that he was right in the middle of the disagreement between Dempsey and Clarkson, he did not know what to do.

_____

_____

_____

3. Although she tried hard to make amends for the errors in the ordering, Ruthann knew that her employers were still unhappy with her performance.

_____

_____

_____

4. Winston went to the copying machine, he made 50 copies.

_____

_____

_____

5. Just between you and me, there will be a surprise party at the office for Alice, she will be 30 years old tomorrow.

_____

_____

_____

6. If Julius is offered the job, he will take it, he wants it very much.

_____

_____

_____

7. In my opinion, the writing submitted by Helen is the best we've seen; she is the one with

   the outstanding grades.

_____

_____

_____

8. In the bookkeeping section, Ms. Palmer is a truly helpful supervisor, she is a person a new

   employee can trust.

_____

_____

_____

9. The decade just ahead, which will be an important one for business, will give us some

   idea of what corporate life will be like in the next century.

_____

_____

_____

10. He knew the result, he had failed the writing test required for the job.

_____

_____

_____

D. Choose a topic—school, fast-food restaurants, movies or television, today's fashions, poli-
tics, popular music, the business world, sports, or any other that strikes your interest—and
write each kind of sentence on some aspect of that topic in the space provided.

   1. S + V

_____

_____

2. S + V + DO

_____

_____

3. S + V + IO + DO

_____

_____

4. S + V + DO + OC

_____

_____

5. S + V + PN

_____

_____

6. S + V + PA

_____

_____

7. Expletive + V + S

_____

_____

E. As in the last application exercise, choose a topic that interests you and write each of the following kinds of sentences. (For variety, choose a different topic from the one you selected in the last application exercise.)

1. Simple

_____

_____

2. Compound

_____

_____

3. Complex

_____

_____

4. Compound-Complex

_____

_____

F. Again, choose yet another topic and write each of these kinds of sentences.

1. Cause-Effect

_____

_____

2. Comparison

_____

_____

3. Contrast

_____

_____

4. Definition

_____

_____

5. Listing

_____

_____

6. Opinion

_____

_____

7. Problem-Solution

_____

_____

G. Refer to the eight sentences with accompanying sentence fragments in Self-Check Exercise 1. Rewrite each to create complete, error-free sentences. You may incorporate the sentence fragments into the independent sentences or add the sentence fragments to the independent sentences.

1. _____

   _____

2. _____

   _____

3. _____

   _____

4. _____

   _____

5. _____

   _____

6. _____

   _____

7. _____

   _____

8. _____

   _____

Challenge Exercise

This summarizing activity asks you to recall all you have studied about sentences. Refer to the materials in the previous chapters as often as necessary as you attempt to write these sentences.

1. Write a simple sentence with a compound subject.

_____

_____

2. Write an opinion sentence.

_____

_____

3. Write an S + V + IO + DO sentence.

_____

_____

4. Write a sentence containing an appositive.

_____

_____

5. Write a sentence containing an introductory dependent clause.

_____

_____

6. Write a complex sentence.

_____

_____

7. Write a sentence containing at least two prepositional phrases.

_____

_____

8. Write a sentence containing two pronouns used after the word *between*.

_____

_____

9. Write a compound sentence requiring a semicolon.

_____

_____

10. Write a sentence containing a correlative conjunction.

_____

_____

11. Write a sentence containing an introductory participial phrase. (Be sure it modifies the subject.)

_____

_____

12. Write a sentence containing a predicate nominative. (Be sure the verb is a linking verb.)

_____

_____

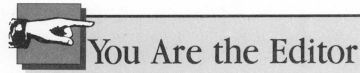

You Are the Editor

Correct all the errors you find in this memo.

TO: Ruby Rodriguez

FROM: Chris Klein

DATE: March 18, 198_

SUBJECT: Recommendation for Shirley Henderson

Ruby, you asked both Dennis Germain and I to write you letters about Shirley. Dennis felt that I was in the best position of the two of us to evaluate Shirleys work. So I am writing you.

Between you and I, Shirleys work is not good. She takes dictation poorly, she types rather badly also. When Dennis and her were working on the Cumberland project, he done most of the work. Expecially in the preparation stages. Shirley may be lazy. If that is her problem, its a big one.

Shirley don't fit into the office staff too satisfactorily. Neither of the other two typists like her very much. She often comes late to work. When she comes at all. Their's not much you can do to help a person who don't seem to want any help or isn't even here to get it.

Frankly, I would be more happier if Shirley could be transferred to another department.

Key to Self-Check Exercises

Exercise 1

1. If they can.
2. By the White House.
3. Standing among the broken sweepers.
4. Administering to the vice president.
5. To gain its favor.
6. After you finish the Trial Balance.
7. Who had recently passed the New York Bar Examination.
8. What he does for the poverty-stricken senior citizens.

Exercise 2

1. seminar;
2. quickly;
3. improved;
4. record;
5. report;
6. head. Now
7. college. Sailing
8. paper. We
9. orchestra. Washington
10. radio. He
11. curriculum, for
12. May, but
13. salary, and
14. university, or
15. San Juan, yet OR San Juan, but

A DYNAMIC BUSINESS VOCABULARY

Here is a list of business vocabulary words. Study them and review all the other business vocabulary lists in this book.

Text

The main body of printed or written matter on a page.

The word-processing operator had difficulty reading the text that was to be keyboarded into the machine.

Title

A document indicating legal ownership of property.

The city of Long Beach secured title to the Fairmont Apartments complex.

Transcriptionist

A person who types documents (letters, memos, or reports) from recorded dictation or shorthand notes.

The transcriptionist found it difficult to understand the dictator's foreign accent.

Trustee

A person appointed to supervise or control the assets of an institution or estate.

Mrs. Crawford acted as a trustee for her father's estate.

Usury

The lending of money at an illegal rate of interest.

The new usury laws make it a punishable offense to charge more than 20 percent interest.

Validation

Verification of actions, research, or statements.

His validation of my testimony concerning the accident was very helpful in court.

Vendor

A seller of goods or a place from which merchandise is sold.

The vendor was able to deliver all merchandise within 30 days.

THE ABC'S OF BUSINESS VOCABULARY

Review the lists of business words that follow each chapter. Test your memory and your ability to use some of these words by completing the following exercise.

1. Write three brief sentences using one of the following words in each sentence: (a) simulation, (b) securities, (c) shareholder.

   _____

   _____

   _____

   _____

   _____

   _____

2. Define the verb *finance*. _____

   _____

3. The meaning of the noun *title* in business is _____

   _____

4. The definition of the noun *tax* is _____

   _____

5. The verb *inherit* means _____

   _____

6. A set of printed queries sent out through the mail or distributed to people by hand is a/an (a) poll, (b) statement, (c) questionnaire, (d) advertisement.

7. The main body of printed or written matter on a page is the (a) graphics, (b) format, (c) foreword, (d) text.

8. A signed statement promising to make payment on a specific date or dates is a (a) check, (b) draft, (c) bill, (d) note.

REVIEW EXERCISE ON CHAPTERS 1–18

Before you study Chapter 19, the final chapter in the book, test your knowledge on the contents of Chapters 1–18.

A. Correct all errors in punctuation in the following sentences. Strike out any punctuation that is not needed. Indicate the correct punctuation on the line provided on the left. Include the correct punctuation mark and the word preceding it. If no changes are needed, write *OK* on the line.

Example:

Biology 101; or Biology 101.   a. John registered for Biology 101, Sandra selected French 10.

_____ 1. While she dictated, he typed, they finished the project in one hour.

_____ 2. We saw the revival of *The King and I.* Which starred Yul Brynner.

_____ 3. Cable television is very popular in my neighborhood. Because we have many sports fans.

_____ 4. Mr. Topol's specialty is tax accounting he teaches two graduate courses at Drexel University.

_____ 5. Atlantic City has many new gambling casinos Brigantine has two.

_____ 6. I will stop at the stationers, and buy yellow, lined tablets.

_____ 7. First I will attend the meeting in New York and then I will travel to Newport.

_____ 8. After I completed the workshop I received my promotion.

_____ 9. No I cannot attend the Saturday session.

_____ 10. I realize however that you are unacquainted with our company's policy.

_____ 11. Our policy is somewhat complex however you should be familiar with it by now.

_____ 12. You Professor Siskind are one of our most effective teachers.

_____ 13. All students who are incoming freshmen must fill in this application.

_____ 14. The Elite program which was made up of ten women and one man was highly successful the first year.

_____ 15. The wallpaper in the foyer was silver gold white and black.

_____   16. Our last reunion was January 3 1985 many graduates attended.

_____   17. The president of our club Manuel Ortiz is majoring in data processing in college.

_____   18. Would you select Phoenix Arizona or New Orleans Louisiana for our regional conference?

_____   19. They are intelligent well-behaved children.

_____   20. Remember to eat Aunt Edythe before you go shopping.

_____   21. With her raise, she will be earning $29000 yearly.

_____   22. His professors were Professor Tarelli for Italian 10; Dr. Ross Hebrew 101, and Dr. Cortez Spanish 235.

_____   23. That biology class was stimulating moreover, it helped me get my present job.

_____   24. Our vacation plans include Lake Placid, New York Bar Harbor, Maine, and Ottawa, Canada.

_____   25. Purchase the following supplies two dozen boxes of Bic pens, three desk blotters, and two reams of Bond stationery.

_____   26. His classes began at 930 a.m. and 1100 a.m.

_____   27. His article The Backlash of the Changing Auto appeared in the *Sunday Inquirer* on July 19, 1985.

_____   28. He inquired Do you have any tax forms left?

_____   29. Did Maria say, "I will have to think it over?"

_____   30. Help, Help, he yelled!

_____   31. The division director asked if we wanted to join the task force?

_____   32. May I arrange for an interview?

_____   33. Have you seen *The Tempest*.

_____   34. He hired his brother in law to serve as assistant manager.

_____   35. Blake Edwards, the well known Hollywood director, is famous for the Pink Panther films

_____   36. She read the latest issue of Fortune magazine in her accountant's office.

_____ 37. She was hired as an au pair by the French family.

_____ 38. Ones diary should be kept secret.

_____ 39. James Casey, Jr.s report was left on the train.

_____ 40. The record book of the graduating class of 85 was the most attractive thus far.

_____ 41. May I have your ten customers saleslips?

_____ 42. Georges photograph was in black and white.

_____ 43. Wont you please call by Monday.

_____ 44. Her article The Modern Woman in this issue of *Redbook* was assigned to the Sociology 101 class.

_____ 45. Have you studied all the principles in this text.

B. Correct all errors in capitalization in the following sentences. Indicate your corrections on the line provided at the right.

Example:

_____ Where _____ a. where are the assigned textbooks?

_____ 1. Will the postal workers strike? we don't think so.

_____ 2. The president of the company remarked, "he is the best-organized comptroller we have ever had."

_____ 3. The CPA said that All the junior accountants had to attend the Tuesday night meeting.

_____ 4. She typed the complimentary close "Sincerely Yours."

_____ 5. The youngster enjoyed "the ugly duckling."

_____ 6. They attend evening classes at Northeast high school.

_____ 7. Miriam and Carl recently purchased a Westinghouse Refrigerator.

_____ 8. My favorite appetizer is a chinese egg roll.

_____ 9. I registered for french, history, and psychology.

_____ 10. The ira has been very active in Ireland.

C. Select the correct answer and write it on the line to the left.

_____ 1. He provided (8, eight) sweaters for the orphans.

_____ 2. (20, Twenty) students attended the seminar.

_____ 3. The picnic was attended by (one hundred, 100) Little Lea- guers and their parents.

_____ 4. We received a copy of your report dated (June 17, 1986, 6/17/86).

_____ 5. They requested payment by January (15, 15th).

_____ 6. His condominium is at (One, 1) State Road in Shakesport.

_____ 7. I may rent the building at 623 South (5th, 5, Fifth) Street.

_____ 8. A filing cabinet to fit your needs costs (one hundred twenty- five dollars, $125).

_____ 9. The infant bibs cost (ninety-eight, 98) cents apiece.

_____ 10. Movie theater admission costs only ($2.00, $2) before 6 p.m.

_____ 11. It took him (½, one-half) hour to finish the test.

_____ 12. It is (twenty-three, 23) miles to the Philadelphia airport.

_____ 13. Dinner has been set for (seven, 7) o'clock.

_____ 14. We will have breakfast at (eight, 8).

_____ 15. I am sure that my grandmother was about (90, ninety) on her last birthday.

D. Some of the lines that follow are complete sentences, and others are phrase or clause frag- ments. Put the appropriate punctuation at the end of the complete sentences. Add words to the fragments to convert them to complete sentences.

Example: When her school day was finished.

Correction: She was tired when her school day was finished. OR
　　　　　When her school day was finished, she went to work.

1. If they can _____

_____

2. Longfellow is one of her favorite authors _____

_____

3. The *Wall Street Journal* will _____

_____

4. Since the program was a success _____

_____

5. After this we'll go on to our next project _____

_____

6. To judge the contest _____

_____

7. Start the timed test at noon _____

_____

8. Walking toward the office building _____

_____

9. Word Processing 100 is a popular course _____

_____

10. Better than the inexperienced typists _____

_____

Correct the comma splices by indicating on the line the coordinating conjunction that should follow the comma.

_____ 11. I will register for the Data Processing Certificate program, I am interested in the field of computers.

_____ 12. She wanted a job as a medical secretary, she did not have sufficient knowledge of medical terminology.

_____ 13. He had acquired the needed office skills, he also had the required two years' experience for the position.

_____ 14. I may become a CPA, I may look for a job in private accounting.

_____ 15. She would have liked to submit the report on time, she didn't want to devote the time to finish it.

E. In the sentences that follow, you will find errors in one of the five Cs of effective communications: *clarity, completeness, correctness, conciseness,* and *courtesy.* On the line, indicate which of the five Cs has been violated.

_____ 1. The three female candidates for the job are Carolina Reyes, Mindy Torillo, and William Johnson, Jr.

_____ 2. Don't get your blood pressure up! We'll send you the form.

_____ 3. Plan to run the workshop for us in August.

_____ 4. We wish to inform you that the equipment will be easy for you to run because all you have to do is talk to someone who has finished the training program and you will see that there is really no problem in learning how to operate the equipment and besides you'll like it.

_____ 5. The effects of the pedantic behavior of the instructor, together with her psychomotor and affective objectives, caused the course to fall far short of success.

F. On the lines to the left, place the letters that represent the correctly spelled words.

_____ 1. (a) necessary, (b) neccessary, (c) necesary, (d) neccesary

_____ 2. (a) greatful, (b) greatfull, (c) grateful, (d) gratefull

_____ 3. (a) privilege, (b) priviledge, (c) privelege, (d) priveledge

_____ 4. (a) convinient, (b) convenent, (c) convenient, (d) convenint

_____ 5. (a) truley, (b) truly, (c) trully, (d) truely

_____ 6. (a) receive, (b) recieve, (c) resieve, (d) reseive

_____ 7. (a) occurence, (b) occurance, (c) ocurrence, (d) occurrence

_____ 8. (a) attornies, (b) attorneys, (c) attornys, (d) atorneys

_____ 9. (a) recomend, (b) reccommend, (c) reccomend, (d) recommend

_____ 10. (a) tommorrow, (b) tomorrow, (c) tommorow, (d) tomorow

19 Business English in Practice

Now that you have studied the basics of business English and have completed dozens of exercises, you are ready to put it all together in various types of written communications.

Although more and more business communication is becoming electronic, mechanical, and computerized, there is still a great deal that must be written out. Such written (or typed) communications permit organizations to maintain records of transactions. They also provide information to managers and executives so that decisions may be made easily and quickly.

Perhaps the most common types of written communication used in business today are memoranda (commonly referred to as memos), letters, and reports. Of course there are others, such as the following:

Proposals	Orientation manuals	Minutes
Policy manuals	Briefs	Agenda
Staff studies	Bulletins	Advertisements

In this chapter, however, we shall concentrate on memos, letters, and reports because they are used so frequently in business.

MEMOS

The business memo is probably the most frequently used intracompany communication. It is called an intracompany communication because the *memo format* is used by communicators to write messages to people or departments in their own company or organization. Communicators change to *letter format,* however, when they write messages to people who do not work for their company.

A memo's basic purpose is to create a written record that may or may not be filed, depending on the recipient and the subject matter. As you know, spoken messages may be misconstrued or forgotten. A memo, however, becomes a record that does much to ensure the completion of the communication between sender and receiver.

MEMO FORMAT

The standard memo format frequently carries a preprinted series of items: *To, From, Date,* and *Subject.* The first two items, *To* and *From,* include the names of the receiver and sender. If company policy dictates, the titles, positions, or departments of the receiver and sender may also be included. In the event a court case arises involving an outside company and the memo is cited or referred to, the title of the sender or receiver may play an important role. For example, the sender may obligate his or her organization on the basis of a statement that is made in the memo. Such a statement may or may not be considered valid, depending on the sender's title as indicated on the memo.

A well-written subject line—inclusive but concise—tells the reader the key topic or topics with which the memo is concerned. The subject line may also permit the writer to skip the standard beginning of the memo, which usually sets the stage.

Figure 19-1. Memo to inform.

TO: All Section Chiefs, Plant One

FROM: Lester Jameson, Plant Superintendent

DATE: February 1, 198_

SUBJECT: New Regulation Concerning Reimbursement for Safety Items

Beginning April 1, 198_ a new procedure will go into effect
concerning company reimbursement for the following items of plant
safety equipment:

> Safety shoes
> Safety goggles and glasses
> Leather safety gloves

All employees will be reimbursed 100 percent for the purchase, after
April 1, 198_, of any of the items listed above.

For each item, Form 205 must be completed and signed by the employee
and his or her section head. These forms are available in the
personnel office and must be submitted within thirty days after the
item is purchased.

gs

Naturally, the date is important as a matter of record.

Modern practice allows flexibility and creativity in the memo heading, so today we see considerable deviation from the standard *To, From, Date,* and *Subject* format.

Standard practice may look like this:

TO: Susan Hayakawa, Sales Representative
FROM: Byron Baer, Sales Manager
DATE: April 10, 1987
SUBJECT: New Memo Style

Today's look in memo headings may resemble this:

TO: S. Hayakawa, Sales Representative
FROM: B. Baer, Sales Manager
           April 10, 1987
           NEW MEMO STYLE
           (Note that the last two lines are not preceded by headings.]

Figure 19-2. Memo to confirm.

TO: Kelly Krachin

FROM: Lester Jameson

DATE: March 4, 198_

SUBJECT: Promotion to Assistant Plant Superintendent

Congratulations, Kelly! This memo is to confirm the decisions we reached at our discussion of March 3, 198_.

1.   As of April 15, 198_, you will assume the duties of Assistant Plant Superintendent with direct responsibility over Units #1, #2, and #3.

2.   Prior to April 15, 198_, you can complete the four-day supervisory management program that is offered periodically by the Industrial Relations Department.

3.   As of April 15, 198_, your new salary will be computed on Company Base Pay Level 12.

4.   As we discussed, this appointment will be on the usual sixty-day probationary basis beginning April 15, 198_.

I have great confidence in you, Kelly, and we all wish you the best of luck as you advance in the company.

gs

PURPOSES OF THE MEMO

Basically the memo has three purposes:

1. *To inform.* In this case information is sent to the addressee or addressees indicated. Such information should be written as concisely as possible (Figure 19-1). If several items of information are included, it is often helpful to the reader if those items are numbered and listed.

2. *To confirm.* At times a specific decision or agreement will be reached at an interview, meeting, or conference. That decision or agreement may be set down in writing in a memo and distributed to all parties concerned (Figure 19-2). The statement giving the decision ensures clear understanding among all parties concerned.

3. *To secure action or record action taken.* Quite often the addressee is requested to take some specific action (complete a task, obtain an item, make a purchase, and so on) (Figure 19-3). In other cases a memo may indicate an action that was taken by the writer.

Figure 19-3. Memo for action.

TO: Kelly Krachin

FROM: Lester Jameson

DATE: May 1, 198_

SUBJECT: Items for Your Action

Because I will be attending the National Association of Plant Superintendents meeting in Detroit on May 6-7, 198_, I would appreciate your filling in for me on the following assignments:

1. Attend company budget planning meeting on May 6 at 10 a.m., Conference Room #3. Secure file from my secretary, Adelina Rodriguez.

2. Meet with Lockheed representative at 2:30 p.m., May 6, regarding wing unit #203 that we have discussed.

3. Hold appraisal interviews with Jane McKay at 10 a.m. on May 7 and Martin Marquez at 11 a.m.

I appreciate your assistance, Kelly, and am confident that you will handle these items in your usual professional way.

gs

QUALITIES OF THE MEMO

Although the memo should reflect the qualities of almost any good piece of writing, it is especially important that the memo be the following:

1. *Brief.* If the memo is typed on an 8½-by-5-inch form (a half sheet), the message should not use more than half the space. The same is usually true when the 8½-by-11-inch form (a full sheet) is used. Again, about half the space is used for typing.

2. *Easy to read and understand.* Every effort should be made to indent key points, list where necessary, use tables for clarity, and use headings—all for the purpose of increasing readability.

3. *Used sparingly.* Some individuals become victims of "memoitis." Memos fly to and from their desks like leaves in an autumn wind. Writing and reading memo after memo takes time away from more meaningful accomplishments.

Memos should be used only when absolutely necessary to inform, to confirm, or to record or secure action. Ideas, statements, comments, and criticisms that can more easily be passed on by phone or in person, and for which no record is needed, should not be reduced to a memo. Memos can also be written that combine information and confirmation, as well as for other purposes. ☑

BUSINESS LETTERS

Although electronic communications of all types are being used more and more in American industry, millions of business letters are still mailed each month. These letters initiate, carry through, and terminate countless business transactions among and between companies, individuals, and organizations in the public and private sectors.

Although the types of business letters and their specific content may vary according to their function (sales, inquiry, claim, credit, and so on), the format of all is similar. See the letter in Figure 19-4 for the standard format.

Self-Check Exercise 1

To be effective, memos should adhere to the five Cs of good communication. As you will recall, these are clarity, completeness, correctness, conciseness, and courtesy. Below you will find sentences taken from memos that violate one or more of the five Cs. First, record all the errors on a sheet of paper. Then, write a brief memo to your instructor describing the errors in the first three sentences. Finally, check your answers with those in the answer key.

1. The four winners of our annual departmental award are Verdette Gregory, Cynthia Foust, Carolina Reyes, and Cynthia Foust.
2. We will have a brief meeting on the handling of incoming mail in Conference Room A or B on either Monday, May 11, or Tuesday, May 12, between 10 a.m. and 11 a.m.
3. The expansion of the Word-Processing Department is really a very simple matter because all you have to do is discuss same with Mary Greenwalt, the new word processing supervisor, and then see the assistant manager, Martha Anderson, who has been in charge of all the office administration departments since last February.
4. Frankly, I don't see why you're getting so excited about our department's sending Form 235 three days late.
5. As the new credit and collection person, you will want to know that any company memos you send should have the following four items in the heading— name of sender, date, and subject line.
6. Our customer service department, for the past several years, has seen fit to research all letters addressed to the president and handle all the matters logically, carefully, courteously, and concisely before sending copies of the letters addressed to the president to the president's office.
7. The next time you are requested to attend a staff meeting at 10:15 a.m., I don't expect you to saunter into the Board Room at 10:45.
8. We will have to bare down on Jonathan Summers because of his latenesses. His personal file indicates that he was formally employed by the FBI.

Figure 19-4. Standard business letter format.

WILSHIRE OFFICE PRODUCTS
388 Marine Drive
Los Angeles, California 90099
(213) 509-1201

March 12, 198_

Mr. Gary Entwistle, President
Personnel Development, Inc.
616 West Watson Place
San Diego, CA 92111

Dear Mr. Entwistle:

It was a pleasure to discuss a management development program with
you on March 6. Certainly the suggestions you made in reference to
our personnel were valuable and perceptive.

We have now secured approval from our Board of Directors to move
ahead with the proposal you made. However, we would like to have the
first session of the program scheduled for July 9 instead of July 2,
198_.

It is our understanding that the total program will consist of 12
sessions (beginning with July 9) and held on Thursdays from 1:30 to
4:30 p.m. in our conference facilities. You will provide all
materials, cases, reprints, and other classroom materials. We will
provide all visual-aid equipment as well as refreshments during the
breaks. The fee you listed will be paid at the final session.

We look forward to the program, Mr. Entwistle, as well as to your
planned trips to our facilities prior to July 9.

Cordially yours,

Robert T. Clifton
President

gr
Enclosures: Copy of signed proposal
             Copy of company annual report

c: Mr. Tom Tower, Training Director
    Wilshire Office Products

GENERAL CHARACTERISTICS

As noted earlier, millions of business letters are sent and received each month in the United States and in foreign nations. Because they serve a multitude of purposes, such as business transactions, information transmission, records of agreements, building of goodwill, and sales, they must be effective. Not only should your letters conform to the format noted in this chapter, but they should also be the following:

Clear	Courteous
Complete	Positive in tone
Correct	Reader oriented (reflect a *you* attitude)
Concise	

TYPES OF LETTERS

Although all letters should reflect these characteristics, they must also contain elements essential to the accomplishment of their specific functions. Some of the ways that letters may be classified are:

Inquiry and response	Adjustment
Acknowledgment	Good news/bad news
Sales and persuasion	Goodwill
Credit and collection	Employment
Claim/complaint	Letters of Transmittal

PARTS OF A LETTER

There are seven standard parts for all business letters.

LETTERHEAD

The letterhead should always answer the questions of *who* (company or organization name) and *where* (street address, city, state, zip code, and telephone). In addition, it may answer the question of *what* (nature of the product or service offered, such as office furniture or computer sales). More ornate letterheads may even contain a photograph or drawing that attempts to convey to the reader a favorable image of the firm.

DATE

Because copies of business letters may be filed to provide a record of communications, it is vital to include the date. That designation should be written out *(December 5, 19—)* to avoid the possibility of confusion or misinterpretation. When the date is indicated as *3-5-87* or *3/5/87,* there is always the possibility that a foreigner may read the date as *May 3* instead of *March 5*.

INSIDE ADDRESS

The first line of the inside address should reflect the recipient's name and title. In the case of women, *Ms., Miss,* and *Mrs.* are all acceptable. If the recipient is a *doctor, commissioner,* or *director,* then the proper title should be used. However, a title and a degree *(M.D., Ph.D.)* should not be used together when they refer to the same designation.

Acceptable

Mr. Clifton Conway
Ms. Betty Kurz
Dr. Mary Callahan
Director Juan Gutierrez
Commissioner Roberta Hale
Judge Timothy O'Connor
Professor Carl Levy

Not Acceptable

   Dr. Martino Vesquez, M.D. [omit the M.D. or the Dr.]

   Dr. Philip Morton, Ph. D. [omit the Ph.D. or the Dr.]

   House numbers and street names that are designated in numerals *(First Street, 29th Street, 123 South 23 Street)* should follow the standard forms established. (See Chapter 17, "Using Numbers in Business English.")
   The name of the city should be written out, not abbreviated:
   Correct: Philadelphia   *Incorrect:* Phila.
   In listing the names of states, the abbreviations established by the U.S. Postal Service (two letters, both capitalized) should be used. (See the complete listing in Chapter 3.) And, of course, the proper ZIP code should always be included.

SALUTATION
Whenever possible, the individual's name should be used in the salutation. Most of us prefer to see our name *(Dear Mr. Martin, Dear Ms. Conroy, Dear Mrs. Karagaski)* rather than *Dear Sir* or *Dear Madam.* It is wise to use a nonsexist salutation when the name is not known, such as *Dear Customer, Dear Madam or Sir, Dear Friends, Dear Colleagues, Ladies and Gentlemen.* Sexist salutations, such as *Gentlemen, Ladies,* and *Dear Sir,* may offend some readers.

BODY
Whether the letter is concerned with sales, credit, claims, adjustments, or any one of several other types of transactions, it should follow the principles of business English. Once again the five Cs of good communication must be mentioned because letters as well as memos must adhere to the principles of Clarity, Completeness, Correctness, Conciseness, and Courtesy.
   In addition, the letter should have a *friendly, natural tone.* All hackneyed, stereotyped, obsolete expressions should be eliminated. Overlong and stuffy expressions may have been effective in George Washington's time, but not today.

Eliminate	Use Instead
Hand you herewith	Enclosed
Brought to my attention	I understand
Enclosed please find	Enclosed is
As per your letter	Your letter of
Prior to	Before
Due to the circumstances	Because
For the reason that	Because

   Wherever possible, a *positive tone* should be used. An effort should be made to arouse a favorable association with your product or service, instead of an unfavorable one.

Negative

   We hope you won't be dissatisfied if you purchase our Supreme Washer-Dryer.

   We don't think you will have difficulty with the Kellogg Converter if you follow the instructions.

   We hope this presentation won't prove to be an imposition on your time.

Positive

   We know you will be satisfied when you purchase our Supreme Washer-Dryer.

   For efficient operation and complete satisfaction, follow the instructions prepared for the Kellogg Converter.

   We know you will find this presentation to be valuable and helpful.

In those instances in which it is beneficial to inject a negative tone, a positive solution should usually follow.

Although you may now have problems with your security system, you may be sure of efficient and satisfactory operations with the new Protectall Lock System.

Still another principle to follow in your writing of letters is to be *reader oriented.* This principle is sometimes referred to as the *you* attitude. Simply stated, it is writing from the reader's point of view, putting yourself in the reader's shoes.

We *Attitude* [Do not use!]

Your purchase of the Clear Kut will help us achieve our sales goal.

Complete the enclosed questionnaire so we may have a successful survey.

This will assure us of a significant profit margin and help our reputation.

You *Attitude* [Use!]

Your purchase of the Clear Kut will assure you of handling a quality product.

The knowledge gained as a result of this survey will assist you as well as other CPAs.

Sales of this item will assure you of a substantial profit margin and increased sales.

COMPLIMENTARY CLOSE

The complimentary close is most frequently written as *Sincerely, Sincerely yours, Yours truly,* or *Cordially yours.* However, there is a trend toward more informality. Friendly statements such as *Warm regards,* and *Best regards,* or even *Yours for the best in furniture* and *For the best in service,* are being used to end effective letters.

SIGNATURE SECTION

Many firms vary their signature section. However, the signature usually consists of three or four parts. When the four-part signature is used, it includes the company name, the handwritten signature, the typed name of the writer, and his or her title. If a three-part signature is used, the company or organization's name is omitted.

```
MORTON MANUFACTURING COMPANY



Avery Morton
Sales Manager
```

or

```
MORTON MANUFACTURING COMPANY



Avery Morton, Sales Manager
```

or

```
Avery Morton
Sales Manager
```

MISCELLANEOUS ITEMS

SUBJECT LINE

It is not unusual to have a *subject line* at the beginning of the letter. The *subject* orients the reader to the content of the letter and assists in filing the letter. The subject line may appear in the upper-right portion of the letter, on-line with the salutation, or below the salutation, indented or centered (Figure 19-5).

ATTENTION LINE

This device is used to direct the letter to a specific individual in the organization who may be the most knowledgeable about your correspondence. If that person is no longer with the firm, his or her successor will take care of your message. If you are certain that the individual you select is available, omit the attention line and place the name first in the inside address. The attention notation should appear on both the letter and the envelope (Figures 19-6—8).

REFERENCE INITIALS

The initials of the typist are placed in the left margin, two lines below the writer's name or position. The trend is to omit the writer's initials in the reference line if his or her name appears in the signature block (Figure 19-9).

ENCLOSURE NOTATION

When items such as duplicate invoices, legal statements, blueprints, or other items of significance are included with the basic piece of correspondence, a notation (*Enclosure(s)* or *Encl.*) is usually made below the typist's initials (Figure 19-10). This alerts the typist to enclose the items referred to in the letter and the reader of the letter to look for the enclosures. The word *attachment* can be used instead of *enclosure* if papers are to be stapled together. The number of enclosures or attachments may be indicated in parentheses after the notation.

CARBON COPIES OR PHOTOCOPIES

At times you may wish to send a copy of your letter to a party other than the addressee. At such times, a photocopy rather than a carbon copy is appropriate. However, it is courteous to tell the reader that you are sharing the information in the letter with another person. That is done by using the designation *cc* for carbon copy or *c* for photocopy plus the name of the individual to whom the copy is being sent (Figure 19-11).

If you wish to inform a third party of the content of the letter but do not wish to let the addressee know the information is being shared, the designation *bcc* for blind carbon copy or *bc* for blind photocopy is used on the copies—not, of course, on the original.

BUSINESS REPORTS

The business report is very often the basis for decision making in the organization. Obviously few company officers can gather information in a dozen specific areas and still carry through their primary assignments. Therefore, other employees are delegated to submit reports that may have as their primary purpose to inform, to analyze, to recommend, to persuade, to compare, or any combination of these.

On the basis of the reports received, important decisions are frequently made. If the report is not clear or complete, or if it is heavily biased, the decisions may well turn out to be poor ones. It is therefore essential that reports, like memos and letters, follow the five Cs of good communication. For your review, they are clarity, completeness, conciseness, correctness, and courtesy.

Figure 19-5. Examples of three subject lines.

December 6, 198_   Subject: Your November 29
                                    Request for Motor Replacements

King Corporation
One North Farrell Street
Atlanta, GA 30352

Ladies and Gentlemen:

December 6, 198_

Mr. Fred Cooper
Production Manager
King Corporation
One North Farrell Street
Atlanta, GA 30352

Dear Mr. Cooper: Subject: Your Nov. 29 Request
                                    for Motor Replacements

December 6, 198_

Mrs. Marie Cooper
Production Manager
King Corporation
One North Farrell Street
Atlantu4 YU 68695

Dear Mrs. Cooper:

Subject: Your November 29 Request for Motor Replacements

Figure 19-6. Letterhead with attention line.

December 20, 198_

Berk and Berk Corporation
101 West Pacific Street
New York, NY 10017

Attention: Ms. F. Gables

Ladies and Gentlemen:

Figure 19-7. Envelope with attention line.

Berk and Berk Corporation
Attention: Ms. F. Gables
101 West Pacific Street
New York, NY 10017

Figure 19-8. Letterhead without attention line.

December 20, 198_

Ms. F. Gables
Berk and Berk Corporation
101 West Pacific Street
New York, NY 10017

Dear Ms. Gables:

Figure 19-9. Reference initials.

Cordially yours,

Robert T. Clifton
President

gr

Figure 19-10. Enclosure notation.

Yours truly,

TEMPLETON COMPANY

Gloria Templeton
President

gm

Enclosures (3)

Figure 19-11. Copy notation.

Yours truly,

TEMPLETON COMPANY

Gloria Templeton
President

gm

Enclosure

c: Ms. Joan Lyons, Treasurer
     Mason and Mason

Reports must also be *objective* and submitted *on time*. Some of the more common types of reports submitted in organizations include the following: ☑

Letter reports	Progress reports
Memo reports	Annual reports
Analytical reports	Formal reports
Recommendation reports	Examinations
Periodic reports	

Self-Check Exercise 2

Here are some sentences that were included in business letters. The sentences may have errors in number expression, punctuation, capitalization, grammar, spelling, or word choice. First, circle the errors in the exercise and correct them on a sheet of paper. Second, write a brief memo to your instructor describing the errors in three sentences. Third, see if your answers are correct by checking them with the key.

1. Our Investigation Department informs me that all unauthorized charges were removed from your balance and the remaining $108.24 is justly due our corporation.
2. The balance on your account, tires and gasoline combined is $516.90 on the 5th of this month we received a $25 payment however that has previously been deducted from the balance just mentioned.
3. We are deeply depressed that you do not understand the billing we sent you on 3/10/87.
4. Upon receipt of your new credit cards please break in half and return in the attached postage-paid envelope your original cards.
5. Immediately following this letter will be an Itemized Statement of your account if you would be kind enough to go over this itemized statement and check your Debits against your Credits to see if a mistake has been made on your account.
6. Please except our apologies with providing you with copies of your August Invoice.
7. We would also like to point out that you are loosing aproximately $145.00 to $150.00 a month by paying so late.
8. Reference is made to your recent letter and your balance of $346.38 is duly noted.
9. The $35.00 past due item as questioned in your letter is resultant from your payment of $161.91 for our September Billing of $196.91.
10. Thank you for your recent letter explaining that the account number did not belong to you but was issued to your son and your formal daughter in law.

APPLICATION EXERCISES

A. Here is a credit letter that was mailed to a customer. Examine the letter and detect as many errors as you can. Describe the errors in the spaces provided on the next page.

All-Company

**203 Sperry Road
Madison, Wisconsin 16303
(608) 362-2779**

July 13, 198_

John H. Smith
235 North Broad St.
New York, NY   10004

Dear Sir:

Writing in reference to our June 198_ statement, which shows a balance due of $5339.87.

After deducting for the open load of gasoline, this reduces the balance to $3072.77.

The reason we are writing this request for remittance is that within the above total is included $1915.92 worth of May charges and June 10th dating which is now past due.

It is our usual policy that any account that is thirty days past due, and is not paid by the 15th of the following month, the account is placed on a temporary cash basis. I do not wish to do this, and would certainly appreciate your efforts in sending us your remittance.

Your kind cooperation and understanding is greatly appreciated.

Yours very truly,

Ira Stein
Creditman

gs

---

1. Errors in inside address and salutation.

2. Errors in paragraphs one, two, and three

3. Errors in paragraphs four and five

4. Ways this letter could be improved

B. Here is a revised version of the credit letter in Application Exercise A. Judge it for content, tone, and freedom from mechanical errors. In a brief memo to your instructor, compare this version with the original letter.

All-Company

203 Sperry Road
Madison, Wisconsin 16303
(608) 362-2779

July 13, 198_

Mr. John H. Smith
235 North Broad Street
New York, NY 10004

Dear Mr. Smith:

For your reference, we have enclosed a copy of our June 198_ statement. You will notice that the total amount due is $5,339.87.

This is to inquire about your overdue payment. Of the total balance $1,915.92 represents May and early June charges. These charges should have been paid by June 10.

It is our policy to place an account on a temporary cash basis when the balance is forty-five days past due. We do not want to do this to your account, Mr. Smith, and would appreciate your prompt payment.

Please place your check in the mail by the end of the week.

Yours very truly,

Ira Stein
Creditman

gs

C. Assume you are a teaching assistant in the fourth grade at the Andrew Jackson Elementary School, 1414 West Compton Street, Evanston, IL 60213. You are planning a geography project on Europe—England as well as the Continent. In an attempt to motivate the children, you want to obtain posters, model planes, model ships, and the like. Write a letter to Pan Atlantic Airlines, 505 Fifth Avenue, New York, NY 10022, and attempt to get a dozen large travel posters of European nations free of charge.

D. Write a memo to "All Office Personnel" in your company in which you ask them to attempt to economize on all office supplies (stationery, file folders, pens, mailing envelopes, clips, containers, postage, photocopies, reprints, and so on). Last year $21,500 was spent on office supplies in the first six months of the year; this year the cost has risen to $28,500.

Challenge Exercise

You are the chief administrator at Bellville Community Hospital. You have just received a courteous letter from Mr. Robert Valdez, assistant principal and instructor in biology at Bellville High School. He asks if he may bring 60 students, all interested in the health care field, to visit the patient floors and labs. He wants his students to see a "hospital in action."

You would like to accommodate him, but 60 students would upset hospital routine and patient care. Furthermore, it would be difficult for such a large number to observe much of value.

Write a brief letter to Mr. Valdez in which you decline his request. Keep in mind that he has sent you many students for your nursing program, and it is important to retain his goodwill. Perhaps he would like to borrow your excellent film titled "A Day in the Life of a Modern Hospital." You could even have your director of nurses introduce the film and answer questions at its conclusion.

You Are the Editor

*A*ccent
*I*mports

5430 Plainfield Street
Pittsburgh, PA 15217
(412) 272-5570

December 2, 198_

Timothy O'Toole

Sixteen South Small Street

Philadelphia, Penn. 19179

Dear Sir:

Subject: Account Number 08967549

Referring to your troubled letter of November 29, 198_.

Since there seems to be some confusion regarding your extended terms balance, we would like to take this opportunity to explain it to you. On your September statement, the balance remaining was $125.89. In October, you were billed for $127.79 in installment charges. This amount was the sum of $107.94 of the September balance plus $19.85 which was the first installment of three for your purchase of $59.55. We have enclosed a photo of both the front and reverse sides of this purchase since you did not seem to have a record of it. In November, you should have been billed the remaining part of the September balance plus the second installment on your $59.55 purchase.

I trust this will clarify the matter to your satisfaction.

Respectfully yours,

Ken Ductoer

Creditman

gs

Enclosure

Key for Self-Check Exercises

Exercise 1

1. The name Cynthia Foust was mentioned twice (a correctness blunder).
2. The time, place, and date are indefinite (clarity and completeness blunders).
3. The sentence is wordy and overlong (clarity and conciseness blunders).
4. The writer seems annoyed and a bit nasty (a courtesy blunder).
5. Only three items are listed (a correctness and completeness blunder).
6. The sentence is overlong and wordy (conciseness and clarity blunders).
7. The writer is bossy and seems irritated (a courtesy blunder).
8. There are three misspellings: *bare* instead of *bear, personal* instead of *personnel,* and *formally* instead of *formerly* (correctness and clarity blunders).

Exercise 2

1. (a) Comma after *balance,* (b) omit the word *justly,* (c) use *company* instead of *corporation.*
2. "The balance on your account covering tires and gasoline is $516.90. This takes into account your $25 payment that we received on the fifth of this month."
3. "We will be happy to explain the billing that we sent you on March 10, 1987."
4. "As soon as you receive your new credit cards, you may destroy your original cards by breaking them in half. The broken cards can be returned to us in the attached postage-paid envelope."
5. "In a few days you will be receiving an itemized statement of your account. By checking the debits against the credits on the statement, you can see if a mistake has been made."
6. "Please accept our apologies. As you requested, we are providing you with a copy of your August invoice."
7. "You are losing approximately $145 to $150 a month by paying so late."
8. "Thank you for your recent letter referring to your balance of $346.38."
9. "The explanation for the $35 balance on your account is as follows:

Our September billing	$196.91
Minus your September payment	− 161.91
BALANCE	$ 35.00

10. Use "son and your *former daughter-in-law*" instead of "son and your *formal daughter in law*"

A DYNAMIC BUSINESS VOCABULARY

Study the following business vocabulary list, and review the other lists in the textbook.

Verdict

The decision reached by a jury, judge, commission, or other party in authority.

In many trials the verdict appears to depend on circumstantial evidence.

Videodisplay terminal

A device similar to a TV screen used to display information electronically when attached to a computer or word-processing system.

The green print on the videodisplay terminal was clear and bright.

Void

Useless; of no effect.

The verdict was declared void by the higher court.

Voucher

A signed document used as proof of a transaction.

The voucher was signed by the controller.

Waiver

A document or statement that changes or voids a right or privilege.

John received a waiver from the dean that exempted him from taking the course.

Warrant

The authorization of an officer to search, seize, arrest, or execute a legal judgment.

The judge signed the warrant, which permitted the police to seize all company records.

Word-processing center

A centralized office area used by technicians who operate word-processing equipment.

The supervisor of the word-processing center had to work overtime three days each week.

Writ

A legal order issued by the court commanding someone to perform a specific act.

The signed writ was served on the company president.

THE ABC'S OF BUSINESS VOCABULARY

You have now completed all the business vocabulary words and terms in the book. Finish this final vocabulary exercise to test your knowledge.

1. Compose three short sentences using one of the following words in each of the sentences: (a) warrant, (b) void, (c) vendor.

    _____

    _____

    _____

    _____

    _____

    _____

2. Define the noun *validation.* _____

    _____

3. The meaning of the noun *voucher* is _____

    _____

4. The noun *usury* means _____

    _____

5. The definition of the noun *trustee* is _____

    _____

6. The decision reached by a jury, judge, commission, or other party in authority is a/an (a) guess, (b) error, (c) verdict, (d) principle.

7. A document or statement that changes or voids a right or privilege is a/an (a) waiver, (b) contract, (c) agreement, (d) decision.

8. A legal order issued by the court commanding someone to perform a specific act is a (a) ban, (b) prohibition, (c) barrier, (d) writ.

9. A document indicating legal ownership of property is a (a) petition, (b) title, (c) report, (d) guarantee.

Index